JUSTIFICATION

*The Doctrine of Karl Barth
and a Catholic Reflection*

by

HANS KÜNG

*40th Anniversary Edition
with a New Foreword
by Hermann Häring*

Westminster John Knox Press
LOUISVILLE • LONDON

Translated from the German *Rechtfertigung. Die Lehre Karl Barths und eine katholische Besinnung* (Johannes Verlag, Einsiedeln, 1957) by Thomas Collins, Edmund E. Tolk, and David Granskou. "Justification Today" translated from the German by Edward Quinn. "Justification: Then and Now" translated from the German by Katharina Gustavs.

Cover design by Mark Abrams

Published by Westminster John Knox Press
Louisville, Kentucky

This book is printed on acid-free paper that meets the American National Standards Institute Z39.48 standard. ∞

PRINTED IN THE UNITED STATES OF AMERICA

04 05 06 07 08 09 10 11 12 13 — 10 9 8 7 6 5 4 3 2 1

Library of Congress Cataloging-in-Publication Data

Küng, Hans, 1928–
    [Rechtfertigung. English]
    Justification : the doctrine of Karl Barth and a Catholic reflection / Hans Küng ; 40th anniversary edition with a new foreword by Hermann Häring.—1st ed.
       p. cm.
    Includes bibliographical references and index.
    ISBN 0-664-22446-6 (alk. paper)
    1. Justification—History of doctrines—20th century. 2. Barth, Karl, 1886–1968—Contributions in doctrine of justification. 3. Justification. 4. Catholic Church—Doctrines. I. Title.
BT764.2.K7913 2004
234'.7—dc22
                                     2003061153

CONTENTS

Part One: Karl Barth's Theology of Justification

A. Justification and Salvation-History

Part Two: An Attempt at a Catholic Response

A. Fundamentals

B. The Reality of Justification

FOR THE 40TH ANNIVERSARY
EDITION OF *JUSTIFICATION*

My book *Justification* was published in 1957, and it made a tremendous impact in the theological world. In fact, after 1957, the churches should have translated the results of the theological reinterpretation of the doctrine of justification into church life. But it was only in 1973, almost a decade after the Second Vatican Council, that a study conference of the Lutheran World Federation and the Roman Secretariat for Promoting Christian Unity would take place on the Mediterranean island of Malta, with a highly welcome result. The Malta Report states clearly that on the question of justification, a decisive convergence had taken place:

Today a far-reaching consensus is developing in the interpretation of justification. Catholic theologians also emphasize in reference to justification that God's gift of salvation for the believer is unconditional as far as human accomplishments are concerned. Lutheran theologians emphasize that the event of justification is not limited to individual forgiveness of sins and they do not see in it a purely external declaration of the justification of the sinner. . . . As the message of justification is the *foundation of Christian freedom* in opposition to legalistic conditions for the reception of salvation it must be articulated ever anew time and again as an important interpretation of the centre of the gospel. (italics mine)

So here is the confirmation from Rome on the question of the message of justification. Moreover, one of the signatories was Walter Kasper, my former assistant, then my colleague in Tübingen and finally a bishop and cardinal. For Karl Barth it was too late to make another pilgrimage to Trent; he had died five years previously. From the agreement reached over the doctrine of justification, it became possible to advance to the understanding of the church as the fellowship of believers which may live anew time and again by the grace and forgiveness of God as the *Ecclesia reformata semper reformanda*. Moreover, there has also come agreement on questions of church ministry and the recognition in practice of the Reformation celebration of the Eucharist, as proposed in my "Theses on the Apostolic Succession" (*Concilium,* 1968) and in the memorandum of the Ecumenical University Institute on "Reform and Recognition of Church Ministries" (1973).

But there, of course, Rome should have joined in. What has happened instead? Instead of joyfully accepting the Malta Report of that official Roman-Lutheran Commission of 1973, the Vatican strictly forbade its publication. Instead of making the liberating teaching of the justification of the sinner by faith fruitful in the proclamation of the church, the Malta Report was pigeon-holed in the Vatican and eventually was made public only by an indiscretion on the part of *Herder Korrespondenz*. Instead of drawing practical conclusions for the freedom of a Christian from the theological results, further progress was deliberately hindered and, wherever possible, freedom was suppressed.

It would take around forty years, until 1999, for the church to sanction the breakthrough already achieved in 1957. C. G. Jung opined that around forty years pass before an idea from the higher levels of the clergy gets down to the person on the street. Did the prelates also count on that? In any event, first of all there was some undesirable theological haggling: instead of taking the results of the book *Justification*, the subsequent discussion, and the Malta document as the presupposition of an official recognition of the consensus, the Vatican, playing for time, set up yet another ecumenical commission with the Lutheran World Federation, which for years had once again to chew through all the statements in the Tridentine decree on justification. Galley slaves' work.

It goes without saying that I remain excluded from such official discussions by commissions under the conditions of an all-too-eternal yesterday—at the wish of Rome and with the assent of Protestants. And I'm pleased: What a waste of time! Here of course the Roman infallibles attach importance to every single statement of Trent: These cannot in any way be false or even wrong, but were "fundamentally" correct or were at least "meant to be correct" (otherwise "everything would collapse"). But of necessity Lutheran biblical scholars responded to the Roman tactics accordingly: They were concerned to demonstrate that as many formulations as possible in Luther or the confessional writings are irreformably correct and, where they can be, are to be pressed into the categories of law and gospel. In a neurosis over confessional profile, some remain caught in the medieval paradigm, others in the Reformation paradigm. As a result, they lose the opportunity of making clear to people in a competitive society in a quite concrete and convincing way how important it is that human beings as persons are not justified by God on the basis of achievements, successes, works of all kinds, but happily by God himself, who expects only trusting faith.

Be this as it may, finally in 1999, despite some shady moves and Lutheran countermoves and after further additional declarations, on October 31, the anniversary of the Reformation, a declaration of agreement was signed in Augsburg. When this happened, vigorous applause spontaneously broke out in the church and went on for an astonishingly long time. For me, watching it on television, it was a great delight; the applause shows those in church and those watching on TV how great the longing was for such an ecumenical agreement. A late triumph, no doubt about it. But should I conceal the fact that at the wish of Rome the name of the author of the 1957 book *Justification*, which was originally top of the list of those to be invited, was again deleted—and as so often without a protest from the Protestants involved? Certainly this pettiness niggles me a little, but I can easily get over it, and in any case I am no friend of long church ceremonies. Did my former assistant and colleague Walter Kasper, now a Curia bishop, no doubt informed about the deletion of my name, perhaps sign for me in spirit? At any rate, to conclude from several reactions, including those of Bishop Karl Lehmann, I was not forgotten by the well-informed. The best sign came a few weeks later at the Cape of Good Hope, on the occasion of my lecture to the Parliament of the World Religions in December 1999. On the stage, the Lutheran bishop of Cape Town, Nils Rohwer, gave me the fountain pen, beautifully engraved by the city of Augsburg, with which he himself signed the Augsburg document. He said that I deserved it more than he did. The lord mayor of the city of Augsburg was kind enough later to send him another jubilee fountain pen at my request. This is practical ecumenism in small matters.

What was politically more important was that the head of the Roman inquisitorial authorities, responsible for the "doctrine of faith," Cardinal Joseph Ratzinger, who otherwise likes to be in the foreground at church celebrations, wasn't present in Augsburg, but he was represented by Cardinal Cassidy and his *adlatus* Kasper. And what a shock: Immediately after the signing, the Vatican, unrepentant and insensitive as ever, announced a new jubilee indulgence for the year 2000. As if Luther hadn't propagated his theses on justification by faith alone, specifically without such pious works, on the occasion of that scandalous jubilee indulgence for the new St. Peter's! This showed some all-too-trusting Lutherans that the harsh Roman core has in no way been converted into honest ecumenical agreement. No, in Rome under this pontificate no one thinks of drawing conclusions for the reform of church structures from the doctrine of justification.

Those who even then still found excuses for the Roman lack of insight and unreadiness to repent, despite the warnings constantly given by me and others, were definitively taught something worse by Ratzinger's declaration of the year 1999. With an almost blasphemous reference to *Dominus Iesus*, again absolute truth was claimed for his own church, and contrary to all the intentions of Vatican II, the declaration even denied that the Protestant churches are churches by nature. My commentary is that this document is a combination of medieval backwardness and Vatican megalomania. At any rate the Augsburg dreams of an ecumenical heyday flew away rapidly after this cold shock from Rome, which was only to be expected. People on the Protestant side should have been on their guard. Honest ecumenism cannot be engaged in with such representatives of the Roman system, the smooth talkers and smooth actors at the head of the Catholic Church. Will we ever experience it?

In the subsequent period I came to know Karl Barth better and better. There is nothing more stimulating than to talk with a man of such character, knowledge, and faith, such humanity and such humor. He would become a fatherly friend to me, something that the cool and intellectual Balthasar never was. As Barth wrote in his letter of introduction [see below, pp. lxvii–lxx], he regarded me in view of my "whole attitude as an *Israelita in quo dolus non est*" (an Israelite in whom there is no guile; cf. John 1.47).

In Basel, in Barth's study up on the "Bruderholz," in a cheerful dispute over the papacy, I finally said to him with an understanding smile, "I leave the good faith to you!" To which he retorts, suddenly quite serious: "Good faith? I would never accept that. And when one day I am called before my God and Lord, I will not come with all my collected theological works in an Älpler-Hutte (rucksack) on my back; all the angels would laugh. Nor will I say in justification of myself, 'I always had good intentions, "good faith."' No, I will stand there with empty hands and only find appropriate those words which I hope may also be my own last words: 'God be gracious to me, a sinner!'"

These are the words of the tax collector, right at the back of the temple. At a stroke it dawned on me how liberating and comforting this message is for my whole life. I hope that I shall always remember it: Christian trust in faith. This is the radical fundamental trust that in the light of Jesus has found its root (*radix*) in the gracious God and has no illusions about its achievements, but needn't be oppressed by mistakes either.

There is no question that the foundations of the strength of Protestant theology and also of the fearlessness, concentration, and consistency of the theologian Karl Barth lies here. This will give me, too, decisive support in all the controversies and form the ultimate foundation for my Christian freedom, which is facing unsuspected tests. Whether I ultimately stand there justified does not depend on the judgment of my environment and public opinion. It does not depend on faculty or university, state or church. Nor does it depend on the pope, still less on my own judgment. It depends on a quite different authority, the hidden God himself, in whose grace I—no ideal man, but human and all too human—may put unconditional trust to the end. *In te Domine, speravi, non confundar in aeternum,* as it says at the end of the *Te Deum*: "In you, Lord, have I trusted; I shall never be confounded."[*]

Hans Küng

---

[*] The above is slightly modified from Hans Küng, *My Struggle for Freedom: Memoirs,* trans. John Bowden (Grand Rapids: Wm. B. Eerdmans Publishing Co., 2003; London: Continuum, 2003), 143–147.

JUSTIFICATION: THEN AND NOW
Hermann Häring
Translated by Katharina Gustavs

On October 31, 1999, the president of the Pontifical Council for Promoting Christian Unity, Cardinal E. Cassidy, and the president of the Ecumenical World Council of Churches, Bishop Christian Kraus, signed a remarkable document in Augsburg (Germany). The doctrine of justification was its subject matter, culminating in the words:

> The understanding of the doctrine of justification set forth in this Declaration shows that a consensus in basic truths of the doctrine of justification exists between Lutherans and Catholics. In light of this consensus the remaining differences of language, theological elaboration, and emphasis in the understanding of justification . . . are acceptable. Therefore the Lutheran and the Catholic explications of justification are in their difference open to one another and do not destroy the consensus regarding basic truths.[1]

What happened there? With great applause from the audience, a high-ranking official of the worldwide Roman Catholic Church (ca. 1 billion Christians) and the highest representative of a council uniting 133 Lutheran churches (ca. 60.5 million Christians) documented that the most contentious issue between the two church communities had lost its dividing sting.

Four hundred sixty-nine years prior to this occasion, on June 25, 1530, the Augsburg Confession (*Confessio Augustana*) had been read at the same church. This latter document was equally intended to make the peace between the churches, but instead had become the foundation for a final division, that continues today. Now, however, the insight and the will for reconciliation clearly seem to predominate. After long discussions among Catholic commissions and hot debates among Lutheran groups, a broad approval could be signaled. Even the Roman Catholic faith community gave up their reservations, and the Lutheran World Federation knew that almost 80 percent of Lutheran Christians were on its side. That there were still over 160 German-speaking theologians and Luther researchers who expressed strong reservations in the end did not spoil the joy of what had been achieved.

Yet caution and thoughtfulness prevailed at this memorable event. After all, a fundamental argument between Catholic and Lutheran traditions was under discussion, which simply cannot be settled with a single stroke of a pen. The Augsburg Confession had been formulated only after tough and prolonged negotiations. It was a well-balanced document that bore the mark of the considerate theologian Philipp Melanchthon and—after the confusion of the preceding 30 years throughout the entire empire—could have become the starting point of a new rapprochement between the two parties. Unfortunately, the voices of reconciliation went unheard in Europe at that time. Instead, one of the most destructive and violent eras began and was ended only 120 years later.

There are two reasons that the will for peace from Augsburg could not succeed at that time. First, the religious enthusiasm with which Luther's doctrine of justification was ablaze shone through even in Melanchthon's balanced wording; it reached a point that left no room for compromises. Second, mechanisms of power politics soon ruled the newly developing churches—now under the leadership of territorial princes—and sometimes even instrumentalized them. And exactly because of having taken an identity-forming shape, the doctrine of justification had become more than a mere polemical argument. It had turned into an ideological power potential. Contrary to its intention, the doctrine of justification would serve as a church-dividing doctrine in the period following.

Against this background, the question arises: What exactly would be the consequences from this initiative? The statements of the document are worded rather cautiously. It speaks only of a "consensus in basic truths," and at another place even more warily of a "differentiated consensus." About the consequences of the relationship the churches have lived so far, the document keeps silent. Would the churches—as a logical consequence of the achievement—not have to recognize each other or at least take up Eucharistic hospitality or communion? Would not all the reasons for a continued separation be destroyed after consensus over this contentious issue has been reached? How could it be possible then that fewer than twelve months later a document of a faith congregation declares that Reformation churches would not even be entitled to bear the honorary title of a church?[2] Or would there be nothing else left to do but to accept the sad realization in the statement carved in the memorial slab of the peace-loving but unsuccessful Pope Hadrian VI (d. 1523) at S. Maria dell' Anima and adapted accordingly: "How much also depends on the spirit in which the message of even the best of documents is received?"[3]

Hans Küng, whose book *Justification* was published in 1957,[4] welcomed the aforementioned signing, yet for a very good reason he was not invited to the celebration at Augsburg. He probably would have asked the audience not only to sign a well-meaning document, but also to think more clearly about its ecumenical spirit and to consult his old book once more. Could anything be learned from Küng and his work?

The Fifties: A Beginning Dialogue

In European theology, the foundations for a Catholic analysis of the justification doctrine were laid during the 1950s. In Germany, Josef Lortz had intensely studied Luther and the Reformation;[5] Hans Urs von Balthasar had made a name for himself with a monograph on Karl Barth's theology.[6] The Jesuit university Gregoriana in Rome was considered the ultimate clearinghouse of theological knowledge, and its connections were far-reaching. Paris was regarded as a place of inspiration for theological history. At that time, both theological places were not only marked by a universal will for Catholic renewal, but also by an interest in ecumenical issues.[7] These conditions were a stroke of luck for the young theologian Hans Küng (b. 1928), who studied philosophy and theology at the Gregoriana from 1948 to 1955 and thereafter went to Paris. He was aware of the fact that the question of justification raised a central and contentious issue between Catholic and Reformation traditions, for whose solution mere detail studies would not suffice anymore. For his "research project" he, therefore, chose the most powerful opponent Catholic theology was facing at this time. It was the Reformed theologian Karl Barth who initiated a thorough revision of Protestant theology in continental Europe and at that time had already published ten volumes of his monumental *Church Dogmatics*. From a debate with him, a leading practice in interconfessional dialogue as well as leading results for a fundamental relationship between Catholic and Protestant churches could be expected. An agreement on questions of justification emerging between Barth and the Catholic tradition would have been a landmark for ecumenical talks.

The work presented here has not only achieved a clear result, but it also offers a detailed picture of the initial years of the debate. Certainly, other members of the Catholic community had already made important contributions, but they did not go beyond general evaluations and offered hardly any constructive rapprochements. With Küng's approach, more determination entered into the discussion because he sought a clear answer to the question of justification. This required a clear vision and a definite method, even if still elementary. Keywords that invite preciseness and carefulness go as follows: Get to know each other, analyze by categorizing, and compare with accuracy. These terms are the key to understanding the method of this book.

The first part of the book is dedicated to the comprehensive and thorough explications of Barth's justification doctrine. For long passages Küng's book can be read as an introduction to Barth's theology. This work corresponds with a time in which each ecumenical challenge was associated with the discovery of unknown and new things and in which—prior to all debate and criticism—the opponent was to be taken seriously and understood. The latter was confirmed by Barth. Instead of isolating the doctrine of justification too quickly and dissecting it into its smallest parts under the microscope, Barth's doctrine of justification is first presented as a whole and within the framework of his own way of thinking. Its roots are traced back to the teachings of Jesus Christ, creation, and redemption. Thus Küng is able to show right from the beginning to what extent this doctrine of justification can only be understood when deeply embedded in theological thinking and placed in an appropriate context. Under further analysis, the content of theological anthropology concerning sin and justice comes second. Against such a comprehensive background, the following questions are meaningful: From which term of justice can be deduced what actually happens in justification? What does it mean that humans are sinners? In which sense may we call them justified? How would sin and justification have to be defined in a theological context? How and in which sense can God's justification result in a worldly and human reality, leading to "sanctification"? How does justification relate to love and action? What is the point of good works when, according to Paul, humans are also saved "without works"? What can and must human action mean when the salvation of every human being depends on God's doing?

With this getting-to-know-each-other and this categorizing, the critical foundation for the future debate was laid. Was it a solid one? Küng's summary doubtlessly bears a Catholic mark, and he does not support his results with ample methodological or hermeneutical arguments, following the Catholic custom of theological discussions in those days. This approach, however, posed no problem, because in his stand against Friedrich Schleiermacher's tradition and within the framework of his

own revelation theology, Barth expressly adhered to the classic dogmatic foundations of the Christian faith as supported in the confessional
traditions of the church. Barth neither tried to reconstruct these foundations historic-critically nor did he subject them to a hermeneutic reorientation. Thus far, no alienation occurred in the process of transferring
it into the language of another church, which might have led to misunderstandings. Thus, for the first phase of the debate, Küng had certainly
chosen an "easy" and appropriate partner.

The task of comparing was then well-prepared. Küng agreed to the
challenge of developing a "Catholic reply" to Barth, which meant, first
of all, again examining critically and categorizing the then-current state
of Catholic discussions. Here the method became increasingly more difficult, because the handed-down, rigid, unhistorical dogmatic system of
new scholasticism had already begun to disintegrate. Though the Council of Trent (1545–1563) flatly refused Luther's approach to justification, knowledgeable council participants who were well versed in St.
Augustine's legacy had created a document (1547) with a more sophis-
ticated line of argument, which now could be taken up again. Furthermore, in the strongholds of Catholic theology, awareness had developed
that the history of ideas within the Catholic Church (certainly the ancient
as well as the medieval legacy) offered a far broader spectrum than had
been officially admitted during the 1950s. Thus Küng, guided more
strongly by the will to build bridges than were others, tried to break open
Catholic bottlenecks. He was fully in line with Catholic thinking by trying to do that with reference to his own "Catholic" roots.

Because of the differing Catholic situation, Küng also tried different
ways of categorizing. He looked into the church's own history of ideas
and refers back to the model of "dogma development" as well as to the
thought of an implicit divine truth, which surpasses all concrete formulations. He also reminded us of the meaning and problematic nature of textbooks as well as the never-resolvable dialectic between logical precision
and life's own practical vitality. He pointed to the limits of Aristotelian
categories, to other keyword and language rules that have a tendency to
develop a life of their own, to the differences between a language geared
toward objective ontological reality and a language focused on the subjective perspective. Last but not least, he also paid attention to the pattern
of interactions between the confessions that was early on set in motion.
The Lutheran-Protestant polemics led to a Catholic theology that limited
itself to anthropological perspectives. He made up a whole bundle of
what will later be called "hermeneutic" considerations in order to bring

momentum to the parties involved. Küng also insisted uncompromisingly on the fundamental importance of Scripture, which—also according to old Catholic conviction—contains the word of God and therefore is in no need for content amendments by tradition. Thus his whole intention focused on presenting the entire doctrine of justification from the sources of Scripture in such a way that with a new directness that does not require Luther as a formal authority, Christians from a Catholic background have a real chance to comprehend and understand it. Küng was well aware that he would best introduce this argumentation strategy very carefully. On formal grounds, however, Catholic theology cannot reject it. Finally, he introduced the last, but probably the most effective, strategy to his line of thinking: He searched for witnesses of undisputed, recognized Catholic theologians who would make an ecumenical dialogue possible. These testimonies are meant to be "illustrations suited to highlight more unusual trains of thought and also suited to show Barth that Catholic tradition cannot be in too bad a shape."[8]

Exactly this mixture of arguments and strategies—the still rather open and natural tone of communication, the determined will to discover true comparables when making a comparison, a basic attitude equally characterized by a healthy self-confidence and a readiness to self-criticism, and finally the complete absence of fear and apologetic reactions—makes the 1950s and 1960s appear so fascinating in hindsight.

After all those clarifications, three starting points emerged from Küng's lines of argumentation. Küng reconstructed and relativized the Tridentine doctrine, which he held in high regard, through exposing its past and rather polemic context. Thus he opened up two new avenues. Similar to his Barth interpretation, he also categorized individual statements on justification from the Catholic side into a comprehensive framework. As a result, their actual meaning can be more clearly assessed. Furthermore, he reintroduced to the Catholic discussion long-forgotten concepts and arguments from patristics and the Middle Ages. In later years a trademark of Küng's theology would be that he often introduced such formative and indisputable core information to the discourse. When, for example, such indisputable authorities as Origen, Hilarius of Poitiers, Basil, Chrysostom, Augustine, and Cyril of Alexandria—and Ambrosiaster and even Bernard of Clairvaux himself—say that salvation cannot be found in works but "in faith alone," it then becomes impossible to take the Tridentine condemnations at face value and in the same breath condemn the basic convictions of the Reformation simply as church-dividing. In the face of strictly

"Catholic"-oriented theologians, this level of argumentation was a major achievement.

Even prior to Vatican II, the model of a self-critical theology geared toward understanding was developed. This model also achieves a remarkable and essentially evangelical result: Whoever takes God's gracious offer seriously—who therefore understands that without our own merit (i.e., "gratis"), God releases us from our guilt and as a response simply says, "I put my trust in you"; who finally discovers that from this experience, without any religious or moral pressure, a uniquely new type of action grows; who can hear this "basic melody" in those detailed discussions—can come to the conclusion that "it is undeniable that there is a fundamental agreement between Karl Barth's position and that of the Catholic Church in regard to the theology of justification seen in its totality" (see 277–78 below).

Important for the discussion at that time was Barth's above-mentioned, highly noticed letter, which Küng put in front of his doctoral thesis. In this letter, Barth had put on record that with Küng's definition of positions, provided his representation of the Catholic side was true, there remains no actual reason to be separated from the Catholic Church. That innumerable Catholics along with Barth were amazed at this new interpretation is quite understandable. Perhaps also understandable was that they shared Barth's question about whether this young man with his apparently new views actually represented the Catholic opinion. Could Küng's older colleagues not have given a clear answer? Only a few actually did so.[9] Other than that, a peculiar reverse effect could soon be observed in the Catholic public. With Barth's Protestant astonishment, their own Catholic reservations were justified whereby the whole situation was turned upside down. The Catholic reaction did not take long to form and the reason for the hesitation in accepting Küng's views became most obvious because Küng himself had clarified the centrality of the justification debate. Now the doctrine of justification was no longer a merely abstract and isolatable single statement, but a comprehensive "teaching" or, better yet, a formative basic conviction that would raise its head in all other areas of faith: whether Jesus Christ or redemption, whether the Christian view of humanity or the relationship with God, whether Christian anthropology or the question of Christian liberty was concerned. As if the compass had made a 180-degree turn overnight, the newly understood doctrine of justification demanded the reorientation of the whole of theology and certainly, above all others, the entire doctrine of office and sacraments.[10] Most amazing is not the fact that this effect took shape, but the fact that hardly anybody seemed to notice. The discussion of this issue was unconsciously suppressed.

The Council and Thereafter: Change and Unnoticed Rediscovery

From the beginning, Küng clearly felt that the tenet of *Ecclesia reformata semper reformanda* belongs to the faith of justification itself, just like the back of a coin. Catholic theology had stated its premise: Given that the doctrine of justification is the main reason for the division of the churches, a reunification will become possible as soon as this reason for division is canceled. Under the pressure of the new status of the discussion, Catholic teaching authorities (including many theologians) rearranged the context: Only when the church's claims of truth, leadership, and hierarchy are settled can we then draw consequences from the doctrine of justification.

In January 1959, the discussion changed abruptly when the Second Vatican Council was announced. The purely theological discussion became eclipsed by a broad range of practical questions and concrete ecumenical hopes, later determined by the council's ecumenical decree (November 1964). Somehow that the central question of justification did not play any role in it went unnoticed. Had the concept been dropped from the ecumenical agenda? A distinction that Küng introduced becomes very important here. Indeed, the discussion about the isolated statement of justification disappeared for a long time. Officially, this question resurfaced only in later documents.[11] But what about the doctrine of justification as a fundamental definition that must influence all other statements and realities of the church?[12] Only one who is familiar with this real function of the justification doctrine as seen from a Reformation perspective can understand why Küng followed the work of Vatican II with a highly critical eye and why he criticized the later inner-Catholic developments with increasing vigor, culminating in 1970 in his intervention on the pope's claim of infallibility.[13] Küng felt it increasingly clear that pope and curia were not willing to accept the critical challenge of the justification doctrine.

What then is the current challenge? Despite the standstill, the horizon of understanding the doctrine of justification has changed fundamentally over the last decades. According to the apostle Paul, who was given center stage in the Reformation, salvation is found "in faith alone" and not in works. In keeping with the common Reformation understanding, this statement applies to the salvation of individual humans, who are always granted God's grace without any merit on their part. At the same time, Luther was quick to discover that the statement also contains an ecclesiological component. According to this view, the church is not allowed to go between God and individual believers as an authority that would then negotiate God's word, will, truth, or salvation on its own conditions. Unfortunately, this aspect of a close connection between ecclesiology and the justification doctrine was neglected during the postcouncil ecumenical dialogue. Though this point was repeatedly mentioned as an open question in the relevant documents, none of them actually named clearly the critical aspect of the Reformation position: Ecclesiology is not just about consequences from the doctrine of justification, but real core questions, through which the exact content of the justification doctrine will finally be determined. Catholic and Protestant Christians could always engage in splendid discussions about the question of what the term "justification" may mean, yet they always clashed over the question of how justification can be practiced concretely within the church. While the doctrine of justification has not been further developed over the last forty years, official dialogue commissions need to be blamed for the lack of development. They were unable to spot and act upon this fundamental issue. That these commissions, officially appointed and usually filled with conservative church representatives, never led a broad and true theological discussion was a mistake. For example, aside from Scripture, official commission texts quote only from earlier commission texts. Thus, the work of these commissions was increasingly overtaken by theological and interchurch developments.

Consider, then, the theological development of Hans Küng, in whose thinking important developments of the Western church are reflected. Here are some highlights.

As early as the 1950s, the question of societal—especially social-ethical—implications was raised. The doctrine of justification does not allow having humans evaluated according to their own achievements and their recognition within society. The societal-critical consequences are obvious. However, they were never reflected in official documents.[14]

Since the late 1960s, comprehensive theological concepts have been developed to a much greater extent. These concepts did away with theoretical deductions. Instead, life experiences and interactions, narrative traditions, hermeneutics, and real-life practical and cultural contexts took center stage. Just think of the new christological approaches, the concerns of the political and feminist theologies, as well as the various liberation theologies. In them the impulse of the doctrine of justification found totally new forms of expression. As a result, the doctrine of justification not only has societal-critical consequences, but also political-emancipatory ones.[15]

Beginning in the 1970s, theologians began to pay increased attention to the aspect of confidence, which is inherent to each and every faith and even knowledge. Seen from this perspective, the message of the justification doctrine highlights a primordial human desire. It lives from the experience that salvation, mercy, and reconciliation can only be given and received without any merit on our part. We need to learn "to accept ourselves as accepted" (Tillich). This discovery means opening up to an unconditional freedom and at the same time rejecting any authoritative and achievement-bound path to salvation. Thus we can impart as a message of salvation the message of the justification doctrine in a secularized culture. The justification doctrine even builds a bridge to a "God-distant" culture.[16]

In the 1980s, the call for an unconditionally well-meaning God grew so radically strong that God could only be seen as a God of all humankind and could only be thought of as a God who is able to break drastically through all particular promises of salvation and all exclusive claims of salvation made by the various religions and salvational systems. Religions can be awarded salvation effects as long as they share the salvation of this God with all humankind. The doctrine of justification unfolds a universal dimension that crosses cultural and religious borders.

The developments of the 1990s led to interreligious and global questions. With extreme intensity and controversy, the following question was put forward: What unites religions in a globalized world that at that same time is threatened to death? Important answers include: The healing effect of religions is to be measured by their ability to show that being human and humanitarian is a fundamental truth as well as by living compassionately and in solidarity with the victims as a gift of God. The truth and mystery of God are that all humans shall have the opportunity to be unconditionally human and to have confidence in their lives. This message reveals that the doctrine of justification is not specific to the Christian faith. On the contrary, the message of justification becomes a very plausible idea as soon as the religions grasp and approve it as a fundamental experience. These developments can only be understood if we distinguish between the justification approach and a fundamental position in which the gift of God always appears to be the greater one.

Divided Situation: Current State of Discussion

In the face of these developments, the contrast with the ecumenical dialogue could hardly be more extreme. The latter still continues to be closely tied to the ecumenical issue as it had been taken up in the past and dealt with by Küng. So far his book on justification is not outdated. Better yet, his thesis of that time has received a late justification. Everyone today agrees that the doctrine of justification no longer divides confessions. Differentiating exegetical as well as theological and dogmatic research has strongly confirmed that notion, especially the studies about the Council of Trent. Research by O. H. Pesch was of the greatest importance because he presented the Catholic and Protestant ways of thinking in their own plausibility and at the same time in their compatibility.[17]

Since 1999, the state of discussion can be easily and accurately shown in the Joint Declaration of Augsburg with its highly detailed style. First and foremost it documents a determined and successful desire to understand each other. With rationality and patience, the contentious questions are differentiated and classified into seven single individual-anthropological points.[18] For all seven problem areas, the points of agreement as well as continuing disagreement are meticulously listed. Each single time, however, the conclusion is drawn that the differences no longer warrant a church division. In light of such a desire for rapprochement and understanding, this document is a masterpiece of patience, reflection, and logical accuracy.

Unfortunately, this masterpiece of sophistication comes with a high price tag. The complexity and technical effort with which the issue is presented as well as the theological jargon, geared exclusively toward inside experts, are unparalleled. In fact, insiders are the only ones who are able to follow up on their own. The majority of believers probably simply follow set phrases without ever advancing to the real story. Provocative contents thus disappear increasingly behind the veil of historical recollections, and each further step along the thought process threatens to tip the overall balance.[19] This fatal dynamic has probably developed because the issue of justification, now finally isolated as a factual statement, does not spur progress for the problem of confessionalism, but is absorbed by the identity problem of the confessions. The justification issue is no longer the expression of a basic emotion of unconditional confidence in real life, but rather the label of the church's self-legitimation. The negotiating partners cannot escape this force of circumstances. The call for justification is no longer an act of language—which changes situations, offers churches orientation, and puts them on the spot—but rather a complicated teaching system that must be preserved. The old heraldic animal of the Reformation, which 450 years ago was still a fierce and storming horse, has now become an ailing nag that obviously requires intense medical attention. Forty years ago, justification was still considered an unwieldy sign of identification, as can be seen in Küng's work, but now it is made to fit the dimensions of ecumenical rapprochement.

The interpretation above may seem exaggerated and unjust. However, it serves its purpose well in illustrating the uneasy feeling that creeps up on committed Christians in the meantime. The interpretation is also meant to explain why the achieved consensus is so strangely fragile. Despite year-long preparatory talks, Rome, as we know, intervened very late and in a rather unfriendly manner.[20] In Germany, the publication of the document was unanimously rejected; the core of the justification doctrine seemed betrayed.[21] As an explanation, the reader is referred to the rather relative value given to the justification doctrine in this document as well as to the self-confidence currently displayed by the Catholic Church. I read those objections as an indication that this strangely divided and fragile situation is not yet clarified. Obviously, simply presenting the justification doctrine as a describing theory or as a statement among others is impossible. It actually lives from the effect it exercises over other statements. If someone accepted the doctrine of justification, would it be possible for the same person to also concede the Catholic understanding of office or the doctrine of the pope's infallibility? To overlook the fact that by nature the doctrine of justification has a critical and judging function, by evaluating religious (church as well as individual) practices and demanding a certain fundamental faithfulness, would be equally impossible. Could someone in the name of justification live with the practice of a church that will hardly ever change? This question is certainly most serious and also very difficult. The ignited conflict hits exactly the distinction that Küng had introduced with his book.

All of its frailness is revealed in a formulation that is meant to represent a compromise between the negotiating partners. The document speaks about the significance of the justification doctrine when it says in its first point that the doctrine of justification is "of central importance for the Lutheran Reformation," that it is "the 'first and chief article,'" "the 'ruler and judge over all other Christian doctrines.'"[22] At No. 18, however, the whole issue sounds much more cautious: Here we find the doctrine of justification only as "an indispensable criterion," even though it remains "in an essential relation to all truths of faith."[23] The lack of clarity and comprehensibility in the current discussion can be explained by the following shortcoming: the context and practice of the statement are not clarified. During the following decades, Küng had increasingly insisted on clarifying the context and practice in the Catholic Church, and for good reason. In the Reformation sense, the doctrine of justification becomes most concrete in the form of church criticism. However, as soon as other practical applications require clarification, the doctrine of justification may not be reconfirmed, but must be newly formulated. No other way exists to open its offensive power.

Paul's Intentions

Regarding Paul, I would like to share the following comments. At a time driven by objectivity and rationality of statements, the doctrine of justification (also in theology) is most deeply misunderstood. An assumption is made that, from an observer's perspective, justification is an intrinsic truth. In contrast, the call of justification is first and foremost an act of language—that is, a call, an interruption, or an intervention—perhaps the hermeneutic instruction as to how human action before God can be understood. The call of justification does not describe, but puts things straight and differentiates. It ensures things are more precisely defined. All words and actions within a Christian framework are subject to God's greater truth and love. Once you understand that concept by way of inner agreement, it appears as the most natural thing in the world and can actually be found in other religious traditions too. Yet it seems to require concrete critical situations so that this drawing up of borders, which in a strictly theological sense I like to regard as "religious" or "referring to God," may be explicitly recognized and voiced. Innumerable contexts offer opportunities for the word "justification" to become concrete. As we are well aware, Luther acted in a different context than Augustine, Pascal, or Barth. None of them could simply foresee what they would be confronted with in the future.

Let's have a closer look at Paul. To the present time, we have innumerable interpretations of Paul's doctrine of justification.[24] Two aspects always tend to be particularly controversial: first, in which sense could Luther actually refer to Paul, and second, how did the two differ from one another? This lack of clarity is inevitable as long as scholars do not reconstruct a specific situation and action, but try to define a doctrine, even though the dramatic situation the early community was facing at that time is well known.

The community of those who wanted to follow the Jew Jesus saw itself confronted with a unique challenge, which probably came as a surprise. The challenge presented itself as crowds of non-Jews, by their cultural heritage mostly Greek men and women, who sought to join the new "way" (Acts 9:2) of the Christians in Jerusalem, but above all in Antioch and other Middle Eastern cities. The amazingly pragmatic solution, which was found in this time of new cultural departures and changes, is also well known. On the one hand, the Jewish tradition was deeply treasured, especially its collective memory, spiritual heritage, and prophetic promises. But on the other hand, most of the instructions of the Torah, by which Jews distinguish themselves from others (up to the present day) and set their daily routines apart, were discontinued. According to the so-called Council of Apostles (Acts 15:1–29), only very few prohibitions remain: the consumption of meat offerings dedicated to an idol, animal blood, and suffocated animals. In addition, the prohibition of "sexual misconduct," whereby primarily the strict and consequent Jewish sexual morality of monogamy (including its patriarchal orientation) is meant, also remains valid. A content justification for such an "axing," as it had to be experienced by Torah-loyal Jews, was not given. Does this ruling not amount to a disaster and a disregard for Moses, especially because for non-Jews even circumcision, the central sign of identification for God's covenant with the Jews, was no longer in force?

Certainly in a postmodern era we can quickly point to the argument of "inculturation" that was in the offing at that time. From our modern liberal perspective, the early communities did not exactly cover themselves with glory in practicing a culture of tolerance, because in later years this issue still caused severe conflicts, even though it had been correctly regulated at the outset. Paul talks about those conflicts in his letters (e.g., Gal. 2–5). Today we can still understand that giving up the holy codes must have plunged the early communities into a severe crisis of identity, which is where the genius of the cultural "border crosser" Paul comes in. As far as I can tell, he seems to be the only one who can make clear that this is not about a convenient (so to say), passive, or empty liberality, but rather a most positive, highly committed religious border experience that will speed up the breakthrough. Paul is capable of bringing this crystal into the light: "A human is justified *by faith* apart from the Codes of the Torah" (Rom. 3:28; Gal. 3:8). At the same time, he is able to root this subject in the Jewish tradition because "Abraham believed God, and it was reckoned to him as righteousness" (Gen. 15:6; Gal. 3:6). Neither contempt nor condemnation of the Torah, and certainly not contempt for the Jewish tradition, is by any means the reason that the Torah becomes dispensable in this situation. Yet in view of the cultural situation of the non-Jewish Christians, Paul sees clearly that the Torah might cover a deeper layer, namely the trusting faith in God.

How can we today understand Paul's breakthrough? I believe the various layers of this process are usually not differentiated and explored in detail. In its most universal form, the acknowledging surface of his statement is very simple: The ultimate rule of judgment is always one of unconditional trust in God. This underlying factor applies to all demands and rules, all claims and rejections, all judgments and condemnations you make. This certainly holds true in any case, no matter which rules of behavior are established in a religion, no matter which lifestyle is at stake and in which cultural space a religion needs to find its identity. Paul's statement, however, is so open at its surface, also so distant and neutral, that hardly anybody could contradict it. With his reference to Abraham, Paul does not contribute anything uniquely new to the problem-solving effort.

Furthermore, nobody should actually be surprised to hear that in all situations for a faithful person, his or her relationship with God is the most important. Who would, by the way, want to dispute that, as Luther stated at this level, all humans misunderstand "works" as their own achievements and can instrumentalize them for their own glory? The controversial formulation of the Joint Declaration is trapped in exactly this scientifically measured and objectively analyzing surface diction: when the justification doctrine is understood as "an indispensable criterion." Paul, on the other hand, goes one step further. He specifically immerses himself in the conflict-laden context itself. The context equals the conflict of two cultures and therefore results in daily individual and collective arguments. The conflict is between two competing cultures and at the same time about their merger. Therefore we find a growing uncertainty over standards, insecurity about motives and possibilities of abuse in all things considered, the constant doubling and ambiguity of symbolic and semantic worlds, and finally the threatening of sacred traditions and taboos. For that reason, Paul not only analyzes, but also takes action, to fight for his own opinion in this highly conflict-laden situation, and to declare his position, to make a judgment and take it back again because he himself has to search for a path. Depending on the situation, he either relativizes the Torah (Gal. 3:25), criticizes it harshly (Gal.

3:3–13), or even dares to distance himself from it (Gal. 2:19), though the children of Israel always remain the "children of promise" for him (Rom. 9:8) while the Jewish faith continues to be the olive tree from which God's promise will go out for all time (Rom. 11:13–36). These different evaluations of the Torah gave rise to a diverse range of interpretations of Paul's writings. From my perspective, they can only be understood as sometimes immature reactions to each of the many different situations. Paul, in fact, exposes very concretely the negative impacts of the Torah, the more it is demanded by his opponents. The Torah leads people to be arrogant and to know it all, and it creates a bad conscience; it then becomes the scapegoat, so to speak, for whatever purposes humans want to abuse it.

In my opinion, Paul's judgments are neither theologically balanced nor meant to be ultimate judgments of the Jewish way to salvation, but confrontation and unmasking techniques *ad hominem*. Thus he also accuses the Christians James and Barnabas of hypocrisy (Gal. 2:13) and initiates an open confrontation with Peter (Gal. 2:11) without condemning them theologically. In the end, he comes to the conclusion that all of humanity is included in the sin (Rom. 9:23). Therefore, Jews and Gentiles are no different (Rom. 3:9). The Torah has such an unmasking function because it is so close to God's will. Why this complicated game of arguments and counterarguments, judgments and relativization? Because Paul interrupts each and every human self-admiration, as religious as it may be, and calls out to everybody: Before God you cannot earn a thing. And what exactly an individual is unable to earn before God will be best known to him or herself.

Now we have reached a third layer, and we are taken to a deeper dimension: to the comprehensive religious experience from which Paul's intervention lives. He does not discover confidence in God as a religious phenomenon, but as an act—that is, a revolutionary force—which as demonstrated in the letter to the Galatians opens up a world of freedom and future. Then what does "justification" as a language act mean in the strict sense of the word? This type of justification does not reveal itself by discovering or understanding those contexts, but by exposing and accepting a specific situation in its ambiguity, as a bone of contention between faith and self-legitimation. Therefore Paul's achievement is not that he pointed out the paradox in relations between confidence and own achievement, but that he unveiled the intercultural conflict between "Jews" and "Greeks" as a test for the evidence of trust toward God. For those historical reasons and in the exact same situation of cultural change, "faith" (πίστις) becomes the new keyword, the *identity maker* of the Christian path. Such detailed understanding of faith is entrusted with the assignment to find a new way, especially in times of cultural change: "For freedom Christ has set us free; stand fast therefore, and do not submit again to a yoke of slavery" (Gal. 5:1). Christian truth, therefore, does not lie in the repetition of such nice words, but in the ability to initiate new interventions when cultural interconnections are at stake.

This is exactly what Luther had realized. At a time of cultural change, Luther put this intervention in concrete terms again, to the discontent of the old church. I am afraid that church and theology only kept analyzing the surface of the factual statements over the past decades of their ecumenical rapprochement, instead of actually reconstructing the intervention itself, getting concretely involved in the confrontation, and making clear where one stands. Only then is it possible to show clearly what "faith" and justification can mean in our time. A church that does not allow other churches to question it about how its practices of faith stand the test of life is probably incapable of realizing the totally new intervention, which at the beginning of an interreligious era can be started from the non-Christian religions.

Conclusions

Let us go back to the monograph on justification by Hans Küng. Does it not follow from the above that his former work is outdated now? A thorough reading makes it clear that Küng not only wanted to portray and describe, but at the same time to intervene. His former work was packed with signs of criticism, including self-criticism. By placing Karl Barth's letter in front of his work, he intended from the outset to cut off any retreat to a further need for interpretation. The year 1957 was a time at which such a movement could still be naturally started. Unfortunately, the Second Vatican Council avoided the core of the challenge. With increasing clarity, Küng repeated and intensified his interventions into the 1970s. His suggestions about how to reform the practices of office and sacraments, his new interpretation of Christology, and his inquiry into the pope's claim of infallibility—all of it should have been understood as the realization of Paul's call for justification. The leadership of the Catholic Church did not seize this opportunity, and the churches of the Reformation did not protest against it. At some point in time, these omissions will have to be addressed. As with Paul's times, the church is again facing intercultural confrontations in the real world, and there is no telling yet where the consequences will take us. Küng has recognized this in his interventions since the 1980s.

"Justification": Is it not a poor and misleading term because of its juridical connotations? Over and over again, this question has been discussed, approved, and answered with new interpretations. In the meantime, scholars discovered that the Hebrew term *zedaqah* together with the term "wisdom" have their roots in a general term, *Ma'at,* which was widely used in the Middle East and was just rediscovered in the Egyptian tradition. Where *Ma'at* reigns, the world exists and people are gathered in the good hands of a world order, a universal meaning. When, with their agreement, they allow themselves to be admitted to *Ma'at,* then the people and the world will straighten things out within themselves.[25] Against this background, justification faith would have to be understood today as the determined "yes" that is ready to confront and willing to carry through with the conviction that humanity can only get things straight with itself through an unconditional, consequent, and self-critical confidence in God. The great symbol for that Paul sees in Jesus Christ, because his death and resurrection brought even sin back into this network of meanings. Couldn't that approach form the foundation for a program of interreligious dialogue, a universal world order, and a religious world peace? If seen from this perspective, the question of justification would again be a highly relevant topic, which would bring the churches back into contact with the agenda of the world—just as in Paul's times.

Notes

1. *Joint Declaration on the Doctrine of Justification: The Lutheran World Federation and The Roman Catholic Church* #40 (Grand Rapids: Wm. B. Eerdmans Publishing Co., 2000), 25–26.

2. "The ecclesial communities which have not preserved the valid Episcopate and the genuine and integral substance of the Eucharistic mystery, are not Churches in the proper sense." See Congregation for the Doctrine of the Faith, *Declaration DOMINUS IESUS on the Unicity and Salvific Universality of Jesus Christ and the Church,* August 6, 2000, No. 17.

3. *Wieviel hängt davon ab, in welche Zeit auch des besten Mannes Wirken fällt* ["How much also depends on the time in which the work of even the best of man falls"].

4. Hans Küng, *Rechtfertigung: Die Lehre Karl Barths und eine katholische Besinnung. Mit einem Geleitbrief von Karl Barth* (Einsiedeln: Johannes Verlag, 1957).

5. Already published at that time, among others: J. Lortz, *Die Reformation in Deutschland,* 2 vols. (Freiburg im Breisgau: Herder, 1949).

6. Hans Urs von Balthasar, *Karl Barth, Darstellung und Deutung seiner Theologie* (J. Hegner: Cologne, 1951).

7. The following works shall be listed here: Louis Bouyer, *Du Protestantisme à l'Eglise* (Paris 1954; 2nd ed. Paris: Éditions du Cerf, 1955.); Yves Congar, *Chrétiens désunis. Principes d'un 'Oecuménisme' catholique* (Paris: Éditions du Cerf, 1937); Yves Congar, *Vraie et fausse réforme dans l'Eglise* (Paris, Éditions du Cerf, 1950); Henri de Lubac, *Surnaturel. Etude historique* (Paris: Aubier, 1946).

8. Küng, *Rechtfertigung,* 124.

9. The responses were analyzed and an inventory was compiled in Christa Hempel, *Rechtfertigung als Wirklichkeit. Ein katholisches Gespräch: Karl Barth—Hans Küng—Rudolf Bultmann und seine Schule* (Frankfurt: Peter Lang, 1976).

10. The thesis can be verified in Hans Küng, *Die Kirche* (Freiburg: Herder, 1967; ET *The Church,* trans. Ray and Rosaleen Ockenden [New York: Sheed and Ward, 1967]).

11. In the year 1972, then again 1983, 1986, and 1994.

12. Luther called them *"Rector et judex super omnia genera doctrinarum"* (Martin Luther, *D. Martin Luther's Werke: Kritische Gesamtausgaber* [Schriften]. 65 vols. in 127. H. Böhlaus, 1883–1993. [WA] 39, I, 205).

13. H. Küng, *Unfehlbar? Eine Anfrage* (Zürich: Benziger, 1970).

14. N. Greinacher, *Christliche Rechtfertigung—gesellschaftliche Gerechtigkeit* (Zürich, Einsiedeln, Köln: Benziger 1973); Jürgen Moltmann, *Theologie der Hoffnung* (Munich: Chr. Kaiser Verlag, 1965, c1964.); Dorothee. Sölle, *Politische Theologie, Auseinandersetzung mit Rudolf Bultmann* (Berlin: Kreuz-Verl, 1971). See also the works of Reinhold Niebuhr and Johannes Baptist Metz.

15. Hans Küng, *Christ Sein* (Munich: R. Piper, 1974); ET *On Being a Christian,* trans. Edward Quinn (Garden City, New York: Doubleday, 1976); Edward Schillebeeckx, *Jezus, Het verhaal van een levende* (Bloemendaal: Nelissen, 1974); ET *Jesus: An Experiment in Christology,* trans. Hubert Hoskins (New York: Seabury Press, 1979).

16. Paul Tillich had already stated that the question of guilt at the time of the Reformation had been replaced in our modern time by the question of the (secularized) meaning of life. This fundamental movement is meant here.

17. Otto Hermann Pesch, *Theologie der Rechtfertigung bei Martin Luther und Thomas von Aquin. Versuch eines systematisch-theologischen Dialogs* (Mainz: Matthias-Grünewald-Verlag, 1967; 2nd ed., 1985); idem, *Hinführung zu*

Luther (Mainz: M. Grünewald, 1982); idem, *Thomas von Aquin. Grenze und Größe mittelalterlicher Theologie. Eine Einführung* (Mainz: Matthias-Grünewald-Verlag, 1988).

18. The individual points go as follows: Human Powerlessness and Sin, Forgiveness and Making Righteous, Justification through Grace, Justified Sinner, Law and Gospel, Assurance of Salvation, and Good Works.

19. Maybe against his own will, O. H. Pesch made this situation clear in a fictitious conversation, which shows clearly that any further discussion can only lead to further entanglements of new detail problems: *Die 'Gemeinsame Erkärung zur Rechtfertigungslehre' Entstehung—Inhalt—Bedeutung-Konsequenzen.* Lecture on January 13, 1998, in Cologne: www.kath.de/akademie/rahner/vortrag/Pesch-Rechtfertigung.html.

20. See reports in the *Herder Korrespondenz* (HK), July 1998, 328; August 1998, 386–88.

21. *Votum zur 'Gemeinsamen Erklärung der Rechtfertigungslehre.'* On *Gemeinsamen Erklärung der Rechtfertigungslehre* see: www.theology.de/rechtfertigungslehre.html and www.lutheranworld.org/Events/LWB-1999-Press_Releases.html.

22. "The doctrine of justification was of central importance for the Lutheran Reformation of the sixteenth century. It was held to be the 'first and chief article' and at the same time the 'ruler and judge over all other Christian doctrines.' The doctrine of justification was particularly asserted and defended in its Reformation shape and special valuation over against the Roman Catholic Church and theology of that time, which in turn asserted and defended a doctrine of justification of a different character. From the Reformation perspective, justification was the crux of all the disputes." *Joint Declaration* #1, 9.

23. "Therefore the doctrine of justification, which takes up this message and explicates it, is more than just one part of Christian doctrine. It stands in an essential relation to all truths of faith, which are to be seen as internally related to each other. It is an indispensable criterion, which constantly serves to orient all the teaching and practice of our churches to Christ." *Joint Declaration* #18, 16.

24. Michael Theobald, *Der Römerbrief* (Darmstadt: Wissenschaftliche Buchgesellschaft, 2000).

25. Jan Assmann, *Herrschaft und Heil. Politische Theologie in Altägypten, Israel und Europa* (Munich: Carl Hanser Verlag, 2000), 202–3. Assmann speaks of a "*konnektiver*" [connective], also of an all-connecting justice, which can be found in all great cultures. It is called in Egyptian *Ma'at,* Vedic *rta,* post-Vedic *dharma,* Chinese *tao,* ancient Persian *ascha,* Accadic *kittu* and *mescharu,* and in Hebrew *sedeq/sedaqa,* Greek *dike* and *themis.* All these terms, especially the

first five, share another meaning: "world order," which means justice according to a "natural right" view (203).

Bibliography

For a bibliography of works by Hans Küng, see: http://www.weltethos.org/dat_eng/index4_e.htm

BALTHASAR, H. U. VON, *Karl Barth, Darstellung und Deutung seiner Theologie.* Cologne 1951.

DULLES, A. "Two Languages of Salvation: The Lutheran-Catholic Joint Declaration." *First Things* 98 (1999): 25–30.

DUNN, J. G. D. *The Theology of Paul the Apostle.* Grand Rapids 1998.

DUNN, J. G. D., and A. M. SUGGATE. *The Justice of God: A Fresh Look at the Old Doctrine of Justification by Faith.* Grand Rapids 1993.

Growth in Agreement I: Reports and Agreed Statements of Ecumenical Conversations on a World Level, ed. Harding Meyer and Lukas Vischer. New York 1984.

Growth in Agreement II: Reports and Agreed Statements of Ecumenical Conversations on a World Level, 1982–1998, ed. Jeffrey Gros, Harding Meyer, and William G. Rusch. Grand Rapids 2000.

HÄRING, H. *Hans Küng: Breaking Through.* London 1998.

HEMPEL, C. *Rechtfertigung als Wirklichkeit. Ein katholisches Gespräch: Karl Barth—Hans Küng—Rudolf Bultmann und seine Schule.* Frankfurt 1976.

Joint Declaration on the Doctrine of Justification, Origins 28 #8, July 1998. Also published as *Joint Declaration on the Doctrine of Justification: The Lutheran World Federation and The Roman Catholic Church.* Grand Rapids 2000.

KINNAMON, M. and B. E. COPE, eds. *The Ecumenical Movement: An Anthology of Key Texts and Voices.* Grand Rapids 1997.

KUSCHEL, K.-J. and H. HÄRING, eds. *Hans Küng: New Horizons for Faith and Thought.* London 1993.

McGRATH, A. E. *Iustitia Dei: A History of the Doctrine of Justification.* 2 vols. New York 1986.

OBERMAN, H. A. *The Impact of the Reformation.* Grand Rapids 1994.

PESCH, O. H. *Theologie der Rechtfertigung bei Martin Luther und Thomas von Aquin. Versuch eines systematisch-theologischen Dialogs.* Mainz 1967; 2nd ed., 1985.

PREUS, R. D. *Justification and Rome.* St. Louis 1997.

REUMANN, J. *Righteousness in the New Testament: Justification in the United States Lutheran-Roman Catholic Dialogue; with Responses by Joseph A. Fitzmyer and Jerome D. Quinn.* Philadelphia and New York 1982.

SEIFRID, M. A. *Christ, Our Righteousness: Paul's Theology of Justification.* Leicester and Downers Grove, Ill. 2000.

SÖDING, T., ed., *Worum geht es bei der Rechtfertigungslehre? Das biblische Fundament der 'Gemeinsamen Erklärung' von katholischer Kirche und Lutherischem Weltbund* (Quaestiones Disputatae 180). Freiburg 1999.

THEOBALD, M. *Der Römerbrief.* Darmstadt 2000.

JUSTIFICATION TODAY
An Introductory Chapter
to the New Edition*

My heartfelt thanks are due to The Westminster Press and Burns & Oates for making available once more to English-speaking readers my first book, *Justification,* on which I had first worked in Rome and presented as a theological dissertation in 1957 in Paris. At that time, almost twenty-five years ago, the foundations were laid for a common Christian understanding of the doctrine of justification; the fundamental question at issue between the Roman Catholic Church and the Reformation may now be regarded as settled.

In this essay I would like to draw attention to the many-sided significance that a common ecumenical understanding of justification has in particular for people today. For in the modern efficiency-oriented society the question of the justification and freedom of a Christian is more than ever relevant

to the personal existence of the individual Christian,
to the reform and renewal of the Church,
to ecumenical agreement between the Christian denominations,
to social commitment in modern society.

Paul: Liberated for Freedom

There is no doubt that Christendom as a whole was made freshly aware of the complex of problems associated with the Bible, tradition, and authority when a devout monk and mystical theologian, almost five hundred years ago, turned into a Protestant, speaking out powerfully for the freedom of a Christian, for the reform of the Church, for the spiritual and political independence of the German nation: *Martin Luther.* After fifteen hundred years of a highly complex history of the Church and theology, he set out with unprecedented thoroughness to ask again about the origins, about the authentic Christian reality, about the gospel. He wanted in this way to remove all the doubts and temptations of medieval

---

*Translated by Edward Quinn.

man, to establish a new certainty, based not on pious works and customs but solely on faith. This was to be a certainty of conscience, a genuine certainty of salvation, founded—outside ourselves—on the gospel of Jesus Christ himself, and—if in God's name it had to be—also against ecclesiastical traditions and authorities.

Here indeed was a new theological paradigm, encompassing the whole relationship of man to God and God to man: a new macromodel of theology, following up to a point in the tracks of the father of his Order, Augustine, and passionately opposed to Aristotelianism and Scholasticism, Roman justification by works and glorification of the Church, Renaissance worldliness and Renaissance papacy. Luther wanted to remain a Catholic, but he was not allowed to be one. Pope and bishops at that time resisted any radical reflection on the gospel and set themselves at first against any reform of the Church. The result of what may be called here—more correctly than with Augustine or Aquinas—this theological upheaval was a schism in Western Christendom that has not yet been healed.

Luther was absolutely convinced that he had done no more than gain a fresh understanding of the old gospel and had thus helped to propagate once more the idea of the freedom of a Christian—in the sense that the apostle *Paul* especially had brought out forcefully against both Peter the Rock and other apostles, and likewise the libertinist fanatics. The parallels could not in fact be denied: Paul himself was opposed on two fronts.

1. On the one side—as we can read in the letters to the Church of Corinth—was a group of enthusiastic, pneumatic *fanatics*. They boasted of being in possession of the Spirit and derived from their elitist "higher" knowledge an absolutely self-confident freedom; they thought they could permit themselves arrogance, dogmatism, lovelessness, self-glorification, even violence and every form of sexual license.

It was Paul who referred these eccentric, utopian libertinists with their fantasies of the future, wanting to anticipate heaven on earth, to the *Crucified*. At this point all pride in talents and abilities, all ruthless attempts to achieve one's aims at the expense of others, all abuse of freedom, and all boasting before God and men are unmasked. Was it not precisely the Crucified—that is, the man Jesus, powerless, incapable of any further achievement—whom God exalted, revealed as his Christ, and so justified? Yes, in the weakness and folly of the Crucified the weakness and folly of God himself seemed to be manifested: a weakness and folly, however, which—in view of the new life of the Crucified with God—was revealed in a paradoxical turnabout as God's power and wisdom. This crucified and living Christ calls man to follow him: to make use in trusting faith of the freedom promised on the cross, not however in a libertinist fashion, but responsibly for his fellowmen; to apply his particular gifts to the advantage of the community; in everything to attempt to follow boldly the path of active love. Thus, according to Paul, the Crucified as the Living One is the criterion of freedom and indeed the center and norm of what is Christian. This of course holds also in regard to the other side.

2. For, on the other side—as can be gathered from the letter to the Churches of Galatia (modern Turkey)—there was the group of pious moralizing *traditionalists,* who—unlike the enthusiasts—did not anticipate the end, but turned back again to the past. The new freedom that Paul had promised them—from the Jewish law and thus also from persistent failure, permanent guilt, even death—they regarded as a dangerous aberration. Faith alone, they thought, was not sufficient. There was a need of religious ritual, of law and order, of moral achievements and pious works, in order to make things right with God.

It was Paul who referred these traditionalists (who had lapsed into the old cultic and moral legalism) also to the *Crucified* as symbol of impious depravity—to the Crucified

who did not want to make the moral more moral, the devout more devout, but turned to the unmoral, the undevout;

who, while submitting to the law, nevertheless radically relativized it and, against a God of the law, proclaimed the God of love and mercy;

who, consequently, appeared to the guardians of law and order to be an outlaw and a fanatic, and in the name of the law was condemned as a criminal and crucified; and

who thus took on himself, for the lawless and godless, the curse of the law.

He it was—this very one—whom the life-creating God himself justified against the law, thus definitively releasing men from the curse of the law and for true humanity.

This was Paul's essential conviction: looking to the Crucified, there need no longer be any human beings blindly subjected to the law, ritual, religious conventions, but only *truly free Christian people* who entrust themselves and their whole fate to God, "in Christ"; that is, who live a Christ-inspired life: "For freedom Christ has set us free" (Gal. 5:1). It is only from this standpoint that we can understand what Paul meant by the "law of Christ," the new law that had replaced the old: no longer heteronomy but true autonomy, not determination by others but a realm of freedom in which a person attains his or her identity in faith and life. From this standpoint it is also understandable that Paul does not plead for any sort of libertinist detachment when he uses the expression about Christ as the "end and goal of the law." Paul attempts in a supremely dialectical fashion to bring together in his interpretation freedom and commitment "in Christ" for the good of man. Freedom is both gift and task. Trusting faith remains its foundation. This way of trusting faith is practicable for the educated and the uneducated, men and women, the powerful and the powerless, even for the devout and those who are not devout. Why? Because it has consequences, but requires no special preconditions or achievements in advance, simply a *commitment of oneself to God* in view of the Crucified—regardless, of course, of all one's own merits or accomplishments.

Anyone who recognizes in this way, without illusions, that he can do nothing for himself in regard to what really matters but is wholly dependent on the grace of a God who does not evaluate people in a human way according to their achievements, accepting, approving, and loving them from the very outset: such a one is at peace with God (and with himself); he is *justified in the sight of God* in virtue of his faith and *solely of his faith.* And, as accepted, approved, justified by God, he is no longer a servant or slave ruled by law and ritual—that is, by other human beings—but is free: truly a child of God and so truly human. As a grown-up son or daughter of God, he or she is called and enabled, without legalism or pressure to produce results, to find and realize a meaning in his or her own life. Here is a new orientation: instead of having our gaze selfishly fixed on ourselves, it means involving ourselves with others living with us, and so—in the practice of creative love—doing much more than fulfilling the law insofar as this aims, according to God's will, at the good of human beings. Liberated for freedom then means for Paul: liberated for love. But back (or on) to Luther.

Luther: Master and Servant

Could not Luther sincerely think that he had Paul completely behind him when, with reference to 1 Cor. 9:19 and Rom. 13:8, he summed up his message *Concerning Christian Liberty* in two dialectically formulated guiding principles:

"A Christian is a *free master* over all things and subject *to no one*";
but also

"A Christian is a *servant* at the disposal of all things and subject *to everyone*"?

Luther made these statements in a dramatic situation. In the same year 1520 the Roman Curia reopened the heresy trial that had been interrupted for political reasons until after the election of the emperor. In June, on the basis of forty-one very unintelligently selected propositions, Luther was threatened in the bull *Exsurge Domine* with excommunication; the burning of all his books and a recantation was required within sixty days. In October, on the advice of the ambitious papal legate Miltitz, Luther agreed to mediation and sent to the Medici Pope Leo X a letter conciliatory toward the pope personally but quite rigid in regard to the issue: recall to the gospel and the necessity of reform. With this letter he enclosed the small treatise *Concerning Christian Liberty,* in Latin and German, to explain how he wanted his reforming program to be understood in principle and to convince the pope of his orthodoxy and good intentions. This last attempt to reach agreement with Rome however remained unanswered. After the nuncio Aleander had had Luther's works burned in Louvain and Cologne, Luther himself responded in December in Wittenberg by burning the papal bull threatening excommunication, as well as books of canon law and scholastic treatises: a signal that stirred the whole nation. Excommunication followed three weeks later, at the beginning of January 1521. At first it was scarcely noticed in Germany, but the die was cast, as was made clear in the same year at the Reichstag in Worms, where Luther had to realize the new freedom of a Christian in practice and in public.

The book with the famous and much misunderstood title *Concerning Christian Liberty*—after the books *To the Christian Nobility of the German Nation* and *On the Babylonian Captivity of the Church,* the third great programmatic Reform work of the year 1520—although composed in a mere two or three days, is a classic document of Lutheran piety and Reformation thought. As Luther himself wrote to the pope: "A little booklet—this is how the paper may be regarded—but it contains the *summa* of a Christian life—that is how its meaning should be understood" (*Werke,* Munich Edition, II, 265). It is then a description of being a Christian, defined in terms of Christian freedom, which for Luther is the essence of salvation: "so that we may know fully what a Christian is and what is the meaning of the freedom that Christ

has won for him and given to him, of which St. Paul writes so much''
(II, 269).

According to Luther, this freedom bestowed by Christ can be understood only if the anthropological dialectic between the outward and
inward, fleshly and spiritual, old and new man, is taken seriously—
without, for instance, wanting to talk of a "pure interiority." In this
respect we may not simply separate opposites, as the older Scholastics
did with the aid of rigid distinctions that did not allow for opposites.
Here opposites must be seen in their unity with the aid of that dynamic
dialectic which describes the complex living reality of man precisely
with the aid of opposites. The relationship of man to God and God to
man is not a static connection but an event in the light of which alone
man and God can be rightly understood at all in their nature: man (*homo
coram Deo*) as sinful man and God (*Deus pro nobis*) as justifying,
saving God. Considered sociologically and politically, master and servant are different persons, but from the theological standpoint one and
the same person is both master *and* servant, free *and* subject. This
requires explanation.

Why, according to the *first guiding principle,* is a Christian *a free
master over all things and subject to no one?* This holds for the inward,
new, spiritual man: for the man of faith. For man becomes really free,
not by any external realities, not by having or doing something externally, not by being concerned with holy things, wearing priestly vest-
ments, performing pious works, observing ecclesiastical customs. No,
man becomes free by the word of God itself, by the gospel, on whose
promises man can rely. Not any kind of human religious law, human
precept, human work, but (and this has scarcely been proclaimed) only
trusting faith makes man a Christian, makes him truly free, and
even—by participation in Christ's kingship and priesthood, in a "joyous alternation"—king and priest, so that there can be no intrinsic
difference between priests and laity, apart from the ministry of bishops
and priests to their communities.

Of course, it is completely wrong simply to appeal to faith—as often
happens—and then assume that nothing more need be done. For the
old, fleshly, outward man has by no means disappeared. Freedom only
begins on earth, man is still *in via,* on the way, tied to the body, which
he has to subdue and control. It is at this point that good works have
their place. They are not a substitute for faith, to justify ourselves in the
sight of God, to make ourselves devout and free. They are a consequence of faith, so that we can follow the example of Jesus Christ, not

constrained by law, but voluntarily imposing discipline on the body, the outward man, and—out of a love that is ready to serve, which spontaneously emerges from this faith—existing for other people. As the good tree bears good fruits, the believer practices good deeds. Good and pious works, then, do not make a person good and pious. On the contrary, the good and pious person produces good and pious works. Freedom *from* (useless) works is simultaneously freedom *for* (useful) works.

For Luther, as at an earlier stage for Paul, man as a person is radically changed by faith. Insofar as it is the expression of God's will, he fulfills the law out of love and consequently goes far beyond what is required. For the believer, God's will is not a coercive, guilt-imposing, accusatory law, but a challenging promise, liberating grace: out of faith proceeds love of God and a free, voluntary, joyous life of service to one's neighbor. For the Christian is not expected to do pious works for his own soul's salvation—as devout people, especially in monasteries and convents, often attempt to do—but with faith in Christ and out of love for his neighbor. Thus for Luther, as for Paul at an earlier stage, freedom also involves commitment. That is why the *second guiding principle* runs: a Christian is *a servant at the disposal of all things and subject to everyone.*

The question arises: although all this was very much disputed at the time, is it not indisputably correct today? In recent times the controversies about Martin Luther have moved out of the field of biography and generally of Church history into that of theology. For Cochlaeus, Luther's first biographer, and for his numerous successors in the subsequent four centuries, the Reformer was a depraved monk and a demagogic libertine, a revolutionary and an arch-heretic, destroying the unity of the Church and of the Empire; it was the same with Döllinger, Denifle, and Grisar. The turning point came only in the 1940's, notably with Joseph Lortz. For this Catholic historian Luther was an inspired, tragic figure, a personally sincere Christian and Reformer, involved in almost insoluble difficulties, but living and praying out of a deep faith, who must be relieved to a large extent of responsibility for the division of the Churches, when the abuses in the late medieval Church and the opposition to reform on the part of pope and episcopate are ruthlessly laid bare. For Johannes Hessen, Luther is a representative of the "prophetic type," continually necessary in the Church, leading a justifiable struggle against intellectualism, moralism, institutionalism, and sacramentalism.

Meanwhile, however, the theological discussion has made progress. For Lortz, Luther, when compared with Aquinas or Bernard, was not, despite everything, wholly a hearer of the gospel: for all his justified ecclesial and theological interests, even in his basic initiative of a doctrine of justification, Luther fell into heresy as a result of his subjectivism and selective quotations from Scripture.

This restrictive thesis of Lortz has proved untenable. As Otto H. Pesch and other Catholic theologians have shown by their criticism, the Lortz school largely excused Luther by referring to his personal assumptions and their background in Church history and the history of theology, but did not take seriously enough the relevant theological questions raised by him. It is not Luther merely to the extent that he remained a Catholic, but Luther precisely as Reformer who must be heard by Catholic theology and subjected to a theological reappraisal.

But—and this is another question—what must be the criterion of such a theological and ecumenical appraisal? The criterion for an objective appraisal, for example, of the book *Concerning Christian Liberty* cannot simply be the Council of Trent or the theology of high Scholasticism, not Greco-Latin patristics, still less modern textbook theology. All of these are at best secondary criteria by comparison with the one primary, fundamental, and permanently binding criterion: the original Christian message, the gospel—before which both the Latin and Greek Fathers, the neoscholastic theologians, and of course Luther also as well as the Council of Trent have to justify themselves. The essential question then is whether Luther in his basic theological initiative had behind him the primordial Christian testimony.

What was a very bold thesis only some twenty years ago (at that time with reference to Karl Barth's doctrine of justification) has meanwhile been largely accepted. In his essential basic statements on justification and the freedom of a Christian, Luther had the support of the New Testament and especially of Paul. This has been substantiated in the meantime by a whole series of Catholic monographs on both Luther and the understanding of justification; it has been confirmed also by the most recent Catholic and Protestant commentaries, especially on the Letter to the Romans (cf., for instance, those of Kuss and Käsemann), which are in agreement on the essential questions of justification and Christian freedom. It cannot be denied that no one—not even Augustine—in the previous fifteen hundred years had come so close as Luther to the meaning of Paul's message of salvation: a message that had quickly ceased to be understood in its original sense after the breakdown of Judeo-Christianity. And this rediscovery of the original Pauline understanding of justification beneath the retouching and the accretions of fifteen hundred years, which doubtless rested on a basic spiritual experience, is at the beginning of that new Reformation paradigm of theology.

Today there is no need to argue in particular about this basic teaching of the Reformation. After the doctrine of *sola fide* (and correspondingly of *sola gratia*)—incidentally well rooted in the old Catholic tradition—had been needlessly disputed for four centuries, recent translations of the Bible—as, for example, the new ecumenical Bible in German—give clear expression to the common understanding particularly of the essential text in the Letter to the Romans: "For we hold that a man is justified only (!) by faith, apart from the works of the law" (Rom. 3:28).

It is not surprising then that a study commission of the Lutheran World Federation and the Roman Catholic Church in a document adopted at Malta in 1971 formally confirmed this convergence: "On this point the discussions of traditional controversial theology were particularly acute. Today a far-reaching consensus can be observed in the interpretation of justification. Catholic theologians also insist in regard to the question of justification that God's gift of salvation for believers is not tied up with any human conditions. Lutheran theologians insist that the event of justification is not restricted to individual forgiveness of sins and they regard it as more than a merely external declaration of the sinner's justification. Through the message of justification, God's righteousness realized in the Christ-event is conveyed to the sinner as a reality that encompasses him, establishing a new life for the believer. As opposed to legal conditions for the reception of salvation, the message of justification as the foundation of Christian freedom must again and again be given expression as a momentous explication of the heart of the gospel" (in *Herder-Korrespondenz,* 1971, p. 539).

The only surprising thing is that this "Malta Report" was kept secret by the Vatican, became public only as the result of an indiscretion, and was never used during the whole of the last decade as the basis for a single conclusion. Has this perhaps again something to do with the tedious question of infallibility and the fact that it cannot under any circumstances be admitted that the thirty or so anathemas (threats of excommunication) pronounced by the Council of Trent against the

Reformation doctrine of justification were based on misunderstanding and lack of understanding; that is, they were mistaken decisions like so many others in the course of history?

As always, it is a scandal (and I use the word deliberately). After four hundred and fifty years of argument about an article of faith with which the Church stands or falls (*articulus stantis et cadentis ecclesiae*), it is established that there had been no need to quarrel and divide the Church on this issue. And what is done? This epoch-making document is filed away and the theologizing, administering, organizing, and celebrating continue as before. And this unfortunately is what happens, not only in Rome but also in Lutheranism.

At the same time we read in the joint Lutheran–Roman Catholic Malta Report: "Lutherans and Catholics are agreed that the gospel is the foundation of Christian freedom. This freedom is described in the New Testament as freedom from sin, as freedom from the power of the law, as freedom from death, and as freedom for the service of God and neighbor. But since Christian freedom is linked with witness to the gospel, it requires institutional forms for its mediation. Consequently, the Church must regard and realize itself as an institution of freedom. Structures that injure this freedom cannot be legitimate in the Church of Christ" (p. 539).

Certainly both the Protestant Church and theology and the Catholic likewise have every reason for self-criticism, and there will be no talk here about a canonization of Luther the man of God, whose veneration in Protestantism occasionally came close to the Catholic veneration of saints. Unbiased ecumenical theology is aware of the fact that Luther admitted not only his uncontrolled (and also depressive) temperament, his tendency to exaggerate, but also a theology one-sided in certain respects and scarcely supported by Scripture. There are important differences between Luther and Paul and—despite all the right initiatives and concerns—writings like *The Bondage of the Will* or the sermon *On Good Works* were and are open to misunderstanding, in need of completion and correction, not infallible. Luther's radical pessimism in regard to sin and morality, under the influence of Augustine, made it impossible for him to remain impartial while taking seriously the world and man, especially pre-Christian man and the non-Christian world. His theology was not safeguarded initially against fanatical and subjectivist misunderstanding (the confusion in Wittenberg even three years after his book on freedom showed him this) in the same way that it had been safeguarded against the hierarchical, institutionalist Roman misunderstanding. The ideal of a free Christian Church, composed of free Christian people, brought out of the Babylonian captivity, was not realized, but supplanted by an abundance of provincial princely and regional Churches. The unity of the Reformation camp was not maintained. And Protestantism became a world power, not through Luther, but through a similarly profoundly devout, but also legally trained, theologian who had more feeling for a clear, comprehensive theological synthesis, ecclesiastical organization, and international spaciousness; who combined works with faith, order in the Church with the freedom of a Christian; and who thus with his doctrine of predestination, justification, *and* sanctification involuntarily conjured up what Max Weber called the "spirit of capitalism." This was Calvin. It was not the Lutheran Wittenberg or any other German city, but Reformation Geneva that became the clandestine capital of Protestantism and eventually the seat of the World Council of Churches.

Marcuse: Personal Freedom—Social Bondage?

This however is the point at which the opposite critique of Luther's conception of freedom begins. It was not by chance that Herbert Marcuse's study "on authority and family," first published in 1936, appeared—together with contributions from Horkheimer and Fromm—in a new edition in *Ideen zur kritischen Theorie der Gesellshaft* ("Ideas on the Critical Theory of Society") in 1969 at the very time of the student revolts. This representative of the Critical Theory and Praxis analyzes there the relationship between freedom and servitude, autonomy and heteronomy, in civic philosophy, the origin of which he finds in the works of none other than Martin Luther.

According to Marcuse, German culture is rooted in Protestantism. The latter enabled emancipated individuals to accept the new social system by helping them to switch their claims and demands from the external world to their inward life, to inwardness. "Civic philosophy"—from Descartes by way of Kant and Hegel to the counter-revolution and the Restoration (de Maistre, Bonald, Burke, Stahl)— "had placed the autonomy of the person at the very center of their theory. Kant's doctrine of freedom is merely the clearest and supreme expression of a trend that had been active from the time of Luther's work on Christian liberty" (p. 55). But, in regard to this work, what Marcuse says at the beginning of his chapter on Luther and Calvin is true: "*Concerning Christian Liberty* brings together for the first time all the elements of the concept specifically of civic freedom and makes them the ideological foundation of the specific form of civil authority: allocation of freedom to the 'inner' sphere of the person, to the 'inward man' with the simultaneous subjection of the 'outward man' under the system of secular authorities; the transcending of this system of earthly authorities by personal authority and reason; separation of person and work (person and office) with 'double morality'; justification of actual bondage and inequality as a consequence of 'inward' freedom and equality'' (p. 59).

For all his indisputable antiauthoritarian tendency, Luther, according to Marcuse, had established Christian freedom as an inward value to be realized independently of any external conditions and to be preserved under servile social conditions, without pressing for practical change or sociopolitical liberation. "The unification of inward autonomy and outward heteronomy, the breakdown of freedom into bondage, is the essential characteristic of the concept of liberty that has dominated civic theory from the time of the Reformation" (p. 56). In this light, inward personal freedom and outward social bondage are mutually dependent and stabilize one another. "Christian teaching on freedom switches man's liberation to before his actual history, the latter then being a history of his bondage, a 'perpetual' consequence of that liberation" (p. 56). It was not at all accidental, therefore, that Luther held out to the peasants revolting in 1525 a kind of "Christian freedom" that in fact would not make then sociologically and socially free, but would positively reinforce their slavery.

This critical view of the Reformation and its subsequent manifestations cannot simply be rejected. In 1830, as Rector Magnificus of the University of Berlin, *Hegel,* the leading defender of civic philosophy, gave the great jubilee address for the third centenary of the *Confessio Augustana* and defined Christian freedom against the clerical two-tier Church as freedom of the spirit: "We take Christian freedom to mean that everyone is declared worthy to turn to God with his thoughts, his prayers and his worship; that everyone establishes with God himself the relationship he has to God and God has to him; but God himself for his own part completes this relationship in the human spirit. We have to deal, that is, not with a Deity subject to nature's dispositions, but with the God who is truth, eternal reason and consciousness of this reason: in other words, spirit" (*Berliner Schriften,* p. 33). Hence religious freedom is the essence of freedom of the spirit in all areas of education, of the liberal arts and of the sciences, as a result of which "the rules of both the state and civic and moral life are changed with the renewal of religion'' (p. 39).

Taking for granted Feuerbach's atheistic critique of religion, *Karl Marx* in his own critique of Hegel's Philosophy of Right could not regard either civil society or even the Reformation itself so positively. For him this was not the true solution, but nevertheless the true setting of the problem. Luther, he maintained, had overcome servitude arising from obsequiousness, but only to replace it by servitude arising from conviction; he had destroyed faith in authority, because he restored the authority of faith; he had liberated man from external observances of religion, because he made religion something pertaining to the inward man. Now, however, after Feuerbach's critique of all religion and in the transition from the critique of religion to the critique of law and politics, the theoretical revolution of the Reformation had to be completed in the practical revolution: "the categorical imperative has to overthrow all conditions under which man is a degraded, subjugated, forsaken, contemptible thing" (Marx, *Werke* I, p. 497).

This critique of a particular kind of interiorization of freedom in Protestantism cannot be rejected out of hand. Was there not, particularly in Lutheranism (Marcuse himself sees some differences of emphasis with Calvin), a widespread theological justification of actual economic and social bondage and inequality? Was not obedience to the secular ruler overstressed and a right of resistance, such as Calvin asserted, rejected? As a result of Christian justification, had not special justice been largely forgotten?

Defenders of Luther—I am thinking, for instance, of the analysis by the Tübingen Protestant theologian Oswald Bayer (in *Zeitschrift für Theologie und Kirche* 67, 1970, pp. 453–478)—have of course rightly pointed to the fact that, according to Luther himself, faith and love must be distinguished, but under no circumstances torn apart as inward freedom and outward bondage.

1. According to Luther, *faith* and the freedom it confers cannot be understood as an "eternal," always existing "inward *a priori*" of man. Faith and freedom are provoked publicly and concretely by the word of the Christian message, not before, but in this history. They are always fragile, can be lost, but can also be found again in encounter with the word. It is therefore a question of a freedom that is active in one's calling, work, and everyday life in the world, but that cannot be derived from these things. In this way—within the framework of a new model of theology—Luther established a new theory of work and calling, of

service of the world and service of God, Church, and office, by which the world at that time was not only differently interpreted but also actually changed: an utterly practical and not merely, as Marx thought, a theoretical revolution. Calvin's theology in particular, with its stress on asceticism in the present world—Marcuse mentions Max Weber's thesis only marginally—had sociological consequences which really laid the foundations of the new industrial society, even though they turned out eventually to be highly ambivalent.

2. Faith and freedom then are by no means restricted to the interior life, but are dynamically and vitally active in the world through what Luther—with the New Testament—calls *love*. The person who truly believes is not concentrated on himself, but gets away from himself and involved with others in a practical way, in a service, a "servitude," the goal of which is not in fact servitude but freedom and alleviation of the needs of others. This is a "servitude" arising from freedom and meant to lead to freedom.

In this connection of course it is scarcely possible to maintain consistently the distinction between the "inward" and the "outward" man. While it is possible to find in it a deeper meaning, as Eberhard Jüngel does in his book *Zur Freiheit eines Christenmenschen* (but only with a great deal of theologico-dialectical dexterity and with the aid of a vertical Christology), it seems to me—with Oswald Bayer and many others—that this static, spatial metaphor is at any rate much more open to misunderstanding—or even dangerous—than the dynamic, temporal "old" and "new" man.

This is true not merely of the present time. It must be admitted that not only Lutheranism but also Luther himself scarcely drew with sufficient clarity the sociocritical consequences—which were certainly possible—from his doctrine of justification, for example, in regard to the enslaved and impoverished peasants. On this point Ernst Bloch has rightly placed Thomas Münzer alongside Luther and in opposition to the latter. In connection with the two-man doctrine, the two kingdoms doctrine decisively simplified the problems and exercised a profoundly negative influence on Lutheranism up to the time of its resistance to National Socialism. The fact should not be overlooked, however, that the Catholic tradition also, laying the greatest stress on works, saw the consequences of justification mainly in the internal ecclesial sphere of pious works of mercy and the reception of the sacraments, but scarcely in a new organization of society or in the liberation of the oppressed. It was, in any case, not a Protestant state but the papal states which came to be regarded as the most socially backward in Europe. Until they ceased to exist, immediately after the definition of the primacy and infallibility in 1870, the authorities in Rome successfully opposed any kind of Catholic social teaching; but as soon as they themselves were no longer faced with demands, they were all the more insistent in making demands on state and society.

As far as Luther is concerned, our modern statements of the questions have perceptibly changed. Today, at any rate, we are no longer—like Luther—full of fear for the world and our own souls, asking how we can find a gracious God. But we are no less in fear for the world, for our existence and the future, asking now: How is our human life to acquire a meaning and direction? How will the history of mankind turn out? How can we survive? At the same time we do not understand God primarily in a legalistic sense, as God the judge declaring man free from his sins and justified, but as God the partner and associate, present in the vast world process, calling man to undertake responsibility for world and history and making us answerable to him in freedom.

In other words, it is a question not merely of individual justification, or purely of saving our own souls, but also of the social dimension of salvation: comprehensive care for our fellow human beings and work on changing the structures of bondage and the constraints of society. We cannot be concerned merely in a spiritual way with salvation hereafter and peace with God, but must be wholly concerned with the common good and the total good of mankind in love of neighbor *and* of those who are far away. Unlike Luther and his contemporaries, we are not so much compelled to justify our life before God, but we are certainly bound to justify it to ourselves, to our fellow human beings, and to society.

And it is at this very point that the deepest problems of the freedom of a Christian today become evident. The urge for self-justification—now not so much before God as before men, before human society—throws us back on the old problems as they emerged, in a different form, even with Paul and again, anew, with Martin Luther.

Freedom in the Achievement-oriented Society

"L'homme est libre, l'homme est liberté" ("Man is free, man is freedom"), wrote Jean-Paul Sartre in his programmatic essay *L'existentialisme est un humanisme* (1948, p. 36), protesting against determinism, mechanistic natural science, and the degradation of humanity by religion, thus defining human existence forthrightly as freedom, since—as he holds—there is no God. But for Sartre this proposition did not imply any naive enlightenment optimism. Aware of what Horkheimer and Adorno had called—about the same time—the "dialectic of enlightenment," Sartre added: "L'homme est condamné à être libre" ("Man is condemned to be free") (p. 38).

In fact, in the process of enlightenment and secularization man has freely taken into his own hands the responsibility for the world and history in all areas, but this responsibility—originally an act of liberation—has increasingly turned out to be a heavy burden. For today man no longer finds in the world traces of his Creator, but only of himself. This is a hominized, but very often not humane world, in which man is continually confronted with his achievements, with his imposing creations, but increasingly also with his horrendous destructions. Many older people, once accustomed to success, cannot understand why there is a widespread aversion to the very idea of achievement among the younger generation. But this is not our situation.

The more man realized his freedom, the more laws were needed for the sake of the common good. The more achievements he demanded of himself in the modern achievement-oriented society, the greater became the danger of losing himself: not only of losing sight of meaning and direction, but of losing himself in the anonymous mechanisms, structures, and organizations of this system. With increasing discipline and involvement, it became impossible for man to become aware of himself; with increasing responsibility, man became wholly involved in his task; the system of norms created by society itself, becoming increasingly close-meshed, mercilessly encompasses and regulates man in his calling and work, but also in his leisure, vacations, and traveling. The thousandfold precepts and prohibitions of modern traffic laws themselves amount to a symbol of modern human life as such. In brief, in all sectors there is an unprecedented *secular system of laws* in which man is losing his spontaneity, initiative, and independence and has less and less scope for himself and for his own human existence. We are faced with what looks like a lethal closed system in which increased achievement drives man into greater dependence, from which he thinks he can escape only through more achievements. It is true: man is condemned to be free.

Does not man thus experience in a modern form what Paul and Luther called the "curse of the law"? Modern life keeps him under pressure to produce greater achievements, to be on the move, to be successful. He must continually *justify himself:* no longer before God's judgment seat, but before the forum of his milieu, of his fellow human beings, of himself. But in this achievement-oriented society he can justify himself only by achievement; it is only by achievement that he is anything.

All of this leads to a diffusion of identity in different social roles, to a crisis of identity, even a loss of identity. Man is compelled to play one or several roles in society. He may then perhaps be a prodigious worker, outstanding in his profession, but is he still truly human? One thing seems to me indisputable: by his wholly secularized devotion to work according to the principle of achievement, by all his diligence, by all his industry in this industrial society, by all his activities, man still does not acquire being, personality, identity, freedom; he does not by any means gain any confirmation of his ego, any justification of his person, or a meaning to his existence. *Self*-justification of this kind cannot lead to the goal.

There is a great deal to be said about all this. But what can we do? Perhaps I may conclude by briefly indicating the essentials in the form of propositions:

1. Certainly we must *not do nothing.* Man does not find himself by renouncing achievement, by acquiescence or fatalism, still less by opting out or refusing to do anything. Achievement is required from everyone, merely in order to survive. An easygoing younger generation—in school, university, or occupation—is no answer to a very uncongenial world situation.

2. On the other hand, man should *not* base his life on *achievements,* on work, career, success. This is not merely because adverse circumstances could at any time destroy much of it, but because none of it, not even money, can make man human, render his life meaningful, or justify his existence. For man is more than his deeds, his work, his calling, his success, his merits; the person is more than his role; achievements are important, but they are not what matters in the last resort.

3. What is important in the last resort is for man to recognize the limitations of thinking in terms of achievement, to break through the pressure for achievement and the obsession with achievement, and to place his life on a *new foundation,* a new basic attitude, a different "awareness," making possible for him a truly human existence, a new freedom. From first to last, in all living and working, he must rely on something that alone can sustain him through all life's successes and

failures, through good and evil; in the midst of all realities up to the last he must place his trust unswervingly in that first and last reality which we describe by the much misused name of "God." But how can the real God be known?

4. As a Christian, man can know the real God in the one *Jesus Christ*. He it was who told the story of the Pharisee intent on achievement, the man who thought his achievements counted for something in the sight of God and men and thus that he was fully justified in his whole existence and position. But Jesus said that this man did not go home justified. On the other hand, there was the unsuccessful man who could show no achievements, or at best only morally inferior ones, but who did not pretend to be justified in the sight of God and presented himself there with all his failure, placing his hopes only in God's mercy: he it was who went home justified. This Jesus, eventually *crucified* because of this message, incapable in his absolute passivity of any achievement, and eventually—unlike the defenders of pious achievement—justified by God: this Jesus for that very reason is and remains God's living sign that what is really decisive depends, not on man and his deeds, but—for man's well-being in good and even in evil—on the merciful God who expects from man in his own passion, looking to the passion of the Crucified, an unswerving trust: *faith,* which alone can make him at peace with God and with himself and *alone can justify him.*

5. In this way man gains the *freedom of a Christian,* which can be rightly understood only in the dialectic of being free and becoming free. If man binds himself in faith alone to the one Absolute, to the one true God, who is not identical with any finite reality, then he becomes free in regard to all finite values, goods, powers, which preserve their true— that is, relative—importance. He recognizes then also both the relativity of his own achievements and the relativity of his lapses. He is no longer subject to the merciless law of having to achieve something. It is true that he is by no means dispensed from all achievement, but he is liberated from the obsessional neurosis of having to justify himself by his achievements. He is no longer absorbed in his role; he can be the person he is and may be the person he can become. And not only in his achievements and roles, but in his whole existence, in his being human, he is *justified,* apart from his achievements. Because of his believing trust in the wholly Other, he knows that his life under all circumstances has a meaning: not only in successes, but also in failures; not only in brilliant achievements, but also in lapses; not only in increasing achievement, but also in declining achievement; not only in happiness,

but also in unhappiness; not only in living, but also in dying.

I am breaking off at this point, in the hope that I have been able to explain a little how justification by faith and the freedom of a Christian can be understood today in a good Catholic sense in the light of the gospel. I may therefore conclude this essay with the words with which Martin Luther concluded his treatise *Concerning Christian Liberty:* "See! That is true, spiritual, Christian freedom which frees the heart from all sins, laws and precepts, which surpasses all other freedoms as heaven surpasses earth. May God give us the power rightly to understand and keep it."

Hans Küng

Eberhard-Karls University (Tübingen)
The Institute for Ecumenical Research
November 1980

Preface to the First English Edition

Along with the American edition of this book it would be tempting to include an answer to the intra-Catholic and ecumenical discussion which has been prompted by this study. However, even an inclusive bibliography of contributions to the discussion would necessitate many more pages in this volume which is already sufficiently ample. A thorough answer which would avoid superficiality would really call for a new book. Such an answer is planned; and my contribution to the volume *Christianity Divided* (ed. by D. J. Callahan, H. A. Oberman, and D. J. O'Hanlon, New York, 1962; London, 1962), entitled "Justification and Sanctification According to the New Testament," should be considered as a small foretaste of this and as an extension of the present volume. Here only a few preliminary remarks are made to provide the reader with an orientation to the discussion.

1. *The interpretation of Karl Barth's doctrine:* Karl Barth is to be interpreted as he interprets himself. Nevertheless, the interpretation of his doctrine in the second, Catholic, section of the book (approved by Barth) is just as instructive as the first section, which is more reportorial. All too often Barth himself feels misunderstood by the so-called Barth specialists—to their astonishment, for they do not take seriously the explicit and unambiguous approval of the Barthian *and* Catholic doctrine which has been presented. In view of his approval one must take exception to an opinion of Barth which has already for a long time been accepted, implicitly used in dogmatics, but never officially approved by him. (This is true of the American edition of Jérôme Hamer's interpretation of Barth [1948], which appeared in 1962 with a new foreword, and which was already superseded by the masterful book on Barth by Hans Urs von Balthasar [1951]). If we do for once have the pleasure of questioning an author who is still living about his own teaching (something impossible, often painfully so, with the "theologians of antiquity"), then we ought not to place our own private, proud

(and not a little unappreciative) interpretations ahead of those which are, after all, interpretations of the author approved by himself—as though we could, in this way, be more Barthian than Barth. Karl Rahner puts it correctly:

It is not the object here to debate with those who know Barth's theology as to whether Küng's meaning corresponds in every respect to the objective data in Barth's *Church Dogmatics*. That would be too difficult a task, which only the specialist in Barth's theology would be entitled to perform. To the uninitiated it is sufficient and objectively most important to say: "Barth himself finds his own views correctly represented by Küng, indeed, in *both* parts of the book." And therefore the layman can only say: "Barth must know best what he himself really meant." The rest of us could believe him and rejoice in this fact and thankfully acknowledge it even when we know that Barth is still not a Catholic. It is, in any case, of secondary importance or completely irrelevant to point a finger and say: "Yes, but Barth has also said something here and here which does not agree with this!" Why should not Barth have understood better, in reading the lectures of Küng, just what he himself intends? Why should not the opportunity have been offered him clearly to acknowledge his concerns as disclosed and to point out the danger to be avoided by Catholics through thoroughgoing formulations in the method of controversial theology? Is the consensus which is arrived at in this way only verbal? (*Tübinger Theologische Quartalschrift*, 138 [1958], pp. 46f.)

And this ought to be added in thankfulness: If Karl Barth were a lesser theologian than he actually is (he is at least the best contemporary anti-Catholic polemicist, and taken very seriously by the Lutherans); if he did not possess a true and deep understanding, which rests on a fundamental and comprehensive acquaintance with Protestant and Catholic theology in history and the present, and an often-proved sense of what is decisive; if he were of the type who always saw all the difficulties, always looked into the problem but never through it—in short, if Karl Barth were not a greater theologian but a lesser critic (there are also great critics!), then he would doubtless not have spoken a large and courageous "yes," but rather a small and hedged-in "yes, but." He would have found fault instead of rejoicing.

2. *Interpretation of the Catholic doctrine of justification:* Until now, no Catholic author has challenged the Catholic orthodoxy of the Catholic doctrine of justification as presented in the second part of this book. J. L. Witte, professor of controversial theology

at the Pontifical Gregorian University, wrote on the state of the discussion:

Küng has succeeded in making his positive answer convincing even for Barth, as clearly brought out in the introductory letter written by Barth himself. A very great service. It is even greater, because in this way he has cleared out of the way stubborn misunderstanding from the Protestant side, or (if that is premature) at least afforded the opportunity for this. Whoever knows from his own experience just how powerful these misunderstandings still are concerning the Catholic doctrine of grace would surely rejoice that here, in a book which will certainly be read by many Protestant theologians, is presented the best fruit of ancient and of modern Catholic theology in a precise way and generally in very fortunate formulations or citations. The difficulty which Protestant theology has in accepting this answer can be heard not only in Barth's introductory letter, where he declares that he waits with interest, "interest and apprehension," as to how this book will be received by the "Catholic specialists," but also from the reviews of many Protestant theologians who have already expressed their doubts about the possibility of a Catholic agreement with this answer. But already an express Catholic consensus has become apparent insofar as all Catholic reviews, with all their criticism of details, are agreed that the elements of the doctrine of justification as developed in the second part of this book do present *a* theological interpretation which is, at least, a possible one in the Catholic Church. That is, the answer given here and satisfactory to Barth, namely, the affirmative answer to the question regarding the real acceptance of justification as God's act of sovereign grace, is understood by all as truly Catholic. Also, a second "cloud of witnesses" has already joined the first which were cited in the book, so that the "Catholic reflection" of this book has a meaning for controversial theological discussion which extends far beyond itself. (*Münchner Theologische Zeitschrift,* 10 [1959], pp. 38f.)

3. *Consensus:* It was expected from the beginning that many objections to the consensus between the Barthian and the Catholic doctrines of justification would be submittted from both sides. And in general one could also suspect just what points would be objected to. These objections are to be tested with care. The author would be the last to feel that his work could not be defined, interpreted, explained, supplemented, and improved at many points. It is also granted at the outset that there are differences, and important differences, between the Barthian and the Catholic doctrines of justification. It is quite correct to stress this in the discussion. However, the conclusion of my investigation did not point to a total, but rather to a *"fundamental"* agreement, namely, to an

agreement which, at this point, would not warrant a division in the Church (cf. pp. 280, 284). This is, of course, what has meaning for an *ecumenical* discussion. Has the previous discussion brought out distinctions between the Barthian and the Catholic doctrines of justification which would divide churches and not just schools of thought (in fact and not just verbally)? No one is therefore underestimating the import of distinctions between schools of thought! Divisions between schools can also be so great within the Catholic Church that, from time to time, the battle among various schools with respect to directions of thought could be carried on with more force and be linked with more to-do and louder anathemas than the battle with heresy. Think for a moment of the Christological and trinitarian debates of the ancient Church, or the Thomistic-Molinistic controversies of more modern times, where the identification of nonbinding opinions of a school and the binding doctrine of the Church was so disastrous because it was largely overlooked (the Thomistic-Molinistic controversy is an example, but not the only one). Either a Catholic or a Protestant theologian can insist that this or that expression is an obligatory part of the Church's doctrine when, in reality, it is only a historically conditioned private opinion or that of a school, as to the doctrine of the Church. This can be done with the best of intentions, often from faulty understandings of Scripture, history of doctrine, or systematics. (Only later, oftentimes decades or centuries later, is it shown not to be binding.)

It is to be assumed from the outset that such a situation does pertain with regard to the doctrine of justification (and, as the reviewers have granted, my book has uncovered such misunderstandings in particular points). One can think of specific theological expressions: "the appropriation of justification," "inner justification," "gratia creata," "the ontological aspect of grace," "the substantial reality of grace," "merit," "the relation of justification and sanctification," etc. Our task must be to discover what is *de fide* (dogma) by using all the means of the theological discipline (*Theologischer Wissenschaft*). With many of the distinctions brought forth by critics it is not clear whether they make distinctions to mark off the Church or to separate schools and theologies. In this connection one ought not also to assume that Karl Barth was so naive in his interpretation as not to have expressly kept in mind the danger of a purely verbal consensus which had no factual substance. One of the first sentences of my introductory chapter states: "We all know that a single word can mean two things and two words one thing."

And now back to the question once again: Does the discussion, to date, between the Barthian and the Catholic doctrines of justification really point out differences which would irreducibly divide not just a school of theology but a church? In full consciousness of the difficulties of many of the questions raised which have not yet been responded to—I must still answer: "*The discussion to date has not brought forth irreducible distinctions between the Barthian and the Catholic doctrines of justification which would divide the Church and not just a school.*"

May the final word of this preface be that of Karl Rahner:

Especially in a controversial theology there is the danger that an overly neurotic anxiety might destroy the unity which could be there, though we might not perhaps yet be one "essentially" or "in the deepest sense." Such an anxiety produces every peculiar endeavor (and such efforts can be observed in controversial theology!) to prove a mutual lack of consensus by means of more and more refined formulations and nuances, where our ancestors in the sixteenth century would have maintained a lack of unity with less subtle formulations which everyone could easily see and express, or they would then have united. Today the situation is that, with many points of controversial theology, only the most refined theological rhetoric is able to clarify for the initiated (but not for the ordinary man) precisely where the distinction exists. In such cases (there are others of a contrasting type) it would be better and more Christian to say that we may be one or definitely could be one. Barth has done just this in a courageous and temperate way. In order to have the right to live in a divided church, one must be certain (to state it strongly) that there is no unity in the truth—and not merely be unsure as to whether we may really be one, or precisely what the other man is intending to say, or whether we have really understood him with precision. (*Op. cit.,* pp. 48f.)

Hans Küng

Tübingen, August, 1964

ACKNOWLEDGMENTS

The following translations of foreign-language works have been used. T. & T. Clark: *Church Dogmatics,* by K. Barth, used by permission. B. Herder Book Company: *The Church Teaches* (translation of materials from Denzinger's *Enchiridion Symbolorum*), used by permission. The Newman Press: *The Spirit and Forms of Protestantism,* by L. Bouyer; *The Theology of St. Paul,* by F. Prat; and *Theological Investigations,* by K. Rahner; used by permission. Lutterworth Press: *The Mediator,* by E. Brunner. The Westminster Press: *Peter, Disciple—Apostle—Martyr,* by O. Cullmann; *Christ and Time,* by O. Cullmann. Thomas Nelson & Sons, *The Revised Standard Version of the Bible.*

In citations from Barth's *Church Dogmatics,* italics are used at points where Küng inserted them in his citations from the original German. Similarly, in biblical quotations italics inserted by Küng have been kept.

ABBREVIATIONS

The following abbreviations are used in this volume:

AAS	*Acta Apostolicae Sedis*
CSEL	*Corpus Scriptorum Ecclesiasticorum Latinorum*
CT	*Concilium Tridentinum* (ed. Goerres)
D	Denzinger, *Enchiridion Symbolorum*
DBS	*Dictionnaire de la Bible, Supplément*
DTC	*Dictionnaire de Théologie catholique*
EphThLov	*Ephemerides theologicae Lovanienses*
GCS	*Griechische christliche Schriftsteller*
MünThZ	*Münchner theologische Zeitschrift*
NRTh	*Nouvelle Revue Théologique*
PG	*Patrologia*, Greek series (Migne)
PL	*Patrologia*, Latin series (Migne)
RechScRel	*Recherches de Science Religieuse*
RevScPhilTheol	*Revue des Sciences Philosophiques et Théologiques*
S.th.	Thomas Aquinas, *Summa Theologica*
TWNT	*Theologisches Wörterbuch zum NT* (Kittel)
ZkTh	*Zeitschrift für katholische Theologie*

Karl Barth's *Church Dogmatics* is cited with volume and page numbers thus: IV/1, 355.

A LETTER TO THE AUTHOR

My dear Hans Küng,

You have asked me to put in writing something about that book of yours—more than once a subject of conversation between us. Why not? And if you really want to incorporate this note of mine into your book, then something novel, something unique, will have come about in theological literature; and why shouldn't this happen, too? Startling things have taken place lately in this area of study—in what used to be called the "Theology of Controversy." And as I reflect on these recent developments, I must confess that your book, dealing with my view of justification, is so especially startling that it would hardly add to the shock if I made a personal appearance in it with a few lines of my own.

First, let me make three comments on the content of your book:

1. I here gladly, gratefully, and publicly testify not only that you have adequately covered all significant aspects of justification treated in the ten volumes of my *Church Dogmatics* published so far, and that you have fully and accurately reproduced my views as I myself understand them; but also that you have brought all this beautifully into focus through your brief yet precise presentation of details and your frequent references to the larger historical context. Furthermore, your readers may rest assured—until such time as they themselves might get to my books—that you have me say what I actually do say and that I mean it in the way you have me say it.

2. The positive conclusion of your critique is this: What I say about justification—making allowances for certain precarious yet not insupportable turns of phrase—does objectively concur on all points with the correctly understood teaching of the Roman Catholic Church. You can imagine my considerable amazement at this bit of news; and I suppose that many Roman Catholic readers will

at first be no less amazed—at least until they come to realize what a cloud of witnesses you have produced in support of your position. All I can say is this: If what you have presented in Part Two of this book is actually the teaching of the Roman Catholic Church, then I must certainly admit that my view of justification agrees with the Roman Catholic view; if only for the reason that the Roman Catholic teaching would then be most strikingly in accord with mine! Of course, the problem is whether what you have presented here really represents the teaching of your Church. This you will have to take up and fight out with biblical, historical, and dogmatic experts among your coreligionists. I don't have to assure you that I am keenly interested in discovering what reception your book will find among them. For my part, I can only acknowledge and reflect upon the fact that you have presented considerable evidence in support of this sort of understanding and interpretation of the teaching of your Church.

3. The negative conclusion of your critique is this: Due to my erroneous (because unhistorical) evaluation of the definitions and declarations collected in Denzinger and of the statements of the Church's magisterium in general, I have been guilty of a thoroughgoing misunderstanding and, consequently, of a thoroughgoing injustice regarding the teaching of your Church, especially that of the Fathers of Trent. Quid dicemus ad haec? If the things you cite from Scripture, from older and more recent Roman Catholic theology, from Denzinger and hence from the Tridentine text, do actually represent the teaching of your Church and are establishable as such (Perhaps this single book of yours will be enough to create a consensus!), then, having twice gone to the Church of Santa Maria Maggiore in Trent to commune with the genius loci, I may very well have to hasten there a third time to make a contrite confession—"Fathers, I have sinned." But taking the statements of that Sixth Session as we now have them before us—statements correctly or incorrectly formulated for reasons then considered compelling—don't you agree that I should be permitted to plead mitigating circumstances for the considerable difficulty I had trying to discover in that text what you have found to be true Catholic teaching? Imagine! So unexpected a view of freedom, of grace, of juridico-real justification and its realization and foundation in Christ's death, of the formulae simul justus et peccator and sola fide, and so on! How do you explain the fact that all this could

remain hidden so long, and from so many, both outside and inside the Church? And now for my own salvation, may I just whisper a question (a very confidential question, but one not liable to detract from your book in the mind of any serious reader): Did you yourself discover all this before you so carefully read my *Church Dogmatics* or was it while you were reading it afterward?

And now I come at last to the most important point, that is, to tell you what great pleasure I have derived from your book.

This is, first of all, simply because of the open-minded and resolute way you seem to have addressed yourself at the Germanicum in Rome to Roman Catholic exegesis and to history of dogma and theology, and then proceeded, like an undaunted son of Switzerland, to study my books as well and to come to grips with the theological phenomena you encountered in them. Then too, I admire and applaud the skill and sound German of your argument. Regardless of the problems touched on above, and regardless of the reception and success your book may have, it is a very noteworthy achievement; and the work you have done will not be wasted so far as your priestly and scholarly future is concerned. Moreover, I do not hesitate to tell you that, so far as your whole attitude is concerned, I feel that I may regard you as a true Israelite, in whom there is no guile.

So then, like Noah I look forth from the window of my ark and salute your book as another clear omen that the flood tide of those days when Catholic and Protestant theologians would talk only against one another polemically or with one another in a spirit of noncommittal pacifism, but preferably not at all—that flood tide is, if not entirely abated, at least definitely receding. "Divided in faith?" It is true, as you yourself know and insist, that the problem seen from either side is beset with such difficulties, that the hour, humanly speaking, would seem still a long way off when both sides no longer would be forced to admit that, yes, unfortunately, we are divided in faith. The idea that I might be a crypto-Catholic or you a crypto-Protestant—let us hope that neither of these foolish notions will occur to any of your readers. Yet it is true, isn't it, that today a few on both sides, you and I among them, are coming to realize that, while we are divided in faith, we are divided within the same faith—the same, because and insofar as we and you can believe in the self-same Lord. Those who begin to see this may and must talk to one another, but with a new approach; they should proceed from points on which they are united to discuss what separates them; and discuss what separates them with an eye to what unites them. And how else can this happen, as you say so well in your Introduction, but by our holding up to each other the mirror of the gospel of Jesus Christ?—not forgetting that on both sides the "converts" will be those who turn to examine their own countenance ever more carefully in that mirror. And what will be the effect of such a mutual use of this mirror, at least initially, but that people will try, as you have tried in your book, to view one another in the best possible light? These are small and perhaps even problematical steps forward, but in any event better than none at all. Involved as you are with a subject so crucial as justification, you have taken a rather sizable step; how feasible a step remains to be seen. When and if this step proves to have been well taken, many others will have to follow. Do not content yourself with the fine beginning you have made in this important search. It will certainly take quite an effort, once (as we hope) the central area has been cleared, to make somewhat plausible to us matters like Transubstantiation, the Sacrifice of the Mass, Mary, and the infallible papacy, and the other things with which we are confronted—pardon me, I could not resist picking up Denzinger again—in the Tridentine profession of faith. But these are for the future to worry about. Significant and sufficiently rewarding for the day is this, that the view in both directions (in this division within the self-same faith between people who believe otherwise but in no Other!) will open up and brighten up again. For this, we on both sides can give thanks. For the rest—Veni Creator Spiritus!

Now then, may God bless you.

Cordially yours,
KARL BARTH

Basel, 31 January, 1957

INTRODUCTION

Dogmatic theology implies, as a matter of course, polemic, controversy, dispute, and rebuttal. But in this book our main concern is with self-appraisal. And self-appraisal, like anything else impinging upon the self, is difficult. This is especially true in the case of the theology of justification, because self-appraisal here involves not only the matter of one's own personal justification but also—and before all else—a profound historical analysis. It was just such self-appraisal which 400 years ago split open the seamless robe of the Lord—a rupture which Christians regard as a punishment and non-Christians a scandal, down to this very day.

Yet this split must not be glossed over with facile distinctions nor condoned in a spirit of easy indifference. The prayer Christ offered before He died—"that all may be one"—makes absurd all fruitless polemic, all mere catalogues of differences, all condescension be it ever so generous, all well-intentioned, ineffectual appeals for return to unity and fullness. Besides, as serious Catholic scholars have carefully pointed out, Catholic guilt for the Reformation burns so deep that we cannot ourselves avoid a thorough soul-searching. Grace, that is, Jesus Christ "who has made us both one" (Eph. 2.14), will heal this division too, terrible as it is. All that is needed is that we listen to His word to us, that we repeatedly reconsider His revelation, that we respond to that commandment of His without any subterfuge.

This is not a business of being for Barth or against Barth. What matters is the indivisible truth of Jesus Christ. And the reason for examining ourselves in the looking glass of Karl Barth's theology is simply that Barth's teaching (as Hans Urs von Balthasar has observed in his excellent book) represents both a most pronouncedly Protestant statement and a most pronounced agreement with Catholic views. Again, we wish neither to write Barth off as a heretic nor to list him as a crypto-Catholic among our hitherto hidden assets. In this sense the issue is not Barth at all—and he would be the first to agree—but the confronting of one another with the mirror of the gospel of Jesus Christ, in earnest and uncompromising theological interchange. And this must never be like the "man, looking at his natural face in a mirror," who "goes away and presently . . . forgets what kind of man he is" (Jas. 1.23f.), but in order to attempt a realistic self-appraisal and to let the truth of *Christ* shine forth for all to see. This is meant to be a *dogmatic* discussion, not an exercise in scholarly "objectivity"; we wouldn't think of pretending to be "uncommitted" observers moving toward an illusory "neutral" arena. We want to express a thoroughly consistent Catholic point of view, and to find ourselves, in the mirror of Christ's gospel, becoming ever more Catholic. And we hope, too, that our Evangelical brothers may find themselves in the same mirror increasingly more Evangelical, so that ultimately we may again find ourselves one in the one gospel of Jesus Christ.

We have opted here for an objective rather than a personal and historical analysis. And so we may be permitted to forego an account of the details of the genesis of Barth's theology of justification. We have kept the personal and historical factors in mind throughout our inquiry, but to treat them explicitly would make this study far too bulky.

The main lines of the general development, as von Balthasar (cf. pp. 67–181) has set them forth, also have validity for the theology of justification. They are: the period of the dialectic; the turn to the analogy; the full shape of the analogy. Especially important for the history of the Barthian theology of justification before the time of the *Church Dogmatics* (1932ff.) are: *Römerbrief* (first edition, 1919), *Römerbrief* (second edition, 1922), *Das Wort Gottes und die Theologie* (1924), *Das Halten der Gebote* (1927), *Rechtfertigung und Heiligung* (1927), *Schicksal und Idee in der Theologie* (1927), *Die Theologie und die Kirche* (1928), cf. also *Rechtfertigung und Recht* (1938).

Seed and bud help us to know a flower. Yet we ought also to be able simply to appreciate the flower itself. And so Barth's theology of justification will be considered here in its fully developed and final formulation, as presented in Barth's *Church Dogmatics*.

A superficial view of the issues would simplify matters a great deal. But imputation, fiducial faith, juridicism, and other such central considerations strike too deep for that. We can really grasp them only if, despite the discouraging difficulties, we do the heavy spadework necessary to turn the subsoil, now so hidden and almost untouched, that it might prove especially productive.

In his dogmatic theology, Barth has never wandered from a radically Christocentric via media, avoiding the detours both of neo-Protestantism and of Catholicism. (Cf. for example, Barth's *Offenbarung, Kirche, Theologie,* pp. 24–27, or the first part of his *Church Dogmatics,* I/1, 38–47, 67–79, etc.) Von Balthasar has emphasized that Barth draws his lines against Catholicism (and against neo-Protestantism) primarily by means of a principle of form, which is however intelligible only in terms of the content of his thought. One can give the typically Catholic viewpoint various names—the appropriating of God, the emancipating of the free creature from dependence on God, the relativizing of God's majesty in allying Him with the human. It can also be called the manipulation of grace, the deformation of grace into a physical event and a material condition, the naturalizing of grace; or natural theology, double-entry bookkeeping, or "the Catholic 'and'." But in the original preface to his *Church Dogmatics,* Barth emphasizes before all else the *"analogy of being":* "I take the *analogia entis* to be *the* crucial invention of the antichrist and *the* crucial reason for not becoming Catholic. In saying this I at the same time concede that all other reasons which one might have for not becoming Catholic are short-sighted and shallow." (Cf. also II/1, 79–84.) This dominant methodological principle is the theological wellspring of everything Catholic. It reasserts itself in a variety of doctrinal contexts:

> "For what else is the establishing of such a system embracing God and the creature, the attempt to see and correlate them on the same level, but the kind of act in which the creature arrogates to itself the ability to control itself and therefore God. . . . This act is the basic act of its doctrine of grace, of the Sacraments, of the Church, of Scripture, and tradition, of the Roman primacy and the infallibility of the Pope, and above all its Marian doctrine" (II/1, 582–583).

Von Balthasar, by analyzing the Catholic mode of thought, attempted to prove that this objection was without foundation in the Catholic system. Meantime Volumes IV/1 (1953) and IV/2 (1955) of Barth's *Dogmatics* were published (Vol. III/4 appeared in 1951, the same year as von Balthasar's study), and in them Barth dealt with the process of justification point by point. We cannot review here all aspects of this fundamental problem. Yet it wouldn't be the *fundamental* problem if we were able to sidestep it completely. It forms the dangerous and ever-present substratum beneath all problems concerning creation, sin, grace, and justification. We cannot get beyond these problems without probing Barth's deepest intentions. *What* a man says is easily stated; *how* he *intends* it is the decisive issue. In Volumes IV/1 and IV/2 Barth does not use the term "analogia entis" when referring to Catholic teaching. This silence is due to von Balthasar's Catholic response. But we must wait and see whether Barth really relinquishes his basic objection in treating justification and the closely related problems of creation and sin. Perhaps then we can reiterate and amplify some points touched on by von Balthasar.

One thing was clearly established by von Balthasar: Although Barth in his *Church Dogmatics* does not give up the urgent issues of dialectical theology characteristic of his commentary on Romans, he *no longer focuses upon "dialectical theology"* in the *Dogmatics*. A few reminiscences in the first two volumes ought not to obscure the fact that Barth had then already completed his transition to analogy, however this analogy may have to be defined. On countless occasions Barth has expressly dissociated himself from the formula, "God is all, man is nothing." Quite apart from all irrelevance, is it not tiresome to be continually reviving the old complaints and mistrustfully to insist on reading a dialectical formula into Barth even in places where he himself never intended it?

PART ONE

KARL BARTH'S THEOLOGY OF JUSTIFICATION

A.

Justification and Salvation-History

1. AN ALIEN LANGUAGE

Barth's theology is unintelligible—so we are often told. It keeps slipping away. Very well, but what does the word "intelligible" mean here? We all know that a single word can mean two things and two words one thing. This is especially true for different languages and styles of thought. If I want to understand a Chinese scholar who does not speak my language and yet may have something valuable to say, there is nothing else for me to do but to learn his language and particularly his way of thought, and to make myself at home in them. This certainly does not mean that I should abandon my own language as though it were less correct or unseemly. The point is that for me to insist, in such a case, upon my own manner of speaking and thinking would be tantamount to my abandoning any attempt to truly understand the other man. If a man can think in several languages, he can often discover a symphony in what another imagines to be cacophony.

Catholic theologians have no small difficulty in trying to grasp the theology of Karl Barth, and this precisely because, quite apart from all matters of content, Barth thinks and speaks otherwise than they do. The vocabulary and the whole system of categories, the choice of words and the pattern of thinking are strange. Whereas the Catholic theologian generally thinks and speaks along Aristotelian and scholastic lines, Barth's thought and language take their shape from German Idealism. Barth has assimilated, especially through the theology of Schleiermacher, the whole development from Kant through Fichte and Schelling to Hegel. He has also drawn upon later Protestant theology, particularly that of Overbeck, Feuerbach, Strauss, and especially the theological existentialism of his own teacher, Herrmann. It is not our intention here to become involved in all the problems connected with the use and transposition of idealistic thought patterns. Hans Urs von Balthasar has quite competently discussed these in his book (*Karl*

3

Barth, Darstellung und Deutung seiner Theologie, Cologne, 1951, pp. 201–259).

We point all this out only because as Catholic theologians we can completely misunderstand Barth's theology if we look at it only through Aristotelian and scholastic glasses. We would never notice what, even in purely formal matters, is Barth's constant and overriding concern: he moves from unity, totality and fullness, from the concrete and particular, from the factual and historical, in which the abstract and universal, the essential and permanent are contained. Thus he accents act, event, and reality—in which, in his view, potency, state, and possibility are implicit. This also accounts for his distaste for that "thinking from below" which begins with the potential, the possible, with nature and essence, and which then comes from beneath to fashion the real. Barth thinks from above, from the real and factual and concrete, and especially from that Concretissimum which is God and his revelation in Jesus Christ. And he does this not in some static and formal fashion, but rather in a dynamic and living thought which affirms while negating and negates while affirming. He never illumines one side alone, nor one side after the other in rigid sequence. Rather he always illuminates the whole from many sides, with an oscillating movement like that of life, lighting reality from within so as to bring out its many-faceted brilliance.

At first sight all this can seem confusing, evanescent, paradoxical, even unintelligible. One who remains within his own, perhaps all-too-static thought patterns will never escape the awkward feeling that in Barth everything is slipping away, that here he can never really get to the bottom of things. He will be tempted to make a rash judgment about the insidiousness of the object or, more rarely, will judge his own powers of thinking deficient. Thus the need to be prudent, to enter in, not to judge rashly but rather to learn patiently.

One can perhaps approach Barth's thought processes most readily from Sacred Scripture. There we find an accent on the concrete and living; there, too, everything is caught up in history and movement. In Scripture much is put in pointed, apparently contradictory antitheses and much is hard to fit into a static thought structure. And there, above all, that omnidominant Concretissimum stands at beginning, middle, and end—God revealed in Jesus Christ. Barth in the long course of his development has found his way back from "pure" philosophy to Sacred Scripture, and there at last, getting rid of nonessentials, has formed his language and his thought. So a man can expect to find in Scripture access to a theological understanding of Barth's writings.

2. JUSTIFICATION: WHAT IS THE CENTRAL PROBLEM?

The firewood for the Reformation was piled up long before Luther. Difficulties ran the gamut from superficial personal piety at lower levels to a frightening ecclesiastical secularization on higher levels, from unscrupulous nationalistic politics to muddle-headed late medieval theology. But need all this fuel have fired up a Reformation *outside* the existing ecclesiastical community? It was Martin Luther's spark which finally kindled it. One finds in Luther that he makes scarcely a single theological statement without its precedent in the late medieval theologians. And yet Luther, in his inexhaustible originality, is profoundly and ultimately independent of this decadent theology. His own Reform theology is rooted in the very core of his personality—in a personal experience of divine justification.

Cf. Lortz, *Geschichte der Kirche,* pp. 259–283, *Reformation in Deutschland;* vol. I, pp. 147–236; and *Reformation als religiöses Anliegen heute,* pp. 13–163; on the question of late medieval theology, see Bouyer, *The Spirit and Forms of Protestantism,* pp. 136–165, esp. pp. 151ff.

Without exaggeration we can say too that it is the theology of justification that lies at the root of the still continuing theological battle over the true form of Christianity, at the root of the greatest catastrophe that has befallen the Catholic Church in her two-thousand-year history.

Luther throughout his lifetime regarded justification as the fundamental and central dogma of Christianity. In his commentary on Galatians (1535) he writes on Gal. 1.3: "If the article of justification goes, everything goes. It is therefore necessary that we daily stress . . . and strongly urge this article. We can never say that we think about it or hold to it enough or too much." With greater or lesser depth and consistency, orthodox Lutherans of the sixteenth and seventeenth centuries also insist on justification as the "article by which the Church stands or falls." And among neo-Lutherans it has once more gained its place of prominence. Barth points all this out (IV/1, 521f.). But does he agree with this view?

What is important for Barth in justification is the passage of man from a state of reprobation to a state of election, from death to life. At stake in this transition is the underlying judgment God makes about man. Barth's theology of justification tries to make this intelligible and comprehensible.

"It is a question of explaining the fact and the extent to which in this history, or in the divine sentence on man which underlies this history, we are dealing with that which is just and right. It is a question of showing the right of *God* which gives right to man, and of the right which is given by God to *man.* The highly problematical point in the history is obviously the notorious *wrong* of man" (IV/1, 517).

After thus posing the problem, Barth stresses the special *significance* of the theology of justification: "It is a matter of the genuineness of the *presupposition,* the inner *possibility,* of the reconciliation of the world with God, in so far as this consists of a complete alteration of the human situation, a conversion of sinful man to Himself as willed and accomplished by God. . . . Therefore the Christian community and Christian faith stand or fall with the reality of the fact. . . . The community rests and acts on this *basis.* Faith lives by the *certainty* and *actuality* of the reconciliation of the world with God accomplished in Jesus Christ" (IV/1, 517f.).

For the same reason Barth feels the special *difficulty* of the theology of justification. Problems here strangely multiply. They begin with the relationship between the two basic concepts of grace and justice, but they finally come to a climax in one single mystery: "In the first and final instance the problem of justification is, for those whom it occupies, the problem of the fact of their own justification. Even when we have done our best, which of us can think that we have even approximately mastered the subject, or spoken even a penultimate word in explanation of it?" (IV/1, 519).

From this, finally, comes the special *function* of the theology of justification. Here must be explained the passage from an existence which is godless and dead to an existence in which man lives for God. On this transition the entire *Dogmatics* is focused. "What we can and must say is that in the doctrine of justification we are dealing with the most pronounced and puzzling form of this transition because we are dealing specifically with the question of its final *possibility*. As we have seen already, how *can* it be that *peace* is concluded between a holy God and sinful man—by grace, but in a way which is completely and adequately *right?*" (IV/1, 520). This special function of the theology of justification breaks through with special force in times of crisis in the history of the Church. It was this way in the time of Augustine, in the time of Luther, in the time of the "Enlightenment" at the beginning of the nineteenth century, and it may very well be this way too in our own "humanistic" century.

Barth then does say with Luther: With the theology of justification the entire theological enterprise stands or falls. But is this the whole truth of the matter?

Granted that the theology of justification is especially important, especially difficult, and especially necessary, nevertheless Barth sees in it only *one special aspect* of the Christian message of salvation. In the Church of Christ justification was not always and everywhere the center and focus of the gospel. Luther and the younger Melanchthon exaggerated when they saw in Paul nothing other than a teacher of justification. And none of the Gospels, nor any of the other New Testament writings, are easy to harmonize with Pauline teaching on justification; the problem is not only with the Letter of James. And history teaches us that the Church of the first century, just as later the entire Church and the theology of the East, knew nothing of an explicit theology of justification. Justification became a burning issue only with the Reformation, but even then, for example in Calvin, it was not unqualifiedly central. Side by side with any Protestant theology of justification it had always been customary—and this was true for Luther, too—to develop a theology of sanctification. And a third element would have to be added as well—a theology of vocation, the special concern of the Eastern Church.

"The *articulus stantis et cadentis ecclesiae* is not the doctrine of justification as such, but its basis and culmination: the confession of *Jesus Christ*. . . . The problem of justification does not need artificially to be absolutised and given a monopoly. It has *its own* dignity and necessity . . ." (IV/1, 527f.).

There are other problems besides justification, yet all of them do decisively depend on it. And so we may ask Barth: Where do we locate this decisive strand in the dogmatic fabric? What does it support and what supports it?

3. JUSTIFICATION IN THE TOTAL CONTEXT OF BARTH'S THEOLOGY

A rough sketch is bound to be a poor expedient, lacking life and depth. But men depend on such expedients in order not to lose their way and not to wander into the wrong room or off at the wrong floor. Let us then attempt an outline of Barth's *Dogmatics* so as to learn the place of justification in his theology.

The center toward which, in Barth's view, everything tends, and from which everything radiates, is *the God-man Jesus Christ*. Dogmatic theology means for Barth a radically Christocentric theology. In the first two volumes (especially I/1 but also I/2) this is expressed in a somewhat abstract fashion, in the central concept of the Word of God, which is of course ultimately identical with Christ. Barth's theology of the Word of God forms the Prolegomena to his *Dogmatics*.

Consistent with the content of the Church's proclamation and consequently also the criterion of dogmatic theology as a scientific investigation of the Church's message is the *Word of God*. The one and only Word of God actually appears in three forms, namely as revelation, as Bible, and as proclamation. The three must however always be seen in their unity, as God uttering, God acting, and God's mystery. The understanding of the Word of God can be achieved only in the recognition of it wrought by the Word itself (I/1, 1-283).

The task of *dogmatic theology* lies in a critical inquiry into dogma, into the Word of God in the Church's proclamation—that is, in the critical problem of the compatibility between the Church's proclamation as promulgated or to be promulgated among men, and the revelation attested in Scripture (I/1, 284–335).

But if the inner structure of revelation, Bible and proclamation is to be made plain, this is possible only on the condition that we analyze the fact of the concrete revelation, as Barth does in the detailed development of his theology of the Trinity (I/1, 339–560), his basic positions on Christology (I/2, 1–202), and on the indwelling of the Holy Spirit (I/2, 203–454). It is from this investigation into the concept of revelation that he gets what he needs for his theology of *Sacred Scrip-*

ture, which he describes to us as God's Word to the Church, as the authority and the freedom of the Church (I/2, 457–740). Here, too, he gets his theology of *proclamation,* which is treated as a responsibility of the Church in its function of listening and teaching (I/2, 743–884).

Barth begins the *Dogmatics* proper with his *theology of God* (Vols. II/1, and II/2). This is developed entirely and exclusively along Christological lines starting from the Council of Chalcedon:

The first and fundamental chapter deals with the *knowledge* of God —its accomplishment through the revelation of Christ in faith (II/1, 3–62), its possibility through the communication of God's truth in Christ to men who share in this truth through grace (II/1, 63–78), its limits in the hiddenness of God (II/1, 179–254).

And what is the underlying *reality* of Him who is here known? It is the living God, who lives from and through Himself and thus seeks and achieves communion with men in both love and freedom (II/1, 257–321). Each of the divine perfections, itself identical with His one and simple essence, is a form of love in which God is free (His grace, His mercy, His patience, together with His holiness, His justice and His wisdom) or a form of freedom in which God loves (His unity, constancy and eternity, with His omnipresence, omnipotence and glory) (II/1, 322–677).

Yet the being of God is not a mere being-for-Himself. God is simultaneously for *us* in Jesus Christ. This is God's *gracious choice*—the eternal election of Jesus Christ, who is the elector as well as the elected (II/2, 3–194), is simultaneously the election of the one community of God, of Israel, and of the Church (II/2, 195–305), whose testimony bears witness that the rejection of individual men is in Jesus Christ made null and void, and proclaims the eternal election in Jesus Christ of the individual to eternal life (II/2, 306–506).

Yet Barth's theology of God does not come to an end with this climactic moment in the *Dogmatics.* Barth treats ethics as an integral component of his dogmatic theology, and he anchors it, as he does all his ethical teaching, directly in a Christian theology of God, the theology of God's *commandment.* Commandment is defined as God's claim, God's decision, and God's judgment (II/2, 509–781).

The theology of God attempts to clarify in faith what God is in himself. The question then follows: What are the *works of God?* In succeeding volumes, with his *Dogmatics* still far from finished, Barth takes up the three great works of God, which include in themselves all the others and ultimately represent the different moments of the one great work of God—creation, reconciliation, redemption (or consummation).

The theology of creation (Vols. III/1–III/4) is, in the deepest sense, a theology of salvation and cannot be developed apart from a context of faith. Creation is, as it were, the first work of the triune God and as such is not yet a reconciliation or a consummation. Reconciliation and consummation, however, do have in creation their *anticipation,* and in that sense they do begin with creation.

In the first part of his theology of creation, Barth treats explicitly of the *work* of creation; first of faith in God the Creator (III/1, 3–41); then of creation as the first of the works of the Trinity, creation and salvation-history, the literary quality of the biblical account of creation (III/1, 42–94); and finally of the central problem of both creation accounts—of the relationship between creation and covenant. Barth considers creation the external basis for the covenant, and the covenant the inner basis for creation. The purpose, therefore, and the meaning of creation is the making possible of a history in which God will join with man in a covenant—and one which has its beginning, middle, and end in Jesus Christ (III/1, 94–329). The work of the Creator continues in the great kindness by which He permits what He has created *to* actually *be* through Him and (as adjusted to Him) *to be good* (III/1, 330–414).

The idea of creation involves not only the Creator's act, but also its result. The second part of the theology of creation deals with the creature, specifically with man *as God's creature.* This is Barth's theological anthropology, and thus it must be rooted in his Christology (III/2, 3–54). It is from the man Jesus Christ that we take our departure in explaining man as the creature of God (III/2, 55–202) and as called to be God's covenant partner (III/2, 203–324). Human existence is being-for-God and being-with-fellowmen. How is this being constituted? Man—in his irreversible difference, inseparable unity and indestructible orientation—is through God's Spirit constituted entirely and simultaneously the soul of his body (III/2, 325–436). And man is all this as a form of being temporally limited by an eternal God, and thus fastened upon that eternal God as the hope of his existence (III/2, 437–640).

The third part contrasts *Creator and creature,* and discusses the providence in the fatherly Lordship of God the Creator in Jesus Christ (III/3, 3–57) through which He preserves (III/3, 58–90: conservatio), accompanies (III/3, 90–154: concursus) and rules (III/3, 154–238: gubernatio) the course of this special creaturely existence. He then discusses the conduct of the Christian under this universal Lordship (III/3, 239–288: faith, obedience, and prayer). To his theology of providence Barth subjoins his teaching on the disturbing element in God's providence, that is, his theology of nothingness or evil (III/3, 289–368: the misjudgment involved, the recognition and reality of evil) and his teaching on God's messengers and their adversaries in the context of God's universal government (III/3, 369–531: the problems of angelology, the kingdom of heaven, angels and devils).

The fourth section of the theology of creation contains the first part of special ethics—*the commandment of God the Creator:* the orientation of creation in Jesus Christ is toward the freedom of man (III/4, 3–46). There follows an inquiry into the freedom that God wills for man in relation to Himself (freedom before God, holydays, confession, prayer, III/4, 47–115), in relation to his fellowman (freedom in the community—husband and wife, parents and children, neighbors and strangers, III/4, 116–323), in view of his temporal limitations and his circumscribed life (freedom within bounds—unique opportunities, vocation, honor, III/4, 324–685).

After creation Barth deals with reconciliation. Volumes IV/1 and IV/2 contain the sections so far published on the *theology of reconciliation*. These volumes require special attention because they deal explicitly with justification. Barth has planned two additional volumes on the theology of reconciliation, after which the series is to be concluded with a treatment of a *theology of redemption* or consummation (eschatology). This sketchy outline must suffice. Barth's theology, with its grandeur and its monumental perspectives, its exciting review of the history of dogma, its sympathetic exegesis, its critical confrontation of a whole range of philosophers and theologians, and most important of all its constructive theological power—a power unmatched in recent times—will come to life only for him who comes to grips with the heavy (and often quite long-winded) volumes—who reads them and judges for himself.

4. THE ETERNAL FOUNDATION OF JUSTIFICATION

It is true that justification is a temporal event, but it is not a chance event, nor is it an arbitrary one. Barth sees this, as he sees all other works of God, as grounded in God's eternity—in the *eternal gracious choice of God made in Jesus Christ*. Only in his eternal and free self-determination in Christ—in which He commits Himself to sinful man and thus commits sinful man to Himself—is God the God of creation, the God of reconciliation, the God of redemption. And it is only through this commitment that He is the God of justification.

On questions of methodology, i.e., on the orientation, foundation, and place of a theology of election in the *Dogmatics,* see II/2, 3–93; on the eternal sonship of Jesus Christ, I/1, 457–512; on the incarnation of Jesus Christ, see I/2, 1–202.

With this eternal beginning of justification we have also the original choice of God, that original decision which is never to be overshadowed, revoked, or corrected by any other decision. From eternity to eternity God chooses Himself in Jesus Christ, in the form of a creature. Without Jesus Christ, who is God's own gracious choice and consequently God's original Word and resolve, there is no choice, no way, no work. Barth develops this in detail on the basis of the prologue to the Gospel of John and parallel passages, notably Colossians 1, Ephesians I, Hebrews 1, et al.

Cf. II/2, 55–58, 95–99, 102–103, 106f., 146–155; for foundation in the history of dogma cf. II/2, 44–49, 60–76, 106–115, 118–120, 127–145. Especially interesting is Barth's position in regard to Augustine, Thomas and Calvin.

It is only in Jesus Christ that the family of man, the community of God in its dual form—Israel and the Church—is elected. And it is ultimately only in this family context that individual men in their private relationships are chosen by God. So, too, the justification of sinners is grounded in the unique eternal election of the individual as a member of the people of God in Jesus Christ. (On the ecclesiological aspect of election, see II/2, 195–305; for the individual aspect, see II/2, 305–506).

Predestination is for Barth not some sort of particular act but rather the whole preparatory dealing of God with men (creation, reconciliation, and consummation), the comprehensive act. "The divine predestination is the election of Jesus Christ" (II/2, 103). This means in the first place that "Jesus Christ is the electing God" (II/2, 103) (in communion with the Father and the Holy Spirit). He chooses from eternity to be obedient to the Father, to give Himself over and become man, so that the covenant with man might become a reality. And this also means that "Jesus Christ is the elected man" (II/2, 116). The choice falls on the man Jesus of Nazareth, and in His life and death and resurrection, in His humiliation and His exaltation, the divine covenant with all mankind is accomplished. Therefore in this one Man all men are elected. "In him" (Eph. 1.4) means not only like Him but also in His person and through His will, through His choice. So that every man has "a participation in the grace of the One who elects, a participation in His creatureliness (which is already grace), and a participation in His sonship (which is eminently grace)" (II/2, 121).

Yet God's original choice is, from all eternity, God's giving of Himself for man, who stands before Him from all eternity as a *sinner*—the giving of Himself for the man who was created good by Him but fell away from Him. And so the eternal divine predestination is *twofold,* "a *praedestinatio gemina*" (II/2, 161; cf. 161–174). Jesus Christ Himself is as much the elected One as He is the rejected One: "God wills to lose in order that man may gain. . . . In the election of Jesus Christ which is the eternal will of God, God has ascribed to man the former, election, salvation and life; and to Himself He has ascribed the latter, reprobation, perdition and death." (II/2, 162f.)

And so, negatively, the gracious choice implies *rejection.* Yet not the rejection of man who, though created good by God, sinned and would indeed have deserved rejection, but instead God Himself in His Son makes the burden of rejection His own. He who is without sin takes sin upon Himself, and with it sin's punishment—

damnation, death and hell. God chose all this for Himself by living and by dying on Golgotha. Christ stands alone, where all men ought to stand. He suffers for all. He is the only one rejected by the Father, in order that in Him all of us might be the Father's elect. This then is what is most important about predestination. This is its purpose and its point—that the gracious election is in its positive aspect revealed and realized in the resurrection of Christ and His ascension. This is the fact of *election*. God chooses for Himself damnation, death and hell, so that He might choose for mankind the overflow of His glory, His blessedness and everlasting life.

But is not God's eternal will therefore a dual will, a Yes *and* a *No?* God's eternal will, even though dual, is in the act of election one and single, because the No of rejection is in every way subordinate to the Yes of election. For man there is no reprobation unto death or damnation, since God in His own Son has taken all this upon Himself. It is only by a malicious misconstruction of the situation that a man could put himself there where, in place of all, Christ stands by Himself alone. But even there such a man— despite and even in the very act of bearing false witness to the rejection of man—would still do obedience to Christ because in his perjury he would represent and accomplish the death of the unique rejected one, Jesus Christ. But the truth is and remains only this— the election of *all* rejected men is in that Jesus Christ who precisely as rejected is the elected One; and the election is to the kingdom of God, to blessedness and everlasting life. This is the foundation for the justification of men.

"God's eternal decree in the beginning was the decree of the just and merciful God, of the God who was *merciful* in His justice and *just* in His mercy. He was just in that he willed to treat evil seriously, to judge it and to sentence it, to reject and to condemn its author, delivering him over to death. But He was merciful in that He took the author of evil to His bosom, and willed that the rejection and condemnation and death should be his own. In this decree of the just and merciful God is grounded the justification of the sinner in Christ, and the forgiveness of sins" (II/2, 167).

So, too, the justification of sinners in time is made possible and real because God from eternity has in His own Son elected condemnation for Himself, yet elected forgiveness for sinners.

Thus it is a foregone conclusion for Barth that justification originates in the *grace* of God, and in His grace taken in its eminent sense, not merely as creatureliness but as sonship (cf. II/2, 121f.), in His sovereignty and the initiative of His particular good will. The theology of election must bear witness to grace as "the starting-point for all reflection and utterance, the common denominator which should never be omitted in any statements which should follow, and which should, if possible, be asserted in some form in these statements" (II/2, 93; cf. II/2, 9f., 91f., 100–103, 117–120, etc.).

Is not the creature annihilated in all this? On the contrary, it is right here within the theonomy and divine dominion of this gracious original choice, that the autonomy, individuality and *independence* of the creature are fully realized. They have their firmest foundation in the eternal and gracious election of God.

"God elects man in order *that man may* be awakened and summoned to *elect God*, and to pray that he may give himself to Him and that in this act of electing and prayer he may exist in freedom before God: the reality *in nuce* which is distinct from God and yet united with Him in joy and peace; man who is the meaning and purpose of the whole creation; man in whom his own sphere can and should have autonomy and a kingdom" (II/2, 180; cf. 175–180).

Justification as a temporal event must not be dissociated from eternity. Does this mean that the divine election—and with it justification—was "fixed" in advance, the consequence of an inflexible eternal decree? In no sense. While the gracious election is the work of the unchangeable God, nonetheless this God is also very much alive. Justification is eternal, yet it is a living and present event (cf. II/2, 180–194). It occurs eternally in time, it occurs precisely at the point where justification comes to men. It is also true that it is precisely in justification that the mystery of eternal election becomes present and manifest in time.

God, too, retains His full freedom in this event of election (cf. Rom. 9–11). "Then in the course of God's eternal deciding we have constantly to reckon with new decisions in time. As the Bible itself presents the matter, there is no election which cannot be followed by rejection, no rejection which cannot be followed by election" (II/2, 186). We are dealing with the "rule of the living God who is free to love where He was wroth and to be wroth where He loved, to bring death to the living and life to the dead, to repent Himself, and to repent of His repenting" (II/2, 187).

This is how Barth regards the justification of men—from the viewpoint of God's eternity. The eternal original commitment of God to men, the gracious election of Jesus Christ and in Him of all men, becomes operative in time. Through God's judgment and verdict on the cross and in the resurrection of Christ, in the rejection and election of the God-man, justification comes to the sinner. Around this central event the entire history of man revolves. All human history is the history of God's covenant with man.

5. THE COVENANT—PREREQUISITE FOR JUSTIFICATION

We have seen that the eternal original foundation for justification is God's gracious election in Jesus Christ. This gracious election is nothing else than God's eternal *covenant* with men. Before and beyond all time God chooses in Jesus Christ to be a covenant God and consequently to have man as His covenant partner. Yet this covenantship does not remain hidden in eternity; rather it is revealed in time. The eternal covenant of God with man is initiated and carried forward in time.

How apart from this covenant could a guarantee be given that in justification (and in reconciliation in general, since justification is only one aspect of reconciliation) we do not have a purely accidental affair of only relative importance, pertaining perhaps only to a certain group of people? The eternal covenant of God, brought into being in time, makes justification an unqualified act, eternally valid and universally binding. Justification is without question a reaction to the sin of man, a nevertheless and in-spite-of reaction to this incident. But the justification we find in reconciliation is "something quite different from the blind paradox of an arbitrary act of the divine omnipotence" (IV/1, 12). It is, on the contrary, God's "affirmation and consummation of the institution of the covenant between Himself and man" (IV/1, 36), the divine implementation of His eternal and original covenant-purpose.

"In Jesus Christ we are not merely dealing with the author of our justification and sanctification as the sinners that we are. We are not merely dealing with the One who has saved us from death, with the Lord and Head of His Church. As such, as the One who fulfils this divine work in the world, which would be lost without Him, He is born in time, at His own time. But at the same time and beyond all

18

that—and the power of His saving work as the Mediator is rooted and grounded in this—He is the 'first-born of all creation' (Col. 1.16)—the *first* and *eternal* Word of God delivered and fulfilled in time" (IV/1, 48).

In Barth's view, nothing of what God has done in time can be isolated from this covenant. Much is involved in the realization that even in the first of God's works, in *creation,* we are faced with this selfsame covenant of grace which is later to be reaffirmed in a new and decisive way in the justification of the sinner.

Creation, while not itself the covenant, is already an expression of revelation and an actualization of God's eternal covenant-purpose. It is a work of the triune God and is accomplished in the God-man Jesus Christ who exists from eternity.

For creation as a work of the Trinity, see III/1, 45–61, especially the proof from scripture, pp. 52–56; see also pp. 363f.; on God the Father as Creator, see I/1, 441–456.

"But if Jesus Christ is the content and form of the first and eternal Word of God, then that means further that the beginning of all things, of the being of all men and of the whole world, even the divine willing of creation, is preceded by God's *covenant* with man as its basis and purpose" (IV/1, 53; cf. III/1, 71–77). The relationship of creation to covenant has to be precisely defined.

Creation is focused on history, and indeed on *the* history: "the history of salvation . . . the true history which encloses all other history . . . the history of the covenant of grace instituted by God between Himself and man" (III/1, 59f. *passim*).
Creation is the beginning of this covenant history. True, creation is not itself the covenant nor is it the cause of the covenant—there is no inner evolution at work here—but it is the way and means to the covenant. *"The creation is the external—and only the external—basis of the covenant"* (the inner basis is God's free love, III/1, 97f.). Creation makes the covenant technically possible; it sets aside the spaces and furnishes the subjects for it. It requires the existence of man and the world, and love presupposes the existence and reality of the beloved. Barth makes all this clear in a long exegesis of the first creation account (III/1, 97–251).
Still the unity must not be lost track of in this diversity. While creation has precedence in history, the covenant has precedence in importance; while creation is the formal prerequisite for the covenant, the covenant is the material prerequisite for creation. While creation is the external foundation for the covenant, *the covenant is the internal basis of creation"* (its external basis is the omnipotence and wisdom of God, III/1, 231): "What God created when He created the world and

man was not just any place, but that which was foreordained for the establishment and the history of the covenant, nor just any subject, but that which was to become God's partner in this history, i.e., the nature which God in His grace willed to address and accept and the man predestined for His service. The fact that the covenant is the goal of creation is not something which is added later to the reality of the creature. . . . It already characterises creation itself and as such, and therefore the being and existence of the creature. The covenant whose history had still to commence was the covenant which, as the goal appointed for creation and the creature, made creation necessary and possible, and determined and limited the creature." Barth demonstrates this for us with the help of the second creation account (III/1, 232–344). Creation does not merely promise, announce and prophesy the covenant, but rather—without being identical with it—prepares for the covenant in anticipating it. It is itself an early and unique covenant-sign, a true sacrament.

Man in creation is thus already entirely and completely under the *grace* of God, and this *in an eminent way*. We can and must recognize a double pattern of grace, without in any way losing our awareness of the unity of the two in fact. Both are grace, creation as well as covenant. Yet the grace of creation is not simply identical with the grace of the covenant, while the grace of the covenant automatically encompasses the grace of creation.

" 'I will be your God': that is the original *emergence* of God from any neutrality, but also His emergence from what is certainly a gracious being and working as Creator and Lord in relation to man. That is *more* than the creation, more than the preservation, accompaniment and over-ruling of His creatures. That is the covenant of God with man . . ." (IV/1, 38; cf. 39f.).

"According to the Christian message 'God with us' means God with the man for whom salvation is intended and *ordained* as such, as the one who is created, preserved and over-ruled by God as man. It is not as though the expectation belonged to his created being. It is not as though he had any kind of claim to it. God cannot be forced to give us a part in His divine being. The matter might have ended quite well with that general grace of being—which even in itself is great enough. But where God is not bound and man has no claim, even more compelling is the will and plan and promise of God. It goes beyond, or rather it precedes His will and work as Creator. Therefore it has to be distinguished from it, as something *prior*, which *precedes* it. The ordaining of salvation for man and of man for salvation is the original and basic will of God, the ground and purpose of His will as Creator. It is not that He first wills and works the being of the world and man, and then ordains it to salvation. But God creates, preserves and over-rules man for *this* prior end and with *this* prior purpose, that there may be a being distinct from Himself ordained for salvation, for perfect being, for participation in His own being, because as the One who loves in freedom He has determined to exercise redemptive grace—and that there may be an object of this His redemptive grace, a partner to receive it" (IV/1, 9f.; cf. III/2, 348ff.).

On the pattern of grace in creation, see in addition III/1, 38–41, 43–46, 62f., 236–239; for the creation of man in particular, III/2, 142–147, 319–323.

With its foundation established in creation, God's covenant with man is *universal* in character. While this universality is only vaguely hinted at in the Old Testament (the covenant with Noah, the vision of Isaiah, the prophecies of Jeremiah, the individual figures taken from the pagan world, etc. (see IV/1, 25–34), it is proclaimed with full force and clarity in Jesus Christ, who reveals "that this covenant with Israel is made and avails for the whole race" (IV/1, 35).

God's work in Jesus Christ is thus wholly and entirely beneficent (Barth makes this point against Marcion and Schopenhauer, see III/1, 334–340); for it is the work of making the creature real and just.

"Making the creature real" (III/1, 344–365): In Jesus Christ the creature is allowed to *have existence,* and therefore *is.* The creature is not just something that appears to be, not just something conjured up or dreamed up; rather it is real and free. Yet this is certain and manifest only through the self-revelation of the gracious God in the glad tidings of Jesus Christ (Barth here speaks against Descartes, III/1, 350–363).

"Making the creature just" (III/1, 366–414): The creature does not merely exist, is not purely neutral in the sense of not being bad. It is all right, it is good, it is even perfect. We are sure of this through God's self-revelation in Jesus Christ (this against Leibniz, Wolff, Lesser, Brocker, Kyburtz, III/1, 388–414). "If the created world is understood in the light of the divine mercy revealed in Jesus Christ, of the divine participation in it eternally resolved in Jesus Christ and fulfilled in Him in time; if it is thus understood as the arena, instrument and object of His living action, of the once for all divine contesting and overcoming of its imperfection, its *justification* and *perfection* will infallibly be perceived and it will be seen to be the *best* of all possible worlds." (III/1, 385; cf. III/4, 39f.; concerning justification as an explanatory principle in the theology of creation, see III/1, 29ff.).

For Barth's present relationship to "dialectical theology" the following ideas are important:

On the self-realization of the creature: in the creation as such (I/1, 105f.; III/1, 25f., 216f., 331f.); especially important is man as the image of God, that is, as true over and against God (III/3, 183–207); on divine preservation (III/3, 71–73, 85–88: conservatio); on divine accompanying (III/3, 44–47, 145–151: concursus); on divine governing (III/3, 165f., 188–190: gubernatio); on providence in general (III/3, 239–288).

On the *freedom* of man: in creation as such (III/1, 262–267, 291–294, 298f.; III/2, 192–198, 267f., 276f.); in concursus (III/3, 104f., 130f., 145–151); in gubernatio (III/3, 273f., 282f., 285f.).

Man then was created good; he was justified through God's actions. He would not have needed any particular, redeeming, reconciling justification; he stood in covenant with his gracious God and was destined for salvation. But man himself forfeited this salvation; he broke the covenant in the insanity of his sin. If he is justified despite this, and yet as a sinner, it is only because God has stood by His covenant, notwithstanding the sins of men.

6. JUSTIFICATION IN RECONCILIATION—THE FULFILLMENT OF THE BROKEN COVENANT

We now make our way with Barth to justification itself, for which the covenant is prerequisite. Justification (and reconciliation in general) must be seen as the *fulfillment* of the covenant.

"It [the fulfillment] consists in the fact that God realizes His eternal will with man, that He makes the covenant true and actual within human history. It consists in the historical proclamation attested in the Old Testament, and the historical existence attested in the New, of the Mediator, that is, of the eternal Word of God and therefore of God Himself in His historical identity with the man Jesus of Nazareth: in the coming of His kingdom on earth. . . ." (IV/1, 67).

Is it then, after all, a harmonious evolution? It would be if it were not the fulfillment of a *broken* covenant. Now it is a matter of overcoming a radical break, a deadly enmity. The partner in the covenant is now beset with wretchedness. From its inception, the history of the covenant is a history of the breaking of the covenant. And so now not just any fulfillment will suffice; a reconciliation is required. Nor does just any justification suffice (not even that of creation); what is required is the justification of the sinner. The justification required for reconciliation is a reaction against sin, a "nevertheless." But this does not alter the fact that the justification involved in reconciliation is a *fulfilling* of the covenant. Precisely as a reaction against sin it is more than a reaction; it is a prolongation and a confirmation of the original action. It is "the affirmation and consummation of the institution of the covenant between Himself and man which took place in and with the creation" (IV/1, 36; cf. 67/71). Barth explains this with an exegesis of John 3.16 and 2 Corinthians 5.19 (IV/1, 70–78).

But Barth must be correctly understood when he says that the justification involved in reconciliation is an enforcement of the covenant and that it is precisely in sin that grace is triumphant. This is no belittling or glossing over of the frightfulness of man's usurpation.

"The sin which abounds is indeed *sin*. As the opposition of man to the God who is in covenant with Him it is *inexcusable*. As the self-opposition of the man who is in covenant with God it is *fatal*. And the fact that grace much more abounds does not alter or limit or weaken this fact. It is a fact which must be included in our praise of the grace of God" (IV/1, 69).

The abysmal depth of our sacrilege and our wretchedness, as well as the power of God's salvific will, is revealed in this—that for the sake of this fulfillment of the covenant through reconciling justification God Himself has become flesh.

Justification in reconciliation and reconciliation in justification —and yet reconciliation is not simply identical with justification. Barth regards the all-encompassing event, which includes justification too, as reconciliation—the central work of God, standing between creation and consummation. Justification is only *one* aspect, if a vital one, of reconciliation. Barth has worked out, with brilliant systematic orchestration, the whole vast intricate pattern of the process of reconciliation. How then will he fit the theology of justification into the complete theology of redemption?

First, a *methodological prenote:* Barth very much wants to counteract an altogether too analytic analysis in the treatment of reconciliation in any revised and unified synthesis. For reasons which we cannot enter into here—reasons having to do with his difference of viewpoint on Sacred Scripture and ancient tradition as well as with the great dangers of abstraction—Barth rejects:

1. A dichotomy between Christology on the one hand and Soteriology and Ecclesiology on the other (IV/1, 123–125);

2. A dichotomy between a theology of the person of Christ and a theology of the work of Christ (IV/1, 126–128);

3. A dichotomy between a theology of the natures of Christ and a theology of the states of Christ (IV/1, 132–136);

4. A theology of sin as something independent of the theology of reconciliation—a theology of sin considered as though in a vacuum between the theology of creation and that of reconciliation (IV/1, 138–142);

5. A priority of the individual Christian over Christianity (the community, ecclesiology) (IV–1, 148–151).

We shall begin with a brief *schematic outline* of the theology of reconciliation, as a complement to the outline given in Chapter 3 above (cf. IV/1, 79–154). In Barth's view of reconciliation there exists a midpoint at which God and man are brought together, i.e., reconciled. This is in the one Mediator between God and man, Jesus Christ. "He is the atonement as the fulfilment of the covenant" (IV/1, 122). It is He, consequently, who is in the theology of reconciliation the acting subject, the beginning, middle and end. Thus the foundation, core and key of the theology of reconciliation is *Christology,* in the limited sense (A). Everything beyond that is Christology, too. Everything else is its unfolding, its proper and necessary unfolding. And the unfolding has three major stages: from Christ to His opposite pole, sin—the *theology of sin* (B); then the "objective" achievement of reconciliation—*soteriology* (C); and finally the "subjective" appropriation of reconciliation—the *theology of the work of the Holy Spirit* (D), first within the community (ecclesiology), and then, through the community, within individual Christians.

Christology, the theology of sin, soteriology, and the theology of the work of the Holy Spirit—these four elements are what we might call the horizontal strata in the building up of the theology of reconciliation. Yet none of these four strata should be considered independent, for they all interlock and coexist in their center—in Christology.

The vertical structure, on the other hand, includes three perspectives, three phases of the theology of reconciliation, which interpenetrate the four horizontal strata. And these three perspectives follow from Christology: Christ is true God, Christ is true man, Christ is in His unity the God-man. And so in the theology of reconciliation we find the following systematic pattern:

(A) The three perspectives constitute Christology in the limited sense. They demonstrate that:

Jesus Christ is the true *God,* that is, the God who humbles Himself and thus reconciles—The Lord as Servant—the High Priest (munus sacerdotale).

Jesus Christ is true *man,* that is, the man who is exalted by God and thus reconciled—the Servant as Lord—the King (munus regale).

Jesus Christ is, in the unity of the two, *God-man,* that is, guarantor of and witness to our reconciliation—the Prophet (munus propheticum).

(B) Christology is developed negatively in the theology of sin:

Against Jesus Christ, the Lord become Servant, man sins by *pride.*

Against Jesus Christ, the Servant who is Lord, man sins by *indolence.*

Against Jesus Christ, the witness and guarantor of reconciliation, man sins by *lying*.

(C) To counter sin there comes the achievement of reconciliation in Jesus Christ:

The pride of man is countered by God's verdict. This happens in man's *justification*.

The indolence of man is countered by God's discipline. This happens in man's *sanctification*.

The falsehood of man is countered by God's promise. This happens in man's *vocation*.

(D) Reconciliation is applied and made real through the work of the Holy Spirit. *First in the community:* The *gathering* of the community comes about through the Holy Spirit as the awakening power of the Word uttered by the Servant who became Lord, and therefore the power of the divine verdict which justifies man. The *consolidation* of the community comes about through the Holy Spirit as the revitalizing influence of the Word uttered by the Servant become Lord, and therefore the influence of the divine discipline which sanctifies man. The *mission* of the community comes about through the Holy Spirit as the enlightening power of the abiding Word, who as God-man is guarantor of reconciliation, and therefore by the power of the divine promise which calls man.

Then in the individual Christian:

In justification, the Holy Spirit awakens him to *faith*.

In sanctification, the Holy Spirit gives him the power to give in *love*.

In vocation, the Holy Spirit enlightens him to *hope*.

In this Barthian schema the *theology of justification* falls within the *first perspective,* it is the achievement of reconciliation in its first phase. It is based on the central fact that Jesus Christ is true God, and that He has revealed His Godhead precisely in His humility, His Lordship precisely in His Servanthood; and that precisely by His humility He has reconciled to Himself the arrogant man who had wanted to exalt himself and consequently had sunk into the depths. Thus He judged the arrogant man and passed the death sentence on him, and then He, as judge Himself, took the place of the man to be judged and sentenced to death, thus man was absolved, saved for life, and justified. So it is that Jesus Christ, through the awakening power of the Holy Spirit, gathered up His body, i.e., the Church, and calls men to faith in Him.

Without doubt this schema is in itself a problem. Barth would admit, of course, that the theology of reconciliation could be dealt with within some other schema. His only claim would be that his own schema, with all its relativity, does make sense. It will be part of our task to re-examine it in connection with the theology of justification—especially the subdivision justification-sanctification, faith-love. Our first duty is to fill out and understand this schema. This is the task of the chapters that deal with the achieving of justification.

The schema indicates the method of procedure for these chapters. As an approach to the theology of justification, we will begin by examining the first phase of the theology of reconciliation, meantime keeping in mind the second phase and briefly referring to this—as well as to the third phase—for corroboration. But before we resume the steep ascent, it is time to pause for a brief rest.

7. PROSPECT AND RETROSPECT

We look backward. What a man says is easily stated; how he intends it is the decisive issue. So we observed at the beginning. We are concerned here with Barth's deepest intentions. Has our emphasis been correct? We must fathom—and here we recall the idea of "thinking from above" from the Concretissimum—what Barth holds closest to his heart: not some process or condition within man but the powerful and yet not overpowering *supremacy of God*. This is Barth's outspoken or unspoken concern on every page of his treatment of reconciliation. The whole process of reconciliation as a fulfilling of the covenant is, like the covenant itself, *God's* free sovereign *accomplishment through grace*. The Christian triad of covenant, sin and reconciliation must not be given a Hegelian interpretation.

"Whatever connexions there may be before or behind, they do not alter the fact that in so doing God makes a completely new start as the freest possible subject. No one who really knows Him in this activity will ever be able to think of Him as bound by these connexions or committed to this activity. He acts to maintain and defend His own glory. But no one and nothing outside Himself could ordain for Him that this should be a matter of His glory. He acts with a view toward the *goal* to which He wills to bring man, but there is not really any necessity which constrains Him to do this. He acts as a Creator to a *creature*, but sin is the self-surrender of the creature to nothingness. If this is what man wanted, God might easily have allowed man to fall and perish. He had and has plenty of other creatures in whose presence man would not necessarily be missed. He acts with the *faithfulness of a covenant-Lord*, but He would not have been unfaithful to Himself if He had regarded the covenant which man had broken as invalidated and destroyed. He *loved* the world of men, but he did not need to continue to love the sinful world of men. We can only say that He *has* actually done so, and that this decision and act invalidate all questions whether He might not have acted otherwise" (IV/1, 79f.).

Barth wants to consider the relations between God's constancy and eternity, His eternal election, His eternal covenant, His eternal fidelity—there can be no chance in God. But Barth wants us to appreciate more than anything else the constancy of God's election, to see this clearly and unambiguously as God's freest grace, as His most triumphantly sovereign act. His election is a gracious election; His covenant is a covenant of grace. Nevertheless the reconciliation is an irreducibly new and sovereign act of grace. "Reconciliation is God's *crossing the frontier* to man; supremely legitimate, and yet supremely inconceivable—or conceivable only in the fact of His act of power and love" (IV/1, 82). It must never for a moment be forgotten that God stands at the opposite pole not only from a creature of His, but from a creature who is sinful.

And this grace is not merely God's grace as something *past*. For Barth grace is not merely a historical memory with perduring symbolic value, but rather the supremacy of God yesterday, today, and forever. *Grace is and remains indivisibly His grace.* His justice, His holiness, His truth in regard to man remain forever indivisibly new and strange. Every morning grace must be something new and strange—a new bestowal which asks of man only that he should long for it without looking around to see what he himself might be able to give God in return.

At this point Barth launches into one of the two major *polemics* of Volume IV/1—if we disregard his ecclesiology—against Catholic teaching (IV/1, 84–88; also see II/1, 353–358). "The heart and guiding principle of the Romanist doctrine of grace is the *negation* of the unity of grace as always God's grace to man, as His sovereign act which is everywhere new and strange and free. It is the *negation* of the unity of grace as His grace in Jesus Christ. It is the *division* of grace by which it is first of all *His,* but then—and this is where the emphasis falls—effected and empowered by *His* grace, it is also *our* grace. Against this view we must at once and quite definitely set our face (for what follows, cf. the survey given in B. Bartmann, *Dogm. Handb.* vol. 2, 1929, 113)" (IV/1, 84).

"What follows in Bartmann" is a detailed and merciless critique in question form in which Barth attacks the classification of grace according to *gratia increata–creata, gratia externa–interna, gratia gratum faciens–gratis data, gratia actualis–habitualis, gratia medicinalis–elevans, gratia praeveniens–concomitans, gratia operans–cooperans, gratia sufficiens–efficax, gratia Dei–Christi, gratia supernaturalis–naturalis* (IV/1, 84–87).

"How dare we split up the grace of *Christ* and the grace of God in this way? Is it not the case that as outward grace, for example (that which is described as the grace of the life and death of Christ, of the Gospel, etc.), it is wholly inward and proper to man, and conversely, that as *inward* grace which is proper to us it is altogether *outward*, the grace of the life and death of Christ and the grace of the Gospel? Similarly, is it not the case that *actual* grace is *habitual*, and *habitual actual?* That *gratia praeveniens* is *concomitans*, and *sufficiens efficax*, and *vice versa?* How can that which is described as the *second* and perfect be perfect except in the power of the *first*, which is regarded as so meagre and impotent as a purely enabling and preparatory grace? How can the *first* not have already in itself the perfection of the *second?* If there is *one* God, and *one* Mediator between God and man, and therefore *one* grace—what place is there for all these abstractions? These are the questions which crowd in upon us as we face the final Roman Catholic distinction. But the Romanist doctrine of grace insists on these abstractions. Naturally it also maintains—rather more emphatically on the Thomist side and rather less emphatically on the Jesuit—that in the last resort there is only one grace. But it merely *says* this: it does not make any use of it. It simply commemorates the fact. It says it as a precaution, e.g., to ward off the kind of questions that we have been putting. When left to itself and following its own inclination it says something very different; it talks about the *division* of grace. It says the first thing as a bracket in which to say the second: but it does not abolish the parenthesis in order to say *it*" (IV/1, 87).

"But we must not omit an irenical and ecumenical word at the conclusion of this confessional polemic. There is a very deep peace (beyond any understanding) between us Evangelical *Christians* and our Catholic *fellow-Christians* who are badly instructed in this doctrine. We *cannot* believe that they do in fact *live* by the grace which is so dreadfully divided in their dogmatics. Rather, we have to believe, and it is comforting to believe, that they as well as we—if only we did it better—do live by the one undivided grace of Jesus Christ" (IV/1, 88).

Looking forward, we can pretty well predict the focus of our discussion. We have to answer *Barth's question:* Does Catholic theology really take justification seriously as the free sovereign act of God? Does it really accept grace as grace? Is its assertion about the unity of grace really more than an assertion? We know that this is not a new question; it was asked by the Reformers. This is the doubt which Barth has continually and forcefully expressed: Do you not covertly, though in all good faith, assert a ruinously un-Christian autonomy of the human, the creaturely, the natural, so that ultimately you make a hollow shell of *God's* incarnation?

Despite the absence of the term "analogia entis" in Volumes IV/1 and IV/2, we can have no doubt that here the same old fundamental question is put to Catholics. But we would mistake Barth's ultimate intention if we simply dismissed all this with the familiar label "dialectical theology." Granted that the supremacy of grace was central in Barth's commentary on Romans, it was misunderstood at the time to mean a doing away with man. In this sense we have today no dialectical theology. This is clear, to cite only one example, from the chapter which follows the anti-Catholic polemic. This chapter focuses on what is at the opposite pole from the sovereign graciousness of God—that is, *graced man*. To be suspicious of these statements rather than seriously to weigh their full import is quite unrealistic.

"In this way God takes care for His own glory. And he does it by bringing man to glory. That is His sovereign act in the atonement. That is the grace of Jesus Christ. It is apparent at once that the formula 'God everything and man nothing' as a description of grace is not merely a 'shocking simplification' but complete nonsense. Man is *nothing,* i.e., he has fallen a prey to nothingness, *without* the grace of God. . . . This creating and grounding of a *human subject which is new* in relation to God and therefore in itself is, in fact, the event of the atonement made in Jesus Christ. . . .

"We cannot say and demand and expect too much or too great things of man when we see him as He really *is* in virtue of the giving of the Son of God, of the fact that God has reconciled the world to Himself in Christ. We underline the fact that it is a matter of a *being* of man. . . . The old *has* indeed *passed* away, all things *are become* new, God was in Christ reconciling the world to Himself, and those who believe in Him *do* not perish but *have* everlasting life. . . .

"We are now looking at *man*. We are speaking of the being of *man* reconciled to God in Jesus Christ. For it is the meaning and reach of the atonement made in Jesus Christ, the power of the divine act of sovereignty in grace, that God willed not to keep to Himself His own true being, but to make it as such our human being and in that way to turn us back to Himself, to create the new man. . . .

"Notice that it is those that know this new being as their own who . . . have always characterised and described it as the being which has met them as their own in Jesus Christ" (IV/1, 89–92; cf. III/3, 53f.; II/1, 353–358).

It is evident to every Catholic, too—as will be more clearly apparent later, e.g., in the treatment of the theology of sin—that the so-called "dialectic" or "Reformation" positions are here abandoned. Of course we cannot be absolutely certain; and we may honestly suspect that it is here that *our question*—the question we would like to address to Karl Barth—has its basis. Does Barth's theology really regard reconciliation and justification as the reconciliation and justification of *man?* Does God's grace really affect man? When Barth asserts that man is given grace, is it more than an assertion? So we see here, too, that this is not a new question. This question has always been put by Catholics to Evangelicals. This is a doubt which we too must express, in regard to Barth: Do you not ultimately assert a ruinously un-Christian view in which man is deprived of grace, an implicit negation of the human, the creaturely, the natural, so that ultimately you make a hollow shell of God's Incarnation—His becoming man?

B.

The Achievement of Justification

Reconciliation in its first phase is found in God's judgment upon the sinner. This judgment is achieved in the death of Jesus Christ on the cross, and the verdict of this judgment is revealed in the resurrection of Christ. This is the process by which man is justified.

It is very easy to misunderstand this statement, and thus to misconceive from the very beginning Barth's whole theology of justification. If someone, without first gaining an inner and living awareness of Barth's concept of justification, hurriedly resorts to one of the common Catholic definitions of justification (like the Tridentine concept) and simply sets this alongside or in contrast to the Barthian concept of justification, he could readily observe the contrast, and then, with a like readiness, discover implicit heresies—imputation and extrinsicism, juridicism and forensicism —and triumphantly vanquish them. But such a man—in the best of faith—would have closed his heart to what followed, and would have ignored what was said in the first chapter about the "alien language."

This does not mean that Barth is automatically right. He is not, after all, a Father of the Church. But it is necessary to begin trying to penetrate Barth's concept of justification. What is his particular color scheme? Why does he paint certain things in such dazzling hues? Is this or that element entirely missing or is it merely obscured, overshadowed by the brilliant tones of others? In what follows we must constantly keep in mind the question: What is Barth consistently trying to elucidate? Is it not the gracious sovereignty of God? Will he perhaps stress this too in his concept of justification? And here will he, at the risk of neglecting other elements, insist exclusively on the "soli Deo gloria"? Won't this involve a practical denial of the "propter nos homines"? When we have put Barth's concept of justification thoroughly to the test, then we shall have a basis for comparing it with the Catholic concept of justification. Where do the differences lie? Does the

Catholic concept of justification say something different, or does it say the same thing in a different way? And is there validity in this "different way"? Has it been given sufficient consideration? Does it proceed from polemic or from history? To answer these questions we first must take a careful look into the mirror of the gospel.

As far as method is concerned, Chapter 6 showed that, according to the Barthian schema, justification is the accomplishing of reconciliation in its first phase but that this view must be complemented by constant reference to the second and third perspectives.

8. JESUS CHRIST—OUR JUSTIFICATION

The accomplishing of our justification is completely dependent upon Jesus Christ. Our justification would be inconceivable without His death, without His resurrection. Justification hinges on the fact that God in His Son has become man. We must therefore begin with Jesus Christ if we want to gain a closer understanding of justification.

What we have said summarizes a small but highly significant fragment from Barth's Christology (considered in the limited sense). On the basis for Christology in Barth's theology of the Trinity (eternal Sonship), see I/1, 457–512; on his theology of revelation (incarnation), see I/2, 1–202; on his theology of election, see II/2, 3–194.

We shall first speak briefly of the person of Jesus Christ and of His work; we shall then consider Barth's transition from Christology to anthropology. We must begin with the proposition that Jesus Christ, in whom our justification is accomplished, is *true God.*

In the *second* phase of the theology of reconciliation, our point of departure will be the fact that Jesus Christ is truly and wholly man (though there are differences), like us in everything except sin. (Here too is a full treatment of the true activity of the human nature of Christ.)

Barth treats the "verus homo" theme with great fullness of detail:

(a) The *origin* of Christ's humanity in God's election (IV/2, 31–36).

(b) The *accomplishing* of this humanity in the incarnation (IV/2, 36–116). The Son of God as subject of the act; unity in existence and duality in natures according to the Council of Chalcedon; the effects of the hypostatic union which are: communicatio idiomatum (the communication of his human nature to his divinity and vice versa), communicatio gratiarum (the donation made to the human nature—electing grace in its various forms: hypostatic union, sinlessness, the good pleasure of the Father and the empowering of the Holy Spirit, the qualifying of the human nature as an instrument of the divine

Mediator, participation in the majesty of the divine nature), communicatio operationum (accomplishments of the divine and human natures working together).

(c) The basis for the manifestation of this human nature (IV/2, 116–154) in the resurrection and ascension.

The meaning of the unity of the God-man will be developed in the third perspective.

Yet, here, in the *first phase* we have to take our departure from the Godhead of Jesus Christ, the indispensable foundation and epitome of all that follows. The whole process of justification hinges on this, that the true God Himself appears on the scene so that in His fidelity to the covenant He may care for sinners. In this context the secret of the true Godhead of Jesus Christ consists in Christ's being true God at the same identical time that He is man, in that His obedience is as Son and that in His obedience He humbles Himself even unto death on the cross. In His humiliation He is Reconciler and thus is true God. What God is concretely, we must discover from our study of Jesus Christ in whom "the whole fullness of deity dwells bodily" (Col. 2.9). Our concrete factual image of God is filled out and interpreted in all its details from the humiliation of Christ chosen in free obedience of Son toward Father.

"In this way, in this *condescension,* He is the eternal Son of the eternal Father. This is the will of this Father, of this Son, and of the Holy Spirit who is the Spirit of the Father and the Son. This is how God is *God,* this is His freedom, this is His distinctness from and superiority to all other reality. It is with this meaning and purpose that He is the Creator and Lord of all things. It is as the eternal and almighty love, which He is actually and visibly in this action of condescension. This One, the One who loves in this way, is the true God. But this means that He is the One who as the Creator and Lord of all things is able and willing to make Himself equal with the creature, Himself to become a creature; the One whose eternity does not prevent but rather permits and commands Him to be in time and Himself to be temporal, whose omnipotence is so great that He can be weak and indeed impotent, as a man is weak and impotent. He is the One who in His freedom can and does in fact bind Himself, in the same way as we all are bound. And we must go further; He, the true God, is the One whose Godhead is *demonstrated* and plainly *consists* in essence in the fact that, seeing He is free in His *love,* He is capable of and wills this condescension for the very reason that in man of all His creatures He has to do with the one that has *fallen away* from Him, that has been unfaithful and hostile and antagonistic to Him. He is

God in that He takes *this* creature to Himself, and that in such a way that He sets Himself alongside *this* creature, making His own its penalty and loss and condemnation to nothingness. He is God *in the fact that* He can give Himself up and does give Himself up not merely to the creaturely *limitation* but to the *suffering* of the human creature, becoming one of *these* men, Himself bearing the judgment under which they stand, willing to die and, in fact, dying the death which they have deserved. That is the nature and essence of the true God as He has intervened actively and manifestly in Jesus Christ" (IV/1, 129f., cf. 159–210).

This then is the true God as revealed in Jesus Christ—the God who goes into exile, becomes flesh (and in fact Jewish flesh), who humiliates himself—the Lord as servant. This is how Christ proves, verifies and reveals His divinity and—insofar as obedience is concerned—His divine Sonship. Now there is the new question: Why does He do this? To what purpose does the Lord become servant?

Surely it is to demonstrate and manifest outwardly the inner riches of the Godhead. This happens in His hastening like a true Creator and covenant Lord to the assistance of the world and man —propter nos homines et propter nostram salutem. The world which was created good is—because of the sin of man—a forlorn and ruined world. God hastens to its deliverance, not because of any obligation to it or to Himself, but only because of His sovereign will to be merciful and gracious.

How does He deliver us, how does He cope with sin? He does this by becoming brother to man and sinner as He makes His way into exile.

"*Deus pro nobis* means simply that God has not abandoned the world and man in the unlimited need of his situation, but that He willed to bear this need as His own, that He took it upon Himself, and that He cries with man in this need" (IV/1, 215; cf. II/2, 733–741).

"In this second and more incisive sense *Deus pro nobis* means that God in Jesus Christ has taken our place when we become sinners, when we become His enemies, when we stand as such under His accusation and curse, and bring upon ourselves our own destruction" (IV/1, 216; cf. II/1, 396–399).

So Christ becomes our Savior by having been our Judge. And in the first phase of Barth's theology of reconciliation this aspect must be given priority. Moreover, it is to this aspect that Sacred Scripture bears explicit witness.

For the scriptural proof see IV/1, 217–219, 224–228, 230f., 235, 238–240, 243f., 250f., 255f., 259–272, 273–283; II/1, 381–406— Jesus Christ as the Judge who is judged. The second perspective of the theology of reconciliation looks no longer to the humiliation of the Lord who becomes servant but rather looks in this humiliation to the exaltation of the servant who becomes Lord—Jesus Christ as kingly man. Barth describes him: (a) in His *attributes* (IV/2, 156–166), unmistakably visible, unmistakably audible, unforgettable, irrevocable, forcing decision; (b) in His *sharing* with God (IV/2, 166–192)—like God Himself held in low esteem, with God bypassing the exalted and heading straight for the humble in revolutionary contradiction of what the kingdom of man stands for—and yet not against but rather for man; (c) in His *life's work* (IV/2, 192–247)—His Word (gospel, teaching, and proclamation) and His accomplishments (the various miracles); (d) in His *cross* (IV/2, 247–264), the cross as crowning achievement and the events preceding (preparation, divine ordination, the surrounding world and the disciples). In the third perspective Jesus Christ is to be seen as Guarantor and Witness of our reconciliation. But now, once again to the first perspective.

God enters into the midst of men in order to judge them. In this appears the thoroughgoing seriousness of the human situation. Unlike sinful man who behaves as though he were his own judge, God becomes flesh in order that the deserved judgment be imposed on Him. This is a divine indictment of and judgment on everybody. And because it is God who judges, it is sinful man who is, from the outset, lost and consigned to ruin. The love of God burns and kills like a fire of His wrath (see II/2, 742–753; IV/1, 216–221).

Yet God remains free even in His judgment. *How* he carries it out is His affair. He can do this so that without any violation of justice it leads to man's acquittal. He can allow grace to rule, not in place of justice but with justice. It is not that He must do it— in fact everything seems to argue against that—but that He has done it. And how has He done it? He the Judge stepped into *our place,* and in place of sinners took the judgment upon Himself.

"He judged, and it was the *Judge* who was judged, who let Himself be judged. Because He was a *man* like us, He was able to be judged like us. Because He was the *Son of God* and Himself God, He had the competence and power to allow this to happen to Him. Because He was the divine Judge come amongst us, He had the authority in this way—by this giving up of Himself to judgment in our place—to exercise the divine justice of grace, to pronounce us righteous on the ground of what happened to Him, to free us therefore from the accusation and condemnation and punishment, to save us from the impending loss and destruction. And because in divine freedom He was on the way of *obedience*, He did not refuse to accept the will of the Father as His will in this self-giving. In His doing this for us, in His *taking* to Himself—to fulfil all righteousness—our accusation and condemnation and punishment, in His suffering in our place and for us, there came to pass our *reconciliation* with God. *Cur Deus Homo?* In order that God as man might do and accomplish and achieve and complete all this for us wrong-doers, in order that in this way there might be brought about by Him our reconciliation with Him and conversion to Him" (IV/1, 222f.; cf. II/2, 748–752).

The "pro nobis" does not merely mean "in relation to us" nor simply "with us," but rather "in our place." He steps as Judge into our place. Though we would want and like to be our own judge, He exercises the power of His divine justice to free us and give us hope. He steps as the One judged into our place. Sinless He takes all our sins upon Himself, and thus He alone is the rejected One. He has been judged in place of us. He has suffered, has been crucified and has died. Thereby He has put an end to us as sinners and to sin itself, and thus also to the indictment, the verdict and the damnation which were ours. He has done what is just in our stead, and in the very act of fulfilling and revealing divine justice He has fulfilled and revealed divine grace, love and mercy (see IV/1, 231–273; II/1, 393–406; concerning Christ and His death, see III–2, 587–640).

This then is the answer to the question about why the true Son of God became man and went into exile and humiliated Himself. Barth would admit that this can be described in other ways. The vocabulary is that of jurisprudence but Sacred Scripture uses other vocabularies, for example the financial (the handing over of payment), the military (battle), and especially that of ritual. Barth deals with this last aspect in a long excursus (IV/1, 273–283): Christ, as the Priest (= Judge) who interceded for us, the sinful people, has given Himself in satisfaction for sin as sacrificial victim (= the one judged) in the sacrifice of the cross (= God's judgment); thus as God-man He has in our stead provided the perfect offering (= has done what is just).

There still remains the question: how do we know that what Christ has done really applies to us? How can we make the transition from Christology to anthropology? Is there any room for us here?

Is the "pro nobis" only an assertion? Can we with good conscience actually re-enact what He has done for us? It is not so much the prob-

lem of the time lapse (between the twentieth century and the crucifixion), but the question whether we as sinners are not done for when
we come into confrontation with Christ. Could not the reconciliation
of God with the world be understood as nothing else than a revocation of its creation? Do we not all deserve the absolute death? After all
we have, all of us, died and been judged in Christ (for the exegesis see
IV/1, 295–296).

"In the fulfilment of the self-humiliation of God, in the obedience of the Son, Jesus Christ has suffered judgment, death and
end in our place, the Judge who Himself was judged, and who
thereby has also judged. In His person, with Him, judgment, death
and end have been visited on ourselves once and for all. Is there
something beyond this coming to us, and above it? Is there a sure
place and basis from which the judgment which has fallen upon us,
the end in which we are posited, and the death which has overtaken us in that Jesus Christ died for us, can be seen in all their
frightful seriousness and yet not accepted as final and absolute, but
only in a certain relationship and connexion and subordination?"
(IV/1, 296f.)

There is a place for us—in the *resurrection of Jesus Christ*. This
act of God, independent and new, though associated with the
death, is the historical, factual Yes of God to men. In it the Father
has recognized the suffering and death of the Son as the fully
juridical deed done for us, and thus as our deliverance from death
to life, and has accomplished it. In the resurrection the verdict
of the Father is proclaimed: "Because Jesus Christ the Crucified
is risen again and lives there is room for us and therefore . . . for
the problems of the doctrine of reconciliation in our own anthropological sphere" (IV/1, 351, cf. II/2, 758–763).

While Christ's resurrection is considered as the judgment of the
Father in the first perspective of the theology of reconciliation, it is
considered in the second perspective as the Son's pointing the way. In
the first the emphasis is on the resurrection as God's act (IV/1, 303–
310) and on its historic nature (IV/1, 333–342); then on its relation
to the death on the cross in its distinctness, connectedness and irreversi-
bility (IV/1, 299–310; 342–357). In the reflections which form the
transition to the second perspective, Barth asks about the power of the
existence of Jesus Christ for the rest of mankind (IV/2, 264–280):
it is from the resurrection of the Crucified that there comes the power
of revelation and its transmission from Him to us. This means light,
freedom, knowledge, peace and life (IV/2, 280–319). This power is
nothing other than the Holy Spirit of Jesus Christ and of the Father
working in man to direct, correct, and instruct in   IV/2, 319–377).

9. THE REJECTION OF THE SINNER

Justification comes about in Jesus Christ in the judgment on the cross where the Judge Himself is judged and killed. The verdict of God revealed in the resurrection proclaims deliverance from death to life. For Barth this is all the result of the eternal gracious election of man in Jesus Christ, the result of the eternal covenant of grace. In the judgment executed in the death of Christ and the verdict revealed in the resurrection there is a *double meaning*. On the left hand of God and negatively, what is signified is the revelation of His wrath, together with the rejection of elected man (in reference to man's own being): man has been killed. God thus shows Himself to be true to Himself for the sake of man's salvation. On the right hand of God and positively, what is signified is the revelation of the mercy of God, together with the election of rejected man (in reference to man as a possession of God): man has been awakened to life. God thus shows Himself—to His own glory—as true to man. This positive aspect is nothing other than justification.

These two aspects cannot, of course, be separated because we are always dealing with the justificatio *impii*. So before we move on to the positive meaning of God's judgment and verdict, we must consider with Barth this dark and gloomy opposite pole to Christ— a pole which has been continually noticeable as a shadowy figure— the impius, the sinner who in God's judgment has been radically rejected.

What sin is, Barth discovers in the mirror of sinners, in *Jesus Christ*. Why? "Because the God against whom the man of sin contends has judged this man, and therefore myself as this man, in the self-offering and death of Jesus Christ His own Son, putting him to death, and destroying him; and because He has revealed and continually reveals him as this one who is judged and put to death and destroyed in the resurrection of Jesus Christ from the dead and in His Being and living and speaking and witness for all ages" (IV/1, 390; cf. II/1, 390–399; II/2, 768–770; III/2, 34–41; IV/1, 358–397; IV–2, 378–388).

In Christ, sin is revealed in its *fully developed,* pure and unambiguous *form*—that is, as hostility and opposition to God, as fratricide and self-destruction.

Man is "in every respect *opposed to the will of God.* He denies God, because Jesus Christ against whom he offends is God meeting him in the flesh in eternal love and for his salvation. He *murders his brother* because Jesus Christ is the fellowman in whose image God has made every man, in whom as the Head of the human race every man is either honoured or despised, and is now actually despised and denied and rejected and put to death. He *destroys himself* because Jesus Christ is the eternal Word of God by whom all things are made, and by the suppression of this Word man causes himself to fall and delivers himself up to judgment. . . . But if it is revealed here in its nakedness, from this point we can see the reality of it always and everywhere" (IV/1, 399).

Furthermore, in Jesus Christ as Judge the reprehensibility of sin is revealed. For sin—hostility to God, fratricide and self-destruction—is truly sin. It is therefore not merely indifferent to or the opposite of good but really evil, as is irrefutably demonstrated by Christ. For what *God* calls evil *is* evil. Our Fellowman, in whom all men are made, and who is Head of mankind, is as judex aeternus for men the lex aeterna, too (IV/1, 399–403).

Again, in Jesus Christ sin is revealed as the *truth of all human actions.* Because Christ has entered into public association with sinners and has undertaken to plead their case before God, it is revealed that *all* men are sinners, and that no man can invoke a restrictive clause in connection with the reprehensibility of sin and permit himself to regard himself or others as more or less sinful. The *whole* man, despite the indestructibility of his nature, is a sinner to his very core. And there is no distinction between sinner and sin as though between subject and predicate, substance and accident (although it is true in Christ that God hates the sin and loves the sinner; see IV/1, 403–407).

Finally, in Jesus Christ the whole meaning and *import* of sin is revealed. God is infinitely superior to sin and so sin has its limits. Nevertheless, between God and sin there is a dramatic contrast, the sharpness of which becomes evident only in the incarnation of the Son of God. Yet it is also true that there is no possibility for man of himself to rise above his sin. For Christ did not just die for us. He died without us and in opposition to us (IV/1, 407–413).

The theology of sin which is part of the second perspective is prefaced by similar ideas—though with the man Jesus as focus—regarding the recognition of sin. The burden of these ideas is as follows: In comparison with the ɹnan Jesus, the sinner is (a) revealed as His opposite; (b) unequivocally disqualified; (c) impaired in his very being by this disqualification; (d) radically removed from any possibility of a relativizing synthesis (IV/2, 389–403).

Sin must be considered in view of Jesus Christ. *What is it* when it is so considered? Barth here describes it in *one* form just as he proceeded from one certain form or phase of Christology and is on his way to one definite form of achievement of reconciliation, namely justification. This one primal form of sin is *pride,* the dark opposite pole to the humiliation of the Son of God (IV/1, 414–418.)

The second form of sin, opposed to the glorification of the man Jesus, is *sloth* (IV/2, 403–409). The third form, opposed to the witness given to our reconciliation by the God-man, is *lying.*

Sin is in its unity and totality always and simultaneously pride, sloth and lying, which are always and simultaneously opposed to the self-humiliation of God, to the glorification of man and to the witness of the God-man. In this way sin always and simultaneously manifests unbelief and disobedience. Yet we were speaking here of the first form of sin. What does pride mean *concretely*—that is, when we look to Jesus Christ? There are four facets to be considered. While Jesus Christ the Son of God becomes man, the man of pride wants to be like God. Jesus Christ the Lord becomes servant: the proud man, the servant, wants to be Lord. Jesus Christ the Judge judges in that He allows Himself to be judged: the proud man wants to be judge himself. While Jesus Christ helped us by becoming helpless on the cross and in the tomb, man wants to attempt to help himself.

Barth draws from the Old Testament a splendid illustrative example of each of these four facets. For the man who wants to be God, it is the breaking of the covenant on Sinai (IV/1, 423–432). For the servant who wants to be Lord, it is the story of Saul (IV/1, 437–445). For the man who wants to judge himself, it is Ahab's act of violence against Naboth (IV/1, 453–458). For the man who wants to help himself, it is the king and people before the fall of Jerusalem according to the prophet Jeremiah (IV/1, 468–478).

Sloth, too, has its concrete forms. It appears as stupidity (the fool in Proverbs and in Ecclesiastes and especially the husband of Abigail, Nabal, see IV/2, 427–432); as inhumanity (described in Amos' prophecy of judgment, see IV/2, 445–452); as decadence (the story of David and Bathsheba, see IV/2, 464–467); and finally as anxiety (the story of the scouts, see IV/2, 478–483). Barth will discuss sin as *lying* in corresponding terms.

What Jesus does in His humiliation is a divine accomplishment, an event of magnificence. The human endeavor is, in contrast, a radical failure, a vain and untenable enterprise. But, despite this, it does take place. It is a fact—something negative and inexplicable to be sure, yet still factual. Man does what is evil. True, he does it in *covert* fashion. In trying to be like God he wants to be "merely man." In trying to be servant-king, he wants "only" to use his power. In trying to be judge he wants "merely to know what good and evil are." In trying to be his own helper he wants "merely to provide modest and necessary self-assistance." All this is, of course, the wisdom of the serpent in Genesis 3.

Cf. IV/1, 418–421, 432–436, 445–449, 458–463. On the concealment of sloth, cf. IV/2, 410–420 (stupidity as "wisdom"); IV/2, 432–441 (inhumanity as "objectivity"); IV/2, 453–460 (decadence as "freedom" and "genuineness"); IV/2, 469–475 (anxiety as "necessary work" and "resignation").

Yet all this concealment is of no avail. In Jesus Christ it is revealed that man does evil and in doing so is monstrously *in error* about himself, his fellowman, and especially about God. He misses precisely what he seeks—himself. He is swallowed up in the achievement of his self-alienation and self-destruction and therefore loses contact with his fellowman, too. In wanting to exalt himself into the heavens he falls into the abyss. And then there is that frightful misunderstanding of God. He makes himself in his pride a false image of the Godhead, an idol. But God is not a God who revolves around Himself, exists only for Himself, as sovereign and lofty God, Lord, Judge and Disposer. No. He is the God who becomes man, the Lord who becomes servant, the Judge who lets Himself be judged, the Helper who becomes helpless. And this is the way that this God has responded in His incomprehensible grace to the criminal endeavors of men. He replies to the humiliated man who wishes in his pride to exalt himself. He speaks to him as the exalted one who in His meekness humiliated Himself (see IV/1, 421–423, 435–437, 448–503, 463–468; IV/2, 420–424, 441–445, 460–464, 475–479).

10. FALLEN MAN

But what remains of the man of sin, what is it to be a sinner? "The man of sin is *fallen* man, fallen to the place where God who does not and cannot fall has *humbled* Himself for him in Jesus Christ" (IV/1, 478). Man falls precisely in his pride; he falls precisely in exalting himself.

What does this fall tell us? We are approaching a point most vital to our discussion. For Barth, the fall does *not* mean that *the sinner is no longer a human being,* that in his sin he has lost his essence, his nature, his capacities. We can cite only a few passages, but they should be sufficient to suppress any irresponsible chatter about the "dialectic" in *Church Dogmatics.*

"We cannot say that man is fallen completely away from God, in the sense that he is lost to Him or that he has perished. . . . Man in his fall cannot cease to be the creature and covenant-partner of God. He could not create himself and he cannot alter or undo his creation, either for good or fortunately for evil. He cannot make himself another being or destroy the being that he is. Again, he has not ordained and established the covenant, and it is not for him to dissolve it. . . . Man has not fallen lower than the depth to which God humbled Himself for him in Jesus Christ. But God in Jesus Christ did not become a devil or nothingness" (IV/1, 480f.).

"Fallen man is dead. But for the miracle of his awakening from the dead, which he needs, and in which his reconciliation with God consists, it is necessary that he should still be there as a corpse, a human corpse. With the *Formula of Concord* we can call him *truncus et lapis* [a log and a stone] in order to describe his whole incapacity to help and save himself, but this does not mean that he has actually become wood and stone, and that he is no longer a man or present as a man" (IV/1, 481).

"And man himself is none other than the one he always was in relation to God, sharing the same creaturely being and capacity" (IV/1, 482; cf. 492f.).

This is repeated by Barth when he discusses the state of being which remains unaltered for the sinner in his wretchedness: " 'Perversion' is the term that we must use—not transformation or destruction. Even in that which he is in virtue of his folly in all its forms, he is the good creature of God. Even in his sickness he does not lack any of his members or organs. All the features which make him a man still remain. He has not become a devil or an animal or a plant. Even in his misery he is not half a man, but a whole man. . . . We do not see deeply enough if we think and say that there is here *only* darkness, want, shame, impurity, sadness, temptation, curse and perdition" (IV/2, 488; cf. 483f., 488).

All this can be found earlier; for example, the section on divine patience (II/1, 406–422), or divine preservation (III/3, 58–90), or the image of God, that is neither totally nor partially destroyed by sin (III/1, 189, 199ff.; III/2, 325; IV/1, 492); "His nature" is "not destroyed" (III/2, 27f., 29–31); it exists as "an essence which even sin does not and cannot change" (III/2, 43, cf. also 205ff., 226ff., 347f., 520f.).

This is, however, intended to be not a dulling but rather a sharpening of the Reformation teaching. Barth continues: There is no escape for the sinner. He cannot sidestep God.

"The terrible thing about the situation in which man finds himself as the one who commits sin . . . is simply the fact that as a sinner man has not in any way escaped from the sphere of the living God, of His Yes, of His gracious will, that he has not escaped from the relationship of Creator and creature and therefore from the covenant which God has instituted between Himself and man. He can fall; he can fall away from God. But he cannot escape God, as Ps. 139.1–12 tells us in a startling way. . . ."

"The grace of God is still turned to man, but this now means that it is *non-grace, wrath* and *judgment* to the one who despises and hates it and will not live by it. God is his friend, but this means that He *must be the enemy* of the one who acts as though He were an enemy. He can still be a human creature before God with all the capacities and powers which belong to a man, but this means that he has continually to live in the disobedience and turning from God in which he has willed to exercise his capacities, in the service of the revolt against God in which he has willed to engage, so that in his relationship with God he is *thrown back wholly upon himself* and delivered up to his own impotence" (IV/1, 482f.; and similarly for the sinner in his second form, IV/2, 484f.).

And the freedom of man? Here, too, Barth consciously develops and revises Reformation positions. He speaks unequivocally of *Christian* freedom. In this way he can clearly protect the will of the sinner from any determinism. The sinner can go on choosing, he can go on determining how to use his will. However, Barth does not permit this type of choice to be called "freedom." Only the choice obedient to God can be called "free" choice. The choice of the sinner is not "free" choice, but the choice of servitude. The sinner's arbitrium is not a liberum arbitrium, but rather a servum arbitrium. Thus we would falsely interpret Barth if we regarded his servum arbitrium as deterministic.

"It is always a mistake to try to establish or understand the assertion of the *bondage of the will* otherwise than christologically. It cannot be either proved or disproved by empirical findings or *a priori* reflections. As a corollary to the confession of the freedom which has been won for us and granted to us in the man Jesus it is a *theological statement*—a *statement of faith*. As such, it has nothing whatever to do with the battle between determinism and indeterminism. It is not a decision for determinism; and the fact that this is not clear in *Luther's De servo arbitrio* is the objection that we are forced to raise against this well-known work and also against the ideas of *Zwingli* and *Calvin*. . . . It does not consist at all in the fact that man cannot any longer will and decide, i.e., that he is deprived of *arbitrium,* that he has no will at all. If this were the case, he would no longer be a man; he would only be part of a mechanism moved from without. This would involve the transformation of man into another and non-human being—an idea which we have exerted ourselves to repudiate from the very outset in this whole context. But the freedom of man does not really consist—except in the imagination of the invincibly ignorant—in the fact that, like Hercules at the cross-roads, he can will and decide. Nor does the bondage of his will consist in the fact that he is not able to do this" (IV/2, 494).

" 'Whosoever committeth sin is the servant of sin' (Jn. 8.34). In this briefest of biblical formulations we have the whole doctrine of the bondage of the will. *Non potest non peccare* is what we have to say of the sinful, slothful man. His sin excludes his freedom, just as his freedom excludes his sin" (IV/2, 495; cf. also, I/1, 521–524; I/2, 257–265).

"The doctrine which makes this *caveat* necessary is the Romanist doctrine of man's *co-operation* in the accomplishment of his justification . . ." (IV/2, 497). Here is found the severest polemic of Volume IV/2 against Catholic teaching. It is directed against the definitions of Trent: ". . . the whole point of which is to maintain man in an unshaken self-consciousness balancing not only the grace of God but also and primarily his own sin" (IV/2, 498).

"Both sin and grace are understood as quantities, and on this assumption they are compared and pragmatised and tamed and rendered quite innocuous. The meaning of the conflict between the Spirit and the flesh, of the new man in Jesus and the old in whose form we confront Jesus, of freedom and bondage as totalities which do not complement but mutually exclude one another, is not only unperceived but actually concealed in a whole sea of obliterating formulae and objections and protests which are directed against every kind of quietism and fatalism, which have nothing whatever to do with what has to be said seriously concerning either the *liberum* or the *servum arbitrium,* and which can only secure us against having to see and say what really ought to be seen and said at this point. The teaching office [of] the Roman Church neither willed nor could say this. It will not and cannot say it to-day. Instead it speaks on the one hand of that *assentire* and *cooperari* of the unregenerate man in his relationship to the obscure *gratia praeveniens* which is arbitrarily invented and cannot be defined with any precision but which results in his capacity for faith and penitence and a turning to grace. And on the other it speaks of the good works of the regenerate man, who is only a little sinner and commits only tiny sins, and who is in the happy position of being able to increase the grace of justification in co-operation with it, and even to augment the degree of his eternal bliss. The practical consequence of all this is that the misery of man is not regarded as in any way serious or dangerous either for Christians or non-Christians. The Reformation communions could not reunite with a Church which held this doctrine, and they cannot accept the call to reunion with it to-day" (IV/2, 498).

Yet, how can the sinner be described positively? How can we discover that fallen man to whom Jesus Christ has stooped? What is his situation, his status corruptionis? What do we see reflected in the mirror of the obedience of the Son of God? Barth responds with three statements.

1. "In so far as this Word is the word of divine forgiveness addressed to man, the corruption from which it calls and takes him consists in the fact that man is God's *debtor.* He is a debtor who cannot pay" (IV/1, 484; on the extent to which he rejects Anselm of Canterbury, cf. 486–487).

Man is a *debtor,* he has failed. In his relationship with his Creator and covenant Lord, he has not fulfilled the duty which has been laid upon him, the obligation of faith and of obedience. He introduces chaos into God's good creation. He thwarts God's plan, opposes His will, diminishes His glory, for God has bound Himself too intimately to man to remain undisturbed by man's failure. And man is responsible and liable for all this and thus is really in debt.

Man is an *insolvent* debtor; this becomes clear in that God simply forgives him, without being compelled to, yet not arbitrarily but genuinely. Man stood wholly and completely in God's grace. He sinned against that grace, he placed himself under God's judgment and forced

God's love to burn, he caused God's graciousness to take an alien form, that is, the form of wrath. But because man has no way of disposing of God's mercy, he cannot reconvert it to its proper form. There is then only one thing that now makes sense—prayer for forgiveness.

2. "The fact that Jesus Christ died totally for the reconciliation of every man as such, for the man who exists in this way, means decisively that this corruption is both *radical* and *total*. That is to say, it means that the sinful reversal takes place at the basis and centre of the being of man, in his heart; and that the consequent sinful perversion then extends to the whole of his being without exception. . . . Man is what he does. And he does what he is" (IV/1, 492).

Does Barth here take the side of the Reformers? Not without qualification. It is important to notice that he does not bother at all with their formulation of the question. It is immaterial to ask about the extent of the deprivation—the change brought about in man through sin. Such a question is too coarse, too materialistic and quantitative; it will not do to balance a quantum of sinfulness against a quantum or kernel of residual goodness. Sacred Scripture indicates otherwise: Man is totally a sinner from head to toe. And Sacred Scripture tells us too that the integrity of human nature and its existence in the covenant relationship with God remain corrupted. So both things are true—man is *not* totally corrupted, and yet he is *totally* corrupted. Positively this means:

"The Bible accuses man as a sinner from head to foot, but it does not dispute to man his full and unchanged humanity, his nature as God created it good, the possession and use of all the faculties which God has given him. . . . Nor can he step out of the covenant which God has made with him, however much he may want to do so and however much he has deserved to be expelled from it *cum infamia*. The *seriousness* of his situation is much greater than can be expressed by the idea of a setting aside or damaging of his nature which is good. It consists in the crying contradiction that he sets himself—his being in the integrity of his human nature and his being in covenant with God—in the service of evil, and that he now has to exist in that service" (IV/1, 492f.; cf. III/2, 28–32; IV/2, 487f.).

But there is a negative conclusion to be drawn simultaneously and for this very reason:

"We certainly *cannot speak* of any *relic* or *core* of goodness which persists in man in spite of his sin" (IV/1, 493)

"It is quite futile to talk about a 'relic of goodness' which remains to man even as a sinner and which is usually identified rather uneasily with the faculty of reason or a religious or moral *a priori* or the like. In answer to this kind of assertion we have to say (1) that the good which remains to man as a sinner is not merely a 'relic' but the *totality* of his God-given nature and its determination, and (2) that in the same totality he exists in the history of the *perversion* of this good into evil, and is caught up in the movement from above to below. His total being in this movement is his *miseria* which has its limit only in the *misericordia Dei*" (IV/2, 489; cf. 485f.).

The radicality of sin establishes its totality: "At *every point* man is in the wrong and in arrears in relation to God. Because he himself as the subject of these activities is not a good tree, he cannot bring forth good fruit. Because his pride is radical and in principle, it is also total and universal and all-embracing, determining all his thoughts and words and works, his whole inner and hidden life, and his visible external movements and relationships. . . . There is, therefore, no 'nature-reserve,' for among his actions there are *none* which are neutral or indeterminate in character; there are no *adiaphora* in which he can act apart from the question of good and evil, of obedience and disobedience" (IV/1, 496; cf. IV/2, 490f.). Yet we should note the way in which Barth develops this: "There can be no doubt that he never has any reason to be proud, but only to be ashamed of his achievements and even of his will and thought and imagination. This is true even in relation to what seem to be the activations of his nature as it was created good. It is true even where he himself and others can ascribe to these activations a certain and perhaps a very high perfection. In such circumstances there will be every reason, and basic reason, to give glory to God the Creator. But at every point . . . we are dealing not merely with any *corruptio,* but with the *corruptio optimi* [corruption of the good man]" (IV/1, 497; cf. III/2, 24f.).

Still more plainly: "The psychical and physical, spiritual and sensual functions in which the evil acts of men are done can be pure as the functions of the pure (Tit. 1.15). They are this in themselves and as such. The good creation of God persists. We are forced to say this finally not only of the functions of those who are healthy but also of those who are sick in body or soul. The evil does not consist in a disposition of the *psyche* or *physis* but in the sloth of their physical and psychic *action* as it derives from the sloth of their *heart*" (IV/2, 491).

On the problem of the distinction between mortal and venial sins, see IV/2, 492f.

3. "The fact that God willed to have mercy on all men in the sacrifice of Jesus Christ, means that 'He hath *concluded them all* in *disobedience*' " (IV/1, 501). He has had pity on all men but all men have been under His judgment and verdict. God passed judg-

ment on every one of them as sinners. The universality of sin must be seen alongside its radicality and totality.

So the whole history of the world—while not removed from God's universal dominion—is afflicted with disobedience. This history is, in itself, not progressive but rather frightfully static; it is a history of pride. And all this is, according to the Bible, linked closely with the original man, with *Adam*. The history of the world began with the pride and the fall of man. Although he was created good, the original man immediately became the original sinner. The developments of Genesis 3 followed hard upon the events of Genesis 2.5–25. And Adam was nothing other than a primus inter pares, though he has a special prominence in that he stands as an exemplar for all and is representative of all.

In regard to Barth's *conception of hereditary sin,* we noted under point 2 above how Barth establishes the radicality and totality of sin. Barth tends beyond this, however, toward a practical identification of peccatum originale with peccata actualia (IV/1, 499). He rejects the expression "peccatum hereditarium" because hereditary sin must be understood not as a sickness inherited by propagation, not as my fate but rather and exclusively as my *act.* Barth therefore prefers the expression "peccatum originale."

"It is not surprising that when an effort is made to take the word 'heir' seriously, as has occasionally happened, the term 'sin' is necessarily dissolved. Conversely, when the term 'sin' is taken seriously, the term 'heir' is necessarily explained in a way which makes it quite unrecognisable, being openly or surreptitiously dissolved and replaced by other and more serious concepts. . . ."

"It is perhaps better to abandon altogether the idea of hereditary sin and to speak only of original sin [*Ursünde*] (the strict translation of *peccatum originale*). What is meant is the voluntary and responsible life of every man—in a connexion with Adam that we have yet to show—which, by virtue of the judicial sentence passed on it in and with his reconciliation with God, is the *sin* of every man, the corruption which he brings on *himself* so that as the one who does so—and again in that connexion—he is *necessarily* and inevitably corrupt" (IV/1, 500f.).

The "connexion with Adam" is, as indicated, the way in which Adam stands as exemplar for all who come after him.

"That is Adam as seen and understood in the biblical tradition, the man who sinned at once, the man who was at once proud man, the man who stands at that gateway as the *representative* of all who follow, the one whom all his successors do in fact resemble (in the fact that they all sin *at once* as well). . . . The successors of Adam are, in the language of the older theologians already quoted, those who are *represented* in his person and deed. They are those whose will is already in *his* will correctly interpreted and expressed as a corrupted will. To put it in another way, they are those whose free will and commission and omission, whose actualisations of their good human nature, always follow the *rule* and perverted *order* which, according to the prophetic witness, is manifested at once at the very beginning of world-history, in the person and act of Adam, which are typical for the persons and acts of all his successors" (IV/1, 510f.).

In this great exemplary sinner we can nevertheless recognize that other man, who also stands—though in a totally and completely different way—as representative of all mankind—Jesus Christ (Rom. 5.12–21). This is the first known, the true man, who is only prefiguratively hinted at in that first Adam.

In all this then we have the negative side of God's judgment and verdict—the rejection of the sinner. Yet, it would be false to regard this left side abstractly. Barth always regards it in connection with the right side. The left side has its whole meaning in the right side, that is, in the justification of the sinner—which will now be more precisely delimited.

11. GOD'S JUSTICE AGAINST THE INJUSTICE OF MAN

Man is, according to Barth, totally and radically *unjust*. He is the sinner. As sinner he stands in judgment before the wrathful God. He is once and for all condemned, dead, finished. He is no longer of any account at all. Yet the incomprehensible happens. The Son of God steps into the place of the sinner. *He* endures condemnation, death, and damnation. In Him the sinner was done away with, killed, buried, obliterated.

And what about man himself whose place was taken by Jesus Christ in death? What becomes of him? Has he so shared in this death that he now no longer lives on? We know that he lives on but this is not self-evident. Reconciliation could also come about by a revocation of the creation; injustice would then be removed from the world in that man himself would finally and in his utter hopelessness be removed from the world.

But the resurrection of Christ from the dead is the sign of hope. It is the guarantee that death is not the end of everything, and in fact that a *positive* reconciliation with God is possible. For Barth, the great and decisive task of the theology of justification is to demonstrate this reconciliation. How is it permissible and possible to conclude a peace (through grace but in an altogether just way) between a holy God and a sinful mankind? How can the depriving and disapproving judgment and verdict of God be at the same time enabling and approving? How can an unjust and dead and godless man become a just man who lives with and for God?

What kind of justness is it which will completely prevail over the injustice of man? The new justness to be asserted can only be the *justness of God* (IV/1, 529f.).

God is not sub lege. There is no law nor any principle of order which is above or outside of God, to which God could be bound.

54

God is fully free. Yet he is not free in the nominalistic sense. God is not sub lege; He is also not ex lex, but is rather sibimetipsi lex, a law unto Himself. And God's justness means this: God is true to Himself; God's justness is the agreement of God with Himself. (For the concept of God's justice and its relationship to mercy and grace, see II/1, 375–406).

Therefore, in justification God is just. He is within his just rights. Justification is not simply a capricious and arbitrary bestowal of favor and disfavor. Rather it is God just precisely in His mercy and merciful in His justice. He remains, in justification too, true to Himself.

"That in the first instance God affirms *Himself* in this action, that in it He lives His own divine life in His unity as Father, Son and Holy Spirit. But in it He also maintains Himself as the God of *man,* as the One who has bound Himself to man from all eternity, as the One who has elected Himself for man and man for Himself. In the action of His grace He executes that which He willed and determined when to man as this creature He gave actuality and his human nature. In executing it He does not surrender *anything.* And in His relationship *to man He* does not *transgress* but *fulfils* His own law, beside which there is no other and above which there is no higher, the law which is Himself. In this respect, too, the grace which He exercises in justification is not one which is foreign to Him. It is not an act in the performance of which He has to alter or correct Himself, in which He has in part at least to cease to be God and therefore true to Himself. If it were otherwise, how could there be a confidence in His grace which corresponds to the deity of God?" (IV/1, 532; cf. II/1, 400–403; II/2, 759–763; IV/1, 530–532).

The injustice of man cannot alter anything in regard to the justness of God. This injustice is great insofar as it is an injustice directed against God but it is small insofar as it is an *in*justice, and as such can establish no just claim. God retains, in this injustice of man, His just claim over man and His just claim to him, His creature and His covenant partner. And man remains, even as a sinner, in the hand of God and under God's jurisdiction. And therefore God can in strict justness let grace take its course. This is the background of the process of justification. In justification the gracious God has a just claim and "is justified"—"is in the right." He is just in Himself, He is true to Himself.

But isn't this perhaps a purely theoretical claim, a valid but inapplicable claim? Does God exercise this just right of His in practice? God *exercises it* because He is a living and not a dead

God. He will not stand for man's injustice; He intervenes. He exercises His just claim in *judgment*. Here the justness of God and the injustice of man truly come into conflict, come to a crisis. "The righteousness [justice] of God means God's negating and overcoming and taking away and destroying wrong and man as the doer of it" (IV/1, 535).

We can see that God is not loath to exercise His just claim. But isn't there here a hint of something else, that is, of the grace of God in His justice? Barth does not tear justice and grace apart. At the core of God's justice is grace. Grace is the beginning and the end of His justice. Out of grace God elected man from all eternity in Jesus Christ; out of grace He created man in time; out of grace, too, He exercised His just claim in justification. He is angry with man. He judges him. He condemns him. And this because He has not given up on him, because He wants to be gracious toward him (IV/1, 563f.; II/2, 733–741).

But for this very reason the judgment and wrath of God ought not to be minimized. The judgment and wrath are genuine. The grace is *hidden* within this and is capable of being unlocked only by God. Sinful man has no desire to know about grace and for this reason is struck by the just wrath of God. He has a wrathful God who judges him severely (see IV/1, 538–542; II/1, 368–406).

What is meant by God's exercising His just claim in favor of sinful man? What does this crisis of judgment mean? It means a radical division in mankind between the rejected man on the left and the elected man on the right. To both the man on the right and on the left, God is truly just as He is truly gracious.

"On the *left* hand, therefore, he is the man who can only perish, who is overtaken by the wrath of God, who can only die, who has already been put to death and done away, and on the *right* hand he is the same man who even in this dying and perishing, even as the one who has been put away, is still the one who stands over against God, object of His purposes, surrounded and maintained by His life. To put it in another way, on the *left* hand man is the one who because of his wrong is condemned and rejected and abandoned by God, and on the *right* hand he is the same man as the one who even in his condemnation and rejection and abandonment is still pardoned and maintained by God, being kept for the fulfilment of His will and plan. We have to say at once that on *both* sides God acts *righteously,* because He acts in consequence of His right, of His faithfulness to Himself, and in execution of His right over and to man. On the *left* hand He acts righteously in His wrath which consumes the sinner, and on the *right* hand He acts righteously in the limitation, or more exactly in the interpretation of His wrath, in His holding fast to the man who even as a sinner that He can only chide is still His man. And God is righteous in this *distinction* as such: for satisfaction would not be done to His right if He could only chide on the left hand or only pardon on the right, if He accepted the identification of man with wrong, and was content simply to banish from the world both wrong and the wrongdoer, or if in spite of the wrong which man has done and his identification with it He allowed him to live at the price of not destroying the wrong which man has committed, of recognising *de facto* its right to exist . . . this *righteousness* would not be the righteousness of *God* if the distinction as such—and that which happens to man on the left hand as well as the right—were not the work of His *grace*. We have seen that even that which God does on the *left* hand is grace. It is not too small a thing for God actually to continue His fellowship with man in the form of the wrath which consumes man because of his wrong. And we have seen that it would not in fact be good for man to continue to be as a wrongdoer, that it is therefore grace if he has to perish and die as such. But how much more the work of God on the *right* hand, in which He does not abandon man even in his fall into the abyss, in which He does not cast him out of His hand, in which He does not annul and extinguish his being as His creature and covenant-partner, in which He remains to him a home even in the far country into which he has wandered, in which even in death He surrounds and maintains him with His own life!" (IV/1, 541f.)

This is all the *work of God* and thus a true and perfect work on both sides. We should note how forcefully Barth makes this point. In each case, "He (God) does not fashion . . . a mere 'as if' but *actualities*" (IV/1, 542f.). The man on the left is not to be only nominally condemned nor his injustice only apparently destroyed. Rather, his injustice is actually brought to nothing, the man must die. And the man on the right does not achieve only a partial justice. He is not only barely spared, rather God brings onto the stage a new, just, and living man. Therefore God's division is something "*real* and *total*" (IV/1, 543).

It would, however, be false to suppose that this division makes of man a kind of dual personality and of God a double-natured being. What the man on the right and the man on the left are involved in is a dynamic, a transformation, a *history*.

"This state of dualism, this static co-existence of two quite different men, can only be the result of a misunderstanding, a caricature, of what we really have to see at this point. But if this is the case, then the only alternative is to understand the work of the dividing of man on the left hand and the right as the putting into effect of a *history* in which the man on the left hand is the *Whence* and the man on the right hand the *Whither* of the *one* man, the former being this man as he *was* and still is, the latter being this man as he *will be* and to that extent already is" (IV/1, 543).

This history is God's justification of sinful man. And it is precisely this history that is for Barth the great riddle of the process of justification. That static contrast of two, perhaps impressive, images of myself (the "empirical" and the "ideal" man) is relatively easy to understand. But justification has nothing to do with this sort of thing. It is a riddle because there is no independent understanding and no independent living-out of this history. The contrast between yesterday and tomorrow is an absolute and qualitative contrast, and we do not go through the experience of ourselves "as dying, and behold we live" (2 Cor. 6.9), nor do we personally experience ourselves as the prodigal son who "was dead, and is alive, was lost and is found" (Lk. 15.32). This is the riddle of justification (see IV/1, 544–547).

Is this an insoluble riddle? Insoluble insofar as man's understanding of himself is concerned, yet solved through God's revelation. Revelation says very simply that all this, even though beyond our experience, is exactly this way. The whole thing is an event in actual fact.

And why is all this so much of a riddle? Because what we have learned from revelation—the transformation from unjustness to justness, from death to life, the justification of sinful man can only be learned in an *Other,* who has made all this true, has made these assertions possible but who Himself stands hidden in the background—*Jesus Christ.* Our justness is a justness alien to ourselves. It is *His* justness, and only as such our justness. Our history is *His* history and only for that reason our history.

"It is all true and actual in Him *and* therefore in us. It cannot, therefore, be *known* to be valid and effective in us first, but in Him first, and because in Him in us. We are in Him and comprehend in Him, but we are still not He Himself. Therefore it is all true and actual in this *Other* first and not in us. That is *why* our justification is not a matter of subjective experience and understanding. That is *why* we cannot perceive and comprehend it. That is *why* it is so *puzzling* to us" (IV/1, 549).

12. AN ALIEN JUSTICE—OUR OWN JUSTICE

Our justice is "Iustitia aliena, because first and essentially it is iustitia Christi, and only as such nostra, mea iustitia" (IV/1, 549). God's justice is the achievement of His rights in opposition to the injustice of man. As such it is nothing but the judgment of God and nothing else in regard to man and the justification of man. All of these—justice (righteousness), judgment, justification—are only understood when they are seen as *what happens in Jesus Christ.*

"But this righteousness, this judgment of God, this justification by God which comes to man, is something which has taken place concretely in *Jesus Christ.* It *had* to take place in Him because in His person as the Son of the Father He is Himself both very God electing and creating man and very man elected by God and as such ordained from all eternity to fulfil all the righteousness of God. It *could* take place in Him, because as very God and very man He was competent and qualified to accomplish and suffer the contest between God and man, to be both the Judge and the judged in this conflict. It could take place *only in Him* because only He as this one person could be both subject and object in this history, uniting the antithesis of it in Himself: Himself the full end which is made in it; and Himself also the new beginning which is made in it; and both in the place and therefore in the name of all other men, for them and in their favour. It *took place* in Him in that He as the true Son of God became true man, and in this unity of His person became the Judge of all other men: their Judge as the One who was judged in their place—delivered up in His death, and reinstated in His resurrection from the dead. As it has taken place in Jesus Christ this is the justification of sinful man" (IV/1, 550; cf. II/1, 396–399; II/2, 758–763).

What happens in justification is that God powerfully puts Himself in jeopardy. The sinner is, of course, in no way fit for the inescapable conflict with the holy, neither as active nor as passive cooperator, neither as subject nor as object, since in this judgment it is a matter of the death of man and of his life out of this death. In this judgment man emerges holy and alive, only because God Himself puts Himself in his place, because God jeopardizes Himself in a death where God, the Lord, Judge, and Helper, is simultaneously man, servant, judged, and helpless. That is how man can and does become, actively and passively, a partner.

The justification of the sinner as God's putting Himself in jeopardy in Jesus Christ means first of all the *turning away from injustice* (IV/1, 552–555)—that is, the annihilation of human injustice and the elimination of man as wrongdoer. This did not happen in us, because we certainly do not cease to be the sinful men of yesterday. This turning away is not discernible in any experience of our lives. It has come about through Jesus Christ. In Him our injustice is truly and finally wiped out and becomes a thing of yesterday and we as wrongdoers are killed and buried, and become ourselves a thing of yesterday.

"In Him our sin and we ourselves have *perished.* In Him we all start at the divine No which has been spoken with such power and carried through with such effect; at the liberation which is an accomplished fact in this No because it is spoken and carried through in Jesus Christ. This liberation which has taken place in Him is the presupposition of our future. And the freedom given to us by this No is our present. In Him our wrong and we ourselves as the doers of it are *behind* us. He *has* taken it away from us. He *has* taken us away from it. He has set aside and cancelled our existence as the doers of it" (IV/1, 553f.; cf. III/3, 73–85).

The justification of the sinner as God's jeopardizing of Himself means secondly *a returning to God*—the raising up of human justness and the fostering of the life of something new, of a man justified before God. But this positive event does not occur in our existence as such. Merely looking at ourselves we cannot help considering such a just man something unreal. But in Jesus Christ this is reality.

"In *Jesus Christ,* the very man who as such is the eternal Son of the eternal Father, this *future* man, the new and righteous man, lives in an unassailable reality. *In Him* I am already the one who will be this righteous man and live as such, just as in Him I am still only the unrighteous man, to the extent that I once was this man. In this positive sense Jesus Christ lives in *our* place, for *us,* in *our* name. As our wrong and death are our past in His name, in Him, so our righteousness and life are our future" (IV/1, 555).

Christ suffered death. But not only in an active achievement, as subject of the process. Rather in Him, Christ—as the object of justice, comes the answer of the gracious God—the raising up of the dead. And all of this happened for our sake, "for our justification" (Rom. 4.25). And this positive aspect of justification is not our affair though it is our affair too—a concern of ours in which Jesus Christ has taken the lead and which He has consummated.

These two aspects of justice and judgment belong together in their necessary distinctness, in their ineradicable unity, in the unalterable context of the single and irreversible history—a history which moves from the annihilation of the unjustness to the establishment of justness, from a turning away from sin to a return to God, from death to resurrection.

Barth therefore sees the justice of man as essentially an alien justice—the justice of Christ. And he sees the justification of man as a history which in essence occurred in an Other—in Jesus Christ. It would be a misunderstanding of Barth to think that this justice would therefore not be man's own justice, that this justification would not be man's own history. It is precisely in being the justice and history of Christ that it is *our own justice and history*.

"His history is as such *our* history. It is our *true* history (incomparably more direct and intimate than anything we think we know as our history). Jesus Christ comes to us. In *Him* we are quite alone" (IV/1, 548).

"It is all true and actual *in Him and therefore* in us. It cannot, therefore, be *known* to be valid and effective in us first, but in Him first, and because in Him in us" (IV/1, 549). "It also happened that in His resurrection from the dead He was confirmed and recognised and revealed by God the Father as the One who has done and been that for us and all men. As the One who has done that, in whom God Himself has done that, who lives as the doer of that deed, He is *our* man, *we* are *in Him*, our present is *His*, the history of man is *His* history, He is the concrete event of the existence and reality of justified man in whom every man can recognise himself and every other man— recognise himself as truly justified. There is not one for whose sin and death He did not die, whose sin and death He did not remove and obliterate on the cross, for whom He did not positively do the right, whose right He has not established. There is not one to whom this was not addressed as his justification in His resurrection from the dead. There is not one whose man He is not, who is not justified in Him. . . . Again, there is not one who is not adequately and perfectly and finally justified in Him" (IV/1, 630).

Barth's anthropology made a special point of insisting that what the whole of human history hinges on is the history of the man Jesus. This is a matter of "realism," a real history even in its derivative aspects: see for example the various aspects of man's true being such as: existing with God (III/2, 134–140), existence as derived from God (III/2, 139–142), being elected (III/2, 142–147), being called (III/2, 147–158), being as history (III/2, 157–164), being in thanksgiving (III/2, 164–173), being in responsibility (III/2, 173–200).

The justice of the man made just is therefore for Barth actually not only an alien justice but one which is simultaneously man's own. This is meaningful for us but it must be spelled out. We will return to this human aspect of justification in the next chapter, especially in demonstrating how Barth understands the subjective realization of justification. The life of faith is indeed "the being of sinful man in which he finds that *he* is really and truly justified, that his sins are forgiven, that he is a child of God, and an heir of the hope of eternal life" (IV/1, 634).

13. THE JUST MAN

The justification of man is the judgment of God. Here God's justice comes about in that His just claim is established. The verdict is accomplished in the death of Christ on the cross and proclaimed in the resurrection of Christ. What is the effect of this incisive verdict? Barth answers, *"The acquittal of man"* (IV/1, 568). It is the election of the new man (the old man is gone)— the just man, the new creature, the new creation. This is possible because it is *God's* verdict as such, that is, as a word of revelation and not as something he himself experiences. Man must accept it, take it to heart, and act upon it. As a word of revelation, the verdict does not have a partial or relative but an entire and absolute authority, power, and validity. It is something that happened *in* us, not just something said *about* us or attached to us like a label. Something factual has been fashioned, a fundamentally altered human situation.

At this point an oversimplification would be disastrous. Man has a *dual orientation*. He proceeds from the before of his unjustness and death toward the after of his justness and life. And the burden of the divine acquittal is this, that man can proceed from there to here: "He becomes the man who in every present has *both* this past and this future; the one as past and the other as future; the one set aside behind him, the other as a promise before him; irreversible in the same sequence as the death and resurrection of Jesus Christ—but in this sequence not merely the one and the other but *both* at once, and in their specific and highly distinctive ways equally actual and equally serious; not intermingled in any present (as though at bottom they were not two-fold) but both distinct in every present; not separated in any present, but—in that sequence, as moments in that history—indissolubly bound together in every present" (IV/1, 573).

First of all we have to look *backwards* (IV/1, 573–577). In the first place justification has to do with the divine verdict as countermand, a divine acquittal of *sinful* man. It is a iustificatio *impii,* a creatio ex *opposito.* Barth here reaches back to the Reformation for a formula: the iustus is simul peccator. Here we must take special pains to understand Barth correctly. We ought not to regard the matter quantitatively. We are not dealing either in the case of the iustus or that of the peccator with a quantum as though we had here something like a fluid in connected tubes which increases on one side while it decreases on the other. In both instances the whole man is at stake. The whole man has arrived at the goal and yet is still at the beginning—he is and he knows it. His justification is an incipient justification.

"There is no man justified by God who does not have to recognise and confess that he is still unrighteous, still the proud rebel before Him, who does not have to grant that God is always in the right against him and therefore that he is always in the wrong against God. If he is not willing to be this; that means necessarily that he does not wish to be pardoned, justified. If he wants to deny that he is this, that means that he denies the promise, that he does not know it, that he is not caught up in this breaking out of acquitted man. Where there is this breaking out, where the justification of man takes place, it is the justification of the *unrighteous,* and the one to whom it comes will not refuse to admit that he is still this one, that as such he finds himself in this breaking out, and that only as such can he do so" (IV/1, 575f.).

The justified man is a work of the divine new creation but in that very fact he knows that he has fallen prey to nothingness and knows that he would fall time and again without this work of God. Whatever he has he does not—for a single moment—have on his own, since he is a sinner. He only has it as a gift of God's grace. All he is, as a justified man, he receives. We would have a secret, sinful effort of self-justification if man wanted to prescind from a consideration of who he was.

"It is the sentence of God in virtue of which man is separated from that *past* and therefore the sentence of God on the man who can go forward from that *past* to quite a different future. In every present he is still the man he was, the man of sin, the man of pride, and as such fallen man. He is not this man to remain such, but to be so no longer, to become another man" (IV/1, 573; cf. II/2, 754–757). As a biblical proof for this Barth makes a long excursus on the exegesis of Psalms 32 and 51 and especially Romans 7 (IV/1, 577–591).

Still we must not merely look backward but at the same time and even more eagerly *forward* (IV/1, 591–596). Justification is, as we saw, a matter of the sinner's *acquittal,* of the *iustificatio* impii, and of a *creatio* ex opposito. It is above all something positive. Unjustness lies behind man, justness lies ahead. Man's course in justification has a direction which must not be reversed. The new has priority over the old, justness over unjustness, the future over the past, life over death. Despite all distinction and classification, it is not at all proper to give equal weight to the two moments in this process. The *consummation of justification* has priority over its initial stage. The divine verdict is pre-eminently a pledge and a promise. It is true that God's verdict taken as God's No does affect man as the sinner he was and to a certain extent still is. Yet it is as true and more important to say that man as affected by the verdict considered as God's Yes is a man who by reason of God's pledge and promise is already established in His justice and in His new life.

Thus the old man is already the new, the unfaithful partner in the covenant is already faithful, the dead already resurrected. The promise refers to the future, but just as the past of man as sinner is man's present, so also his future as justified man is already his present too. The promise is pledged now, here, today, in the midst of this present time. It is entirely certain, direct, and real. Man even now possesses the totality. So what we have is not merely the beginning of justification but also and more especially its consummation. So present and future are neither simply equalized or identified, nor mutually opposed. Nor is anything achieved by using quantitative concepts:

". . . as though that which is ascribed to the justified man with the promise and therefore in the present is only a little thing, whereas that which we expect in the future is a greater, as though the one is only a part and the other the whole. When an inheritance reverts to a man, and it is quite certain, it is not smaller because he has not yet entered into it (except in the form of a first instalment or a pledge). The moment it becomes his it becomes his altogether. The wrong which according to the divine sentence is behind man is all his wrong. The death from which he comes is his whole death. So, too, the right and life which are before him according to the same sentence are his *whole* right and life. In his past, as it reaches into the present, he is wholly in the wrong and dead. So, too, in his future as with the promise it reaches into the present he is *wholly* in the right and alive. The only thing is that as long as he lives in time and considers his own person, he is both together: *simul peccator et iustus,* yet not half *peccator* and half *iustus,* but both altogether. And the pardon of man, declared in the promise concerning him, the reality of his future already in the present, is no less than this: *totus iustus"* (IV/1, 595f.; cf. II/1, 627; II/2, 756f.).

The fact that man is totus iustus is illuminated by the *content of the promise* whose reception consummates the justification of man. The promise comprises three somewhat identical yet different aspects:

1. The forgiveness of sins: Man receives a *promise* of this, thus it is something future. The fifth petition of the Lord's Prayer is intended for every moment of man's life. Man has always to pray for and await forgiveness of and thus freedom from his sins.

Forgiveness of sins does not mean the undoing of events. This is impossible. God sees and knows man's blemish but He does not take it into consideration. He overlooks it and covers it over, in that He does "not reckon it" (2 Cor. 5.19). Thus he pardons; not out of weakness but rather in an act of divine power and defiance; not extra-juridically but according to the strictest justice. This forgiveness is *in no way a purely verbal* pardoning, but a pardoning which *obliterates* sin.

"As pardoning, it is the effectual and righteous alteration of the human situation from its very foundation. If God's sentence concerning man *is* that He will know nothing of this stain, then the stain *is* washed away and removed, and although man still bears it, in spite of it he *is* without stain, in spite of his wrong he *is* in the right. The divine pardoning is not a remission 'as if' man were not a sinner. As pardoning, it is the creative work of God, in the power of which man, even as the old man that he was and still is, is *no longer* that man, but is already another man, the man he will be, the new man. That is the forgiveness of sins as the final stroke under man's past" (IV/1, 597).

With this a new and positive starting point is fashioned, a new freedom and a threefold opportunity—to hold fast to God's grace and justice, to learn meekness and to reject sin. This is our future, and yet it is *already present to us.* "Your sins *are* forgiven you." What is announced and promised to man does not remain merely an announcement or a simple promise. It really *happens* now.

"Where and when man trusts the promise, where and when he dares to treat it as directed to himself, to apply it to himself, to accept it as true of himself, there the forgiveness of sins takes place, that line is drawn, the new situation from which he can set out is created. There absolution is not simply pronounced to him. It takes place. There he receives forgiveness, the divine pardon, and the freedom of a new and the only true capacity. There he already has it, and he can and should dare to live as one who is forgiven" (IV/1, 599).

2. Reinstatement into the just claims of the children of God: man's re-establishment in his just rights, not merely those of creature and covenant partner, but those belonging to a child of God. This indicates that the goal of reconciliation lies beyond any co-existence of God and man, in a graced community of *being* between man and God in an unprecedented, new ontological relationship, a belonging to God *in the order of being*. God *is* the Father of man, man *is* His child. God has paternal rights in regard to man and man has filial claims on God—including all human rights. But this too is future and promise. We are "born anew to a living hope" (1 Pet. 1.3) of this existence. We have here not merely a distant goal—for it touches the present and is here and now already lived. "We *are* children of God" (Rom. 8.16; 1 Jn. 3.2).

"It may be covered over and concealed by that which overshadows and burdens and harasses us from our past, and basically so, so that there can be no question of any perception. 'It doth not appear what we shall be' (1 Jn. 3.2). But this cannot alter the fact. This cannot either remove it or diminish even a fraction of its relevance. What we are according to God's promise, those to whom God has bound Himself, calling them His children, what we have, the right to hold to this and to appeal to it, the right to cry 'Abba, Father' (Gal. 4.6; Rom. 8.15) . . ." (IV/1, 600f.; cf. I/1, 523–526; I/2, 214–223, 235–240).

3. Man's establishment in a condition of hope and inheritance: the capacity to hope and truly hope for the forgiveness of sin and for divine sonship—like the capacity to pray and actual praying—must in all seriousness come through hoping in God. Man does indeed have the promise that he may hope, yet it all points to the one great hope of the *final* goal, where man no longer travels but comes to rest. The great beyond where man is no longer anything else than totus iustus—the goal of glorification of the servant of God in eternal life and in eternal salvation. These things will *then* be fully present but even now, in every *present situation,* we have though in a hidden way the future as something present. "We are already children and also *heirs*" (Rom. 8.17).

" 'Inheritance' is the decision, the *hidden* thing in all the decisions in which here and now the justified man can have the full forgiveness of all his sins and be a full child of God. 'Inheritance' is the being which is the *hidden* thing in the righteous being which here and now is promised to him without reserve in the divine promise. 'Inheritance' is the present of eternal life which is the *hidden* thing in every temporal present in which he finds himself in this transition. The entry into and taking possession of the inheritance will be the revelation of this hidden thing, the drawing aside of the veil by which it is now concealed, the removing of the contradiction, the solving of the riddle, the dispersing of the mystery of his temporal being. To have the forgiveness of sins and to be a child of God means to be one who awaits this inheritance and moves towards it. To be justified (Col. 1.12) is to be 'made meet to partake of the inheritance of the saints in light' " (IV/1, 604; cf. I/1, 530–533; II/2, 772–781).

14. JUSTIFICATION AND SANCTIFICATION

It must first be formally stated that Karl Barth clearly teaches the *interior justifying* of man. Not that he has denied the forensic justification of the Reformers but that he has revised and deepened it, taking it seriously in its divine character. We saw in Chapter 12 how Barth regards justification in Christ as our own most personal history and Christ's justice as our justice. We saw further on in Chapter 13 how the consummation of justification surpasses its initial stage. We also saw how the forgiveness of sins, the sonship of God and the inheritance of heaven are ontological realities—realities which though hidden away like a deposit are already ontological actualities. Though they are promises, they do not remain mere promises. But rather, if man accepts them as valid for himself, they are fulfilled for him here and now. We may summarize simply by stating that for Barth what is juridically pronounced just is ontologically made just.

"There is no room for any fears that in the justification of man we are dealing only with a verbal action, with a kind of bracketed 'as if,' as though what is pronounced were not the whole truth about man. Certainly we have to do with a *declaring* righteous, but it is a declaration about man which is fulfilled and therefore effective in this event, which corresponds to actuality because it creates and therefore reveals the actuality. It is a declaring righteous which without any reserve can be called a *making* righteous. Christian faith does not believe in a sentence which is ineffective, or only partly effective. As faith in Jesus Christ who is risen from the dead it believes in a sentence which is absolutely effective, so that man is not merely *called* righteous before God, but *is* righteous before God. He believes that God has vindicated Himself in relation to man, not partly but *wholly,* not negatively only but *positively,* replacing the old man by a new and obedient man. He believes that by calling that One His own dear Son in whom He is well pleased, God has set up not a provisional but a *definitive* order in the relationship between Himself and man" (IV/1, 95; cf. II/2, 756f.).

What it means to be made just ontologically in the "subjective" sphere—in the actuality of the individual man—will be discussed in more detail in Chapter 17 which deals with the foundation of Christian being (the Holy Spirit's taking possession, the constituting of the Christian subject, the creator-like character of faith).

To proclaim just is to make just: Would Barth maintain that justification and sanctification are the same thing? Not unequivocally. Barth has treated the relationship between justification and sanctification in a very discriminating fashion (IV/2, 499–511). Justification and sanctification must be seen in the unity of their diversity. The point is that it is *one* divine act, with, however, two quite distinct aspects: "As we now turn to consider sanctification in and for itself, we are not dealing with a second divine action which either takes places simultaneously with it, or precedes or follows it in time. The action of God in His reconciliation of the world with Himself in Jesus Christ is unitary. It consists of different *'moments'* with a different bearing. It accomplishes both the justification *and* the sanctification of man, for it is itself both the condescension of God *and* the exaltation of man in Jesus Christ. But it accomplishes the two together. The one is done wholly and immediately with the other. There are also different *aspects* corresponding to the different 'moments.' We cannot see it all at once, or comprehend it in a single word. Corresponding to the one historical being of Jesus Christ as true Son of God and true Son of Man, we can see it only as the movement from above to below, *or* the movement from below to above, as justification *or* sanctification. Yet whether we look at it from the one standpoint or the other our knowledge can and may and must be a knowledge of the one *totality* of the reconciling action of God, of the one whole and undivided Jesus Christ, and of His *one* grace" (IV/2, 501f.).

"It is one thing that God turns in free grace to sinful man, and quite another that in the same free grace He converts man to Himself. It is one thing that God as the Judge establishes that He is in the right against this man, thus creating a new right for this man before Him, and quite another that by His mighty direction He claims this man and makes him willing and ready for His service" (IV/2, 503).

"But we have to say that to ignore the mutual relationship of the two can only lead at once to *false* statements concerning them and to corresponding errors in practice: to the idea of a God who works in isolation, and His 'cheap grace' (D. Bonhoeffer) and therefore an indolent quietism, where the relationship of justification to *sanctifica-*

tion is neglected; and to that of a favoured man who works in isolation, and therefore to an illusory activism, where the relationship of sanctification to *justification* is forgotten" (IV/2, 505).

And how shall their mutual relationship be described? It is involved in a before-and-after arrangement—an ordering which is not chronological but natural:

"In the *simul* of the one divine will and action justification is first as *basis* and second as *presupposition,* sanctification first as *aim* and second as *consequence;* and therefore both are *superior* and both *subordinate.* Embracing the distinctness and unity of the two moments and aspects, the one grace of the one Jesus Christ is at work, and it is both justifying and sanctifying grace, and both to the *glory of God* and the *salvation of man*" (IV/2, 508f.).

In keeping with this definition of the relationship, Barth describes sanctification in all its detail: (1) as participation in the holiness of Jesus Christ—the Holy One and the holy ones (IV/2, 511–533); (2) as a call to follow Him—a call which is a command, a binding of a person, a first step, a break with the given situation (IV/2, 533–553); (3) as an awakening to repentance—a returning from the sleep of death, a conversion and renewal of the whole man, battle and conflict—all of these being an unforced opportunity through the grace that is in Jesus Christ (IV/2, 553–584); (4) as the praise given by works—these good works are performed, not as though they were humanly burdensome, but out of pure grace and in response to God's command (IV/2, 584–598); (5) as a carrying of the cross—sanctification is consummated in communion with the life and death of Christ; there is a cross for humility, a cross for punishment, for discipline, for strength—in persecution, weakness, and in temptation (IV/2, 598–613).

15. THROUGH FAITH ALONE

Barth sees as the decisive factor in the process of justification the fact that it is a work *of God*. It is *His* justice, His justifying, His judgment, His verdict, His acquittal. Thus far we have talked of this primary and decisive aspect of the theology of justification—often referred to as "objective" justification. But Barth does not overlook the fact that God's justice has its scriptural counterpart. This counterpart is not some kind of concurrence, since self-justification is entirely out of the question here; yet this counterpart, too, is based on the work and gift of God. Yet precisely as a gift it is a truly *human* work. This counterpart is *faith*. Faith is that "which is *adapted,* which *corresponds* on the human side, to His divine justification" (IV/1, 615). But it corresponds only because God gives it validity. Here then we must turn to a consideration of the so-called "subjective" content of the theology of justification, a matter which had special significance in the Reformation.

We learn through faith, and only through faith, that the justified man is not just a beautiful idea, an illusion or myth—but a reality. It is fundamentally impossible for anyone to prove himself by his own power, for only in humble faith can we give an affirmative answer to the question of the reality and existence of the man justified by God—though the answer is not merely for the inquirer himself, but for others as well (see IV/1, 608–614).

Faith is man's realization, acknowledgment, and acceptance of God's verdict upon man, and is the accomplishing of his submission to this verdict. This faith is in the final analysis *humility,* the resignation of a proud man in the face of his pride. Not that man conquers himself and abandons his pride. He is and remains a proud man—who believes. The proud man sees the folly of his pride, loathes it and despairs of it; he has become a man of humbled pride. Faith is thus neither personally chosen humility (it is not a matter of his choice), nor forced humility (it is not a matter of external coercion). Rather faith is the humility of *obedience*. We have here a decision which in the real necessity of its obedience is free, and which in its need for real and thus free obedience is necessary. Hence faith is a despair *full of trust* (IV/1, 614–621).

In speaking of faith here, we mean especially "justifying" faith. Faith as Christian living has, of course, dimensions other than those which are associated with man's justification, and forms other than those involved in recognizing, reaching for, and realizing God's newly established justice. Central to faith, however, is its relation to justification, and this is what we are discussing here. We will return in the next chapter to the problem of faith in its full scope.

For faith as a whole, cf. faith and the Word of God (I/1, 260–283); faith as the knowledge of God (II/1, 3–254); faith in God the Creator (III/1, 3–41); faith and providence (III/3, 246–253); faith and the Church (IV/1, 650–660).

What does justification *"through faith alone"* mean for Barth? It means "the *opposition* of *faith* to all and every *work;* the two statements (1) that no human work as such either is or includes man's justification (not even the work of faith as such), but (2) that the believer is actually the man justified by God" (IV/1, 621). The second, affirmative statement presupposes the first and negative one with which we shall begin our discussion.

"The negative statement of Paul and the Reformers is that *no* human works, not even those which are demanded by the Law, which can be seriously expected of man and regarded as good, either are or include his justification. As works to advance his justification they are *not* expected of him and they are *not* good" (IV/1, 621).

To Barth the term "works" means "thoughts and words and achievements of sinful man . . ." (IV/1, 621). These works have to be completely dissociated from justification. Faith as obedient humility denies the power and worth of any human actions done for the purpose of attaining justification.

The deepest reason for the sola fides is the *solus Christus*. It is He alone in whom man is justified and revealed as justified. Faith is faith in *Him*. Faith is justifying insofar as it recognizes and realizes the justification which comes about in Christ as the verdict of God, and insofar as it expects everything from Christ and nothing from itself, everything from grace and nothing from its own thoughts, words, and undertakings (1/1, 280–283; IV/1, 629–633).

This must not be thought to mean, however, that faith itself could be a work of such a kind, so that man would, after all, justify himself, through the act of faith. This would be the most despicable sort of pharisaism, the pharisaism of the publican. There is no place for human self-glorification here; man can glory neither in his faith nor in his works. A Christian may and should glory in the justness of his faith, but one who is justified by faith must never take his justice to be something acquired under his own power.

Barth knows very well that *Paul* understands "works" as primarily the works demanded by Old Testament law, and that he in no sense despises works as such, to say nothing of rejecting them. Barth also knows that the weakness of the *Reformation* on this point lies in:

". . . a too hasty identification of the biblical situation with its own, and therefore as a result of its own impetuous understanding of the present a failure to see many of the nuances, and the other aspects and parts of the biblical texts, or conversely, because of its impetuous exposition of the texts, a lack of many of the necessary nuances and differentiations in its judgment of the present. Only those who have tried to understand and expound the Bible, and especially Paul as a man of his own day, only those who have happily escaped the dangers which threaten us on these two sides (exposition and application), are entitled to cast the first stone. Certainly in Galatians (not to speak of other parts of Paul's writings and of Scripture generally) there were and are many more things to be discovered than what Luther discovered then. Certainly there was and is much more to be said of the Roman Church and Roman theology both then and since than what the Reformers said then within the *schema* of Galatians. We do not need to consider ourselves bound either in the one respect or in the other by their attitude" (IV/1, 622f.).

Nevertheless the Reformers were one with Paul in holding that no work performed constitutes or entails the justification of any sinful man. Works which are supposed to justify man, works which are supposed to take their place alongside faith as though they were its necessary complement—these plainly connote a falling from faith. There is here only an either-or. And the Reformers sided with Paul in rejecting all works in favor of faith.

"The *sola fide* does not actually occur in the Pauline texts. Yet it was not an importation into the texts, but a genuine interpretation of what Paul himself said without using the word *sola,* when Luther translated Rom. 3.28: 'Therefore we conclude that a man is justified by faith *alone* without the deeds of the law.' Say what we will about the possibility and the freedom and the right and the compulsion and the practical necessity of the doing of works—the works of the Law or the works of faith—according to Paul a man is not justified by the fact that he does these works, and therefore to that extent he is *justified* χωρὶς ἔργων νόμου, without them. And the faith by which a man is justified stands *alone* against this 'without,' even though it is not without works, even though it is a faith which 'worketh by love' (Gal. 5.6). But if he is not justified by the works of the holy Law of God, but by *faith,* then obviously he is justified *only* by faith, by faith *alone, sola fide*" (IV/1, 622).

At this point Barth opens up with the second major polemic against Catholic teaching to be found in Volume IV/1 (we have referred to this earlier in connection with the first polemic against the Catholic theology of grace). This is the excursus on the *Tridentine teaching on justification.* Barth reacts very strongly against the decree of Session VI:

"The decree itself is theologically a clever and in many respects a not unsympathetic document which has caused superficial Protestant readers to ask whether there might not be something to say for it. But if we study it more closely it is impossible to conceal the fact that not even the remotest impression seems to have been made upon its exponents by what agitated the Reformers or, for that matter, Paul himself in this whole question of faith and works" (IV/1, 624f.).

What is the basis for this objection? In Barth's view the teaching of Trent does not leave intact the sovereign character of justification as a *divine* work done for man. The parallel to Barth's first polemic against the general Catholic teaching on grace is obvious. Here as there, Barth's greatest objection is that the Catholic Church does not take seriously the *sovereignty of God;* it flounders in *anthropocentricity.* Barth regards the decree of Trent as impaired by this lack of light from above. This, he contends, reduces divine justification to a physical process taking place within the human subject.

It is on this basis that Barth makes his judgment about individual features of the Catholic teaching on justification—about the death of Christ as merely the causa meritoria justificationis, about the Church as a salvific institution, about human co-operation and human acts of preparation, about Baptism as causa instrumentalis, about the link between justification and sanctification, about the nature of justifying grace, about the repetition of justification in the sacrament of Penance, and especially about the condemnation of fiducial faith.

"The decisive polemical sentence of the Tridentinum is as follows: '*Anathema sit,*' whoever maintains ['that justifying faith is nothing else than confidence that divine Mercy remits sins for Christ's sake, or that it is confidence alone that justifies us' (Can. 12: *D* 822)]. Now Paul certainly spoke of love and hope as well as faith, and if our thinking is to be Pauline we must follow him in this. But in the matter of man's justification he spoke only of faith. And if faith undoubtedly has for him other dimensions than that in which in relation to man's justification it is *fiducia divinae misericordiae peccata remittentis propter Christum,* yet there can also be no doubt that in the contexts in which he connects δικαιοσύνη and אמונה faith is just this and nothing but this: the confidence of sinful man in the demonstration of the undeserved faithfulness of God as given in Jesus Christ, a demonstration in which he finds that his sins are forgiven. If there is any corresponding faithfulness of sinful man to the faithful God, it consists only in this confidence. As he gives God this confidence, he finds himself justified, but not otherwise. That was what the Reformers maintained.

"They did not have the unequivocal backing of Paul for all their statements. But they undoubtedly had it for this statement" (IV/1, 626).

The reading of this excursus makes the cleft between Barthian and Catholic theologies of justification seem hopeless and unbridgeable. Are not all points of common agreement ruthlessly obliterated here?

We shall have to return later to this excursus. For the time being let us insist again that Barth's concept of justification—and this is the norm by which he measures Trent—denotes the divine judgment executed in Christ's death on the cross and revealed in His resurrection, a work which is totally divine. Only by keeping this in mind is it possible to understand the violence of Barth's reproaches. And all this raises a question. Is Barth's concept of justification founded in revelation? Does the Catholic Church have another concept of justification which cannot be harmonized with the Barthian? Are we talking of two different things and therefore talking over each other's heads? Or of different aspects and thus unwittingly talking to one another?

The second and affirmative statement concerning justification by faith alone was this: The believer is, in point of fact, the sinner justified by God (IV/1, 633–637). Room is made for him by the negative statement. Faith had first to be purged of all sorts of veiled self-justification. Nevertheless in that negative form, faith (as the humility of obedience, as empty hand and empty cup, as pure openness to Jesus Christ and to His justice) remains, too, what it was in its positive form—*the faith which truly perceives, reaches out for, and realizes the justification of man.* Thus the sinner may take his existence entirely from Jesus Christ, and trust firmly that the interchange between God and man which took place in Jesus Christ has in its fullest reality taken place for him, and that the alien justice of Jesus Christ has become his—has become man's own justice. Thus in faith man finds himself truly justified through the forgiveness of his sins, finds himself as a child of God, finds himself as an heir of the hope of everlasting life. Faith is not imitatio Christi, insofar as man does not justify himself; yet it is imitatio Christi in one true sense: it is an imitatio Dei inasmuch as trustful faith (πιστις) is the appropriate counterpart to the fidelity (πιστις) of God as actualized and revealed in His judgment and verdict, and it is particularly an imitatio Christi insofar as the obedience of humility is a true reflection of divine condescension, a human re-enactment, a human mimesis and imitation. Not as if this human re-enactment itself justifies man, since all of this is merely *man's* doing, yet without this re-enactment faith would not be justifying faith, and would not be a concrete response to Christ.

"It is not a mere figure of speech to say that in faith man finds that the history of Jesus Christ is his history, that his sin is judged in Him, that his right is established in Him, that his death is put to death and his life is born in Him, that he can *regard* himself as justified in His righteousness because it *is* his own righteousness, because his faith is a real apprehension of his real being in Christ. It is, therefore, quite unavoidable that there should be a correspondence to his being in Christ in the sphere of his own being as differentiated from it, his being in the *flesh* and therefore his walking in *faith*" (IV/1, 636; cf. on the exegesis of Galatians, IV/1, 637–642).

Thus, precisely in its negative emptiness and passivity, justifying faith is found in most positive abundance and *activity* (see I/1, 228ff.; IV/1, 636f.). This point will be further developed in the following chapters. Jesus Christ is indeed not only the Author and Finisher of faith but also the Former of faith. Christology is the crown of justification.

16. LOVE AND WORKS

In Barth's theology of justification faith is strongly accentuated. This does not mean that love is devaluated. As justification relates to sanctification, so faith must be seen as related to love. Here, again, we have two moments in *one* act.

"*Love* as self-giving stands contrasted with *faith* as reception. Yet on the divine side we do not have in the humiliation and exaltation of Jesus Christ, and therefore in justification and sanctification and the work of the Holy Spirit which reveals them, two separate divine actions, but two undivided and simultaneous, although distinguishable, moments or forms of the one divine action. Similarly, on the human side faith and love, reception and surrender are two indivisible but distinguishable moments of the one vital movement and act which constitutes Christian existence. The contrast, then, is only relative, and we can hardly speak of love without (in other terms) making use of the views and concepts with which faith has also to be described, or of faith without attributing to it certain features which in the strict sense are those of love" (IV/2, 730f.).

On this Barth refers to the exegesis of Gal. 5.6; 1 Col. 13.13; Rom. 13.10 (IV/2, 731–733).

Compare further: "And faith itself would not be faith if it did not work by love, if it were not as Luther put it 'a living, active, busy thing' " (IV/1, 627). "Where there is faith, there are also love and works. The man who, justified by faith, has peace with God has also peace with his neighbour and himself. That he lives as one who is righteous by faith to the exclusion of all works is something that he will establish and attest in his works—the particular doctrine of justification that we find in the Epistle of James. If in relation to justification no work is important and every work indifferent, in relation to this conformation every work is important and none indifferent" (IV/1, 627f.).

Faith and love are to be distinguished as two moments of a single act. Justification comes about through faith and sanctification through love. In Barth's view, the erroneous teaching of Trent leads to the falsification of both. Justification as the accomplishment and revelation of God's verdict upon man is the presupposition for sanctification as the placing of man under God's direction. Justification and faith form the foundation. Sanctification and love, building on the foundation of human justness, signify an enlisting of this just man in the cause of the fulfillment of the will of God, an enlistment in active existence, in the task of witnessing and implementing justification through works (see the above citations together with the allusion to the teaching on justification in the Letter of James). This does not imply a supplementing of justification in the sense of some independent self-sanctification. All good works in which love becomes manifest stem from the free grace of God.

"But this carries with it the fact that there can be *no* question of a *justification* of man by his love to God—perhaps as a continuation or actualisation of his justification by faith. Certainly the divine direction, the direction into love to God, can never be lacking in the man who has subjected himself to the divine sentence in the knowledge of it. But it is the pardoning sentence of God *alone* which is the basis of fellowship between God and man, and which therefore justifies man. And the fact that he is justified is something which he finds to be true and actual *only* in faith. That he can love, i.e., seek God, is his freedom to live in that fellowship on the basis which has been laid down by God and God alone. But because we are here dealing with human activity, with the sum of the Christian *ethos* and its always doubtful fulfilment, it can as little contribute to the setting up of that fellowship and therefore to justification as can faith itself as the human recognition that it has been set up.

"It amounts to this, that in *love* man is occupied with something *else,* and he ought always to be so. It would completely destroy the essential character of Christian love as the freedom given to man and to be kept by man if we tried to burden it with the, in itself, impossible and superfluous task of accomplishing or actualising or even completing the justification of man. No one can and will love God who does not believe. No one can and will love God except in the grounding of his being in the fellowship with God realised in that divine judgment. If we are to be justified by faith, in faith we will not look either at our works or our sins. Similarly in love—in the works of our love to God—we will not consider the possibility of trying subsequently to fulfil or to complete of ourselves that grounding of our being" (IV/1, 104f.).

Barth treats love in great detail. His main themes are concerned with the distinction between eros and agape (IV/2, 733–751), and are: God's love is the basis of our love; the love of the Trinity within itself, and its love of the world as an electing, purifying, and creative love (IV/2, 751–783); the love of man as a new accomplishment, as participation, and as joy; and as love of God and neighbor (IV/2, 783–824); the nature of love as decision (love alone matters), as victory (love alone conquers) and as eternal promise (love alone remains): IV/2, 824–840.

Given such a view of love it is not strange that Barth stresses good works. There are good works, and according to Sacred Scripture they have the promise of reward, but there are no works which justify; in fact every work requires the justification of God. It is only in faith that their goodness is perceived; the last word regarding them will not be spoken until God's judgment. And nevertheless good works truly do and *must* come—works which God praises and which for their part praise God. This is the "praise of works" (see IV/2, 584–598). These works of man are good only in their participation in the good work of God. They are good in Jesus Christ, good purely because of grace. Clearly there can be no question of any merit being claimed or falling due to any human agent because of his achievement. On the other hand, no Christian can consider himself blameless if his work is not good work. The Christian cannot be good without good works.

"The divine judgment on all men is very sharply formulated in the Bible. . . . Yet what man does and does not do is never described, either in a recognition of the universal sinfulness of man or an acknowledgment of the sovereign mercy of God, as a night which makes all things dark. Just because God alone is righteous and holy, not remotely but in His acts among and to men, there are also righteous and unrighteous, holy and unholy men, goodness and evil, good works and bad, in the life of each individual man (including the holy and righteous) . . . There are also good works—good because they are praised by God and done to His praise. If we are to accept the witness of Scripture, we cannot ignore this, let alone deny it" (IV/2, 586).

17. THE FOUNDATION OF CHRISTIAN EXISTENCE

We need now to deepen our previous discussion about faith, and with Barth to go further into the matter of the "subjective" realization and appropriation of justification, into the being of the man justified in Christ, into the foundation of the Christian existence of the individual man. This founding comes about in *faith* and is essentially a *work of the Holy Spirit*. The assimilation of the grace given us in Jesus Christ presupposes and includes the present moment, presupposes and includes the gift and its reception, the actions and achievements of His Holy Spirit. The existence of Jesus Christ Himself is already grounded in the being and action of the Holy Spirit (conceptus de Spiritu Sancto). Thus, too, the uniqueness of Christian being, as distinct from the being of the world, lies in its foundation in the Holy Spirit. The awakening power of the Spirit of Christ is what makes men Christians.

On the foundation of pneumatology in the theology of the Trinity see I/1, 513–560; in the doctrine of revelation, 1/2, 203–454; on the work of the Holy Spirit in justification, IV/1, 643–650; in sanctification, IV/2, 360–377, 614–620.

In discussing the being of the Christian we must not forget that what is said of the Christian man is valid for *all men:* that is, it could be said to follow for all other men too, that they are willed in reference to Jesus Christ, and that they know how to believe in reference to their being in Him. Christians have an exemplary kind of existence, as representatives and forerunners of all the other men to whom is given the self-same being in Jesus Christ—even when they do not yet experience it. For the work of reconciliation has been done for all men. Christ was born, died, and has risen for the sake of all. God's verdict has affected them all and "objectively" speaking all of them are justified. However, they have not as yet heard and seen, received, and assimilated. They are as yet not all moved by the Holy Spirit of Christ. Only Christians are moved by the Holy Spirit in the sense indicated; the rest of the world still lacks this Holy Spirit. In this particular sense Christians and only they have turned back to God, because *they themselves* have seized hold of His grace.

Since the Holy Spirit is not a private Spirit but the Spirit of the Church, the appropriation of the grace of Christ donated to us occurs for the individual *only within the community*. In *it* and only through it will salvation be applied to the individual. The "subjective" realization of reconciliation—accomplished "objectively" in the death and resurrection of Jesus Christ—occurs first within the community, as a work of the Holy Spirit of Jesus Christ. The Word and verdict of God which come with actual justification constitute the community—and individual Christians are in turn constituted within the community. It is within the community, it is through and for the sake of the ministry of the community, that the individual is awakened to faith.

This is what induced Barth to give *ecclesiology,* the theology of Christianity, *precedence* over the theology of individual Christian manhood.

In the first form of the theology of reconciliation Barth considers the *gathering* of the Christian community, and in the first place the *being* of the Christian community (IV/1, 650–725): faith in the Church (the Church is at once visible and invisible), the nature of the Church as the Body of Christ (that is, the earthly and historical form in which Christ exists), and the four attributes of the Church (una, sancta, catholica, apostolica). The being of the Church reveals itself in time; the *time* of the Christian community (IV/1, 725–739) is characterized as the between time. This is its weakness and its strength. It is the time God gives the Church as her own but it is also a time delimited by God—the time for her gathering, actualization, and apostleship (cf. I/2, 101–121).

In the second form of ecclesiology, the *upbuilding* of the Christian community is considered as follows: Jesus Christ makes the community fit for the preliminary presentation of that sanctification of the whole human world which is accomplished in Him (IV/2, 614–641). The inner direction of this upbuilding is toward the community's extensive and intensive growth; it lives as the communion of saints (IV/2, 641–660); the outward direction of this upbuilding is toward the community's preservation against the dangers of pressure and tolerance, the dangers of secularization and sacralization (IV/2, 660–676). Her form is the form of order, and therefore of law: the foundation of Church law and its principles as law of service, liturgical law, living law, model law (IV/2, 676–726).

The last part of ecclesiology, its third form, will follow—under the rubric of the *apostleship* of the community.

In the Christian community, however, the grace given the *individual* in Christ is actually assimilated by him. What is important here—and this is incidental to the establishing of Christian existence—is the *active participation of man in God's justifying action*. And this is what happens in that fundamental action of Christian life which is *faith*. In faith occurs the "subjective" realization of salvation. And in faith salvation acquires reality and importance in a definite activity of the individual human subject. But this must not be taken to be a faith which creates its own object, as though the object acquired reality and importance only through faith. All this Jesus Christ, who is the object of faith, already has of Himself without any faith. Faith derives entirely from its object. It lives wholly from Jesus Christ (I/1, 174ff.; II/1, 5–10, 12–16; IV/1, 740–743).

Faith is oriented toward Jesus Christ. Believing man, in his heart, in what is most unique to him, is no longer independent but dependent on Christ and for precisely this reason more than ever independent. Faith is a human activity, taking place in confrontation with the living Jesus and with His work, ineluctably yet in the utmost spontaneity and freedom. Christ is not only the object but also the origin of faith. Faith in His work and His gift. Only through Him and through His Holy Spirit does sinful man become apt for faith and through Him faith becomes a necessity for sinful man. This then is what makes the being of the Christian. He believes in Him of whom and from whom he is.

Thus through the believer's orientation toward Jesus Christ as his object and his foundation in Him as his origin, the *"constitution of the Christian subject"* occurs (IV/1, 749). Faith is a human action. Yet it is at the same time true "that in this action there begins and takes place a new and particular *being* of man" (IV/1, 749). It is within the Christian community, and exclusively there, that the individual subject is awakened to new being. There is no communion of saints without individual saints, no hypostatized Body of Christ without members.

As to how this new man comes into being, Barth wants to be correctly understood. Faith as a *human* act has only a *cognitive* character (IV/1, 751f.). It is (as in a different form love and hope are too) the fundamental act of the Christian life, at work in all individual actions, embracing and defining everything, the most interior and decisive act of the Christian heart (IV/1, 757f.; I/1, 229–233). As the fundamental act of the Christian life, it is a cognitive process which simply takes cognizance of the already completed being and work of Jesus Christ—faith is a *knowing*. But this knowing is spontaneous, free, active. The active element comes into focus in that faith is an *acknowledging*, a *knowing*, a *making-known*.

Christian faith is an *acknowledging:* It is essentially a docile and submissive acceptance of knowledge and thus of Jesus Christ Himself (see II/1, 23–31; IV/1, 758–762). In this acknowledgment there is implied, however, a *knowing*. Obedience as the fundamental act of faith is not a mere emoting, not a mere act of the will; it is not blind and devoid of understanding. Faith knows the person and work of Jesus Christ as these are witnessed to in Scripture and in the Church's proclamation. It thus involves a wisdom, too—not abstract but concrete and existential, a wisdom marked by recognition and obedience. Faith knows in Whom it has believed (see I/1, 230f.; II/1, 12–14; IV/1, 761–776).

This taking cognizance entails, however, a passing on of knowledge. Thus acknowledging and knowing are simultaneously a *making-known*. The faith of the heart has an urgency toward public revelation. Hidden faith has an urgency to communicate. It wants to be visible and audible in the community. This requires no special action; it simply happens when a man is truly Christian. So it is true that a Christian who would only acknowledge and know without making known would actually be no Christian at all. A Christian is by his nature a witness to justification. He is a confessing Christian in a confessional community (I/1, 233–237; IV/1, 775–779).

To this extent then faith has only a cognitive character and yet in faith a *new being* comes to exist. Faith really involves the creation of a new man, a new creation, and a being born again. The just man, despite the simul peccator, is ontologically different from the sinner. This clear teaching of Barth must not be overlooked.

"New being, new *creation* (Gal. 6.15, 2 Cor. 5.17), new *birth*—they are all predicates which are ascribed only to the Christian, and they are all too strong to be taken only as figurative expressions to describe the changed feelings and self-understanding of Christians. Christians do not lose their character as members of the race which God created good and which fell from Him. But in these predicates they are addressed as something other than those with whom in other respects they are still bound in the twofold solidarity of creatureliness and sin" (IV/1, 749).

The term πιστος involves a "*being* of which they are *real* and *objective* participants in the fulfilment of this act and as the subjects of it. Just as the sinful man *is* what he does as such, so he *is* what he does when as a sinful man he is awakened to *faith* and can *live* by it" (IV/1, 750).

And so, despite all of this, faith does have a *creator-like* character. How is this possible? A believing man acknowledges, knows and makes known what has already happened, that is, the justification accomplished and revealed in the crucifixion and the resurrection of Jesus Christ. But how is man really capable of such a cognitive affirmation of what has happened—man the sinner? Sinful man must after all be able to act in regard to this. He must be so constituted as to be really capable, disposed, and ready to make such an affirmation. The act of faith itself—as a *human* act —does not produce new being and thus is not of a creator-like character. But the act of faith is possible and effective only on the *presupposition* that in man this act establishes a new being, that is, that there comes about for this man a new creation, a new birth. And so we may say that through faith man becomes a Christian in fact and that through faith man is created and born again to new manhood.

"It belongs to the alteration of the human situation as it has taken place in Jesus Christ that it now has at least the confirmation of its witness in certain human subjects. Not because they believe, not in the power in which they do believe, but *as* they do *actually* believe (in strength or weakness), *as* they do it and are in a position to do it, they *become* and *are Christians* in the midst of all other men—men with this particular characteristic as men. To this extent we cannot deny to the event of their faith a certain *creative* character" (IV/1, 752).

If faith does not, of *itself*, possess this creative, creator-like power, where does it get it? From its object and origin, *from Jesus Christ*. It is He who through His Holy Spirit calls men to faith and who, at the same time, through the creation of a new being, makes man apt and ready to believe.

"He owes it to Him that he can believe at all, and that he does believe. He believes as one who is confronted and apprehended by Him (Phil. 3.12), as the one in face of whom He is the stronger and has proved Himself to be the stronger. In face of him He is the stronger in virtue of what He has done for all men and therefore for him in His death, and of the fact that God has manifested Him for all men and therefore for him as the One who has done this in His resurrection from the dead. And in face of him He *proves* Himself to be the stronger by the irresistible awakening power of His Holy Spirit. In this strength and in this proof He calls him to *faith*. And in so doing He creates the presupposition on the basis of which the sinful man can and actually does believe. He introduces him as a new subject which is capable of and willing and ready for this act, as a witness of His act and revelation, as a *Christian*. Because the faith of this sinful man is directed on Him and effected by Him, the event of his faith is not merely cognitive as a human act but it is also *creative* in character. The new being effective and revealed in it, the new creation, the new birth—they are all the mystery of the One *in whom* he believes and whom he can acknowledge and recognise and confess in faith" (IV/1, 752f.).

Jesus Christ can do this because He meets every man as this particular individual. For me, and precisely for me, God became man. The Lord became servant, the Judge the one judged, the Helper the helpless. It is precisely I whom He justified, I for whom He is Reconciler and Savior. And because Christ *is* for me I am therefore the new subject, the new creation, the new birth of the Christian.

Does faith achieve, in this fashion, any representation or re-enactment of the saving event which occurred in Jesus Christ? Certainly not in such a way that *God's* saving act could be identified with faith as a free act of *man*. The true representation and re-enactment of this history of salvation in Jesus Christ is the one which Jesus Christ Himself accomplishes in us through His Holy Spirit—so that He makes Himself into, He is and remains Himself the object and source of faith. The act of man *answers* to this act of God.

On this occasion Barth makes his one and only reference to Hans Urs von Balthasar's interpretation and criticism of his work. He praises not only the author, but also what he calls the "Christological renaissance" in contemporary Catholic theology. What is interesting for us is that Barth appears not to understand von Balthasar's fundamental criticism of a "Christological confinement" (Engführung); at least this has made no impression on him. Barth only seems to have "an inkling of something which at first I could not understand" and in the process hits upon "the spiritual splendor of the saints who are supposed to represent and repeat Him (Jesus Christ)" (IV/1, 768).

What does this mean? Has von Balthasar expressed his objection with insufficient clarity, or does Barth choose not to understand, or is there, in the final analysis a hidden identity between the two ideas? The question is very difficult to answer. In the second part we will indirectly touch on it.

But once we have made the fundamental distinction between God's act of salvation and man's act of faith, we can then speak analogously of faith as representing Christ's act of salvation. For in faith there occurs a total change in the entire human involvement with the world, a change most directly related to the death and resurrection of Jesus Christ. Man is, in his being, determined and shaped by Christ. In faith man as it were switches himself in on a circuit parallel with Christ. He patterns himself in correspondence with Him so that he is able and willing to exist from now on only in the *likeness* of Jesus Christ as the One who died and rose for him. This happens on the one hand in the correspondence to Christ's death in man's *mortification*. The analogy between the two lies in the overcoming of pride and of the fall; thus man's faith implies *repentance* and *penitence*. It happens on the other hand in the correspondence to Christ's resurrection to be found in man's *vivification*. The analogy between the two events lies in the restoration of law and of life. Thus faith implies essentially *confidence* and *trust* (IV/1, 770–776).

18. THE JUSTIFICATION OF MAN AS THE SELF–JUSTIFICATION OF GOD

God's eternity was our point of departure—God's eternal election in Jesus Christ. In this all the works of God have their absolute beginning. In this, too, lies the eternal basis of justification. We return to this again when we ask with Barth: What does the justification of man mean *for God Himself?*

It doubtless has the *highest* meaning for God or His Son would not have become man. The high significance it has for God is the basis for the ultimate certainty and importance of the justification of man. *What* meaning then does the justification of man have for God? Barth says in reply: The great importance of man's justification for God lies in the fact that in the justification of man God also and above all *justified Himself.* This is the answer given in Rom. 3.26: "It was to prove that he himself is just" (see IV/1, 559–564).

In justification God acts in His own interest. Justification is of course divine grace bestowed on man. But it is more than that. In justification God executes His own eternal will with regard to man. He acts out of His eternal fidelity and His eternal justness. He carried this forward to victory against the infidelity and unjustness of man and thereby re-established the justice and fidelity of man and made man honorable again. He also and above all established Himself in justice and thus brought Himself to honor.

In the justification of man, God justifies Himself as the Creator of man and as His covenant-Lord. He confirms and manifests His just right as *Creator.* He will not tolerate the chaotic intervention and blemish of sin in His creation. Man is His. Man remains His work and His possession. God has this right to him and will not allow this to be called in question. God furthermore confirms and manifests His right as *covenant-Lord.* Man is God's covenant part-

ner, elected from eternity. God had a special right to this elected
creature and He will not allow the pride of man to put this right
in doubt. He will not have His covenant partner torn away from
Him. He intervenes. In justification, He rejects the man of injustice
and elects the new, the just man. Thus in His justness He demonstrates His grace. Precisely as gracious God He permits no one to
mock Him. It is precisely in His justice that He carries His grace
to its goal.

This becomes clear in its profundity only when we consider
justification as the work of God *in Jesus Christ*. The justification
of man *begins* with the action of the Son of God, with the humble
act of obedience, in which He humiliated Himself for us. This act
is, for Him, in no sense an alien or unworthy thing, assumed by
Him only with reluctance. Christ here rather exercised, confirmed,
and manifested His just *right as* divine *Son*. It is the divine right of
the Son to be humbly obedient to His Father. This is the way He
exercises the divine prerogative which is also His. In acknowledging and executing His Father's right, He exercises His own right
as Son. So we can say that "in the act of His obedience, and therefore of His substitutionary death and passion, in the first instance
He justified Himself" (IV/1, 565).

The justification of man was *consummated* in the acceptance of
the Son of God, that is, in His (and therefore our) resurrection
from the dead. Here, too, there was no arbitrariness involved. The
issue was the exercise, confirmation, and manifestation of the divine
paternal right—a right of grace, of wisdom, and of omnipotence.
By virtue of His fatherly right, and not of any tyrannical arbitrariness, He calls for the obedience of His Son and in revelation of
this same just right raises Him, and thereby raises us, from the
dead. So we may say: "The fulfilment of *our* justification was also
the *self-justification* of God" (see IV/1, 567).

Nevertheless, in God's exercise of His right as Creator and
covenant-Lord and His rights as Father and as Son, God's *freedom*
is in no way impaired. He in no way needs his self-justification.

"God does not owe anyone anything—least of all an account of the
righteousness of what He does or does not do. But as the *living* God—
as distinct from all the godheads of philosophies and religions—is He
not free and able to justify Himself? May it not be that of His own
good pleasure He did in fact (and in the first instance) *will to* justify
Himself, and actually *do* so, in our justification (and supremely in the

fact that it took place in Jesus Christ)? What, then, can we bring against it, especially if we appeal to His freedom or argue that He does not need anything of this nature? A quite unnecessary concern for His majesty? Certainly God is—and was and will be—righteous without having to prove Himself righteous. But seeing He *willed to* and *did* prove Himself righteous, it is only right to count on it that He did not do so in vain" (IV/1, 567).

In the justification of man which is God's self-justification, God's glorious and gracious *sovereignty* emerges fully into view. He appears as "the Sun" of justice. This gives the theology of justification its correct orientation. *God* must have precedence in all things. In whatever is, He is of first and primary importance. To Him is due all honor and all praise. Not until the sovereignty of God— His eternal choice in Jesus Christ and His mightily gracious self-justification—breaks through in all its radiance in the theology of justification, can man live as just man in the hope of the glory of everlasting life wherein he, too, in the light of God's justice, will, as a just man, shine "like the Sun."

19. OPEN QUESTIONS

Until now our intention has been to listen to Barth. We had him speak, where possible in his own words. We had him review for us his theology of justification in its breadth and depth. We sought to follow him with understanding and to understand him as he would understand himself. If we have interrupted him with some brief questions, it was only to hear and understand him better.

In this way we hoped to have arrived at one thing, that is, to have understood what his questions are in regard to Catholic teaching. Even this is not altogether easy. It is easy to understand these questions as reproaches but it is difficult to understand these questions as questions. Reproaches invite counterattack. Questions invite self-appraisal. We have by now sufficient material for self-appraisal and with that the goal of our first part is essentially attained. Barth was to confront us with a mirror so that we, in the mirror of the gospel of Jesus Christ, could understand more deeply the Catholic answer. This is why we permitted ourselves to be questioned.

In the course of the first part it has become clear—it would seem to us—that all questions put to us, both spoken and unspoken, were really only *one* question. It was the question which made itself heard even before we began to study the process of justification. Then it was sketched only in outline. By now it stands before us vividly, etched in firm and heavily shaded strokes. The one continually recurrent question is: *Does the Catholic theology of justification take justification seriously as the sovereign act of God's grace?* The innermost concern of Karl Barth, motivating his whole development from liberalism via existentialism to the *Church Dogmatics*—that is, what von Balthasar called his consuming zeal for God—has persisted too as the decisive concern of his theology of justification. The soli Deo gloria! In his theology of justification, too, Barth's concern is to rouse our understanding and love of this fact: We are dealing with *God*. We men are, after all, not that important. We must not persist in our ancient and vicious tendency always to think first and foremost of ourselves. It is *God* whom we should praise and glorify in the justification of men—*His* justice and love, His fidelity and mercy, His omnipotence and wisdom which we should admire and glorify. It is *His* grace, sent to us sinners in His incarnate Son, which we are to cling to. It is *His* indictment that threatens, His verdict that decides, and His acquittal that liberates. To Him alone be all glory! It is only thus that man gets a justness of his own through the process of justification. Only when God receives His full and unreserved honor will man be given his full honor. Only if full and entire justice is done to God will full and entire justice be done to man. This is why Barth reacts with such unusual sharpness to Catholic teaching, in an almost emotional way. This is why his questions are so full of irritation and so vehement—why his judgment is so hard, and at first glance, so one-sided and unjust: Barth sees the sovereign majesty of God's grace threatened. In the Catholic theology of justification, is God not displaced from His central position? Is He not restricted to the function of a simple if indispensable basis for the possibility of man's being made just? Is not all emphasis primarily on man, on the creature?

In the Catholic theology of *sin,* is God really taken seriously? When man breaks away from his Creator and Sustainer, what happens to him as man? When he loses his "cloak of grace," is it not in the final analysis really only a secondary—though important —accident? Doesn't this homo nudatus stand there, after all, looking thoroughly respectable—a free, good, natural man, wounded perhaps, but unimpaired in his most inner and most personal being? And is redemption any more to him than an accident is to a substance?

And in the Catholic teaching on *grace,* here again, is God really taken seriously? Does it not primarily concern the man who has received grace rather than the gracious God? Do we not prefer to speak, and to speak almost exclusively, of man's state of grace and his life of grace, instead of God's acts of grace? Or about the gifts of grace disposed of by man rather than about the gracious favor which has disposition over man? Hasn't grace become something physical instead of being and remaining something personal? And in the Catholic theology of *justification,* how much talk there is of *man's* becoming just, of *his* transition, of his transformation, and how little talk of the judgment of the punishing and liberating *God.* Are the death and resurrection of Jesus Christ any more than a distant conditioning for anticipation of what today is pre-eminently important, namely, the infused, indwelling justice of man? Is not justification—that stupendous achievement of God's justness—trivialized and reduced to the dimensions of an organic process of reaction and growth within man? Is there not incessant talk about what is creaturely, about various graces and various infusions, with an unbroken silence in regard to God's judging and sentencing? Don't we find everything turned upside down with God doing the bidding of man rather than man the bidding of God?

And as to Catholic teaching on the *justified man,* has it not in practice been forgotten that this justified man was a sinner? With all his grace does he not have only a very loose bond to the gracious God? Does not grace dwell within him in such a way that he really needs God only as Creator and Sustainer? Is the grace which justified him not something which he "has," rather than something he receives afresh at each new instant?

And in regard to the Catholic teaching on *faith:* Isn't faith also trust? And what does the Pauline "faith without works" mean? Are not works, good works, even before justification—are they not co-ordinate with faith? Don't we find that man really justifies himself insofar as he co-operates in effecting justification? As far as justification is concerned, doesn't love make faith superfluous? What is faith with "merits" supposed to be?

Finally, is God in *Jesus Christ* taken seriously in Catholic theology? Is not the word "Christian" very often mere historical reminiscence, a symbol or predicate used to distinguish Christianity from other "ideologies"? Is Christ for all places and all times the principium et finis, Alpha and Omega, the beginning and end of all the ways of God? Does Jesus Christ have a role to play in the "Christian" teaching on creation in Catholic dogma? Is sin examined with reference to Him or to an abstract God? Is gratia Christi only a label for various graces or are all graces really the grace of Jesus Christ? Is Christ more than a necessary extrinsic condition for our justification? And is faith dependent on abstract truths or on Him personally?

Do not all these things taken together still amount to the manipulating of God, the managing of grace, the relativizing of the majesty and sovereignty of God? Do we not find too, in the Catholic theology of justification, an exclusive stress on an analogia entis which is not subordinate to the analogia fidei? And a simple juxtaposition of God and man, set beside each other on the same level, rather than an absolute subordinating of man as something beneath God and His grace? Is this not *the* crucial reason why the Reformers wanted to have nothing more to do with the Catholic Church? Is this not *the* reason why even today one cannot become Catholic?

These questions should suffice to suggest the gravity of the problem and to dispel any inclination to play with facile distinctions. They call us to a serious and responsible reconsideration and evaluation of our teaching.

When we have done that, and not before, then we can put forward *our* questions. We can in our turn ask Barth: Is not God given too little credit in his theology because too little is credited to *man?* Is not God's dignity belittled because the dignity of His creature is belittled? Is not the Lord God diminished because sin is made too powerful? Is not God's act of grace a weak and unconvincing act because man is not truly endowed with grace? Is not divine justification, after all is said and done, only a verbal process, an "as if," because God does not really get the justified man up on his feet? Is not man so radically the *peccator* that the term "iustus" has the value only of etiquette? Do we not find a faith deficient in power because the love associated with it is so superficial?

Taking all of this together, then, do we not find that *man* and thus the incarnation—the *becoming man—of Jesus Christ are perhaps not taken quite seriously?* In the final analysis is the creature not deprived of partnership with God? Is Barth's intercession on the creature's behalf only another gesture of commemoration, a preventive against questions like those asked here? Is all the talk of the value and greatness of man perhaps mere verbalizing not followed up by any action?

These questions are legitimate. We must put them in the same uncompromising fashion as Barth puts his to us. They are, after all, only the reverse and hidden side of his own questions. Once more, no facile distinctions or threadbare dialectic will do at this point. What counts here is careful reflection.

And now a transitional observation. Everybody on both sides

feels the importance of these questions. The answer will be no more than tentative. As such it may pass but never as the comprehensive and cut-and-dried solution. Everything to be said in the second part is meant to be material for discussion and further reflection.

PART TWO

AN ATTEMPT AT A CATHOLIC RESPONSE

A.

Fundamentals

20. THE THEOLOGY OF JUSTIFICATION PAST AND PRESENT

Are we standing today "at a turning point in the theology of justification"? (Asmussen, *Lutherische Kirche,* p. 338.) Yes, we might answer with a sigh of relief, inasmuch as the age of antitheses is over. It took over four hundred years for the two sides to spell out clearly their differences. But today serious theologians in both camps see that the task of unity will not be made essentially easier by antitheses of this sort. Should the era of antitheses then give way to an era of irenic syntheses? Certainly not. But is it not possible to take a different approach? Instead of talking to adversaries we might be able to talk to partners. Instead of mere dialectics we might like to try congenial dialogue.

On the *history of the theology of controversy:* when the controversy began the argument was a mixture of the personal and the objective, of arguments advanced by individual theologians and those advanced officially by churches. On the Catholic side, Franz Veronius, in his *Règle générale de la foy catholique séparée de toutes autres doctrines* (1646), has the merit of overcoming subjectivism in polemic through the formulation of church dogma in its objective form. This approach was continued in Bossuet's *Exposition de la doctrine catholique sur les matières de controverse* (1671) as well as by H. Holden's *Divinae fidei analysis* (1652). From there the lines of progress lead to J. A. Moehler's *Symbolik* (1832). See J. R. Geiselmann, *J. A. Möhler. Die Einheit,* pp. 110ff. concerning this development.

F. Staudenmaier's *Der Protestantismus in seinem Wesen und in seiner Entwicklung* (1846) represents a further step forward. Protestantism was treated synthetically according to a principle—not plural and negative disintegrating principles but a single positive one which tended to lead back to the Catholic Church ("The struggle of the fragments of Catholic truth left in the Protestant churches for their reintegration").

The development of the last century followed in this direction. It is characterized by two features. First, a major part of what was once only Staudenmaier's individual opinion has today become more or less a consensus of theologians. Then, too, there was objectively a tremendous advance in the theological understanding of Protestantism. We have only to compare Staudenmaier's work with Hans Urs von Balthasar's *Karl Barth* (1951), L. Bouyer's *Du Protestantisme à l'Eglise* (1954), .Th. Satory's *Die ökumenische Bewegung und die Einheit der Kirche* (1955), and H. Fries' *Bultmann–Barth und die katholische Theologie* (1955).

A development parallel to that made in the theology of controversy was made in Catholic Church history, especially in its judgment of Luther's personality. Our evidence for this is in the advance from Eck, Cochläus, and Bellarmine, on to Möhler and Doellinger and via Denifle and Grisar to Lortz and Jedin.

Barth has repeatedly shown himself to be a master of congenial dialogue. See, for example, his Schleiermacher essay (*Die Theologie und die Kirche,* pp. 136–189); his appreciation of the traditional theology of election (II/2, 3–145); his interpretation of Hegel (*Die protestantische Theologie im 19. Jahrhundert,* pp. 343–378); his recent study of Bultmann, and so on. In his studies he draws the lines soberly and without compromise but always with a sympathetic consideration of historical elements, with careful probing and loving circumspection of judgment.

So one may well be astonished at Barth's failure to display the spirit of sympathetic dialogue in dealing with the Catholic teaching on grace and the Council of Trent. No one would expect him to whitewash things from irenic motives. However, when Barth in his "irenical and ecumenical word at the conclusion of this confessional polemic" (IV/1, 88) gives vent to the suspicion that Catholics do not *live* this theology of grace, why did he not go one step further and suspect that the *living* Catholic *theology* of grace looks perhaps something less than "scandalous"? And in characterizing the Council of Trent's decree on justification as "theologically a clever and in many respects a not unsympathetic document" (IV/1, 624), why couldn't he have answered some of his impatient questions by showing a like sympathy and empathy for the history of theology? This might have helped him realize that the Church whose "official decisions are infallible" (IV/1, 626) never looked at these decisions as rigid and frozen formulations, but rather as living signposts for continued research into the inexhaustible riches of the revelation of Jesus Christ.

It is not our intent to throttle objectively justified questions by plaintive regrets about Barth's lack of understanding in regard to Catholic theology. Many of Barth's questions are anything but glib and the answers must be even less so. Still the reproachful questioning of Barth makes necessary some introductory observations on the development of Catholic dogma, on the place of the Council of Trent in the history of dogma, and on the sources of Catholic dogmatic theology, before we can tackle the theological problems proper.

The Church maintains that the preaching of the Apostles closed off the entire Christian revelation and that for the Church there were no new revelations afterward (*D* 2021). At the same time, however, it is expressly taught by all contemporary theologians, on the authority of Vatican I (*D* 1796, 1800), that not all the truths of faith were always and at all times *expressly* believed, but rather that a *development of dogma* in the sense of explication (not in the sense of Modernism, see *D* 2057ff., 2080) is possible and really takes place, no matter how much the concrete explicitation which happens under the influence of the Holy Spirit may have to be explained.

Against the Modernistic falsification of the development of dogma see especially *D* 2021, 2054, 2059, 2062, 2080. Individual Catholic solutions seek a middle road between rationalism and anti-intellectualism. See the bibliography of Karl Rahner, *Schriften zur theologie,* I, pp. 49f.: for the earlier works, Newman, Franzelin, Bainvel, Ch. Pesch, Gardeil, Rademacher, Tuyaerts, Marinsola; for the contributions to the discussion preceding the Encyclical *Humani Generis* (Charlier, Boyer, de Lubac, Bouillard, Rondet, Michel, Leblond, Spedalieri, et al.); and finally for works dealing with Marian dogma (Altaner, Balic, Ternus, Philips, Garrigou-Lagrange, Dillenschneider, Filograssi, et al.). Also among the most recent essays consult M. Flick as an introduction to the present-day statement of the problem; and further R. Spiazzi, G. Rambaldi, A. Bea, C. Balic, G. Filograssi, Ch. Boyer (all of these articles are lectures delivered during the week of theological studies at Rome in September 1951); and finally E. Dhanis, *Révélation explicite et implicite,* and A. F. Utz, *Kommentar zur Deutschen Thomasausgabe,* vol. 15. For the philosophical clarification of the question see J. B. Lotz, *Zur Geschichtlichkeit der Wahrheit,* and compare the excellent treatment by Karl Rahner, "Zur Frage der Dog-menentwicklung." H. Bouillard, *Conversion et grâce chez S. Thomas d'Aquin,* is especially noteworthy for the development of dogma in regard to justification.

The Encyclical *Humani Generis* stated: "Besides, each source of divinely revealed doctrine contains so many rich treasures of truth that they can really *never be exhausted.* Hence it is that theology through study of its sacred sources *remains ever fresh;* on the other hand speculation which neglects a deeper search into the deposit of faith proves sterile, as we know from experience" (*Humani Generis,* Paulist Press tr. 1950, p. 11; *AAS,* 1950, p. 568). The *one* truth of faith, its one fundamental structure, is capable of articulation for man in *many* structural patterns—varying the one same fundamental structure through shifting emphasis among the essential traits. Dogmatic definitions express the truth infallibly and precisely (not just approximately) and thus irrevocably. As such they have become involved in the historical reality of everything human. They add to it irrevocable yet historically conditioned accents, expressing a definite objective perspective. But because they are finite statements which never express absolutely everything, they never wholly exhaust the fullness of truth. That is why dogmatic formulations are not at all incapable of being refined and perfected, just as the Church cannot be tied to any particular short-lived philosophical system (*AAS,* 1950, p. 566). As St. Thomas had said, quoting Isidore: "An article (of faith) is a perception of divine truth which *tends toward that truth*" (*S. th.,* II–II, q.1,a.6).

It in no sense follows that every traditional formula can be replaced by some other one *chosen at random.* The intellectual refinement achieved through centuries and the univocal general use of many such formulas warn against any frivolousness in this matter (see the Encyclical *Humani Generis, AAS,* 1950, pp. 566–567). But this much is sure: The implicit truth-content of any formula, insofar as it is divine truth, always exceeds its explicit formulation—and therein lies its character as mystery. For this reason a truth of faith can always be articulated in formulas which are (conceptually as well as terminologically) more complete, more adequate, and more perfect. Truth then is not restricted to some particular (time-bound) manifestation and can be embodied in a more comprehensive (though again finite) historical perspective. This embodiment of revealed truth in a new form of thought and utterance fashioned by the Church does not come about primarily through human theological brainwork, but rather—in consequence of the incarnation—through the Holy Spirit of Jesus Christ working in the Church.

In taking the definitions of the Church as frozen formulas, Barth himself petrifies what the Catholic Church—fully cognizant of its pilgrim status—regards as a thoroughly living gift of the Spirit.

Is the development of dogma then no more than a harmless harmonious and organic flowering? Any such conception would be too simple. In the development of dogma we see an embattled confrontation of the Church of Jesus Christ and His Holy Spirit with the spirit of the world. The majority of dogmatic definitions are *polemic formulations* pronounced against heresies. As Thomas had already strongly emphasized, they are walls raised in defense against error (see *S.th.,* II–II, q.1 a.9 ad 2; a 10 co; a 10 ad 1, ad 2). The homogeneous basic structure and the continuity of dogma remain untouched. But the Church concentrates all its energy at the point where divine revelation is in jeopardy, illuminating the dark spot with its searchlight and unambiguously exposing everything through a sharp, clear and universally intelligible formulation.

With the dark spot exposed to the brightest possible light, other areas move out of the bright cone of the beam—though not into total darkness—back into what, at least for the human eye, is twilight or even obscurity. These hidden truths are not lost to the Church but continue to be and to be believed as before. It is only that they no longer shine so brightly until the human eye, once it has adjusted to the new light, recaptures the full view and value of what surrounds and supports these truths. Any heresy involves a strengthening and a weakening of the Church. A strengthening, because of the deepening of reflective dogmatic consciousness through a sharpening of concepts and heightening of certainty through clearer distinctions. A weakening, because of the danger of one-sidedness and particularity, with theologians helping to petrify and foreshorten revealed truth and with heretics contributing to the impoverishment (as St. Augustine had already noted) by dragging truths out of the Church. And just as heresy has this double effect, so too a dogmatic formulation. It gains in theological precision only at the risk of loss of vitality.

Karl Adam: "Of course there are apparent shifts in the inner balance, especially in times when heresies arise and force the Church to deactivate certain truths which the heretics abuse and to mobilize truths which they deny. The exclusively anti-Gnostic, anti-Arian, anti-Lutheran, anti-Modernist position is not the representative Catholic position. It is rather a time-bound and temporary shift in equilibrium—a shift imposed by the need for counter-attack against the particular heresy. The living strength of Catholicism, in all its unshakeable soundness and truth, becomes evident precisely when it readjusts—even when this happens only after long centuries—back into its original balance . . . It would be worthwhile to demonstrate how readily Catholicism repels erroneous deviating teachings with their entire conceptual framework and all their paraphernalia. In order to prevent any impairment of the Church's consciousness of revelation and once the danger of being thrown off balance is passed, those elements of truth misappropriated and given perverse emphasis by the heretics are, after the necessary correction of accent in correspondence with the total context of revealed truth, consciously reincorporated into the Church's proclamation and preserved there." (*Wesen des Katholizismus,* pp. 178f.; see also Schmaus, *Dogm.,* I, 65f., 68, 76f., 131; Congar, *Chrétiens désunis,* pp. 355–357; Utz, *Kommentar,* pp. 458f.; Van Leeuwen, *Regula credendi,* pp. 350f.).

Is Barth himself entirely immune from the rabies theologorum he so often deplores when he scolds the *Council of Trent* because the plea of the Reformers did not seem to make the slightest impression on the delegates there? (IV/1, 624f.) Is this not a deliberate overlooking of the historical nature of dogmatic formulations as well as of the polemical and defensive character of Trent? Barth seems to forget what he himself once wrote (I/2, 627ff.) regarding the militant character of the Church's "Confessiones"—that is, that these are not "abbreviated summa theologiae."

We will return to specific questions involved in understanding Trent. We do not intend to develop an apology for Trent and for its decree on justification in particular. See in this connection the great source book, *Concilium Tridentinum diariorum, actorum, epistularum, tractatuum nova collectio* (concerning the decrees on justification, see especially Volume V).

On the decree on justification, compare the works cited in the bibliography of J. Hefner, H. Rückert, A. Prumbs, F. Hünermann, M. Premm, J. Henninger, E. Stakemeier, A. Stakemeier, V. Heynck,

A. de Villalmonte, V. Beltran de Herredia, J. Olzaran, J. Rivière, H. Rondet, and F. Cavallera.

In the great work of G. Schreiber, *Das Weltkonzil von Trient,* are pertinent articles by M. Grabmann, J. P. Steffes, E. Stakemeier, F. Buuck, F. J. Schierse, F. Stegmueller, and V. Heynck.

On the general history of the Council of Trent see: L. Cristiani, and especially H. Jedin's *Geschichte des Konzils von Trient.* Continual bibliography is in the "Archivo Teológico Granadino," in *Rev. d'histoire ecclésiastique* (Louvain) and in the *Theologischen Revue* (Münster, Westfalen).

Hence there is no need to show in detail what pains individual participants in the Council (largely Italian and Spanish) took to understand the Reformation's grievances. For instance, how writings of the Reformers were studied by men like Seripando, Pole, Salmeron, Soto, Vega, Castro, et al.; how the fathers were requested by the papal legate, Cardinal Pole, to read the writings of the Reformers impartially and not to argue, "Luther has said so, ergo it is false" (*CT,* V, 82); how the formulation of the relatively short decree on justification took seven months of intensive work (from June 21, 1546, to January 13, 1547); and how the drafts were thoroughly discussed and continually revised.

The preparatory work lasted from June 22 to July 23 (*CT,* V, 261–384). 1. Draft of *"Cum tuba caeli"* from July 24 (384–391), discussed at length and on August 28 referred back (419). 2. Draft of *"Cum hoc tempore nihil"* from September 23 (420–427), referred back (509). 3. Draft of *"Cum hoc tempore non sine"* from November 5 (634–642), completely revised and still twice again put before the fathers on December 7 (691) and on January 9 (780). Only on January 13 was the definitive decree approved (790–802; 817–820).

Barth is no friend of Adolf von Harnack, but what should have made him think twice is that this scholar was obliged to say, "Although it is a work of artifice, the decree on justification is in many respects admirably worked out. One could even speculate on whether the Reformation itself would have developed if this decree had been issued by the Lateran Council at the beginning of the century, and if it had overflowed into the life and blood of the Church" (*Dogmengesch.,* III, 711).

The Council was faced with a very difficult task. The fourteenth and fifteenth centuries were dominated by a decadent scholasticism. Although we must not take too negative a view of the theology which held sway immediately before the Council of Trent (particularly in Italy and Spain—on this whole question, see H.

Lennerz, *Das Konzil*), still this theology was rife with unenlightened late-scholastic discussion, ill-considered appeals to school theories and Aristotelian categories. In many ways Thomism and Scotism had come to a dead stop and had been stifled by Nominalism (Cavallera, *Bull. de Litt. eccl.*, 1943, pp. 229–239; Bouyer, *Protestantism*, pp. 136–165; esp. pp. 162ff.; Lortz, *Reformation in Deutschland*, I, pp. 61f., 137f.) And the long discussions at the Council itself are an indication that before it things were not entirely at their best.

With all of this in mind it must be admitted that Trent accomplished a considerable amount of work. Barth himself acknowledges that not all the statements made by the Reformers and their teaching on justification had St. Paul behind them (IV/1, 626). This is something many of today's leading Protestant theologians recognize very well (see the position of Asmussen on the Augsburg Confession or of Stählin on the "alone"). In this connection did not Trent bring authentic Christianity clearly into focus? Should not *those* things *too* have been said that were said in the decree?

Yet no one will use such considerations to deny the limitations of Trent. Our remarks earlier about the narrowness of human formulations, and especially polemic ones, hold for this Council too. And the limits of Trent might have been less noticeable had the theologians from northern Europe, and especially the Protestants, accepted the invitation and appeared in Trent. (The historical difficulties involved are not under discussion at this point.)

The Reformers actually provoked a certain anthropocentricity in the decree on justification through their own deficient interpretation of Christian revelation. Wasn't it necessary to say *also*—precisely if the honor of *God* was to be saved—that *man* is truly justified, that in his sin he did not totally lose his creatureliness, that grace does not work wholly in the dark, and so forth? Also, should not the accents here (truly a thankless theological task) be placed clearly on the danger that other legitimate aspects of justification would be relegated to the background? Does this give anyone the right to maintain that the Council denies other aspects of Christian revelation? Did the Council insist that it had said *everything* to be said about the justification of man? Does not Barth confuse "the infallibility of the magisterium with an imaginary charism of universal insight"? (G. de Broglie, "Letter to the author" in Bouyer, *Protestantism*, p. ix.) Does he not overlook the fact that the history of theology is "not simply the history of the progression of dogma, but also a history of forgetting"? (K. Rahner, *Probleme,* p. 127.)

In similar discussions about Trent one is likely to be asked with a malicious grin whether such explanations do not produce "a bad historical conscience" among Catholics—the point being that Trent did after all wish to present a comprehensive theology of justification. It is true that Trent was not simply a discussion among confessions or simply a controversial theology but rather a cohesive, positive presentation of Catholic truth. And the Council, especially in Session VI de justificatione, did not limit itself (as it did in Session IV and for the most part in Session V) to restudying and refining texts already promulgated nor did it simply list errors in order to judge them (as did Session VII), but rather dealt directly with the problem of justification as such.

All this is true and indicates the noble and objective spirit of this ecclesiastical assembly, yet we have here no reason for historical pangs of conscience—because the point of departure and the target of Council discussions, as well as the never-absent shadow over them, was clearly the Reformation teaching. The decree on justification too, was motivated not by the desire for an unbiased scholarly peace-time declaration but by heresy convulsing the Church. The introduction to the decree notwithstanding its irenic style, is clearly polemical in purpose: "Since at this time a certain erroneous teaching about justification is being broadcast with the consequent loss of many souls and serious damage to Church unity . . . this Council of Trent . . . intends to set forth for all the faithful of Christ the true, sound doctrine of justification" (*CT,* V, 791; *D* 792a).

Whereas in scholastic manuals justification used to be treated as a footnote to the theology of grace and sacraments, or dealt with in scattered references, it now becomes—following the lead of the Reformers—a complete and independent doctrinal treatise. And it is because of the Reformers too that biblical terminology is used extensively in place of scholastic. A study of the Acta of the Council leaves no doubt about this. One can read, for example, the six questions presented before the theologi minores (*CT,* V. 261), the discussion on double justification (486–675), or those on "fide iustificari, gratis iustificari" and the certainty of grace (724–778).

The Lutheran Rueckert concedes that "the six articles do demonstrate that the Council proceeded to treat the theology of justification exclusively with the idea of answering Luther and to this end directed its interest only to *those* points in which the opposition of Luther to the old faith appeared in sharpest relief. Indeed it even chose to adapt itself to the Lutheran outline of the doctrine" (*Die Rechtfertigungslehre auf dem Trienter Konzil,* pp. 91f., cf. 85–100; cf. E. Stakemeier, *Glaube und Rechtfertigung,* pp. 2–6).

Not just Trent but every Council from Nicea to Vatican I had concrete opponents in view and had a single *specific* polemical objective. It is not for no reason that Denzinger generally brackets the names of opponents of a given teaching (contra Arianos, Macedonianos . . . contra Novatores saec. 16 . . . contra materialistas, pantheistas). One should compare Councils which defined the same doctrine in a variety of connections, for instance, Ephesus (*D* 111a—contra Nestorianos) and Chalcedon (*D* 148—contra Monophysitas). The Acta of the Vatican Council report the continuing battle fought by the commission presidents to prevent sundry "interesting" addita. Especially enlightening is the lecture of the late Cardinal Franzelin before the Deputatio de fide (*Coll. Lac.*, VII, 1611f.): "It has never been the purpose of the Councils to expound Catholic doctrine per se while it was possessed in peace . . . But the purpose of the decrees . . . has always been the exposition and rejection of threatening errors by the declaration of Catholic doctrine *in direct opposition* to those errors. Hence there are almost always two parts to decrees: one in which the error is given its appropriate expression and condemned, and another in which Catholic doctrine is declared *under that precise formality in which it is opposed to the error* . . . Given this aim of the Councils in their definitions of faith, it is clear that not only the choice of the chief points of doctrine . . . but also the essential form itself of the exposition necessarily depends on the nature of the errors to be exposed and refuted. Of course Catholic doctrine must be set forth and declared according to that form of argument and thought by which the error, seen in its peculiar nature, will be refuted, for otherwise the error is not sufficiently exposed and effectively rejected by the declaration of the truth . . . Whenever doubt arises concerning the true sense of expressions in the Councils generally and the decrees of Trent in particular, is not the canon of interpretation assumed by all theologians to be the form and sense of the opposed error?" Similarly the commission's essayist Gasser: "It was not therefore to learn truth that general synods were necessary, but to check errors" (*Coll. Lac.*, 397).

Finally, for his presentation of Catholic teaching, Barth has recourse not only to Councils such as Trent, but also to *textbooks* —in our case, for example, the dogmatic writings of Bernhard Bartmann. His right to do this is incontestable for surely one can find Catholic teaching there too. But Barth appears to have overlooked the problematic character of these contemporary manuals. And this oversight has not gone unnoticed on the Catholic side. We refrain from expressing our own judgment and quote instead the observations of an expert like Karl Rahner in regard to this deficiency of our present-day manuals.

"The textbooks are—textbooks . . . no one can deny that in the last two centuries cultural and spiritual transformations have taken place which, to say the very least, are comparable in depth and extent and power to mould men's lives, with those which took place between the time of Augustine and that of the golden age of scholasticism. If we hold that theology is an endeavour of the spirit and a science which has to be of service to its own time, just as it has, or should have, grown out of its own time; and if we hold this because it has to serve salvation and not mere theoretical curiosity (granting always that pure understanding as such is itself a part of salvation) and salvation is always the salvation of individual men here and now; if we hold in faith that divine revelation is a source of such treasures of truth that it can never be exhausted (*D* 3014): then we should have expected to find at least as pronounced a difference between a theological compendium of today and one of, say, 1750, as between the *Summa Theologica* of St. Thomas and the writings of Augustine. What are the facts? We might just as well look up the average *tractatus* of Billuart or the Wirceburgenses as a modern treatise. Where it is properly dogmatic theology—that is to say, neither history of dogma or its pitiful crumbs, nor *haute vulgarisation*—such a modern theological treatise in no way differs from its predecessors of 200 years ago. Let no one say that of course it could not be different from its predecessors in view of the immutability of the *depositum fidei*. That is simply not true. We need only try to form an idea of the historically contingent character of the uniform canon which has regulated the choice of topics and treatises in a theological textbook for over two hundred years, in order to see that such an assertion concerning the unavoidable immutability of our textbooks is false."

A note on this: "The vicious circle of a Denzinger Theology is beginning to threaten us here. However 'objective' Denzinger may be as to actual texts chosen and collected there, it is equally subjective as to their choice and collection. It is obviously affected by the canon which regulates the questions and theses of current seminary theology: what it has collected and selected is what is needed in the way of authoritative doctrinal pronouncements in just this context. May not much else be found in Denzinger's sources (Papal letters, bullaria, etc.) if only this other material were thought to be as important as this or that question on which Denzinger does in fact supply explanatory material? Now that Denzinger with its selection (and its *Index Systematicus*) is in existence, the theologian feels almost instinctively that it is the canonical norm for what questions are to be treated of in dogmatic theology; for other questions, no evidence may be adduced from Denzinger. The vicious circle is complete" (Karl Rahner, *Theological Investigations,* vol. I, pp. 2–3, and footnote 2, p. 3).

There is no dearth of similar statements by Catholic dogmatic theologians. These would show Barth how utterly wrong it would be simply to equate the full and living Catholic teaching with the theology found in modern textbooks—let alone equate it, as Barth does, with the one textbook by Bartmann which, after all, even in the Catholic camp is by no means the most prominent. Much which cannot be found in textbooks is nevertheless still Catholic teaching. In regard to many Barthian concerns for which there is no place in the textbooks, the authors in question would answer that they "really" always have shared these concerns and that "as a matter of fact" these concerns are their own. This is not likely to be different in the case of Barth's central concern. The all-embracing sovereignty of God in Jesus Christ is certainly not a target any Catholic dogmatic theologian would care to assault. Of course there are obviously great difficulties involved in this problem, a problem which no immediate amiable agreement can be expected to solve. But it may be confidently assumed that all Catholic dogmatic theologians not only do "have" this concern but in one way or another have expressed it. The only criticism we might offer is with the manner in which this is done. The theologians are either not sufficiently clear or explicit or vivid, or they not infrequently deal with the matter in merely ascetico-pastoral rather than theological terms, or they commemorate in domestic seclusion what should rather be shouted from the housetops. He who would walk in the shade of an oak tree is instead presented with an acorn. There are shortcomings there for all to see and some of them are very serious and have far-reaching and fatal results—and for the pastorate too. And yet these shortcomings are *correctible*. They are things that brothers can discuss and—most important of all—they are not things that warrant a separation from the Church.

These remarks are not intended to interfere with any objective discussion of pending problems, but to prevent any looking for debate where there is no real quarrel. The positive question remains: From what sources is Catholic theology to be drawn?

In the not too distant past no Protestant theologian visited the "cemetery"—as Catholic theology was once called—if he could help it. Karl Barth had the courage to sweep away the myth that "Catholica non leguntur." Many followed Barth's example, and today Protestant theologians have learned that even with Denzinger and the manuals in hand, it is not so easy to go hunting the high prey. And some can be heard asking, not without irritation, where does this Catholic theology hide out anyway? But the question is a step forward—indicating some realization here of the dynamic and inexhaustible riches in Catholic teaching. In fact, Catholic teaching is too Catholic (καθ' ὅλον) to be readily spotted in any one place, for it still lays claim to *all* truth.

However, it has to be somewhere. It must somewhere have its source. The well from which Catholic doctrine and Catholic theology draw is the Word of God. The Word of God, in the *strictest* sense, is *Sacred Scripture* alone. The Tridentine "with the same sense of devotion and reverence (the Council) also accepts and venerates traditions" (*D* 783)—we shall shortly return to this—does with full right defend tradition against the Reformation. We find that today there are second thoughts on this among evangelical Protestants too.

Barth's *Church Dogmatics* is, in its entirety, an example of this. For the meaning of tradition in principle, see especially I/2, 538–660; see also the various publications of O. Cullmann, in particular *Die Tradition als exegetisches, historisches und theologisches Problem*. The reconsideration of the first ecumenical councils, of the Reformation and even of pre-Reformation tradition, the rising interest in patristic studies are of general significance for this development in the Protestant church.

But the "with the same sense of reverence" was never taken in the Catholic Church to imply that tradition like Sacred Scripture could claim divine inspiration (see the exact definition of scriptural inspiration in Vatican I: *D* 1787). There was never any tampering with the fundamental truth, that is, that even the most important documents of tradition such as infallible papal and conciliar definitions—despite all the positive things that can be said about them (for example, the negative assistance of the Holy Spirit)—still constitute no more than a *human* account of divine revelation (see also *D* 1800).

So there is this vital difference between any—even the most exalted—document of tradition and a text from Sacred Scripture. Only in the latter do we possess the outright and unmediated testimony of God Himself, and in its original idiom and its primal source. That is why Sacred Scripture has an absolute precedence which no other theological argument can whittle away. And that is why from time immemorial Scripture has been the *first* font of Catholic dogmatic theology.

This is what G. de Broglie insists in his brilliant note on the "inalienable primacy of importance and value" of the argument from Scripture in theology (in Bouyer, *Protestantism*, p. 230). "Consequently, Scripture has always had a place apart in the teaching of the Church. For, if the essential function of a theologian is to transmit the divine message in its entire purity, and, if Scripture is in fact the sole *immediate* source at his disposal whence he can derive that message in the very words of the God who sent it, his primary concern must needs be to recur continually to that source to the fullest possible extent, and so to refer in the first place to the testimony of Scripture in preference to any other. So it is that Pope Leo XIII (whom no one will accuse of underestimating the importance of the Magisterium!) could well observe that recourse to Scripture should be, as it were, the 'soul' of all theology; and he continued: 'This was, in all periods, the doctrine of all the Fathers and the greatest of the theologians, one which they followed out in their own practice. *They set out to establish and confirm, primarily by the sacred books, all the truths of faith as well as those which follow from them*' (Encyclical *Providentissimus Deus*)" (in Bouyer, pp. 230f.). Cf. Scheeben, *Dogmatik* I, p. 147.

Zapelena says in his treatise on tradition: "Scripture is formally the Word of God; tradition *is* not formally the Word of God but *contains* the Word of God" (*Eccl.*, II, 274); see Van Leeuwen, *Regula fidei*, pp. 341f.

The customary distinction between revelatio, inspiratio, charisma infallibilitatis, and so forth, can be found in every treatise on tradition or inspiration (for example, S. Tromp, *De inspiratione*, pp. 27–34, 66f.).

Barth himself should have no illusions and in Volume I/2—despite all his attempts at disengagement—he comes dangerously close to the Catholic conception when he defines the relationship between Scripture and tradition.

And as God's word, Sacred Scripture is a source free of error, valid for all times and places, and most important of all, inexhaustible. The theologian can never readily fashion it into a system. Time and again it springs new surprises, problems, and solutions which the theologian did not previously suspect were in the texts. More like an ocean than a spring, it gets deeper the further out a scholar goes. Therefore Sacred Scripture is not just a mine of arguments for theologians, or an instrument panel for orthodoxy, but rather is the foundation of theology and the taproot of its power. It is the theologian's primary norm, even when it irks him. And that is true for theological terminology too. Not that the use of extrabiblical categories should be forbidden to theologians. Even biblical utterance is determined by certain well-defined Hebrew and Greek categories, though these two languages are in no way absolute prototypes (as the medieval grammarians thought). Theology is not just a repetition but rather an elaboration of revelation, and there was never any theology without some kind of philosophy. Yet it must be borne in mind that once it is agreed that Sacred Scripture must be the primary source of theology and that, consequently, theological elaboration is concerned not with just any teaching whatsoever but precisely with what Sacred Scripture teaches, then all theological and philosophical categories must necessarily be conformed and oriented to the Word of God itself (see chap. 25).

Compare the article by M.-D. Chenu, *Vocabulaire biblique et vocabulaire théologique* and especially the papal bull of Gregory IX to the Sorbonne, cited on p. 1029.

But the questioning will continue. We, and Protestants too, find our teaching in Sacred Scripture. Where then is to be found what specifies Catholic teaching? This is the moment to refer to *tradition* and to return to the "same sense of reverence."

The Evangelical theologian is likewise compelled to go back to some kind of tradition, if he wants to give a historical and dogmatic exposition of specifically Protestant doctrine (or exegesis). Thus Barth makes plentiful reference to the meaning of the Church's creeds and decisions, to the Councils, and to the fathers and doctors of the Church (I/2, 585–660).

Sacred Scripture can be rightly read only within the Church. Sacred Scripture and the Church belong together. This means Sacred Scripture and the tradition of the Church belong together. Tradition in the Catholic sense is in no way the vague entity it so often appears to be from the Evangelical viewpoint. A treatise on tradition is not part of our purpose here. Two major studies on the subject are about to be published (a volume of essays edited by Schmaus and a three-volume study by Geiselmann). However, four remarks would seem to be appropriate.

See the classic treatise *De Traditione* by Cardinal Franzelin. On Trent's inconclusive answer to the question of the nature of tradition see Van Leeuwen, *Regula fidei*, pp. 333–337; for the conception of tradition by Franzelin, Scheeben, the Tübingen theologians, Perone, Newman, and certain contemporary theologians (Deneffe, Koster, Ternus), see the historical investigation of O. Müller; for the Tübingen school in particular (Drey, Möhler, Kuhn, Berlage, Staudenmaier) see J. R. Geiselmann, *Lebendiger Glaube aus geheiligter Tradition.*

1. To define tradition correctly as a *source of revelation,* we must eliminate all purely human and ecclesiastical traditions (apostolic as well as post-apostolic). Trent's only concern was with divine tradition as revealed by Jesus Christ or the Holy Spirit

(*D* 783). The Catholic Church believes that these divine words have not faded away without effect. It is quite apparent that tradition is of radically reduced value as a font of faith.

For the distinction *traditio divina* (*dominica* + *divino-apostolica*), *simpliciter apostolica, ecclesiastica,* cf. Franzelin, pp. 12–15: ". . . only divine traditions are in the strict sense and per se the revealed Word of God and therefore capable of being the object of divine faith" (p. 15). Scheeben, *Dogm.,* I, 150; Zapelena, *Eccl.,* II, 264; A. Michel, *Tradition DTC,* XV, 1314–1318; Ch. Baumgartner, *Tradition et magistère,* pp. 165f., 176ff.

2. Tradition is not simply co-ordinate with Sacred Scripture. Forgetting for the moment that tradition is too narrowly defined if it is associated with scripture as a purely residual concept, we can say that the task of tradition is not something absolutely independent. It revolves around, in fact gravitates toward Sacred Scripture, to which is entrusted the full content of Christian revelation. Scripture has to guarantee, expound, and specify tradition. With these reservations, however, tradition too must be taken very seriously: "with the same sense of devotion and reverence" (*D* 783).

De Broglie: "The position of the Catholic Church, it will be seen, is perfectly clear and precise. It admits, on the one hand, as traditional doctrine, that the apostles (and their associates, the evangelists) have in fact expressed in their writings *all the principal part* of the message they possessed to hand down to us; and it follows that tradition, by its essence, is obliged always to gravitate, as it were, around Scripture, guaranteeing to us its divine origin, interpreting and commenting on it, clarifying and completing its teaching. Yet, on the other hand, the Church can never forget that, if we desire, by the exercise of our faith, to make contact with the divine Word as it springs from its source, it is not enough to question the text of Scripture alone; we must interrogate, too, all that conveys an exact and authentic reflexion of the unwritten teaching of the apostles" (Note in Bouyer, *Protestantism,* p. 233).
Compare Bouyer, pp. 128–135; Scheeben, *Dogm.,* I, 148f.; Moeller: "This tradition is not an autonomous source of revelation, but together *with Scripture comprises a* logical and ontological *unity*" (*Tradition,* pp. 341f.). According to Congar the ancient and medieval exegetes held all truths of faith to be at least implicit in Holy Scripture, as *divinae traditionis caput et origo* (*Vraie et fausse réforme,* pp. 492, 495). Van Leeuwen, in line with Ortigues, Smulders, Bakhuizen, and Van den Brink, carefully observed that in the Tridentine decrees (*D* 783) the "partly-partly" is omitted on the ground that "the whole of

evangelical truth was written down, and therefore not just a part of it" (*Regula fidei*, pp. 344f.). According to him it is a matter of *one* source of revelation in two types of manifestation: "Scripture and tradition are the manifestations of the source of which Trent speaks" (pp. 359f.). Tradition does not necessarily imply that there are truths of revelation not contained in scripture (pp. 362–365). It is more appropriate to speak of the "incompleteness" of Sacred Scripture than of its "insufficiency." In a similar vein see Moeller *Tradition*, pp. 341-346, Scheeben, *Dogm.*, I, 148f. For the position of the great Scholastics with respect to Holy Scripture: Mersch, *L'objet de la théologie*, pp. 134–136 (theology as *"scientia de divina pagina"*); Moeller, *Tradition*, pp. 340f.; Scheeben, *Dogm.*, I, 149.

Most recently we have an article by J. R. Geiselmann (newly reprinted and substantially expanded in the symposium edited by Schmaus) dealing with "the misunderstanding about the relationship between scripture and tradition and its revision in Catholic theology" (*Una Sancta,* 11 [1956], pp. 131ff.). From this it is clear that "partly in sacred books, partly in unwritten traditions," and the accompanying stress on the *incompleteness of the content of Sacred Scripture was not officially approved in any way by the Council of Trent* (pp. 132–139). The (very late) author of this "partly-partly" formula is not Pseudo-Dionysius as has been assumed, but rather his humanistic translator, Ambrosius Camaldolensis (1431). The only pre-Tridentine witness of "partly-partly" is Melchoir Cano. While the Council's theologians and the preliminary draft of the decree had no "partly-partly" tradition behind them, the fathers of the Council, who brought about the replacement of "partly-partly" by a neutral "and" with their thesis that Sacred Scripture was complete as to content, formed part of a sound and long tradition reaching from Irenaeus via Vincent of Lerins right on into the scholastic period and continuing throughout this era. Ignorance of the historical genesis of this "and" (Geiselmann cites other factors too) was the main reason for the post-Tridentine theologians, especially influential ones like Peter Canisius and Robert Bellarmine, circulating the "partly-partly" as the intent of the Council (pp. 140ff.). Geiselmann traces the way in which, during the development from the enlightenment to classicism to romanticism, the formula was corrected—the process being concluded only with the Tübingen dogmatic theologian, J. Kuhn (1858): pp. 143–149. On the basis of this historical survey Geiselmann concludes: "Now that the victory over the post-Tridentine theology of controversy has been won, we have a chance to make a Catholic beginning toward an interconfessional dialogue on scripture and tradition:

"(1) God's Word is by nature a speaking to man, but God speaks to us through the living proclamation of the Church.

"(2) In the living proclamation of the Church the apostolic kerygma, suitably expounded and adjusted to the understanding of the listener, is made present for us.

"(3) Sacred Scripture is the work of the Holy Spirit giving testimony to the living apostolic kerygma, and is in accord with the essential features of that kerygma. Thus, while it is absurd to speak of the incompleteness of Sacred Scripture, there is a real need to interpret it.

"(4) This interpretation is, in matters of faith and morals, entrusted to the Church on behalf of the community of faith. Its interpretation is authoritative in nature and hence binding on the community of the faithful." (pp. 149f.).

3. This tradition—carried forward by the total Church of all centuries in the obedient consciousness of faith given it through the power of the Holy Spirit—is deposited in the various ecclesiastical documents and monuments (creeds, papal, conciliar, and episcopal decisions, the writings of the Fathers of the Church and of theologians, in catechisms, liturgies, ecclesiastical custom, and art). And yet these documents (even the celebrated and infallible ones) do not as such represent divine tradition. They are nothing but human ecclesiastical aids (instruments) for the preservation of divine tradition. Here again, the absolute pre-eminence of Sacred Scripture is evident—because it *is* the unmediated and manifest Word of God in every sentence, while the documents of tradition only *contain* the Word of God. With only this single reservation the "same sense of reverence" is valid.

Franzelin: "Granted that besides the scriptures there are other documents of the Church which contain the Word of God and which were composed with the assistance of the Holy Spirit infallibly guarding them against error, nevertheless there are not other inspired monumenta in addition to scripture" (*De Trad.*, p. 364). It is a matter of "helps for the preservation of tradition" (see pp. 164, 169, 171). Even the "writings of heretics and enemies of the Christian religion" can in an oblique way be considered among these helps (p. 165). (Baumgartner, *Tradition,* pp. 171–185; Deneffe, *Traditionsbegriff,* p. 161.)

There is, naturally, wide variation in the specific character and witness-value of individual documents of tradition. See in this connection the handbooks of dogmatic theology; for example, Scheeben, *Dogm.,* I, 151–187; Schmaus, *Dogm.,* I, 114–128; Zapelena, *De Eccl.,* II., 263–298.

4. *Official* ecclesiastical doctrinal documents in particular represent an extremely valuable aid (since they are not subject to discussion) to the Catholic theologian who is examining the tradition of the Church. For the Protestant theologian, it is true, they are likely to appear to be petrifications of Catholic truth. There is obviously the danger of involvement in an anemic, purely apologetic theology, and of the theologian's immuring himself in these mighty

towers and thus foregoing the opportunity for a dependable and comprehensive view of the theological countryside. But it doesn't have to be that way.

De Broglie: "Actually, we are too much inclined to blame the blind obstinacy of our opponents for the failure of our arguments to convince them; whereas this is often due to the narrowness of our aims and vision, even, nay especially, when we have recourse to the utterances of authority to conceal our defects of method.

"Admittedly, the teaching authority of the Church has its particular function in this connection, and it discharges it admirably when, in stigmatising a heresy, it selects for condemnation a list of propositions containing its chief errors. The harm arises when the apologist imagines that his task consists simply in taking these condemnations one by one and vindicating them by a series of sound arguments" (G. de Broglie, "Letter to the author" in Bouyer, *Protestantism,* p. ix).

What Karl Rahner has said about the Christological formula of the Council of Chalcedon (*Probleme,* pp. 169–174), will apply analogously to the decree on justification of Trent. Such a formulation is an end, a result, a victory. But everything depends on whether the most is made of this victory, on whether this end is at the same time a beginning. The formula has to be *one particular* truth, unfailingly creating a context of freedom for *the truth—* which always counts for more. "Whoever takes seriously the 'historical' character of human truth (in which is also incarnated the truth of God and His revelation) realizes that neither the elimination of a formula as antiquated, nor its preservation as a petrifact, does justice to human understanding. For history is not simply an atomistic, ever-fresh beginning, but rather is (to the degree that it is spiritual history) the coming into being of the new which yet preserves the past and indeed preserves the past *as* the old—the more so the more spiritual history is. But this conservation which recognizes a true thing to be true once and for all, is historical conservation only provided history goes on and the train of thought departs from the achieved formulation in order to rediscover it— that is, to rediscover the real, the old, to rediscover itself" (p. 170). We must therefore continually strive to move away from the formulation—not in order to give it up, but rather in order to understand it, to understand it "according to the Spirit." In passing beyond the formula we will continually rediscover that "God is always greater." And by thus moving away from it we will never stop returning to it.

While it is thus quite true that scripture can be rightly understood only in the light of the Church's documents, it is equally true that the usefulness of the documents, as Thomas had seen, lies in their being simply a *"means of defence* of dogma against heresies, or an *auxiliary* which makes more accessible to the unlearned the content of Scripture and Tradition" (de Broglie, "Note," in Bouyer, *Protestantism,* p. 232).

"If then, for St. Thomas, the fundamental aim of theological science is to establish the truths of revelation by having recourse (as far as possible) to *the very sources* whence the Church derives them, it becomes clear that the argument based on ecclesiastical documents (even infallible ones) cannot be considered by him as having a right, in theological 'science,' to a superior or an equal rôle to that of the argument from Scripture (even to that from Tradition). For, to say that the purpose of 'definitions' is not to create or reveal new dogmatic truths, but simply to attest with clarity and certainty truths *already possessed by the Church's faith and already discernible as such,* implies that the theologian discharges his office imperfectly if he confines himself to the establishment of dogmatic truths *by means of* 'definitions'; whereas he would fulfil it in the best possible way by establishing all the 'defined' truths *without direct recourse to the argument drawn from the definitions themselves.* The 'definitions' lose none of their value by being considered by the theologian in the light of 'confirmations' which he could, strictly speaking, dispense with; on the contrary, that would be the best way to justify their existence, to arrive at their proper understanding, and to shed the clearest light on the study of the meaning and application of each" (*Ibid*).

The concentration of theology on Sacred Scripture further does not exclude but includes an obligation to the true authoritative teaching of the Church. Church tradition, and in particular Church documents, are for us not signposts in the history of dogma which simply help a man find his way, but signposts which help him decide which way he is going to take. The Catholic theologian feels bound at this point not only in a relative but in an absolute way. Hence he does not begin by investigating scripture as an independent Christian individual and subsequently consulting the Church's dogmatic proclamation (as a negative norm). Rather, he carries on his investigations into Sacred Scripture while remaining at the same time positively aware that he is absolutely bound to the teaching of the Church. Nevertheless—and there is no getting away from it—he is searching *Sacred Scripture,* around *which* as the immediate, tangible Word of God, all other things must revolve. Here and nowhere else is the center of his theology.

These brief remarks on the sources of Catholic dogmatic theology may explain to the Evangelical theologian how difficult it is to see Catholic teaching in its fullness. Although it considers every and all truth its property, Catholic teaching *as a whole* is to be found only in the totality of the Old and New Testament revelation. It can never be conveniently localized in any one human place, where it might be conveniently ferreted out and hunted down by an adversary. The Protestant theologian could not be more mistaken than in asserting that this or that is *not* Catholic teaching.

These same remarks serve to remind the Catholic theologian how difficult it is for himself to become aware of the fullness of Catholic truth. Although it is easy for the believer to confess Catholic truth in its entirety, the theologian is able to determine accurately only after an intensive and broad study of the sources of faith what at a given point is and is not Catholic teaching. All in all, even the most solid theology cannot but be a theology for wayfarers and thus incomplete and capable of improvement. The Catholic theologian has more reason than anyone else to be modest.

These observations give us the *method* for our presentation down to the last detail. In the first place, we will draw our Catholic answer from Sacred Scripture with full openness to the Word of God, even if it reveals things less frequently noticed. Sacred Scripture is to be read within the Church and within its binding tradition. And so we shall cite witnesses from Catholic tradition whenever necessary. There can be no question here of strict proofs from tradition. For such a task, an endless number of special studies would be necessary. Rather, these will be in the nature of *illustrations,* useful to clarify trains of thought which are perhaps unfamiliar; and useful, too, to show Barth that the Catholic tradition cannot be in quite such a bad way. This is why we try to cite the greatest possible number of texts verbatim.

It is because of the great number of topics we must touch on in these short chapters that we venture to speak only of an *attempt* at a Catholic response.

"For whatever is true and by whomever it is spoken, it is spoken by the Holy Spirit" (Ambrosiaster, on 1 Cor. 12.3; *PL,* 17, 245; cited in *De Ver.* q. I. a. 8 sed c). All our discussions of the development of dogma and the sources of Catholic theology show one thing: The Catholic theologian faces truth wherever it happens to be without reservation, and if possible with self-critical openness. He knows full well that the Christian separated from him often comes to him, not with empty hands, but rather with a genuine contribution enriching the Christian substance. He may even look for Catholic truth in Karl Barth, as long as this is not done in too human a manner. For the Catholic theologian also knows that, notwithstanding all the searching, he has found the truth. The idea should never arise that the Church—simply because she accepts *all* truth, wherever it may be found, as *her own*—could ever be dependent on Barth or any human being, as though she saw the star of wisdom rising only now, as though she had not already found *the* Wisdom, and hence *all* Truth in Christ. The idea should never arise that the Catholic dogmatic theologian has a need for something besides the Church and her teaching office, as though someone would have to hold up to him the mirror for him *to be* a Catholic. The Catholic theologian may and must learn, may and must search, but never except in the confident knowledge that he has already found the truth through Christ in the Church.

And therefore the search of the Catholic theologian is as noted above, a *committed* search (and for this very reason free). This is also the one major element which the Catholic theologian painfully misses in Barth's theologizing, that is, the final obedient and faithful commitment. True, there is a search going on here, courageous, free, and broadminded, into all centuries and into all areas, into theologians and philosophers, Catholic, Orthodox, and Protestant, into the Church's proclamation, and especially into Sacred Scripture. We are reminded of I Thess. 5.21: Everything that is true ought to receive its place. And yet the Catholic theologian asks himself how it is possible for an obedient commitment to become *concrete* here. *Who* is it who decides what is right and just, calls the parties before his chair, pronounces judgment on all philosophers and theologians, and on the total tradition of the Church? Is it the man committed to Sacred Scripture? But who then passes judgment definitively—by means of a spiritual and free interpretation—on Sacred Scripture itself? And so—in good faith certainly—passes judgment even on Christ? Is it not this one isolated *human being,* who may invoke his Holy Spirit and yet in every case decides with his "natural" reason whether at this point, through him, the Holy Spirit and not the spirit of the world is speaking?

"I therefore speak against you that you may possess the whole. Perceive the concordant contention, perceive the contention of love." Would it be honest for the Catholic theologian not to give voice to his impression that—despite all the sympathetic notes, despite Barth's searching and his judgments when he discovers he is only all too human—this freedom is disguised arbitrariness? How could he fail to be moved when Barth speaks so powerfully of Christ, of Sacred Scripture, of grace, and of faith? But time and again it pains him that despite these pronouncements other elements seem to predominate—that is, that assurance comes not from grace but from man himself and his reason. This is an act not of believing but of knowing, since it is man who decides what is believed. Barth criticizes Catholic theologians a great deal, with great intensity, and in the final analysis it is always for the same reason—for being altogether too human. Yet Catholic theologians ask themselves (in all humility and aware of the extent of their insufficiency): don't they really concretely express (and precisely through their often very marked subordination to the teaching office of the Church) what it means to rely faithfully, in obedience and free commitment, on grace, on the Word of God which rules in and through the Church?

The problem of the ecclesiastical and especially the papal teaching office, certainly must not be taken lightly on the Catholic side. It cannot be disposed of with a superficial apologetic if only because precisely at this point the theoretical and dogmatic problems are intricately intertwined with practical ones (concrete administration in church government, church politics, and development of dogma). And it is not only Reformation history which testifies to this. Here, too, everything hinges always on whether the Catholic Church and the papacy in particular are able, in their total concrete being and life, to furnish "proof of the Spirit and of power" in a way which is generally valid. And who could overlook the fact that for different men and different times there can be great differences in the difficulty of hearing the voice of the Good Shepherd from the chair of Peter? On this score we must not be deluded by the great number of individual converts who after all often have extraordinary gifts of grace.

But on the other hand, one ought not to make demands from the Protestant side which do not seriously see the incarnation and the Church as a divine-*human* configuration. Barth has seen very clearly the problem of the Church which, hidden from view and encrusted with all kinds of human frailty, can nevertheless still be a sign and witness. Could he not have considered the primacy in this connection?

It is truly startling to read, for example, Barth's section on the Church as a hidden and manifest sign of the divine governance of the world (III/3, 198f., 205–210). All that is needed is to substitute hypothetically for the word "Church" the word "papacy" (as the shepherd who represents this Church: Jn. 21) in order to see the papacy as "sign and witness" which indeed "can be overlooked, but which can still be seen" (p. 198f.). It is clear that Barth's three criteria for the sign-character of the Church in world events can be applied in an analogous way to the papacy as the shepherd representing the Church: "We think of the remarkable *claim* with which the Church (the papacy) exists. We think of its (his) capacity for *resistance* and *renewal*" (205). "And *also* if we consider it from this always possible standpoint, we have to say something rather *more* about Church (papal) history than that it is merely a part of secular history" (206). It is not possible to cite fully such statements, so important for Barth. But here are just two more, in which the reader may make his own substitutions as above: ". . . And this means that he will not be too greatly shocked at it, or too full of criticism and complaint. For he also sees that in and through it all the Church has continually *resisted*, that it has continually been snatched from its anxieties and preserved at the last from a complete submergence in its temptations, that suddenly or after a period its wounds have been healed, that its Babylonian captivities have ended, that its enemies and persecutors have one day vanished from the scene, that it has continually been raised up from the dead to newness of life. He sees in its history something persistent and persisting—a continuity" (208).

"And then perhaps we shall ask whether the process of *de*formation, the distortions and disturbances which are caused in the Church by human error and ill-will, must not be regarded as necessary reactions against what have come to be dominant over-emphases, or as beneficial challenges to a new and better faithfulness. The fathers were perhaps right when along these lines they tried to find a positive meaning even in the existence of heresies and schisms. Certainly, if we are members of the Church participating for ourselves in its daily renewal we learn to be amazed at the *economy* which rules in its history, not merely modulating and correcting but constantly reviving, so that it seems to be ordained that a secularised Christianity should always be followed by the counter-thrust of a vigorously eschatological" (209f.).

Barth, from the perspective of the Gospel, considered the existence of a papacy as "not impossible" (IV/1, 672f., cf. I/1, 108–111, 115f.). Its existence would be a matter of the "proof of the Spirit and of power." Barth rightly demands this proof of the papacy. However, his own statements could have restrained him from asking *too much* of the papal office.

With this the introductory chapter comes to a close. What has to be shown is the fact that—and just how far—a theological discussion of justification is possible and necessary today.

21. THE REDEEMER JESUS CHRIST

"Those therefore who correctly understand admit a three-fold operation, not indeed of free choice, but of divine grace in themselves or concerning themselves. The first is creation, the second reformation, the third is consummation. For in the first place we are created in Christ unto freedom of will, secondly we are reformed through Christ unto a spirit of liberty; with Christ, finally, we are to be consummated unto a state of eternity. For that which was not, had to be created in Him who was; that which was deformed, had to be reformed through Form; the members could not be perfected without the Head" (Bernard of Clairvaux, *De gratia et libero arbitrio, PL,* 182, 1027f.).

This statement of Bernard brilliantly illuminates the one context in which the theology of justification is seen in its true proportions. Justification is not the central dogma of Christianity. This has always been Catholic teaching and Barth continues it against Luther in the best Catholic tradition. The central *dogma* of *Christ*ianity is the mystery of *Christ,* the mystery in which is revealed the mystery of the triune God as well as the mystery of the total creation, which was created good, fell, was redeemed, and is to be consummated (1 Cor. 2.1f.; Col. 4.3; Jn. 17.3; 14.6; Rev. 22.13). Christian theology is the theology of revelation. The theology of revelation looks to the revealed God. God reveals Himself in and through Jesus Christ. Only when the *whole* of dogma is seen in Christ and hence in the Trinity is it truly Christian dogma. Like theology as such, the theology of justification (and in its context the theology of creation and sin) must be an enduring concentration on Jesus Christ. Only in this way can the division between Christians caused by the theology of justification be overcome.

What Prat said about the teaching of Paul is in the final analysis valid for scripture as a whole: "The first bird's-eye view of this immense field is enough to convince us that its centre is Christ. Everything converges on this point; thence everything proceeds, and thither everything returns. Christ is the beginning, middle, and end of everything. In the natural order, as in the supernatural, everything is in him, everything is by him, everything is for him. . . . Every attempt to understand any passage whatever, if we should eliminate the person of Jesus Christ, would end in certain failure.

"This is forgotten by those theologians who make the foundation of the doctrine of Paul either the metaphysical notion of God, or the abstract thesis of justification by faith, or the psychological contrast between flesh and spirit" (Fernand Prat, S.J., *The Theology of Saint Paul*, II, pp. 13–14).

A Christocentric theology is obviously not to be pitted against a theocentric one. If the total fullness of the Godhead is to dwell bodily in Christ, and if the Father is to be manifest in His incarnate Word, then theocentric theology and Christocentric theology cannot, in reality, be contrasts. The more theocentric a theology the more Christocentric and vice versa. And Christocentric dogmatic theology always means at the same time Trinitarian dogmatic theology. The Father thus remains the beginning and end of the total process of salvation. Yet the bond between all the mysteries of faith is Jesus Christ. As the universal Mediator, Jesus Christ is the central mystery of Christianity. Jesus Christ—God and man, Head and body.

Even the non-Catholic theologian can observe that the Christocentric orientation has in recent Catholic theology become again a major interest. Initially stimulated by the demand for a "theology of proclamation," this development is primarily due to a renewed awareness of Sacred Scripture and patristic theology. It makes itself felt not only in dogmatic theology, but with equal force in moral theology too.

Along with J. A. Jungmann (*Die Frohbotschaft und unsere Glaubensverkündigung,* esp. pp. 20–27) and F. Lakner (*Das Zentralobjekt der Theologie,* with many historical examples), it is E. Mersch who has especially urged this emphasis in his "Le Christ mystique centre de la Théologie comme science"; "L'objet de la Théologie et le Christus totus" (especially important on account of the historical sketches: patristics, pp. 129–132, 134–135; scholasticism, pp. 132–150).

In *moral theology* the following are noteworthy: E. Mersch, *La morale et le Christ total;* J. Leclercq, *L'enseignement de la morale chrétienne* (esp. pp. 37–48); G. Thils, *Tendances actualles en Théologie morale* (esp. pp. 3–19); G. Ermecke, "Die Stufen der Sakramentalen Christusebenbildlichkeit als Einteilungsprinzip der speziellen Moral"; G. Gilleman, *Le primat de la charité en théologie morale* (pp. 185–224); F. X. Arnold, "Das gott-menschliche Prinzip der Seelsorge und die Gestaltung der christlichen Frömmigkeit"; A. van Kol, *Christus' plaats in S. Thomas' moraalsystem.*

Witnesses to the realization are—together with many exegetes—in *dogmatic theology:* E. Mersch, *Théologie du corps mystique;* R. Guardini, *Das Wesen des Christentums;* M. Schmaus, *Katholische Dogmatik; Konzil von Chalkedon, Geschichte und Gegenwart* (esp. vol. III). And in *moral theology:* E. Mersch, *Morale et corps mystique;* F. Tillmann, *Handbuch der katholischen Sittenlehre* (esp. vol. III: "Idee der Nachfolge Christi"; vol. IV: "Die Verwirklichung der Nachfolge Christi") ; B. Haering, *Das Gesetz Christi.*

Not to be overlooked in this connection is the ever-mounting number of excellent *books on Christ,* also of great theological significance. To name only some of the most important among contemporary authors (cf. our bibliography) : K. Adam, G. Bichlmair, H. Felder, R. Guardini, J. R. Geiselmann, J. Sickenberger, F. M. William, M. J. Lagrange, F. Prat, J. Lebreton, J. Bonsirven, L. de Grandmaison, Y. de Montcheuil, Th. Quoidbach, H. Daniel-Rops, F. Mauriac, J. O'Brien, A. Fernandez, G. Ricciotti, G. Papini, I. Giordani.

The theology of justification must be distinguished from Christology (in the limited sense) but a theology of justification considered in itself would be a severed branch. In Christology and with it in the theologies of creation and sin, the decisive questions of the theology of justification are answered. So these foundations of the theology of justification must first be discussed. But let us state the goal of the following five chapters as modestly and concisely as possible.

Not within our scope are an evaluation of Barthian Christocentricity, an outline of a corresponding Catholic counter-image—let alone a plan for Christology, or an inclusive presentation of the biblical teaching on Jesus Christ, creation, and sin.

Rather what is to be made clear in bare outline is how, for the Catholic, the theology of justification is not suspended in mid-air but rather integrated into the all-encompassing mystery of the redemption of Jesus Christ and defined from this viewpoint.

In these chapters we consciously avoid references to Barth's theology. The essentials of the Catholic theology of justification are to be presented as unpolemically and thus as briefly as possible. A comparison with Barth's theology will follow in a special chapter.

The New Testament contains very many statements about the *eternal pre-existence* of Jesus Christ. This fundamental aspect of Christology is presupposed rather than expressed in the Synoptic

Gospels, but is brought fully to light by Pauline and Johannine theology—yet here with perfect matter-of-factness. It is not enough to consider these statements in Trinitarian theology, for they are of central significance for the theology of creation and redemption. These hints, taken from the Catholic theological context, may suffice. We will put aside for the moment the work of Jesus Christ in time.

The origin of Jesus Christ is in God's eternity. For *Paul,* Jesus Christ is "the power of God and the wisdom of God" (1 Cor. 1.24), "the image of the invisible God" (Col. 1.15; 2 Cor. 4.4), and therefore "the foundation . . . which is laid" (1 Cor. 3.11), the "first-born of all creation" (Col. 1.15), "before all things" (Col. 1.17). "For in him all the fulness of God was pleased to dwell" (Col. 1.19). He is, in short, "God's mystery" (Col. 2.2; cf. 1 Cor. 2.1).

According to *John,* Jesus Christ is the one Word of God, in which the Father, before and unto all eternity, fully expresses himself: "In the beginning was the Word, and the Word was with God, and the Word was God. He was in the beginning with God" (Jn. 1.1f.); therefore, he is "Life," "Light" (Jn. 1.4). He is from eternity as "the only Son of God" (Jn. 1.14, 18; 3.16, 18; 1 Jn. 4.9), "in the bosom of the Father" (Jn. 1.18). "Before Abraham was," he is (Jn. 8.58). The Father has Him in His "love . . . before the foundation of the world" (Jn. 17.24). He is thus the one "who is from the beginning" (1 Jn. 2.13f.): "the first" (Rev. 1.17; cf. 2.8; 22.13), the "Alpha" (Rev. 22.13), "the beginning" (Rev. 22.13).

The topic here is Jesus Christ in the eternity of God. Jesus Christ, who has not yet become man, but who—and this is important—will become man. The topic is the *Word to be incarnate* whose incarnation is already real, not in time but in God's unalterable, eternal, and powerful decree: "Christ . . . a lamb without blemish or spot. He was destined before the foundation of the world but was made manifest at the end of the times for your sake" (1 Pet. 1.19f.). It is "the Lamb slain from the foundation of the world" (Rev. 13.8 KJV).

The literal translation of Rev. 13.8 is defended by many older and by various modern exegetes: "Immolated from the time of creation, because fixed there in the counsels of God, and consequently in some sense already accomplished." Bonsirven cites among modern exegetes in favor of this translation, Charles, Eichhorn, Alford, Bulgakov (*Apocalypse*, p. 224). The reason given is the order of the words and the parallel with 1 Pet. 1.20; so also Lohmeyer, p. 112; Charles, pp. 354f., Swete, p. 164.

These passages speak of the eternal pre-existence of the Redeemer. And so the redemption in Jesus Christ can be described in Sacred Scripture as an *eternal* mystery. What occurs in history is only the *revelation* of this *eternal* mystery—which is not new, only newly proclaimed: "The mystery *hidden* for ages and generations but now *made manifest* to his saints. To them God chose to make known how great among the Gentiles are the riches of the glory of this mystery, which is Christ in you, the hope of glory" (Col. 1.26–27). It is the "revelation of the mystery which was kept secret for *long ages,* but is now disclosed" (Rom. 16.25f.) "to make all men see what is the plan of the mystery hidden *for ages* in God who created all things; that through the church the manifold wisdom of God might *now* be made known to the principalities and powers in the heavenly places" (Eph. 3.9–11), "a secret and hidden wisdom of God, which God decreed *before the ages* for our glorification" (1 Cor. 2.7).

On the concept αἰών (αἰώνιος), cf. Mussner, *Christus,* pp. 24–27; Prümm, *Sammelbericht,* p. 267; also cf. Sasse, *TWNT,* I, 197–209; Cullmann, *Christus,* pp. 38–42.

So it is true to say of the Redeemer: "Jesus Christ is the same yesterday and today and forever" (Heb. 13.8); *He* is "before all things" (Col. 1.17), "in the beginning" (Jn. 1.1), "before Abraham was" (Jn. 8.58), "the first" (Rev. 1.17; 2.8; 22.13), "the Alpha" (Rev. 22.13), "the beginning" (Rev. 22.13). "That which was *from the beginning,* which we have heard, which we have seen with our eyes, which we have looked upon and touched with our hands, concerning the word of life—the life was made manifest, and we saw it, and testify to it, and proclaim to you the eternal life which *was with the Father* and was made manifest to us—that which we have seen and heard we proclaim also to you . . ." (1 Jn. 1.1–3).

The words of scripture about the pre-existent Christ must consequently not be taken as philosophical, metaphysical speculation about the Logos or about the hypostasis (for example in the sense of Philo); they must be taken in the context of salvation. These words occur only in connection with the redemption.

Bonsirven remarks on *Pauline* theology: "How can we maintain unity among the different states of Christ? By the dogma of the incarnation, which is the entry of a divine being into human becoming. We encounter here the idea of pre-existence. It is real pre-existence, not pre-existence only in thought such as the Jews attributed to certain beings. It is not, however, a pre-existence such as that conceived by a number of theologians—that of the Word not yet clothed in humanity. St. Paul does not know this Word existing in the bosom of the Trinity. When he considers pre-existence, he always speaks of Jesus Christ as mediator of creation, for example, in the time before his appearance on earth" (*Théol. du NT*, p. 254). See also Cerfaux, *Le Christ*, pp. 373f.; Mussner, *Christus*, pp. 28, 42.

Commenting on the Prologue to John, which is especially important in this connection, Spicq says (*Le Siracide*, pp. 194f.; as G. Kittel, emphasized before him, *TWNT*, IV, 134–139): "Actually what is most characteristic and least debatable in the prologue is that it is void of any speculative and metaphysical preoccupation. At the same time the Logos is a real concrete and historical person, whom the disciples have beheld in the Christ. This double character excludes in St. John the notion of an abstract reflection on a pre-existent essence affirmed by faith. It is not then from the viewpoint of the theology of wisdom that the apostle has hypostasized the Word. The evangelist takes as his point of departure the person of Jesus whose luminous, glorious radiations were visible, and from this concludes to his divinity and pre-existence . . . The novelty of the prologue . . . consists less in identifying Jesus with the Logos than in affirming the pre-existence of this Christ-Word and of showing His coming on the plane of history."

Similarly in Dupont, *Christologie*, pp. 48f.; Boismard, *Prologue*, p. 122 (the Johannine prologue theology is a "théologie fonctionelle"); Starcky, "Logos," in *DBS*, V, 494; Berbuir, *Zeugnis*, pp. 7–9 (cf. also Menoud, *L'évangile*, p. 53; Cullmann, *Christus*, p. 79).

Sacred Scripture emphasizes the absolute significance of a redemption which appears to be purely relative and temporal by showing the divine and eternal origin of redemption; it looks, so to speak, both backward and upward. It bases the existence of the God-man in the eternal decree of God's power, and thus emphasizes the absolutely unique historicity of the incarnation (in contrast to all other historical events) in a manner not to be surpassed. While every temporal event must be conceded a certain ("ideal") eternity in the counsel of God, it is only in Christ that the one totally different thing takes place. For this event involves not just something that is in itself temporal and extra-divine; it also involves the eternal divine being Itself. What we have here is a complete union between a creaturely temporal nature and the unchangeable eternal God.

J. Dillersberger in his commentary on John 1.1, "It is a matter of a 'backward look'; this first sentence is from the perspective of the 'man Jesus' " (*Wort vom Logos,* p. 48: cf. p. 67). Bonsirven, *Théol. du NT,* p. 264: "The incarnation is the principle and the first step in the mediation. This obliges us to regard it in a way different from other historical events, limited as they are in time and space. It has happened at a point in the visible history of the world. But it is, in invisible history, a fire which radiates all through the centuries. In brief, the incarnation has in chronology only a support. In the world of spirits the incarnation is at the center, and human history throbs within it. It is the only mediation, the only effective divine activity. Through it the eternal comes to the aid of the temporal, and the temporal takes its place in the eternal." Bonsirven refers in this connection to J. Guitton, *Le Temps et l'Eternité,* p. 323. Important here is the Old Testament tradition about the pre-existence of the Son of Man; see A. Feuillet, *Le Fils de l'homme de Daniel et la tradition biblique.*

Because the incarnation was prepotently willed from eternity in God's decree, it could make that redeeming power radiate even before it became a historical event. And thus the grace of Jesus Christ was already able to operate in the Old Testament. Abraham rejoiced because he "saw the day of Jesus" (Jn. 8.56); Isaiah prophesied about Jesus because he "saw his glory" (Jn. 12.41); the Patriarchs drank from the Rock, Christ, which followed them (1 Cor. 10.4); there was a "cloud of witnesses," who "practised justice" and "received (the) promises" (Heb. 11.33; 12.1) and "saints" who died before Christ (Mt. 27.52; cf. 1 Pet. 3.19; Eph. 4.8). Therefore too, as we shall see later, the grace of Jesus Christ could intercede when men fell through sin, and could already be present in a mysterious way in creation.

These scriptural passages on the pre-existence of Jesus Christ have a significance for the theology of justification that can hardly be overrated, as the next chapters will show. The theological explanation of this pre-existence is, however, one of the real difficulties of theology. We will attempt a further elaboration of this in an excursus at the conclusion of the present investigation—in order to keep in proportion the chapter here presented, and especially in order to remove from the present discussion any semblance of dependence on our particular, and thoroughly arguable, interpretation. Sufficient to say that the pre-existent Christ, not yet incarnate Word, already had something to do with redemption, that the incarnation was effectively willed in God's eternal decree.

It must be pointed out here that the excursus cannot involve an assimilation of gnostic-rationalist theories, nor a decision regarding the Scotist-Thomist controversy on the motive of the incarnation, nor an answer to the question whether the cited passages refer to Christ as man or Christ as God.

Jesus Christ, in his pre-existence, does not stand alone in the Father's sight. According to the words of Sacred Scripture He stands before the Father together with the Church and, in fact, together with *mankind*. Then too, we men were chosen in God's eternity with and in Jesus Christ. The prologue to Ephesians makes this point (hinted at in Jn. 1) most emphatically: "Blessed be the God and Father of our Lord Jesus Christ, who has blessed *us in Christ* with every spiritual blessing in the heavenly places, even as he chose us *in him before the foundation of the world,* that we should be holy and blameless before him. He destined *us* in love to be his sons *through Jesus Christ,* according to the purpose of his will, to the praise of his glorious *grace* which he freely bestowed on *us in the Beloved.* In him we have redemption through his blood, the forgiveness of our trespasses, according to the riches of his grace which he lavished upon us. For he has made known to us in all wisdom and insight the *mystery* of his will, according to his purpose which he set forth *in Christ* as a plan for the fullness of time, to unite all things *in him,* things in heaven and things on earth. *In him,* according to the purpose of him who accomplishes all things according to the counsel of his will, we who *first* hoped *in Christ* have been destined and appointed to live for the praise of his glory" (Eph. 1.3–12).

This unity of ours with Jesus Christ stands therefore, before the foundation of the world, as God's one eternal decree and plan of salvation. God maintained this decree—against sin—for our justification and glorification. This eternal decree has to do with *all* men, indeed with the whole world ("heaven and earth"). God accomplishes it, however (as the following chapters of the Letter show) through the *Church,* which is called the "mystery of Christ" (Eph. 3.4).

Together with the studies of Cerfaux, Gossens, Soiron, Warnach, Wikenhauser, Kaeppeli, Journet, the exegetical work of F. Mussner, *Christus, das All und die Kirche,* is important for the ecclesiological aspect of Ephesians; Mussner takes issue with the "gnostic" interpretation of H. Schlier (1930) and E. Käsemann (1933). However, Schlier has in the meantime re-expressed his own interpretation in two excellent articles. We cite from the latter of these ("Die Kirche als Geheimnis Christi"): "What is meant by the apostolic assertion that the Church is the mystery of Christ? It means first of all . . . that in the Church the mystery of the eternal will of God makes itself felt, that is, that everything in heaven and on earth is restored again in Christ (Eph. 1.9f). When the Church came, what came to light was this mystery—God's eternal will again to raise up man and his world. And wherever the Church is, she puts design into her work. What is present in her and through her is what God has always seen, wanted, and resolved upon—that is, the elevation in Christ of a fallen and crushed mankind and of its world. But what this implies is that the essence of the Church is not rooted in history nor in creation. The Church is not a product of men and of powers, of their times and places; but rather represents, in her form and activity, essentially a will which antedates everything in the history of this world of ours, transcending even creation, committing the world's ages to Christ and to His salvation as to their antecedent (cf. 3.11). And it implies something else besides. The Church by nature aims once and for all at the whole of humanity and the human world . . . In her there governs the mystery of a will of God which embraces and is concerned with heaven and earth. She is once and for all ordained for and intent upon all times and climes, all men and powers. Being and acting in this manner, she accomplishes the salvific will of God . . . When the Apostle speaks of the mystery of Christ, he has in mind first that the Church is the mystery of the will of God which in Christ precedes everything, is concerned for everybody, and raises up everybody in peace" (pp. 385f).

For the pretemporal aspect of the Church, cf. especially: Pilgram, *Physiologie,* pp. 31–48, 115f.; Wikenhauser, *Kirche,* pp. 49–51; Soiron, *Kirche,* pp. 214–216; Bonsirven, *Théol. du NT,* p. 266; Malevez, *L'Eglise dans le Christ;* Congar, *Sur l'inclusion de l'humanité dans le Christ;* Warnach, *Kirche im Epheserbrief,* p. 33; Beumer, *Altchristliche Lehre einer präexistenten Kirche.*

And so the Church also is—in Christ and in her own way— an *eternal* mystery: "He chose us in him *before the foundation of the world*" (Eph. 1.4). We were called through *"the grace* which he *gave us* in Christ Jesus *ages ago,* and now has manifested through the appearing of our Savior Christ Jesus" (2 Tim. 1.9f). God has chosen us *"from the beginning* to be saved" (2 Thess. 2.13). We have "eternal life which God, who never lies, promised *ages ago* and at the proper time manifested in his word" (Tit. 1.2–3). And to us will be said: "inherit the kingdom prepared for you *from the foundation of the world*" (Mt. 25.34). The worshippers of the beast are those "who dwell on earth, . . . every one whose name has not been written *before the foundation of the world* in the book of life of the Lamb that was slain" (Rev. 13.8, cf. also 17.8).

Because God, from all eternity, ponders in himself this mystery, the primitive Christian tradition—going back to biblical foundations—attributed to the Church an eternal existence in the decree of God, and even considered her a pre-existent divine being which became manifest on earth in the fullness of time.

The most famous passage in the earliest Christian literature is found in *The Shepherd of Hermas,* Vis. II, IV, 1 (The Loeb Classical Library, *The Apostolic Fathers,* I, 25): "Who do you think that the ancient lady was from whom you received the little book?" I said, 'The Sibyl.' 'You are wrong,' he said, 'she is not.' 'Who is she then?' I said. 'The Church,' he said. I said to him, 'Why then is she old?' 'Because,' he said, 'she was created the first of all things. For this reason is she old; and for her sake was the world established.' "

Orbe has in his article investigated in terms of the history of religion the relationships involved in the marriage of Jesus Christ with his Church before history began: "From the very dawn of Christian literature there has clearly been a different understanding of this marriage, projecting it into the prehistory of visible creation. This interpretation had to find, in the spiritual union of Christ with the Church, the type and model of marriage, existing long before the incarnation of the Word, on a level which could very well serve as pattern for the first couple living in Paradise—could give us a visible realization of a superior and spiritual prototype" (p. 300).

Cf. the Fathers cited in Warnach, especially Ignatius, 2 Clement, Clement of Alexandria, Epiphanius (*Kirche im Epheserbrief,* pp. 75f.). The classical passage, however, can be found in Origen, *Cantic. Comm.* 2 (*GCS,* 157–158). Concerning this Orbe stated: "Accordingly, from the historical point of view, his is an extraordinary exegesis. The final word has not yet been spoken concerning the Pauline doctrine of the Church as the mystical body of Christ, despite the extensive literature to which it gave rise in the last decades. Its products in the main follow either the paths of speculation or historical ways that are clearly orthodox. Therefore it is not strange that precisely those who historically spoke the first word concerning the Church, the body of Christ, have been absolutely silenced or at least are hardly studied in their true importance and significance" (p. 344).

Obviously the Church cannot be credited with the same kind of pre-existence as her Head, Jesus Christ. As we have already said, it is only with Him that a "substantial" uniting of the eternal God Himself (in His Son) to a temporal nature takes place; only in Him is there any question of a "hypostatic" union.

Therefore we must avoid at all cost any suggestion that something like a fourth hypostasis is surreptitiously to be introduced into the Godhead. We refer to K. Prümm's criticism regarding certain formulations by Warnach (*Sammelbericht,* pp. 268f.). Aside from this, Prümm thinks the material from tradition adduced by Warnach (cited above) "very instructive in showing the development of the idea of consistency in the divine plan of salvation" (p. 268f.). F. Mussner seems correct in stressing that while the Church participates in Christ, who through the "anakephylaiosis" exercises a cosmic dominion (which in *this* particular sense might entitle us to speak of "cosmic dimensions" in the Church), she is never to be simply identified with the cosmos ("bringing the cosmos into the Church"; pp. 671f.).

In the excursus on Jesus Christ in the eternity of God an attempt will be made to differentiate more accurately between the pre-existence of Jesus Christ and "the pre-existence of the Church."

But this much may be correct in the idea of a "pre-existent" Church: God, from eternity, in his Son destined to be man, had in mind mankind and the good of all mankind (1 Tim. 2.4 and so forth); the Church—being the "mystery," "body," "bride" of Jesus Christ—cannot be thought of except as an integral part of this plan of salvation. From the very beginning the whole of the history of the world is in fact determined by this Christ-and-Church-oriented plan of God for salvation. Secular history turns (through God's special grace) into a history of salvation, into a history of Christ, indeed into a history of the Church (which obviously is no basis for a "Christian" integralism or an "ecclesiastical" totalitarianism). Here is the legitimate place for the idea of a "Church from the beginning"—an idea which runs through all of Catholic tradition. This Church would be understood as the historical realization (beginning with the very dawn of creation) of the Church "pre-existent" in the eternal decree of God. "Thus we must say that if we take the whole time of the world in a general way, Christ is the Head of all men, but according to their different levels." The reason is that "the body of the Church is made up of men who have existed from the beginning of the world right up to its end" (*S.th,* III, q. 8, a. 3).

M. Pribilla (*Kirche von Anbeginn*) cites for this "Church from the beginning" in the widest sense: Justin, *Apol. 1,* 46; *PG,* 6, 397 (according to him "all are Christian who have lived with the logos, even if they were taken for atheists" as Socrates, Heraclitus, etc.; *Apol.* 2, 8 and 13; *PG,* 6, 457, 465; then 2 Clement 14, I, 202); Hippolytus (*Danielkomm.,* I, 17, (ed. by Bonwetsch, vol. I, 1897, p. 28); Origen, *Cantic. Comm.* 1.2 in 1.11, 12 (*PG,* 13, 134); Eusebius, *Eccl. Hist.* 1.4 (*PG,* 20, 75–79); *Demonstr. evang.* 1.5 (*PG,* 22, 43). And then especially, and in many places, Augustine, by whom Thomas seems influenced in this point: e.g. *Retr. 1,* c. 13, 3 (*PL,* 32, 603); *De. bapt. 1,* 24 (*PL,* 43, 122); *Ep. 102,* 12 (*PL,* 33, 375); *De cat, rud. 19,* 31 (*PL,* 40, 333); *C. duas Ep. Pel. 3,* 11 (*PL,* 44, 595); *Enchir. 118* (*PL,* 40, 287); *Ep. 190,* 6 (*PL,* 33, 858); *De nupt. et concup.* 2, 24 (*PL,* 44, 450); In Ps. 128, 2 (*PL,* 37, 1689); *De. civ. Dei* 18, 47 (*PL,* 41, 609); *Ep. 164, 2; 190,* 8, (*PL,* 33, 709, 859); In Ps. 36, 3, 4 (*PL,* 36, 385). And finally one more witness from the end of the patristic period: Gregory the Great, L.5, *Ep. 18* (*PL,* 77, 740); *Hom.* 19 in *Ev. n.* 1 (*PL,* 76, 1154); In Ezech. II, 5 n. 2 (*PL,* 76, 985).

For the valuable statements of Augustine before the Pelagian heresy, cf. also J. Guitton, *Le temps,* pp. 306–317.

For the theological problems of these texts, cf. Capéran, *Le problème du salut des infidèles* I, 31–132 (patristic period).

On the reconciliation of these teachings with the Encyclicals *Mystici Corporis* and *Humani Generis,* see the many commentaries, in particular that by K. Rahner, *Die Gliedschaft in der Kirche* (esp. pp. 72–74).

This then is God's decree concerning salvation, efficaciously worked out in God's eternity. God chooses Himself in His Son to achieve the salvation of all men through the Church.

22. CREATION AS A SALVATION EVENT

What God has resolved upon in eternity happens in time. All temporal development comes about as an achievement due to the one eternal plan of salvation in Jesus Christ. All—that is, not only reconciliation and consummation, but also and above all creation. Bernard of Clairvaux had profound insight when he linked justification in Jesus Christ with creation in Jesus Christ. If we lose sight of this we will easily warp our perspective. While creation is neither reconciliation nor consummation, redemption and consummation are grounded in creation in Jesus Christ. While Jesus Christ is essentially the Redeemer and Consummator of the world, creation too took place in the same Jesus Christ. What Catholic theologian could be deaf to the impact of the scriptural testimony to the *mystery of Jesus Christ in creation?*

This mystery is very closely linked to the mystery of the pre-existence of Jesus Christ in the bosom of the Father. It is not surprising, then, that it should be Paul and John again—and once more with clear matter-of-factness and clear dependence on Old Testament (and Hellenistic?) wisdom theory—in whom the cosmic significance of Jesus Christ comes through with marvelous brilliance. The first explicit New Testament witness is perhaps 1 Cor. 8.6: "Yet for us there is one God, the Father, from whom are all things and for whom we exist, and one Lord, Jesus Christ, through whom are all things and through whom we exist." And perhaps in close connection: "All are yours; and you are Christ's; and Christ is God's" (1 Cor. 3.22f.), and "For no other foundation can any one lay than that which is laid, which is Jesus Christ" (1 Cor. 3.11). The classic Pauline witness, however, is Col. 1.15–17: "He is the image of the invisible God, the first-born of all creation; for in him all things were created, in heaven and on earth, visible and invisible, whether thrones or dominions or principalities or powers—all things were created through him and for him. He is before all things, and in him all things hold together." The Letter to the Ephesians follows along the same lines (cf. 2.10, 3.9), although here the accent shifts from the cosmological to the ecclesiological. The Letter to the Hebrews echoes this Pauline witness, according to which Jesus Christ is the one "whom he [God] appointed the heir of all things, through whom also he created the world. He reflects the glory of God and bears the very stamp of his nature, upholding the universe by his word of power" (Heb. 1.2–3). So it is said of Him: "Thou, Lord, didst found the earth in the beginning, and the heavens are the work of thy hands" (Heb. 1.10); "now in putting everything in subjection to him [man], he left nothing outside his control" (2.8, cf. 3.1–5).

Finally, the cosmological role of Christ finds equally plain expression in John: "All things were made through him [the Logos], and without him was not anything made that was made. In him was life, and the life was the light of men" (Jn. 1.3f.). And so He came to "his own" for "the world was made through him" (Jn. 1.10f.). And: "the Father loves the Son, and has given all things into his hand" (Jn. 3.35; cf. 13.3). At the end of the New Testament it is again repeated: Jesus Christ is "the beginning of God's creation" (Rev. 3.14). In this light we perhaps gain a better understanding of the Christ of the Synoptics saying, for example: "All things have been delivered to me by my Father" (Mt. 11.27), and "all authority in heaven and on earth has been given to me" (Mt. 28.18).

So Jesus Christ (and through Him the Father and the Holy Spirit), constitutes, according to scripture, the origin and foundation of being, the archetype and prototype, the light and power, the meaning and the value, the support and the purpose of creation. All creation, being Christoform, has a hidden Trinitarian structure. But we must never forget that neither Paul nor John engage in cosmological theorizing for its own sake. These texts too are in keeping with the perspective of salvation. And a review of the contexts will show that they are always embedded in the mystery of redemption.

We refer to the statements of exegetes quoted in the preceding chapter since they too have their place here (especially in relation to the prologue of St. John). There are only some additional brief remarks to be made in connection with the locus classicus, Col. 1.15–17.

1.15–20 is a hymn of redemption: Käsemann even considers it a baptismal hymn (a primitive Christian baptismal liturgy). In 1.12–20 Paul carries his line of thought to a conclusion. It is the one and the same Jesus Christ in whom we have redemption and forgiveness of sin (14); who is the image of the invisible God and the firstborn of all creation (15); in whom, through whom, and for whom everything is created (16); who is before all, and in whom everything has its permanence (17); who is the Head of His Body the Church, who is in the beginning and is the firstborn from the dead, so that in all things He is the first (18); in whom God allows Himself to dwell in all His fullness (19); in whom God has reconciled everything to Himself through His blood on the cross (20).

The decisive cosmological loci (1.15–17) are even philologically very closely tied up with the soteriological context. They depend upon the relative pronoun ὅς ἐστιν, which is generally translated "Who indeed is" (*der ja ist*). J. Huby comments: "Paul has explained the role of Christ in the creation and government of the world, not to engage in cosmological speculation, but to emphasize strongly His place at the center of religion and the unequaled fullness of His redemptive mission" (p. 43). And Bonsirven: "Theologians tend to attribute this participation in the creative act to the Word as subsisting within the Blessed Trinity. We have already said that Paul does not choose to put it that way. Rather what he shows here is Jesus Christ, the firstborn from the dead, the Head of the Church. These related phrases have the same subject" (*Théol. du NT*, p. 264). F. Prat, *Théol. de S. Paul*, I, 345–349; A Duran, *Le Christ*, pp. 57f.; E. Walter, *Christus und Kosmos*, pp. 666f.; J. Lebreton, *Trinité*, I, 402f.; O. Cullmann, *Christus*, p. 79; E. Percy, *Kolosserbrief*, p. 71. "Faith in creation is here made part of faith in salvation," p. 313.

Still we shall not here deal with the important problem (which is not pressing in this context and is not touched upon by Paul himself) —that is, whether this passage speaks of the divine or the human nature of Christ (see on this the excursus of the pre-existence of Jesus Christ).

Thus it comes as no surprise that it is precisely the mystery of the *Church*—or the mystery of Christ—that is hidden in *creation*. Although not identical with creation, it is "the mystery hidden for ages in God *who created all things*" (Eph. 3.9). God's plan of salvation was already operative in creation. He conceives the plan in Jesus Christ, for the salvation of all men through the Church. In creation God maintains His will for salvation even against the rebelling creature.

Schlier: "Now this mystery is, in a certain way, also the mystery of the Creator. As such it is hidden before all ages in God who created the universe (3.9) . . . History only allowed *its* mystery to be revealed, the mystery of 'the age of this world.' In spite of this the mystery of Christ was there, and it is always there wherever creation is at work. It is also the Creator's mystery, and has its being not only in God's eternal salvific will but also in His will as Creator. After all, according to the Apostle, Christ is also the one in whom 'all things were created' and 'hold together' (cf. Col. 1.16), so that the creature does affirm this mystery in its own way. And to the extent that creation is present in the world, in which men 'by their wickedness suppress the truth' (Rom. 1.18), and exchange 'the glory of the immortal God for images resembling mortal man' (cf. Rom. 1.23,25)—to that extent the mystery of Christ is operative and manifest as the mystery of the Creator. As terrible as the course of world history is in the Apostle's eyes, creation and God's will to create are nevertheless always based on it, and ultimately on the fact that it happens. But this means that the Mystery, though largely obscured and falsified by men and powers, in Christ enlightens creation in a new and unique fashion. As the Apostle insists in this passage in opposition to the Gnostics, the Redeemer is none other than the Creator. Therefore, when the mystery of Christ comes to light in the Church, it also brings forth the mystery of creation." ("Die Kirche als Geheimnis Christi," pp. 386f.); see also Soiron, *Kirche,* p. 215.

It is scarcely possible to enumerate all the passages in Catholic tradition (especially in the Fathers of the Church) which speak of creation through Jesus Christ. The chapter in the history of dogma dealing with this truth of faith remains to be written. It will turn out to be a meaningful history of development, but probably also one of forgetting. It is not that this truth of faith absolutely disappeared but that it did not always remain in the forefront of consciousness. The Fathers' preoccupation with the pertinent passages strikes every reader of patristics. But it cannot be maintained that these same passages still played the same role in the medieval summas.

To quote but one example: In St. Thomas' *Summa Theologiae,* the fundamental texts about creation in Christ are cited with the following frequency: Col. 1.16 was cited three times (I, q. 46, a. 3 co; q. 108 a 5 sed c; a. 6 co; of these passages only the first deals with the creation in Christ, the other two are on the order of the angels); Col. 1.17 was not cited; Jn. 1.1–2 was not cited; Jn. 1.3 was cited four times (I, q. 18 a. 4 sed c; q. 39 a. 8 co; q. 74 a. 3 arg. 1; III, q. 10 a. 2 ad. 1—the first passage does not deal with Christ). To sum up: of those scriptural passages in the *Summa* which are fundamental to creation in Christ, we can find only two quoted in the corpus of the articles (and neither of these quotations is in the Christological part of the *Summa*).

This truth of faith is more in focus in Greek writers, because their theology of the Trinity, in direct continuation of Sacred Scripture, centers primarily on the various Persons and only incidentally on the one nature. And so, even in the theology of creation, their sights are set directly on the three Persons, acting concretely as individual persons in the divine operations ad extra— each Person acting in His own way and acting personally (although the work of the three Persons is as much one in its origin as in its effect, and although the principle of the unity of action is protected): the Father acts through the Son in the Holy Spirit. This teaching is found in the ante-Nicene (Greek and Latin) Fathers (and is already present, with great beauty, in the writings of Irenaeus). It is found again in the Greek Fathers of the third and fourth centuries up to John Damascene. Moreover, this development of Trinitarian doctrine is no mere development of appropriations in the scholastic sense. (See on this development of doctrine, the very fine work of de Régnon, *Théol. positive sur la Sainte Trinité,* esp. I, 335–365.)

We need then to know the reasons why creation in Christ, although not forgotten, receded more and more into the background. This trend in the development of dogma would require a thoroughgoing investigation, but three possible reasons suggest themselves: the influence of heresy, the influence of Augustinian Trinitarian speculation, and the inclination (also present among the Greeks) to view this saving truth metaphysically rather than from the viewpoint of salvation history.

Gnosticism so completely separates its God from everything creaturely that nothing remains but a silent abyss. The Gnostics compensate for this by filling in the space between the distant God and creation with intermediary beings, the aeons, whose task also includes the creation of the world. As proof of their thesis the Gnostics used scriptural passages about Christ as Creator of the world. This, of course, compelled the Fathers to speak a great deal about such passages. At the same time they had to fight against the intermediary beings (according to the Gnostics these were also hinted at in scripture). It is quite possible that at that time the use of these scriptural passages had already taken on a somewhat suspiciously gnostic flavor. For the ante-Nicene Fathers, Sabellianism is still a major antagonist. Against its unification of the Trinity, the formula "per quem" (together with theophanies and the mission of the Son) continued to be a most potent argument for the distinction of the Son from the Father.

In the meantime, however, *Arianism* broke loose, reshaping the confused gnostic theories about aeons into a rational and clear theory about Jesus Christ as a created intermediary being. As proof Arianism misappropriated the anti-Sabellian arguments and therefore interpreted the "per quem" to mean "not numbered together with but sub-numbered." Christ was now the firstborn, that is, the first created. He is God's only unmediated creation; through whom, subsequently, all else was created. Precisely because the Logos is the creator of the worlds, the Arians argued, He is essentially lower than the Father, who is enthroned high above all creation in solitary majesty. There-fore, the Nicene Fathers felt that it was urgent to shift the emphasis from the special role of Jesus Christ (and the Holy Spirit) in creation to the identity in nature between Jesus Christ and the Father. We can find traces of the anti-Arian struggle even in the liturgy, though by nature it is much more traditional than the language of theologians. Where possible the mediating role of Jesus Christ was made to recede in favor of His unity with the Father. In the doxologies we note an obvious shift from διά-ἐν to μετά-τον (cf. Jungmann, *Stellung Christi im liturgischen Gebet,* pp. 151–168). Basil himself tells us how the new creedal formula at first scandalized the faithful (de Régnon, *Trinité,* III/1, 120f.).

On top of this came the new psychological interpretation of the theology of the Trinity introduced by Augustine. Markedly dependent on the school of Antioch, which (because of its strongly anti-Arian orientation) suppressed distinctions of persons as much as possible, Augustine consciously took the one divine nature as his point of de-parture moving from this into his treatment of the individual persons (cf. de Régnon, III/1, 141f.). Therefore he quite understandably placed very great stress on the unity of the divine activity in its action ad extra. What the Greeks saw as the personal activity of distinct Persons (though accomplished completely within unity of nature), was now regarded as pure appropriation. Thus the neglect of the special concrete way in which the one indivisible divine action is proper to each distinct person. This is how the "by himself" (per ipsum) comes to be minimized.

On the other hand, the Greeks did their share in causing the per ipsum to be taken less seriously, at least inasmuch as they did not always sufficiently keep in focus the *perspective of salvation-history.* These texts were often all too readily attached to neo-Platonic philoso-phumena. And obviously a general Logos-speculation could no longer claim the same attention as the truth of salvation.

Scholasticism, on the whole, stuck to the line projected by Augustine in this regard. Not that the truth of creation in Christ was no longer an object of speculation in the Middle Ages. It was this, but in a rather more indirect way, that is, in connection with Trinitarian speculation and discussions of the motive of the in-carnation, where creation in Christ gained its place of special honor particularly in the Franciscan school. Alongside the great medieval scholastic theologies there were other medieval streams —theologies which were more mystically oriented and which deserve special attention. The modern development has thus far not gone substantially beyond Scholasticism.

As for the mystical and existential but nevertheless eminently theological orientation in medieval theology, a major part of these theological works have not been investigated nor even published. Among them the exegetical writings are especially significant. See the valuable catalogues of F. Stegmueller, *Repetitorium biblicum medii aevi* and *Repetitorium commentariorum in Sententias Petri Lombardi.*

Among known examples of what these unknown works are like, let us point to the profound Christian mysticism of Bernard of Clairvaux, of Richard of St. Victor and Rupert of Deutz, and to the *Soliloquia Animae ad Deum.*

From modern times we have worthwhile contributions on creation in Christ based on patristics in Petavius (for example on man created in the image of Christ in *Theol. dogmata,* III, 200–202; IV, 156f., 239f.); see Dieringer, *Dogmatik,* p. 144; Staudenmaier, *Lehre von der Idee;* Berlage, *Dogm.,* IV, 68f.; Baader, *Uber den paulinischen Begriff des Versehenseins;* Scheeben, *Dogm.,* II, 440, and so on; Schmaus, *Dogm.,* I, 329; II, 45–55; Dillersberger, *Das Wort vom Logos,* pp. 53–58; Berbuir, *Natura humana,* pp. 110–112.

It would take the equivalent of a book to develop conceptually the theological implications of the ontological presence of the whole creation in Jesus Christ, so this must be omitted here. And related problems in Trinitarian theology on this point (especially the principle that the operations of the Holy Trinity ad extra are one) also fall outside the scope of this study. In any event the problem cannot be one of Greek versus Latin or Latin versus Greek Trinitarian theory. Both have their traditional place in the Catholic Church. Since both explanations have their limitations and special difficulties, we need a review in depth which would do more justice to both perspectives (cf. de Régnon, *Trinité,* I, 432–435). Yet the significance for salvation of Christological and cosmological scriptural statements (see the next chapter) strikes us as more important than speculative exploration of the causality of Jesus Christ. On this latter, we limit ourselves to two citations, both bearing in the right direction.

The first indicates the context within which such an exploration should be conducted. Karl Rahner's statement about the special relationship of the justified man to the individual divine persons can be applied analogically to the special relationship—clearly enunciated in Scripture—of creation to the Father, the Holy Spirit, and especially to Jesus Christ.

"It would have to be proved in the strictest possible way that it was impossible for there to be this kind of communication of the divine Persons each in his own personal particularity and hence a non-appropriated relation to the three Persons. There is no way of producing such a proof. Consequently there can be absolutely no objection to maintaining on the basis of the positive data of Revelation that the attribution of determinate relations of the recipient of grace to the three Divine Persons is not merely a matter of appropriation, but is intended to give expression to a proper relationship in each case. In Scripture it is the Father in the Trinity who is our Father, and not the threefold God. The Spirit dwells in us in a particular and proper way. These and like statements of Scripture and Tradition are first of all 'in possessione'. It would be necessary to prove that they may be merely appropriated, on the grounds that they can be understood merely as such and that the contrary is impossible; it cannot be presupposed. So long as this has not been achieved, we must take Scripture and the expressions it uses in as exact a sense as we possibly can" (Karl Rahner, *Theological Investigations,* vol. I, pp. 345–346).

The second citation from J. Huby calls attention to the fact that the categories of exemplary cause and final cause do not reflect the language of Sacred Scripture (which here is unexcelled) in a manner really worthy of God. Scripture suggests that when we treat the question of the causality of Christ, we start not from a necessary minimum but rather from a possible maximum.

On Col. 1.16f., Huby writes: "Is it necessary to see in this expression 'in him' an assertion of the theory that creatures find in the Son of God their ideal image and their pattern? This exemplarist doctrine does not seem to be present in the thought of St. Paul. We interpret ἐν αὐτῷ in verse 16 as in verse 17: in him all things have been created as in the very principle of their existence, the supreme center of unity, harmony, and cohesion, which gives the world its meaning, its value and thereby its reality, or to use another metaphor, as the nucleus, 'the meeting-point' (Lightfoot) where all the threads, all the life-giving forces of the universe converge and are co-ordinated. If we could instantaneously see the entire universe, past, present, and future, we would see all beings ontologically suspended in Christ and definitively intelligible only in him" (*Ep. de la captivité,* p. 40).

Everything originates and exists in *Jesus Christ.* Until the present time, this was what Catholic teaching sought to explain. What must be stressed now is that *everything* originates and exists in

Jesus Christ (and so in the Trinity). Therefore, His is the primacy in everything (Col. 1.18). Therefore, His is *the* way, and *the* truth, and *the* life" (Jn. 14.6); therefore He is "the light of the world" (Jn. 8.12; 9.5); "the door" (Jn. 10.9); "the bread of life" (Jn. 6.35, 48, 51); "the vine" (Jn. 15.1, 5); "the resurrection and the life" (Jn. 11.25); the one "in whom are hid *all* the treasures of wisdom and knowledge" (Col. 2.3). As we observed, the Holy Scripture speaks about τὰ πάντα on every occasion. And, therefore it is impossible to overstate the importance of this "everything."

Cf. the lexicons of F. Zorell, and W. Bauer on τὰ πάντα. Cf. Mussner, *Christus,* pp. 29–39, on the extent to which the τὰ πάντα formula (especially in Colossians and Ephesians) has a cosmological connotation. At any rate it means "the whole creation" (p. 31). See in addition, Schlier, *Kirche im Epheserbrief,* pp. 88f. ("the total existence of the world"); Huby, on Colossians 1.16, p. 40 ("the sum total of creatures without any exception"); Dillersberger, *Wort vom Logos,* p. 50 (on Jn. 1.3).

Another order, not created in Christ, is *possible* only on the supposition that the strictly supernatural character of the present Christian order is guaranteed. But once this is granted there is no reason to exclude any given thing in this concrete existing order from having its existence in Christ. *Everything* is in Christ, through Him and unto Him. *Everything* continues to exist in Him. Sacred Scripture explicitly warns against excluding anything: "And without him was *not anything* made that was made" (Jn. 1.3), and "now in putting everything in subjection to him, he left *nothing* outside his control" (Heb. 2.8). The expression "everything" includes man, his nature, his reason, his philosophy, his natural law. And this involves creation, creatio ("in him all things were created"—Col. 1.16); preservation in being, conservatio in esse ("in him all things hold together"—Col. 1.17; cf. Heb. 1.3); co-operation in activity, concursus in operationem "(apart from me you can do nothing"—Jn. 15.5; cf. 5.17). Everything, the world of angels, men and matter, in its being and in its history, the original just man and the sinful man, the justified man and the beatified man—absolutely everything has its continued existence in *Him.* Without Him it "could" be, but without Him it is nothing.

On συνεστηκεν (Col. 1.17) cf. the lexicons of Zorell and Zerwick ("hold together and are preserved"), Bauer ("to have its continuity, to exist"), and Huby ("in Him all things hold together and are held together"), p. 42. Cf. also ἔκτισται ("The creation continues, conservation in being"): Berbuir, *Zeugnis,* pp. 26, 30 ("the ground of the possibilities of its continuing being and existence outside and above nothingness"). Prat (*The Theology of Saint Paul,* I, 291): "Without him . . . all creatures, incapable of enduring by themselves, would be scattered about, would crumble to pieces and again be lost in nonentity through mutual conflict. He it is who preserves them with their existence, cohesion, and harmony."

Certainly creation has its own being: yet the ground of this being is actually Jesus Christ. General structures of being also exist in the Christian world order. Yet the root of these structures is Jesus Christ. All things have their specific nature and this nature has its natural structure. Yet the foundation of nature is Jesus Christ. "For no other foundation can anyone lay than that which is laid, which is Jesus Christ" (1 Cor. 3.11).

Let us insist again that God could have made a purely natural order not created in Christ. (Enc. "Humani Generis," *AAS,* 1950, p. 570). We must therefore distinguish a double gift (creation and creation in Christ): otherwise the specifically supernatural character of the order created in Christ would not be guaranteed. We cannot avoid this theological thesis (G. de Broglie, *De fine ultimo humanae vitae,* pp. 126f.). Yet we must not forget that this natural order is "pure" order *as* "pure" order. In no case must the use of this necessary and helpful thesis be allowed to mislead us into "profaning" anything concretely existing by lifting it out of its "continuing" in Christ and setting it up as an absolute.

Once everything (human nature too) is seen in Jesus Christ, then it also appears that the autonomous theoretical and practical naturalism of modern times, to which H. de Lubac (*Surnaturel,* pp. 150–155, etc.) drew attention and which not one Catholic theologian was ready to defend in the excited debate about this book, is devoid of any theological foundation (and even the semblance of any). On this, cf. the work of H. U. von Balthasar (*Karl Barth,* pp. 278–335); K. Rahner (*Ein Weg zur Bestimmung des Verhältnisses von Natur und Gnade; Bemerkungen über das Naturgesetz und seine Erkennbarkeit; über das Verhältnis des Naturgesetzes zur übernatürlichen Gnadenordnung*); I. P. Kenny (*Reflections on Human Nature and the Supernatural*); L. Malevez (*La gratuité du surnaturel*), E. Gutwenger (*Natur und Übernatur; Der Begriff de Natur in der Theologie; Zur Ontologie der hypostatischen Union*); J. Fuchs (*Lex naturae; De valore legis naturalis*); et al.

To what extent, from the christological point of view, is "everything", the whole real man, tinged with the "supernatural"? We do not want to go into this question. It cannot—as the above works testify—

be disposed of in a few sentences. Our point here, which according to revelation can in no way be compromised, is that in the present dispensation, man is man only through *Jesus Christ* but even in Jesus Christ man is *man*. Whether one should designate this man as "supernatural" or "natural" appears to be more of a semantic and therefore a secondary question. There seem to us to be good reasons for using the term "natural" as well as for using the term "supernatural." If the term "supernatural" is to be applied to the essence of creation in Christ as such, it should be with the awareness that the word is being used in a wider (though not necessarily a figurative) sense than customary up to now; and this could easily result in confusion. It would then be indispensable to establish the various meanings of "supernatural." On the other hand, applying the term "natural" to creation in Christ can be just as confusing. So we avoid taking a stand on the semantic question. A great deal of work remains to be done in refining our concepts here and perhaps it will turn out that we do not have, as yet, the words to express ourselves unequivocally.

So the traditional and also the modern distinctions (cf. the above authors, especially Rahner, von Balthasar, Fuchs) used in Catholic teaching on grace did have their importance in the christological context too. They are too well known to need enumeration. Let us simply note what Fuchs has formulated as follows: "The possibility of a theological distinction, and a necessary distinction, in man between a natural sphere of being and one surpassing nature obviously ought not to be understood as though there actually were in man anything purely natural, not realized in a supernatural way, not affected by the supernatural sphere . . ." (*Lex naturae,* pp. 45f.; cf. Gutwenger, *Ontologie,* p. 409).

All is in Jesus Christ. This does not preclude but rather implies that being in Christ reveals decisively different *stages.* As pointed out above, being in Jesus Christ is not simply identical with being just.

Pure material being is unconscious of its being in Jesus Christ, and hence not oriented toward the visio beata (though it is mysteriously affected by sin and grace and it does wait with sighs and travail for the redemption—see Rom. 8—and is thus mysteriously oriented to the revelation of a new heaven and a new earth—see 2 Pet. 3.13; Rev. 21.1; Isa. 65.17; 66.22). But pure material being is in Christ in a manner different from that of men or angels who are (actually or potentially) conscious of their being-in-Christ.

The sinner, who revolts against his being-in-Christ (who, however, in his sinful turning away from Christ, does not get rid of this Christ who is his destiny) is in Christ in a manner different from that of the justified man, who as a living member of Christ lives as a temple of the Holy Spirit in the justifying grace of God.

And the homo viator, who knows and loves Christ "in a mirror dimly" (1 Cor. 13.12), but who despite everything already possesses "his spirit . . . as a guarantee" (2 Cor. 1.22), as "the guarantee of (his) inheritance" (Eph. 1.14), is in Christ in a manner different from the homo beatus, to whom it is given to see Christ and in Him to see the Father and the Holy Spirit "face to face" (1 Cor. 13.12) and to serve Him in unending bliss.

And the man who is damned, who has renounced Christ for good, who is willfully away from Christ, who has his irrevocable existence through Christ, and his ontological orientation toward Christ, senselessly torn asunder—he must despite this bend his knee to Jesus Christ and honor him (Phil. 2.9–11) who is the Head of all mankind and thus is and remains his Head (Eph. 1.19–23). Here a terrible difference of fathomless depth is revealed. For the lost man is in Christ in a manner contrasting with that of the saint, who has found, in Christ and through him in the Holy Spirit and the Father, the infinite and thus completely self-transcendent fulfillment of his being, and who may serve and praise God in eternity.

These decisive differences stand; and being in Christ, far from attenuating them, serves to exhibit them in all their intransigence. To avoid all misunderstanding we will not attempt here a comprehensive review of the meaning of the concepts. Despite all the discussion of the point, the τα παντα should never be called in question.

The problem which spontaneously suggests itself is this: *Why* did God create everything in Jesus Christ and why does everything have its enduring existence in Him? God has acted in freedom, in a way that is not arbitrary but rather full of deepest meaning. What is the meaning of this divine activity?

It is odd that this question, so obvious and so meaningful, is raised rather infrequently and then most often indirectly. And the attempted answers tend to be superficial. Certainly, God has acted thus in order to add to the revelation of His glory: Jesus Christ is the utter brilliance, the peak of creation. But should this thought tempt us to consider being "in Christ" as merely a beautiful and wonderful addition to creation? By the very fact that creation is in Jesus Christ, it is more than an ingenious notion of God, something adding to the perfection of the universe; it is more than a marvelous but ultimately idle caprice. Deus ludens is no homo ludens! Jesus Christ is, as was shown, not only the culmen et finis of creation, but primarily and above all its principium et fundamentum. He is its "enduring existence." He does not exist for the sake of creation but creation exists for His sake.

Why then does creation have its foundation in the God-man? Why not simply in one God, the unique Creator? Wouldn't this be "possible in itself"? Was not the answer implied in the two chapters on Jesus Christ in creation, with their accent on the perspective of redemption? The next chapter will attempt to make this answer explicit and at the same time show what has already been hinted at. In our Catholic answer to the question of the motivation of the incarnation we have no need to take a stand against either the Scotistic or the Thomistic thesis. Rather we can, without cheap compromise, approve both of them.

While the Thomistic and Scotistic theses tend to speak in hypothetical categories (for example, what *would have* happened *if* Adam had not sinned?), we will speak as Scripture does, exclusively of the order of fact (what *did* happen?). Cf. H. U. von Balthasar, *Karl Barth,* pp. 336f.; *Begriff der Natur,* p. 456; E. Mersch, *Théol. du Corps mystique,* I, 170.

Yet the controversy between Thomists and Scotists concerns a question which is *by no means purely* hypothetical. It is in the final analysis a question of the inner meaning (the motive) of the incarnation. Therefore, when we turn now to the meaning of creation in Christ, we shall have occasion to refer once again to the traditional controversies.

23. SIN AND DEATH IN THE PLAN OF SALVATION

God's plan of salvation in Jesus Christ dominates the whole of human history. Sin has over the world no absolute dominion. This does not of course mean that sin is justified but rather that it is condemned. God's plan of salvation, His eternal decree in Jesus Christ, is not in favor of but against sin. And the sinner inevitably encounters the wrath of God. God's punishment for the sinner is death.

Death? Really death? We must take pains to look straight from the Old Testament into the New, so as not to take this matter too lightly. The death of the sinner is something highly spiritual, it is true. But the Old Testament warns us against any trivializing spiritualization.

The death of man is a great mystery. It is not even easy to discover from Scripture whether this is a mystery of light or of darkness. In the various biblical passages light and darkness seem to alternate. Note the contrast between the serene belief in resurrection of Maccabees and the agnostic pessimism of Ecclesiastes or Sirach. Or between the happy death "surfeited with life" of the patriarchs in the priestly tradition and the ceaseless dread of death for Adam and Eve in the Yahwist. And even in the same identical author—in the one letter to the Romans—light and shadow tend to fuse.

We are not of course attempting here to present a general theology of death but rather to make one thing plain: Death is punishment for sin.

Cf. the following works on the theology of death: Féret, *La mort dans la tradition biblique;* Freundorfer, *Erbsünde und Erbtod beim Apostel Paulus;* Guillet, *Thèmes bibliques;* Michel, "Mort," in *DTC;* K. Rahner, *Zur Theologie des Todes* (cf. also "ζωη," in *TWNT,* von Rad, Bertram, Bultmann; "θανατος," Bultmann; and the older works cited there by L. Duerr, H. Schmidt, G. Quell).

On sin in general, see Deman, "Péché," in *DTC;* Gillon, *La Théorie des oppositions et la théologie du péché au XIIIe siècle;* Haas, *Die stellung Jesus zu Sünde und Sünder nach den vier Evangelien;* Kirchgaessner, *Erlösung und Sünde im NT; and in TWNT,* "ἀδικια" by Schrenk and "ἀμαρτια" by Quell, Bertram, Stachlin, and Grundmann.

The mode of death, the punishment of death, and the concept of death in the Old Testament have to be evaluated as facts of cultural history. Especially here, we must base our understanding on common oriental conceptions, without unduly harmonizing the various sources. But may we for a moment forget that these cultural and historical facts—even those in the sober Levitical or Deuteronomic legal passages on violations worthy of death—in their very character as facts of cultural history, have *theological* significance in that they are intended to appeal to us as the inspired word of God? Sacred Scripture sees death in connection with sin, and it presents this truth without glossing over it. Thus in sin the sinner earns for himself instantaneous death—instantaneous death in the massive Old Testament body-soul sense of the word. The sinner does "deserve to die" (Rom. 1.32).

Man dying a sudden death because of his sin is a common occurrence in the Old Testament. Regardless of how the individual texts may be interpreted the various traditions of the historical books, all the way from Genesis to 2 Maccabees, demonstrate with poignant detail (too drastic for human reasoning) what the sinner deserves—death. So it comes as no surprise that among the Israelites premature death "in the middle of one's days" was considered a punishment for personal sin (e.g. Ps. 55.23; 102.24f; Isa. 38.10; Jer. 17.11).

We shall cite some examples verbatim to show their grim earnestness: "But Er . . . was wicked in the sight of the LORD; and the LORD slew him." (Gen. 38.7); "And what he [Onan] did was displeasing in the sight of the LORD, and he slew him also" (Gen. 38.10); "Now Nadab and Abihu, the sons of Aaron . . . offered unholy fire before the LORD, such as he had not commanded them. And fire came forth from the presence of the LORD and devoured them, and they died before the LORD" (Lev. 10.1f.); "While the meat was yet between their teeth, before it was consumed, the anger of the LORD was kindled against the people, and the LORD smote the people with a very great plague" (Num. 11.33); "The men [spies] who brought up an evil report of the land, died by the plague before the LORD" (Num. 14.37); "And as he [Moses] finished speaking all these words, the ground under them split asunder; and the earth opened its mouth and swallowed them up, with their households and all the men that belonged to Korah and all their goods" (Num. 16.31f.); "Then the LORD sent fiery serpents among the people, and they bit the people, so that many people of Israel died" (Num. 21.6); "But they [the sons of Eli] would not listen to the voice of their father; for it was the will of the LORD to slay them. . . . And the ark of God was captured; and the two sons of Eli, Hophni and Phinehas, were slain" (1 Sam. 2.25; 4.11); "And when they came to the threshing floor of Nacon, Uzzah put out his hand to the ark of God and took hold of it, for the oxen stumbled. And the anger of the LORD was kindled against Uzzah; and God smote him there because he put forth his hand to the ark; and he died there beside the ark of God" (2 Sam. 6.6f.).

And there is a long additional list: 1 Kgs. 13.26 (the disobedient man of God); 13.34; 14.12, 17; 15.29 (the extermination of the family of Jeroboam); 16.12 (Baasha); 16.18 (Zimri); 20.36 (the sons of the prophet); 22.35–38 (Ahab; cf. 21.19); 2 Kgs. 9.30–37; 10.1–25 (Jezebel and the last descendants of Ahab, cf. 1 Kgs. 21.23), 2 Kgs. 1.10, 12 (the soldiers in front of Elijah); 1.17 (Ahaziah; cf. 1.4); 2.24 (the boys who jeered Elijah); 7.19f. (King of Israel); 2 Chron. 13.20 (Jeroboam); 2 Macc. 13.21 (Rhodocus); Jer. 28.16f. (Hananiah); compare in this connection also 2 Sam. 24.15–17; 1 Kgs. 16.34f.

These are all examples which stand for "the many" who in turn stand for all men "swept away with all their sins" (Num. 16.26). The Lord can speak of all sinners: "I may consume them in a moment" (Num. 16.45); and "now those who died by the plague were fourteen thousand seven hundred" (Num. 16.49).

Against this background one must understand the punishment of *banishment,* the judgment of destruction commanded by Yahweh (Deut. 7.1f.; 20.13f.; 1 Sam. 15.3): "And [he] requites to their face those who hate him, by destroying them; he will not be slack with him who hates him, he will requite him to his face" (Deut. 7.10).

The *legal death sentence* especially must be seen against this background. Of course, the Israelite legal code must be evaluated in its "Sitz im Leben," in its development, in its connection with the common law of the ancient Near East and its affinity with the Assyrian collection of laws and the Hittite Code. However, this does not derogate in the slightest from the theological fact that in the given context it stands as a declaration on death as punishment for sin against Yahweh's law. That is how the inspired author represents the death penalty to us—as something dictated and established by Yahweh as punishment for the infringement of the charter of Yahweh's covenant (for example, the establishment of the death sentence for breaking the Sabbath; Ex. 31.12–17). That all the criminal laws of punishment should be considered together with the whole civil law is part of the covenant charter. This seems actually to set Israelite law apart from other ancient Oriental codes, despite all the similarities. The catalogue of violations deserving death is especially impressive when compared to the Pauline catalogues of vices.

The following are to be killed: whoever strikes or curses his parents (Ex. 21.15, 17; Lev. 20.9); whoever uncleanly eats sacrificial meat belonging to the Lord (Lev. 7.20–21), the sacrificial fat (7.25), blood (7.27), or tainted sacrificial meat; whoever approaches gifts consecrated to the Lord while unclean (22.3); whoever transgresses against the integrity of the slaughtering place of an animal to be sacrificed (17.4) or against the unity of the place of offering (17.9). Besides these, death is the punishment for: murder (Ex. 21.12, 14; Lev. 24.17, 21); kidnapping (Ex. 21.16); idolatry (Ex. 22.19; Deut. 13.2–19; 17.2–7); child sacrifice (Lev. 20.2–6); blasphemy (Lev. 24.15); violation of the sabbath (Ex. 31.14; 35.2); magic (Ex. 22.17); acting as medium or wizard (Lev. 20.27); divorce, homosexuality, bestiality, incest (Lev. 20.10–18; Ex. 22.18, Deut. 21.22); the prostitution of a virgin (Deut. 22.20f.); raping of an engaged woman (Deut. 21.23–27); and the manufacture of anointing oil (Ex. 30.33) or incense (30.38) in the same proportions as those reserved for the sanctuary. Also to be condemned to death are: false prophets (Deut. 18.20) and the owner of a goring ox which has killed a man (Ex. 21.29). Cf. also Gen. 9.6; 20.7; Ex. 19.12.

We have also included in this catalogue passages which do not speak of a formal "death sentence" but of "being cut off from the people." Even if we grant that "cutting off" was not simply identified with the death penalty but rather that it refers to some form of excommunication, as Pirot-Clamer rightly observes (Lev. 7.20, art. "Excommunication," in *Dict. de la Bible*, II, 2133), nevertheless what Cazelles remarks (Lev. 7.20. Cf. also *Bibl. de Jérus.*) is also to the point, namely, that "for a nomad in the desert to be cut off from his clan is equivalent to a condemnation to death."

For the Old Testament law, cf. A. Cazelles, "Loi," in *DBS*.

Just how seriously these laws must be taken is shown by some representative narratives of how the death sentence was executed: the Levites killed 3,000 Israelites who practised idolatry (Ex. 32.27–29); the violators of the sabbath were stoned (Num. 15. 32–36); the thief Achan was stoned (Josh. 7.16–26). How seriously death as such must be taken as the penalty for sin is shown in general by the elementary catastrophes of ancient salvation history; the destruction of the human race in the flood, the destruction of Sodom and Gomorrah, the destruction of the Egyptians in the Red Sea, and finally, the destruction of Samaria and Jerusalem can be seen correctly only in this theological perspective: Sacred Scripture sees destruction as the direct result of sin.

What God wanted to make tangibly clear, as it were, in the history and law of Israel—this He had His *prophets* cry out among His people. This unmistakable outcry can be heard not only through the countless threats of annihilation directed against sinful peoples, against Babel, Assyria, Egypt, Edom (for example, Isa. 1.27f.; 10.25–30; 13.9–22; 14.22–23; Ezek. 5.5–17; 21.13–22, and so on), but also through the clear words of God directed to individual men.

Thus God let it be clearly said to His favorite, David: "The LORD also has put away your sin; you shall not die. Nevertheless, because by this deed you have utterly scorned the LORD, the child that is born to you shall die" (2 Sam. 12.13–14). And we find in Job what God can threaten the sinner with: "Pour forth the overflowings of your anger, and look on every one that is proud, and . . . bring him low; and tread down the wicked where they stand. Hide them all in the dust together; bind their faces in the world below" (Job 40.11–13). Equally clear are the words of the angel in Tobit 12.9–10 ("For almsgiving delivers from death . . . but those who commit sin are the enemies of their own lives") and in Zech. 5.3 ("This is the curse that goes out over the face of the whole land; for every one who steals shall be cut off henceforth according to it, and every one who swears falsely shall be cut off henceforth according to it").

As might be expected, however, the classic witness is found in Ezekiel, the prophet whose preaching is, in a special way, directed to the individual and his personal responsibility: "Behold, all souls are mine; the soul of the father as well as the soul of the son is mine: the soul that sins shall die. . . . But if a wicked man turns away from all his sins, . . . he shall surely live; he shall not die. . . . Have I any pleasure in the death of the wicked, says the Lord GOD, and not rather that he should turn from his way and live?" (Ezek. 18.4, 21, 23; cf. 18.13, 19, 20, 31–32; 33.10–15). That this means physical-spiritual death is shown in the total Old Testament context and that of these verses in particular. Knabenbauer (*Cursus s. Scr. zu Ez.,* 18.4) remarks: "He mentions 'death,' . . . because death embraces, so to speak, the sum of all the penalties appointed by the law against transgressors, just as life is promised to him who keeps the law. Not in vain do Pradus and a Lapide advise concern about temporal punishment and death: 'for he replies to the Jews who unjustly complained that they were being scourged and punished with death and other disasters not on account of their own sins but for the sins of their parents.' " Cf. von Rad (*TWNT*, II, 847): Ezekiel obviously counted on the sinner's quickly dying. Here the linking of the natural life process to the Word of God is complete. . . ."

It goes without saying that these Old Testament ideas have their after-effects in the New Testament. Among the most striking are the deaths of Ananias and Sapphira (Acts 5.10) and of Herod Agrippa (12.22–23). But there are other examples of the same truth; 1 Cor. 11.30 (death because of an unworthy eating of the body and blood of Christ); 2 Pet. 2.1 (the destruction of false prophets); and Jude 5 (the three Old Testament examples of punishment). Also in Paul the principle of understanding the New Testament as far as possible from the Old Testament is borne out. Together with 1 Cor. 11.30, Rom. 5.12ff. and 1.32 show that Paul thinks also of bodily death when he speaks of death as the penalty for sin. Indeed he sharpens the Old Testament declarations inasmuch as he conceives of death not merely as punishment in the traditional and juridical sense (Rom. 1.32; 6.16, 23) but beyond this as a necessary and so to speak connatural result of sin (Rom. 8.6, 13; 1 Cor. 15.56; 2 Cor. 7.10), the harvest of the seed of sin (Gal. 6.8), the fruit of sin (Rom. 7.5, cf. 6.21). We have, he says, a body of death (Rom. 7.24).

Yet while it essentially retains the Old Testament view of death, the New Testament evidences a fundamentally new viewpoint, a spiritualization of death in the good sense. This will be discussed shortly.

So much is clear from Sacred Scripture. The sinner has forfeited his life—and with it, according to the true biblical conception, has forfeited salvation (Num. 17.13). The sinner does truly "deserve to die" (Rom. 1.32); he deserves to be "cut off" from the earth (Zech. 5.3). He has no reason to complain about this judgment of God. It is not the good Creator and Conserver, but the sinful creature himself who brings about this judgment of God.

Sin is a fall from the covenant, a fall from God. Sin is separation from God; that is its essence. Man, whose whole existence depends on God's love, turns away in sin from the foundation of his existence, and thus this foundation is for him—lost. He does not possess this foundation in himself. Aversio a Deo et conversio ad creaturas. Man, who has his source and goal, his continuance and support in God alone, turns away in sin from his source and goal, from his continuance and support, by claiming to have these within himself. But since he does not have these things in himself and is nothing when not dependent on his divine source and goal, his continuance and support, he gravitates toward his own nothingness instead of finding his everything in God. Thus man merits to be "cut off" from the earth. He merits and deserves his instant condemnation, his fall into hell.

This fundamental Scriptural statement was not overlooked in Catholic tradition.

The Greek Fathers especially fathomed the depth of the fellowship of man with God and hence the frightfulness of separation from God. As Origen expressed it, the souls of the just are in God's hand while the souls of sinners really "do not exist" (cf. Voelker, *Das Vollkommenheitsideal des Orig.*, p. 32).

The patristic texts will be referred to shortly. As for modern Catholic theology, F. A. Staudenmaier (a student of J. A. Moehler) who worked out this aspect of sin with a special acuteness deserves particular attention: "We have acknowledged above that sin is a deviation and fall from what ought to be; this deviation and fall expresses itself first of all as a *negation,* and indeed a negation of all that ought to exist and of what we call the Good. What ought to exist, the Good, is what we can comprehend within the eternal divine idea. Sin acts by means of its inherent spirit of negation as *negation of the divine idea, its content and its point of view;* it negates at the same time all that is put into the idea by God. Consequently it negates, together with the idea, *being, truth, order* and *law,* and negates the *goal* and *function* of things. By turning from the idea, the sinful spirit turns away from the *divine* and *eternal.* But it is characteristic of the dynamism of sin, which drives toward total apostasy and total deviation, that it is not satisfied with mere negation but that it wants to *liquidate,* to *annihilate,* to *destroy,* what it negates. This is precisely the sense of the remark that sin is not purely, i.e., exclusively, a negation of good, but also a *privation* of good. By sin as privation we understand, first of all, not a condition in which the creaturely spirit is deprived of the Good, although such a condition would be the result of sin; but rather the word 'privation,' just as the word 'negation,' is to be taken primarily in an active sense, so that privation implies an *actual real* robbing, after which the state of having been robbed occurs only as result." (*System der Christl. Dogm.,* II *Teil* 2. *Unterabt.,* "Die Lehre von der Sünde"; Frieburg i. Br. 1852, pp. 91f., cf. also *Encyclopedie,* p. 560).

But M. Schmaus also asserts, under the title "Sünde und Selbstzerstörung": "He (man) can only come to his own self in the 'thou' which encounters him, ultimately only in the 'Thou' of God. Whoever shuts himself up in himself, whoever revolves around himself and within himself, shutting off the 'Thou,' does violence to his own nature which is akin to and aspires toward God. He destroys himself." (*Dogm.*, III/2, 157). "Loss of God is loss of self" (1, 200). "In the cross of Christ, God's behavior toward man reached a climax of earnestness. God has man experience, with the highest degree of intensity, what he stands guilty of. In the cross of Christ God reveals to man who he is—a rebel and hence destined for death. In it God Himself gives man his authentic interpretation" (II, 767).

Cf. F. Baader on the connection between religion and politics (Sämtl. *Werke*, VI, 13).

The scriptural sayings are unequivocal. And yet the doubt persists. Is this not a case dramatization? Are these expressions not unnecessarily forced? Don't they contradict all appearances and the whole of everyday experience? After all, the sinner as a rule does not die; he is not cut off; he continues to exist in an average situation and even to enjoy it. In fact, the whole "order of being" remains intact.

What constitutes the most mysterious aspect of the mystery of sin is not that the sinner deserves to die, which is rather self-evident, but rather that the sinner, in the average situation, continues to exist. Here we must again have recourse to the Word of God. Why does the sinner continue to exist?

The answer is plain and simple: "Have I any pleasure in the death of the wicked . . . and not rather that he should turn from his way and live?" It is the same Ezekiel, who spoke so inexorably about the death of the sinner, to whom we owe this statement of such incomparable beauty (Ezek. 18.23). God spares the sinner, and that is the answer. He does not allow him to carry his work of destruction to its conclusion. He wishes to give him time to repent. Salvation time is testing time. Ezekiel is only one voice in a chorus of praise for the divine mercy.

"The Lord is merciful and gracious, slow to anger and abounding in steadfast love. He will not always chide, nor will he keep his anger for ever. He does not deal with us according to our sins, nor requite us according to our iniquities. For as the heavens are high above the earth, so great is his steadfast love toward those who fear him; as far as the east is from the west, so far does he remove our transgressions from us. As a father pities his children, so the Lord pities those who fear him" (Ps. 103.8–13). "Their heart was not steadfast toward him; they were not true to his covenant. Yet he, being compassionate, forgave their iniquity, and did not destroy them; he restrained his anger often, and did not stir up all his wrath" (Ps. 78.37–38). "The Lord

upholds all who are falling, and raises up all who are bowed down
(Ps. 145.14).

Yet God's actions speak louder than His words. Israel's history
is a continuing Passover of the Lord, a forbearing passing by of the
Lord (Ex. 12.11; cf. 12.13, 23, 27). The whole of the history of
salvation does now become a history of healing, from beginning
to end. It means the healing and saving of sinners. This is true of
the murder of Cain (Gen. 4.1–17), of all of mankind in the flood
(Gen. 6–9; esp. 9.15f.), of the sons of Jacob (Gen. 42–50), and
of the people of Israel at Sinai (Ex. 32.10–35), after the return
of the spies (Num. 14.11–25; cf. Deut. 9.25–29). The history of
the wandering in the wilderness is an almost irritating history of
unfulfilled divine threatening, of which Paul was to say: "And
for about forty years he bore with them in the wilderness" (Acts
13.18; cf. Ezek. 20.13–17). But even after this the whole of the
era of the judges is described as a constant alternation of fall, punishment, and forbearance (cf. the general scheme in Judg. 2.13–
23). Is not the end purpose of the prophecies of destruction in the
time of the prophets really the proclamation of salvation? Does
not Jeremiah's mission really culminate not in "destroying" and
"overthrowing", but in "building" and "planting" (Jer. 1.10)?
And likewise Isaiah's mission in regard to the tree "whose stump
remains standing when it is felled" (Isa. 6.13)? And Ezekiel's mission in making sure that man "shall surely live" (Ezek. 3.21)?
Compare Amos 9.8–10; Hos. 11.8f.; and so forth. For pagans
there is the example of the sparing of Nineveh despite the ill humor
of Jonah beneath the castor oil tree. Finally the ultimate meaning
of Israel's national catastrophe—the Babylonian captivity—is,
through all the punishment, still the saving of the people. Therefore the Israelites give thanks on their return that God "did not
totally destroy" them.

Ezra's prayer of repentance, Ezra 9.13–14: "And after all that has
come upon us for our evil deeds and for our great guilt, seeing that
thou, our God, hast punished us less than our iniquities deserved and
hast given us such a remnant as this, shall we break thy commandments again and intermarry with the peoples who practice these
abominations? Wouldst thou not be angry with us till thou wouldst
consume us, so that there should be no remnant, nor any to escape?"
Nehemiah 9.30–31: "Many years thou didst bear with them, and
didst warn them by thy Spirit through thy prophets; yet they would
not give ear. Therefore thou didst give them into the hand of the peo-

ples of the lands. Nevertheless in thy great mercies thou didst not make an end of them or forsake them; for thou art a gracious and merciful God."

The most complete Old Testament witness, Wisdom of Solomon 11.15–12.27, is in all its forms a "presentation of God's method of punishment, which restrains his omnipotence in favor of his wisdom, kindness and patience" (Feldmann on this text).

Actually, the Wisdom of Solomon shows us two fundamental facts: sinners deserve "destruction"—but they go on existing because God spares them for the sake of their repentance. God could have sent animals against the sinful Egyptians. Not only could their poisonous breath have *exterminated* men "but the mere sight of them could *kill by fright.* Even apart from these, men *could fall at a single breath* when pursued by justice and scattered by the breath of thy power. But thou hast arranged all things by measure and number and weight. For it is always in thy power to show great strength, and who can withstand the might of thy arm? Because the whole world before thee is like a speck that tips the scales, and like a drop of morning dew that falls upon the ground. *But thou art merciful to all, for thou canst do all things, and thou dost overlook men's sins, that they may repent.* For thou lovest all things that exist, and hast loathing for none of the things which thou hast made . . . thou *sparest all things,* for they are thine, O Lord who *lovest the living.* For thy immortal spirit is in all things. Therefore thou dost *correct* little by little those who *trespass,* and dost remind and warn them of the things wherein they sin, that they may be freed from wickedness and put their trust in thee, O Lord. Those who dwell of old in thy holy land . . . these parents who murder helpless lives, thou didst will to *destroy* by the hands of our fathers, that the land most precious of all to thee might receive a worthy colony of the servants of God. But even these thou didst *spare,* since they were but men, and didst send wasps as forerunners of thy army, to destroy them little by little, though thou wast not unable to give the ungodly into the hands of the righteous in battle, or to *destroy them at one blow* by dread wild beasts or *thy stern word. But judging them little by little thou gavest them a chance to repent,* though thou wast not unaware that their origin was evil and their wickedness inborn, and that their way of thinking would never change. . . . For thy strength is the source of righteousness, and thy sovereignty over all causes thee to spare all. For thou dost show thy strength when men doubt the completeness of thy power, and dost rebuke any insolence among those who know it. Thou who art sovereign in strength dost judge with mildness, and with great forbearance thou dost govern us; for thou hast power to act whenever thou dost choose. Through such works thou hast taught thy people that the righteous man must be kind, and thou hast *filled thy sons with good hope, because thou givest repentance for sins*" (Wisd. of Sol. 11.19–24, 26; 12.1–3, 6–10, 16–19).

With the commentary by Feldmann, compare the exegetical interpretation and the commentaries of Pirot-Clamer and Cornely-Zorell.

For an exact translation of the decisive words, cf. esp. Osty (*Bibl. de Jer.*).

Cornely-Zorell observes on Wisd. 11.24: ". . . It is plain that mercy is introduced here as a kind of controller of omnipotence, inasmuch as it is suggested that mercy moves Wisdom not immediately to inflict the punishment due the sinning creature, and to grant it time for repentance (cf. Rom. 2.4)." And on 11.26: "He seems certainly to be alluding to the Egyptians, whom Wisdom would have loved were it not for their terrible cultic practices; and he suggests that this is apparent from the fact that if they had not been supported by Wisdom, they could not have existed but would have fallen back into the nothingness from which they had been called." (Cf. pp. 425f., 428f.) Cf. also 12.8; 12.19, and so on.—*On the terminology, see R. Schuetz, Les idées eschatologiques du livre de la sagesse, pp. 110f.*

Shouldn't this lengthy series of considerations from the Old Testament shed at least some light on the Yahwist's obscure account of the fall, especially on the much discussed threat of death in Genesis 2.17? Is not an imminent death threatened, which then mysteriously fails to materialize? Is it not a sign that even in original sin, the forbearing mercy of God is operative?

On the difficulties of the Fathers, cf. Petavius, *De opificio* II, c. X (*Theol. Dogm.*, IV, 275–280).

We must acknowledge that this exegetical explanation is at least useful. It does justice not only to the Old Testament context but also to the verbatim passage taken by itself: " ביום means literally "in the day that," but also often means "as soon as, then." The LXX (and with it, the Greek Fathers) literally translated it ἠ δ'αν ἡμερα as does the Vulgate also: "in quocumque enimdie." In general the passage is also interpreted this way by modern exegetes. And no matter how it may be translated there remains this significant difficulty—the difficulty that it is insisted that man should die the moment that he sinned, whereas in truth he did not die until long after his sin" (Hummelauer, *Gen.; Cur. S. Script.*, I, 141). Symmachus already saw this difficulty and so he translated מות תמות as θνητος εση and not θανατω αποθανεῖσθε as the LXX did (Vulg: morte morieris). This translation is, however, contrary to the text (it disregards the fact that Adam was "mortal" whether or not he sinned). And the translation "thou wilt be guilty of death" (*Targ., Jerome*) is not exact. To take death to mean the beginning of a slow process of death appears to be too far-fetched.

It is probably best to hold to the original sense of the words and adopt the solution of Hummelauer and others: "The clearest solution is for us to say, insisting upon the obvious sense of the words, that God really threatened Adam that he would die at the very moment he sinned. But a person does not forsake truth and fidelity when he grants a reward greater than he had promised, nor does he who inflicts a lesser punishment than he has threatened. God had threatened death on the spot and he graciously deferred the execution of this sentence." (On this passage see Pirot-Clamer, and on Ps. 77.38 see Knabenbauer.)

On this passage Gunkel remarks (*Göttinger Handkomm.*, I, 10); "This threat is not ultimately realized; they do not die at once. These facts, rather than being explained away (e.g., B. Dillmann: toil and suffering are the beginning of death), are to be plainly acknowledged. The difficulty which the modern expositors have with the nonfulfillment of the divine words was hardly experienced in that way by the ancient expositor, who would simply answer: God is and remains the Lord of His words and so afterwards He 'repented' His word. More than that the expositors probably saw it as a special act of mercy that God later on did not make this word come true. Very similar is 20.3, where God threatens to kill Abimelech, but eventually lets him live." Similarly Skinner (*Internat. Critic. Comm.*, Genesis, p. 67); von Rad (*TWNT,* II, 845: "Gen. 2.17 is a threat that was not carried out; it suggests instantaneous death"). Freundorfer calls attention to the fact that the Pauline explanation of the Genesis account does not necessarily exclude our interpretation: "It would not be inconceivable that a death which would not have occurred at all except for sin was threatened in Gen. 2.17 for the very day of transgression but finally postponed by the merciful God" (*Erbsünde*, p. 26). Freundorfer, on the basis of philological and contextual considerations, is correct in rejecting the interpretation which holds for a spiritual death. Cf. Gen. 3.22 (p. 22).

While New Testament revelation offers substantially more than just a clarification of this Old Testament line of thought—as will appear later—it does offer this too. The Redeemer Himself is the one who declares anew that it is not we who deserve mercy.

According to Him all sinners deserve death: When Jesus heard of the murder of some Galileans He said: "Do you think that these Galileans were worse sinners than all the other Galileans, because they suffered thus? I tell you, No; but unless you repent you will all likewise perish. Or those eighteen upon whom the tower in Siloam fell and killed them, do you think that they were worse offenders than all the others who dwelt in Jerusalem? I tell you, No; but unless you repent you will all likewise perish." (Lk. 13.2–5) And then He told them the parable of the fig tree, where the Lord said: " 'Lo, these three years 1 have come seeking fruit on this fig tree, and I find none. Cut it down; why should it use up the ground?' And he answered him, 'Let it alone, sir, this year also, till I dig about it and put on manure. And if it bears fruit next year, well and good; but if not you can cut it down' " (Lk. 13.7–9).

The Apostles repeat in their own way the words of the Lord. In 2 Pet. 3.9: "The Lord is not slow about his promise as some count slowness, but is forbearing toward you, not wishing that any should perish, but that all should reach repentance." Paul referred to the Wisdom of Solomon when he said in Romans 2.4 (cf. 3.26): "Or do you presume upon the riches of his kindness and forbearance and patience? Do you not know that God's kindness is meant to lead you to repentance?" (Cf. Wisd. of Sol. 15.1; 11.23). And again in Romans 9.22: "What if God, desiring to show his wrath and to make known his power, has endured with much patience the vessels of wrath made for destruction?" (Cf. Wisd. of Sol. 12.20). Concerning this, Huby says: "The punishment has not gone as far as the total destruction of the guilty. The patience of God has curbed the full exercise of His wrath, but at the same time allowed it to become manifest in history" (p. 351).

The sinner, although "guilty of death," continues to exist. Although he has himself removed the ground from under his feet, he is not "cut off." Although he has torn himself away from his Creator, from the foundation of his being, he is not "annihilated"; he remains on this earth. The sinner remains man even in and despite his sin. Why? Because God does not will the destruction of the sinner, but spares him for his change of heart. And why can God spare him? Because He has chosen from eternity to take upon Himself the death of the sinner. Redemption is the reason for the sinner's continuing to exist. From redemption the sinner draws the possibility of remaining in existence and of remaining man, even in and despite his sin. Thus the sinner, remaining and remaining man, already participates in the grace of his redemption.

Ambrose: "But Adam did not look for the Lord—for how should he have looked for Him, he who fled from Him and was afraid to show himself? Therefore the Lord did not deign to see him; 'for the eyes of the Lord are toward the righteous' (Ps. 34.15). But to such an extent He was unwilling to see him that He asked, saying, 'Adam, where are you?' (Gen. 3.9). He who is sought is considered to be absent. It is faith that renders us present to God, wickedness that causes the godless to be banished from Him. No one therefore is absent to God but he who renders himself absent; and He [the Lord] says, 'According to your faith be it done to you' (Matt. 9.29); for whoever does not know Him will not be known. Therefore, Adam like a sinner could not save his home: he was cast out of Paradise and banished into exile, that he might repent. He received a deferral of sentence that he might not perish utterly forever; that Eve might be saved through the birth of children, through the faith of holy Abel, the grace of the prophets, and the future of the church" (on Ps. 37.20; *CSEL*, 64, 87).

And these had pointed in the same direction: Theophilus, *ad Auto-lycum* II, c. 26 (*PG*, 6, 1092f.); *Ep. Barnabas*, c. 12 (*PG*, 2, 760f.); Theophilus, *ad Autolycum* II, c. 29 (*PG*, 6, 1097); Justin, *Dialogue with Trypho*, c. 39 (PG, 560); *2 Apol.*, c. 7 (*PG*, 6, 556); Irenaeus, *Ad. Haer.*, III, c. 23 (*PG*, 7, 961); Tertullian, *Scorpiace*, p. 5 (*CSEL*, 20, 155); Cyprian, *De bono pat.* c. 4 (*CSEL*, 3, 399); Lactantius, *De ira Dei*, c. 20 (*CSEL*, 27, 1290); Ambrose, *De sacr.*, II, 17–19 (*CSEL*, 73:32–34).

Among modern Catholic dogmatic theologians, for instance, B. Heinrich: "Supposing that God had not had mercy on fallen man and had not elected him from eternity, would both *bodily* death and eternal damnation have happened at once, and thus the propagation of the human race have become impossible? This question, like those developing from it, cannot be answered since the answer is dependent solely on God's freewill. We can only thank God that He did not will the death of sinful man but rather that he should be converted and live. Presupposing the divine mercy it is, however, certain that *bodily life,* which continues despite the soul's death, constitutes a great natural grace given to fallen man (despite what he deserves and for the sake of the Redeemer), a grace which all other graces presuppose" (*Dogm.*, VI, 705). Similarly F. X. Dieringer, *Dogm.*, 337.

Berbuir: "The man who begins to steal from God and instead of accepting his sonship through God's grace grasps at a sonship of nature —before God this man in his envy has become a senseless, a contradictory thing. But does God proceed to annihilate him? There is something yet more mysterious here: He does not carry out the annihilation. In a promise of the incarnation and crucifixion of the Son still obscurely expressed, in the cursing of the serpent, the cursing of the personified envy of man, He proclaims His own victory to be achieved in the ongoing history of man—a victory over the tempter of creaturely self-will, the victory of his incarnate mercy (Gen. 3.15). . . . And in the same breath, so to speak, He visits upon Adam and Eve, and upon the whole of human nature, a merciful punishment, an existence in suffering, even to the sorrowful extremity of death. What is the mysterious reason for this? . . . If man through sin declares himself free from and rid of the Son, still the Father does not say that the Son is rid of man, nor does the Son Himself rid Himself of man" (*Natura humana*, pp. 113f.).

The holier the man, the more shocking his sin appears to him, and the more necessary the grace of Christ. Of the great Spanish mystics we shall cite only one, Ignatius of Loyola. At the end of the first week of his *Spiritual Exercises* he tells the participant: "Here the petition should be for shame and confusion, because I see how many have been lost on account of a single mortal sin, and how many times I have deserved eternal damnation, because of the many grievous sins that I have committed" (*The Spiritual Exercises of St. Ignatius*, p. 26). And at the end of the consideration of his own sin: "This is a cry of won-der accompanied by surging emotion as I pass in review all creatures. How is it that they have permitted me to live, and have sustained me in life! Why have the angels, though they are the sword of God's justice, tolerated me, guarded me, and prayed for me! Why have the saints interceded for me and asked favors for me! And the heavens, sun, moon, stars, and the elements; the fruits, birds, fishes, and other animals—why have they all been at my service! How is it that the earth did not open to swallow me up, and create new hells in which I should be tormented forever! . . . I will conclude with a colloquy, extolling the mercy of God our Lord, pouring out my thoughts to Him, and giving thanks to Him that up to this very moment He has granted me life. I will resolve with His grace to amend for the future. Close with an *Our Father*" (*Ibid,* p. 30). And the liturgy echoes this: "Oh God, you who manifest your almighty power chiefly by sparing and by showing pity . . ." (Collect for the Tenth Sunday after Pentecost). "O God, whose nature it is always to pity and to spare . . ."

The Redeemer, Jesus Christ, makes it possible for the sinner to remain in existence and to remain a man. *He* thwarts the "annihilation" which man in his sin is heading toward. He holds him, He cuts short his fall, so that his downfall will not become a final falling away. Jesus Christ, as the one significant prevenient grace (gratia praeveniens), prevents the annihilating work of sin. From eternity God has foreseen the fall of man and has taken precautions. And so the "enduring existence" of everything was committed by Him to Jesus Christ—to Jesus Christ, precisely with a view to its redemption. Creation in Jesus Christ is not redemption but, as its prerequisite, it is the hidden beginning of redemption. This is the reason why, despite everything, God did not have to "repent" that He had created man. He doesn't have to "destroy him completely from the face of the earth," nor finally revoke His creation of man (cf. Gen. 6, 7, 13).

Let us touch briefly on a question whose answer leads too far afield. Does "to be cut off," "to be destroyed," and so on, mean that the sinner deserves immediate condemnation to hell or annihilation? Sacred Scripture (even the crass terminology of the passages cited from the Wisdom of Solomon), it appears to us, gives no certain answer to this question. Scripture speaks rather of death, so we did too. In any answer, the question of the immortality of the human soul would demand first consideration. The Fifth Lateran Council decreed in opposition to the Neo-Aristotelians that the soul was de facto immortal (*D* 738). It was not expressly defined there that it was de iure immortal, but this is accepted as true by all the Catholic theologians. However, this de iure, according to the general consensus, implies not an essential or absolute immortality (i.e. an absolute or metaphysical impossibility of death); such an immortality belongs only to God. Rather it implies only a natural immortality (which is grounded in the "nature" of the living organism, in contrast to gratuitous immortality). As a spiritual and simple being the human soul cannot die (in the sense of privation of life through corruption). Nevertheless, as a contingent and not necessary being, the human soul can cease to exist: "Although the intellective soul is 'by nature' immortal, nevertheless as a contingent being it can, speaking absolutely, be annihilated and thus lose its life. Granted this absolute possibility, we affirm that . . . God will in fact not annihilate the intellective soul. And so for the intellective soul, which enjoys natural or 'intrinsic' immortality, we claim also 'extrinsic' immortality." So the philosophical point of view is explained (according to P. Siwek, *Psych. metaphys.*, pp. 403f.). While not contesting the reasons put forth on a philosophical level, we must consider it an open question whether on the level of salvation history a new factor does not break in, that is, mortal sin, which could justify annihilation. Some have sought arguments against this (especially from the relation between sin, punishment, and hell), but they are not conclusive enough to decide the question. Of interest in this connection are some remarks of Thomas, for example the reference in *De Pot.* q. 5, a. 4, ad 6: "Although in justice God could deprive of existence and annihilate a creature that sins against him, yet it is more becoming justice that he keep it in existence to punish it: and this for two reasons. First, because in the former case justice would have no admixture of mercy, since nothing would remain to which he might show mercy: and yet it is written (Ps. 25:10) that all the ways of the Lord are mercy and truth." According to this, annihilation is *de facto* impossible, because justice would then no longer be tempered with mercy. Or in *S.th.*, I, q. 104: first a. 3, on whether God can annihilate anything. "I answer that . . . just as before things were, God was free not to communicate esse to them and thus not to make them, so after they are made He is free not to give esse to them, and thus they could cease to exist; and this would be to annihilate them." Then in a. 4: ". . . But the natures of creatures show that none of them is annihilated . . . Moreover the annihilation of things does not pertain to the manifestation of grace, since the divine power and goodness are rather shown by the fact that God preserves things in esse. Thus it should simply be said that nothing at all will be annihilated." (From this point of view perhaps even the mysterious working of the mercy of God, bound as it is to operate even in hell—in and through all justice—could appear in a clearer light). This then may be enough by way of reference to a difficult question which cannot be disposed of in a few sentences.

What then is the answer to the puzzling question we posed at the end of the last chapter? Why is everything created in Jesus Christ and why does it have permanence in Him? Certainly not because of some genial caprice of a playful God. Rather in anticipation of sin, "for us men and for our salvation" a merciful God created everything beforehand in the one Jesus Christ, our Redeemer, and He has placed in Him the unforfeitable existence of all that is. "The counsel of the Lord stands forever, the thoughts of his heart to all generations" (Ps. 33.11), and "where sin increased, grace abounded all the more" (Rom. 5.20).

The Fathers have very explicitly connected creation in Christ with the redemption. Generally they expressed the relation in this way: He through whom we had already been created had to come to re-create us. Irenaeus gave this an especially pointed formulation in *Adv. Haer.* III, c. 22 (*PG*, 7, 958): "Paul called Adam a type of the one who was to come (Rom. 5.14) since the Word, the maker of all things, had predetermined the future disposition of the human race in reference to the Son of God—God predetermining that the first man should be of animal nature so that he should be saved by the spiritual man. For, since He who was to be Savior pre-existed, there had also to be that which was to be saved, so that the Savior's existence would not be empty of meaning." Other examples are: 2 Clement c. 1 (Funk, p. 69); Athanasius, *De incarnatione Verbi*, c. 7: 10, 13, 20 (*PG*, 25, 108f., 112f., 117, 129f.); *Orat. c. Arianos*, II, c. 53 (*PG*, 26, 257f.); Gregory Nyss., *Oratio catech.*, c. 8 (*PG*, 45, 37f.); Ambrose, *Explan. Ps.* 36.20 (*CSEL*, 64, 225); *De paradiso*, 10, 47 (*CSEL* 32, 1, 305); Augustine, in *Ps. 23 enarr.* III, n. 16 (*PL*, 36, 239f.); Leo the Great, *Serm. 64*, c. 2 (*PL*, 54, 358f.). Other passages can be found in Petavius, *De Trin.*, VI, c. 5 (*Theol. dom.*, III, pp. 200f.); *De Inc.*, II, c. 15 (*Theol. dogm.*, V, pp. 351f.).

This tradition is also taken up by the scholastic theologians, e.g., Bernard of Clairvaux, *De gratia et libero arbitrio*, c. 10 (*PL*, 182, 1019f.); Thomas Aquinas, *S.th.*, III, q. 3, a. 8, *Contr. Gent.*, IV, 42, III *Sent. dist.*, I, q. 2, a. 2; Bonaventura, *Breviloqu.* q. 4, c. 1: "The incarnation of the Word was most becoming for our restoration, in order that, as the human race had come into being by the uncreated Word and had fallen into sin by departing from the inspired Word, it might arise from its guilt by the incarnate Word."

An especially illuminating text is found in Cyril of Alexandria (*Thes. assert.*, XV, *PG*, 75, 292): "God, who knows what is to come and does not have to wait for it to happen, knew before the creation of the world, what would come to be even in the last times and so, just as he did not begin reflecting on us merely when we had come to exist, but made individual things real before the earth and the world were in existence—so, too, He had already premeditated ahead of time everything which concerns us. And with this foresight He set His Son as the cornerstone on which we were to be erected, thus to arise anew unto incorruptibility, we who through our own mortal failure would have fallen prey to corruptibility. For He knew even this, that through our own wickedness we would make ourselves mortal" (Cited in Schmaus, *Dogm.*, II, 492). See the citations from Athanasius and Leo at the end of this chapter.

So a powerful light shines back upon the chapter concerning creation. This is the reason why all the many passages on creation in Christ are always found in a redemption context. The reason why the Christian mystery of redemption is already present in a hidden way in the mystery of creation "hidden for ages in God who created all things" ("through Jesus Christ" as is very fittingly added in the majority of codices. Eph. 3.9). This is the reason why "we have redemption, the forgiveness of sins" explicitly in Him "in whom . . . all things were created" (Col. 1.14ff.), the reason why "the head of the body, the church" is He in whom "all things hold together" (Col. 1.17f.). For this reason creation is mysteriously pointed towards the Church. In fact, in creation the eternal salvific decree of God is already mysteriously pre-established—a decree which God, in Jesus Christ, had decided on for the good of all men through the Church.

Soiron (Kirche, p. 218): "This however does not mean that creation, and in it especially man (in sin) has ceased to be an incarnation of the *Word* even if only in a natural and naturally enfeebled and distorted form. Creation could not help sinking into nothingness if the Father were to take back the Word of Creation which He spoke in His Son—and if the Son were to take back the Word to which He creatively gave form in the creature—and if the Father and the Son were to take back the Holy Spirit which they breathed into creation. Burdened and corrupted by sin as creation and especially all men are, they continue to be incarnations of the divine Word—even if distorted and dishonored. And since they are still incarnations of the divine Word, the Father, Son and Holy Spirit have not totally drawn back from creation and from mankind, allowing them to sink into that nothingness. Therefore, even after the sin of Adam, creatures are incarnations of the divine Word, joined and bound in unity in the Word of God through His spirit. They still have an appointment to undergo integration in Christ the Logos into the one Christ, Head and body. Cf. also E. Walter, *Christus*, p. 68f.; F. Baader, *Werke* IV, 376; III, 349f.

It is indeed marvelous how God's singular plan of creation in Jesus Christ actually includes *all* His works since "*all* the paths of the Lord are steadfast love and faithfulness" (Ps. 25.10), and how creation is already included in the "for us men and for our salvation," being a work of God's divine mercy and grace, as is proclaimed by the antiphonal choirs of Ps. 136.

With Christ as the point of reference, the death of man can mean not only darkness but also light. The death of man takes on a positive or negative significance in reference to Christ's death. By His death we sinners are again reconciled with God (Rom. 5.10). Christ was uniquely without sin and uniquely not guilty of death. Nevertheless He was "made. . . . to be sin" (2 Cor. 5.21; cf. Rom. 8.3, Gal. 3.13f.). One "has died for all" (2 Cor. 5.14). He died "once for all" (Rom. 6.10).

Thereby He annihilated the power of death (2 Tim. 1.10; Heb. 2.14) and set us free from the law of death (Rom. 8.2). Whoever dies to sin and dies in Christ, that is, whoever by faith conforms himself in Baptism to His death (Rom. 6.1–14, Phil. 3.10) has actually left death behind. He must indeed die in a physical sense but this is only a consummation of the death of faith, and it has lost its sting for him (1 Cor. 15.55). In Christ the believer has already conquered death (1 Cor. 15.55). Whoever believes in Him has already passed over from death to life (Jn. 5.24; 1 Jn. 3.14). He will live even if he has died, he will not die in eternity (Jn. 11.25f.). So death will be overcome by sin's being overcome. Death, once a threat of damnation and a revelation of sin, turns into the opposite through faithful dying unto Christ, becoming an event of salvation leading to everlasting life.

This is—in shadow and figure—already mysteriously proclaimed in the *Old Testament*. In fact the Priestly text in Genesis hints at the disintegration of life on which the Yahwist puts such ominous emphasis. The Priestly writer teaches this by stressing a continuing decline of length of life among the Patriarchs; but the other possibility of death, death unto salvation, is dominant in this very same writer in the way in which he has the Patriarchs dying after a happy old age, "sated with life" (Abraham, Gen. 25.8; Ishmael, 25.17; Isaac, 35.29; Jacob: 49.33) This is hinted at later on in the phrase "gathered to his fathers," spoken of Moses (Dt. 31.16), David (2 Sam. 7.12; 1 Kgs. 2.10, 11.21; Acts 13.36), Solomon, (1 Kgs. 11.43) et al. The explanation of this is found in Heb. 11.13: "These all died in faith."

In the *New Testament* the hidden mystery has become manifest. Jesus Christ, who is the life, has appeared. In His life-giving death He has taken on Himself the death of all of us and so freed us from the law of death (Rom. 8.2). With this has ended the general law of God's punishment by immediate death, although the death of the Israelites remains as a warning (1 Cor. 10.5–12, 11.30; cf. also Acts 12.22f.; 2 Pet. 2.1, Jas. 1.15).

And so Jesus rescued from death the woman caught in adultery (Jn. 8.1–11) not because she did not deserve death—indeed stoning was what was commanded for this in God's law—but because *all* deserved it (" 'Let him who is without sin among you be the first to throw a stone at her'. . . But when they heard it, they went away, one by one. . ."). And the incarnate mercy of God has saved all from the death they deserved (" 'Neither do I condemn you, go and do not sin again' ").

The wish of the disciples that the sinful Samaritans be destroyed by fire was thoroughly justified in the light of the Old Testament ("As Elijah did" Lk. 9.54—God fulfilled it for Elijah). Jesus says in response: "You do not know what manner of spirit you are of" (9.55). This is certainly not the spirit of Jesus Christ. His Spirit is the Spirit of the saving justice of the merciful God: "The Son of Man came not to destroy men's lives but to save them" (9.56). He is "the resurrection and the life" (Jn. 11.25). "The passion of Christ is communicated to every baptized person so that he is healed just as if he himself had suffered and died" (Thomas, *S. Th.*, III, q. 69, a.2).

Whoever will not repent but would rather die in sin, whoever to the end of his life, given him despite his sin, does not utilize the respite—this man in his insolence calls down upon himself the judgment of death, the definitive judgment of damnation (Rom. 2.6–13). Now there takes place the full death, the death which man brought on himself by sin and whose effects were only held in check by the prevenient grace of Jesus Christ—the second death, the sea of fire (Rev. 20.14f.). The time of testing has run out, death has become final—against the desire of God—it is a death unto damnation and the denial of the grace of Jesus Christ becomes definitive. Death unto damnation is confirmed by the fearful judgment of God on the sinner: "Your will be done in eternity."

Even the damned sinner will have a continued existence in Jesus Christ. Where else would he have it unless he wants to sink back into nothingness? The τα παντα keeps its validity even here. But this being in Christ here implies an enforced and grudging genuflection before the one who remains the Lord of His being (Phil. 2.9–11; Eph. 1.19–23). It means being absurdly torn between his sinful and vain "wishing-to-be-in-himself" and his undeniable "being-in-Christ." Yet it remains a mystery, unsolved by any theology, how God, who here as always is at once just and merciful, can give being and permanence to those who have missed the goal for good.

At the end of this chapter let us cast another glance at the traditional controversy between Thomists and Scotists not insofar as it concerns the hypothetical order (cf. the chapter on creation), but in its bearing on the actually existing order. Is it possible to avoid using harmonizing expedients to achieve a facile compromise, and yet to do full justice to the concerns of both parties?

The concern of the *Scotists* is the irreducible primacy of Jesus Christ in all things, even before His historical incarnation. Christ is not for our sakes but we are for His sake. The primacy of Christ, far from being just a result of the fall into sin, is already a full reality in God's eternal counsel and in creation. One can do justice to this concern by colorfully and convincingly emphasizing the eternity of the one Jesus Christ and the being of creation in Jesus Christ—a fact that is ultimately to be based on the eternal character of the decision regarding the incarnation. This decision is, in reality, identical with the decision regarding redemption.

The *Thomistic* concern is with the incontrovertible redemptive character of the incarnation of the Son of God. Christ has come into the world not for Himself but for us—"for our salvation." The redemption is not a more or less necessary phenomenon accompanying the incarnation. We can do justice to this concern by seeing the existence of Jesus Christ as given in the counsel of God, and the being of creation in Christ as given in His redemptive character—a fact that is to be based on the eternal character of the decision regarding redemption which is in reality identical with the decision regarding the incarnation.

Féret: "The two theologies (Scotist and Thomist) are quite in accord in affirming the absolute pre-eminence and the universal kingship of Christ in the actually realized creation. Pre-eminence in the entire created order of nature and grace, pre-eminence also in the uncreated and divine order, that is, in divine predestination, in the predestination of all things in God" (p. 70). "Thomistic theology is far from laying less stress than others do on the absolute primacy of Christ. Its originality and value in this matter derive from its refusal, in full accordance with its realistic point of departure, to speculate on this pre-eminence in abstraction from the redemptive function of Christ. There are some treatises which proceed by dialectical analysis from the created act considered as, in a way, a priori. And they quite hypothetically put first among the decrees thus obtained an incarnation of the Word. Thus they easily give the impression that they attribute this pre-eminence to the incarnate Word as such, and not to the Word as it became incarnate in fact, that is, in a suffering and redemptive humanity." ("Apropos de la primauté du Christ," p. 71; cf. also Féret, "Creati in Christo Jesu").

In this way the *dangers* of either system, whenever they are too narrowly represented, are obviated. In other words, there can be either a platonizing consideration of Christ as a primal idea, and so forth, in relation to creation, a consideration which does not take full account of the *one* person of Jesus Christ the *Redeemer* (in an extreme Scotism); or the danger of a conception of the fall into sin which puts the unalterable eternal plan of God in question, and which knows very little of what to do with the statements of Sacred Scripture on Jesus Christ in creation (in an extreme Thomism). By avoiding these extremes, we remain in the factual and historical perspective. We avert hypothetical problems and at the same time come close to the mediating attempt at a solution (for example that of Molinas) which tries to stress the unity and the uniqueness of the divine decree.

Cf. P. Galtier, *De incarnatione,* pp. 456–482; M. Scheeben, *Dogm.,* V/2, 221–226; E. Mersch, *Théol. du corps mystique,* I, 165–170.

A classical patristic text, Athanasius, *Contra. Arian.,* II, cc. 75–77 (PG, 26,306ff.), may serve to summarize what we try to say about Jesus Christ, creation and sin. Similar texts can be found in Leo the Great, Sermo 22 in Nativ. Dom II, c. 1f. (*PL,* 54, 193ff.) and in Cyril of Alexandria (*Loc. cit.*).

"The expressions 'before time', 'before He made the earth', and 'before the earth was established', ought not to mislead anyone for he connected these words correctly with the expression 'He founded' and 'He created' because *it, in turn, touches upon the order of salvation in the flesh.* For the grace brought to us by the Redeemer has recently made its appearance as the Apostle had said and with His coming it has fallen to our share. It was prepared before we were in existence or rather before the foundation of the world, and the reason is totally good and wonderful. It is not proper that God should have come to our aid later, so that it would look as though He did not know our condition. The God of all things, *who created us through His Word,* knew our condition better than we and knew beforehand that after our initial justice we would later become transgressors of His law and on account of disobedience would be driven out of Paradise. *Therefore, out of His kindness to man and his goodness in the Word through which He created us, He prepared this our order of salvation in order that we would not remain totally dead though we had fallen (deceived by the serpent). But rather, in possession of the redemption and salvation prepared for us in the Word—we should again rise up and remain without death because He Himself was created for us as the beginning of ways and has become first born among brethren* and He Himself arises as first fruit from the dead. The blessed apostle Paul teaches this in his letter . . . How would He have elected us before we were, if we were not preformed beforehand in Him as He Himself has said? And how would He ever have predestined us for sonship before man was created if the Son Himself had not been established before time and had not taken over the order of salvation for our sake? Or how can we be, as the apostle asserts, like "those predestined to partake of the inheritance" if the Lord Himself were not constituted before time so that He could have the intention to take upon Himself, in the flesh and for us, every consequence of the Judge's condemnation of us so that we could, from then on, obtain sonship in Him? And how did we become receivers before all ages, when we were not yet in existence, coming into existence only in time, unless the grace coming to us was deposited in Christ? Therefore He will say at the judgment, when each one will receive on the basis of his acts and deeds: 'Come, O blessed of my Father, inherit the Kingdom prepared for you from the foundation of the world.' And how and in whom was it prepared before our beginning if not in the Lord, who moreover was established before time in order that we might partake of His life and grace, being built upon Him as well-hewn stones? And this has happened, as those even with a modest share of piety one after another realize, *so that, risen from a brief death, we might be able to live eternally. For earthly men this would be impossible if the hope of life and salvation had not been prepared before all time in Christ. . . .*

"Nor was it feasible that our life should be established in any other than in the Lord who is before all ages and through whom the ages have come into existence so that we, too, could inherit eternal life as it existed in Him, for God is good. And since He is always good, He willed this—He who found our helpless nature in need of His help in salvation. *Just as a wise builder,* intending to build a house, *at once takes counsel how he could restore the house in case, after its construction, it should suffer damage. Just as he takes precautions,* making all necessary materials available to the contractor for the restoration, so that even before its erection preparations are made for the restoration of the house—thus too *before our own day the renewal of our salvation was founded in Christ, in order that we might also be re-created in Him.* The counsel and intention was prepared before all time but the work was performed when necessity demanded it and the Savior arrived. For the Lord in Heaven Himself is going to stand in place of all of us, taking us into eternal life" (*Ath.* I, 225ff.).

24. THE WRETCHEDNESS OF SIN

Even sin stands under the control of God's plan of salvation in Jesus Christ. In creation, God in Jesus Christ had already obviated sin so that its fatal power could not have its full effect. Man, by sinning, has plunged into the abyss and he owes it to the restraining grace of Jesus Christ that he can remain on earth and remain human.

This divine order of salvation, full of marvelous mysteries, so far from being an excuse to take sin any less seriously, is reason to take it all the more so. Certainly man remains man even in sin. He "lives" on but his life lacks what is vital, lacks what makes life worth living, the grace and peace of the Lord. The one life not worth living is the life of the sinner. With good reason sin has always been designated mors animae (*D* 175, 798). This man, seemingly alive, lives off his death, lives a life the core of which is attacked by death. For this reason the sinner is called a corpse by Sacred Scripture—even though by the prevenient grace of Jesus Christ he continues to exist in the body. (Eph. 2.1, 5, Col. 2.13).

Cf. also the strong expressions of Augustine; on this, see M. Strohm, *Der Begriff der "natura vitiata" bei Augustin,* and N. Merlin, *St. Augustin et les dogmes du péché originel et de la grâce.*

Precisely because God has from the beginning established the permanence of all in Jesus Christ, it is even truer here than elsewhere to say that there is no peccatum philosophicum in this order (merely unsuitable to rational nature and right reason, *D* 1290). Rather any sin is also a sin against the Creator of this nature. For this reason too, it is a principal truth that in this order sin is never sin merely against God or subsistent being, but also and always (consciously or not) against God incarnate. It is never just sin against an order of nature or creation, but also and always and principally against the One in whom this order of nature or creation has its permanence (Col. 1.17). It is never merely a sin against a general law but always and principally against the One who is *the* Way and *the* Truth (Jn. 14.6). We have all helped kill the Son of God. What happened on Golgotha happens in every sin. It is for the sins of the whole world that He has died.

Rondet: "Saint Paul's morality is based less on natural reasons (1 Cor. 6.9; Rom. 1.28) than on the great principles of his theological and spiritual teaching. To sin is to extinguish or to grieve the Spirit (1 Thess. 5.19; Eph. 4.30). To be virtuous is to please God, to offer Him a holy sacrifice in a body and a spirit without blemish (Rom. 12.1), to imitate Christ (Rom. 15.3–7). Fornication is condemned for reasons which are entirely mystical (1 Cor. 6.15–20). The morality of marriage (Eph. 5.21–33) and the family (Eph. 6.1–9) and social morality in general (Eph. 4.1), including the condemnation of lying (Eph. 4.25), is based on the fruitful concept that Christians are members of one another and members of Christ" (*Gratia Christi*, pp. 60f.).

Since God has from the beginning established the permanence of all in Jesus Christ and since as a result the whole of mankind in its Head stands before God from the beginning as a unity, any sin against the Head is also a sin against the body. Even the most personal and secret sin is not a private sin but rather a sin of social, that is, antisocial character. Every sin has an ecclesiological aspect, is an attack on the other members of the one body, a burden for the Church. The direct and visible damage caused by man and the consequences of his evil are only the surface phenomena of a deep-seated process which destroys the communion.

The Catholic Church has at all times taken the social and ecclesiological character of sin very seriously. Evidence of this— besides the Confiteor of the Roman mass—is the early Church's practice of penance. The latest research in the history of dogma has shown that in the primitive church's practice of penance, the reconciliation with the Church (pax ecclesiastica) played a decisive role.

Cf. A. Landgraf, *Sünde und Trennung von der Kirche in der Früh-scholastik;* B. Poschmann, *Paenitentia Secunda; Busse und letzte Ölung;* M. Schmaus, *Reich Gottes und Busssakrament;* K. Rahner, *Vergessene Wahrheiten über das Buss-Sakrament*, and the articles cited there on the Sacrament of penance, Tertullian's, Cyprian's, Origen's, and that of the *Didaskalia Apostolorum*. The ecclesiological aspect of sin has been stressed, too, by B. Häring, *Gesetz Christi*, pp. 124f., 354,

et al.; J. Beumer, "Die persönliche Sünde in sozial-theologischer Sicht";
de Lubac, *Katholizismus als Gemeinschaft,* pp. 78–79, etc.

Whether consciously or unconsciously sin is always sin against
Jesus Christ. That is, man sins against the One in whom he and all
men have been created and in whom he has permanence together
with all men. But he is spared by this One so that even in sin he
will have permanence in Him and will not perish. Indeed, the One
in whom he and all men have their permanence from the first—
this One will, in the fullness of time, become a man among sinners
in order to make His creature live for Him anew and more fully.
Herein lies the mystery of the incomprehensible sentence in the
Wisdom of Solomon (15.1–2): "But thou, our God, art kind and
true, patient, and ruling all things in mercy. For even if we sin we
are thine, knowing thy power; but we will not sin, because we
know that we are accounted thine."

As Bernard of Clairvaux expressed it: "But neither in this age could
a like similitude (of the divine image) be found anywhere, but the
image would still have been lying prostrate here foul and ugly if that
woman of the Gospel had not lighted a lamp—that is, if Wisdom,
appearing in the flesh, had not swept the house clean of its blemishes,
seeking the coin which He had lost (Lk. 15.8)—that is, His image,
which, robbed of its pristine beauty, lay, as it were, hidden in the dust,
dirty under a hide of sin. When He had found it, He cleaned it and
removed it from the realm of dissimilitude; and restoring it to its
pristine splendor, He made it like in glory to the saints, yes, made it
like Himself in every respect as of yore; for that Scripture, indeed, was
fulfilled: 'We know that when he shall appear, we shall be like him;
for we shall see him as he is' (1 Jn. 3.2). And in truth, to whom should
this work more fittingly belong than to the Son of God, who, being
the brightness of the glory and the very stamp of the Father's nature,
upholding all things by His word, readily equipped both to transform
the unsightly image and to strengthen the weak creature? And putting
to flight the darkness of sin, He made it wise again, and by the power
of the word He made it strong against the reign of demons. There
came therefore that very beauty to which free will had to be conformed; for in order to have its pristine beauty restored, it had to be
transformed by that beauty from which it had also been formed. But
the beauty is Wisdom. . . ." (*De gratia et libero arbitrio,* chap. X;
PL, 182, 1019f.).

And in the *Soliloquia Animae ad Deum,* then ascribed to
Augustine, it says: "Chap. 5: . . . All things that were made were
made by the Word. And how well were they made? 'And God saw
everything that he had made, and it was very good' (Gen. 1.31). All
things that are, were made by the Word. And all things that were

made by the Word, are very good. 'And without him nothing was made' (Jn. 1.3), because there is nothing good without the highest good, but evil is where good is not, which certainly is nothing, because nothing else is evil than what is free from good, just as nothing else is blindness than what is deprived of light. Evil therefore is nothing, because certainly it was made without the Word, without whom nothing is made. But that is evil which lacks that good by which all good things were made—namely, the Word, by which all things that are, were made. But the things that are not were not made by Him, and therefore they are nothing. And therefore evil things are those which were not made, because all things that are, were made by the Word; and all things were made good by the Word. Since therefore all things were made by the Word, evil things are not by Him; it remains therefore that all things that were not made are not good, because all things that were made are good. And therefore evils are not, because they were not made; and therefore they are nothing, because without the Word nothing was made. Evil therefore is nothing; because it was not made. But of what nature is evil, inasmuch as it was not made? Because evil is freedom from the Word, by which the good was made. Therefore to be without the Word is evil, which is not being, because without the Word there is nothing. But what is it to be separated from the Word? If you wish to know this, hear what the Word is. The Word of God says, 'I am the way, the truth, and the life' (Jn. 14.6). To be separated from the Word, therefore, is being without the way, without the truth, without life. And therefore without Him there is nothing and therefore evil, because it is being separated from the good, by which all things were made very good. But to be separated from the Word, by whom all things were made, is nothing else than to be wanting and to cross over from having been made to being abandoned, because without Him there is nothing. As often, therefore, as you deviate from the good, you separate yourself from the Word, because He is good; and therefore you accomplish nothing, because you are without the Word, without which nothing is made. . . .

"Chap. 6: . . . I am wretched; I did not understand; and this because I was without Thee, O Word, without whom nothing was made, by whom all things are preserved, without whom all things are annihilated. For as all things were made by Him, and without Him nothing was made, so by Him all things that exist are preserved by Him, whether in heaven, or on earth, or in the sea, and in all the abysses. Neither does part cling to part in a stone nor in any creature, but they are preserved by the Word, by whom all things were made. Let me therefore cling to Thee, O Word, that Thou mayest preserve me; because when I withdrew from Thee, I perished within myself, unless Thou who didst make me hadst made me over again. I sinned, Thou didst visit me; I fell, Thou didst lift me up; I was ignorant, Thou didst teach me; I did not see, Thou didst enlighten me" (*PL*, 40, 868f.).

The theology of justification slowly emerges again. It is probably clear by now that the discussion of Jesus Christ and of creation had their point. Now it will be possible to interpret correctly the starting point of justification, the sinner, and to assay sin in its final power and in its ultimate impotence.

Sin is described by Trent as the rule of the devil and of death through which man loses his innocence and becomes a child of wrath (*D* 793). Sin, as *aversio a Deo et conversio ad creaturas*, drives directly toward total death and the ruin of the creature. It means much more than deprivation of an ornamental accident or of a white robe of grace. It means an attack on substance and heart. And because it is an attack on God it is really an attack on man, an attempt at sinful *self-destruction*. That is *the final radicality and power of sin*. Yet, this is the place to state clearly with Trent: "If anyone says that after Adam's sin man's free will was destroyed and lost . . . let him be anathema" (*D* 815; see *D* 793, 797). The Council did not wish with this to gloss over sin as something harmless. If the sinner remains man and retains his human nature, it is not because he pursued his destruction half-heartedly (man had indeed sinned sufficiently in a fundamental way); it is not because he himself destroyed the indulgence of God (man has indeed deserved to be cut off by God); it is not because he himself saved a final trace of goodness (for he is indeed evil in his heart, in his very center.)

"*For my name's sake* I defer my anger, *for the sake of my praise* I restrain it for you, that I may not cut you off" (Isa. 48.9; see Ezek. 20.13–14). Here with all its sharpness is the pronouncement of the Second Council of Orange, can. 22: "*Those things which are peculiar to men*. No one has anything of his own except lying and sin. But if man has any truth and justice, it is from that fountain for which we ought to thirst in this desert, that having drunk some drops of water from it, we may not falter on the way" (*D* 195). Man remains man because the mercy and grace of God spared him and in patience preserved him for justification, that is, through the merciful power of Jesus Christ which already had in creation a preventive and inhibiting effect. Canon 14 says: "No wretched person is freed from misery, however small, unless he is first reached by the mercy of God, just as the Psalmist says: 'Let thy mercy, Lord, speedily anticipate us' and also: 'My God, His mercy will prevent me'" (*D* 187. See *D* 189).

Gregory the Great: "Holy men know that they were born of corruptible seed after the fall of their parent, and not because of their own virtue but by grace from above, which came to them first, they were changed for better vows or works. And whatever of evil they recognize as being in themselves, they perceive to be because of their mortal ancestry; but whatever of good they see in themselves, they recognize as a gift of immortal grace, and, for the gift received, they become debtors of Him who by His prevenient grace enabled them to want the good they desired; and, by continuing His blessing, granted them the gift of being able to do what they wish" (*Moral.*, XXII, 20; *PL*, 76, 225).

The order of being remains intact because the One in whom it has permanence from its beginning conquers any dissolution with His mercifully active No. The destroying power of sin comes to nothing, not through the firmness of man but rather through the cornerstone Jesus Christ, who in the very core of sin allows grace to be "victorious" (Rom. 5.20). "Although we were displeasing we were loved so that there might be produced in us (something) by which we might please" (*D* 198). In this the *ultimate impotence of sin* is revealed.

In regard to the interpretation of *II Orange* (and, correspondingly, of XVI Carthage and of the Index of Celestine, which follow the same line), it is obvious that there is, of necessity, a vital difference of purpose and emphasis between the ancient anti-Pelagian documents and the modern anti-Protestant and anti-Jansenist ones. But to distort this into a real contradiction, should this idea occur to anybody, is entirely out of order because Trent, for instance, consciously takes II Orange for its point of departure (for instance, in the first three canons of the decree on justification, *D* 811–813). The Catholic dogmatic theologian cannot but take the old as well as the new documents in their unrestricted and undiminished meaning and try to articulate them. II Orange can be correctly seen only in the light of Trent, and Trent can be properly evaluated only in view of II Orange. That is why we have attempted to take such seemingly opposite statements as *D* 815 and *D* 195 and, without any diminution of the one or the other, take them together at face value. Another example of this follows below.

The dogmatic value of II Orange is disputed. For it is doubtful whether only the professio fidei or also the canons, and again whether all the canons or only the first eight, were approved by Boniface II (*D* 200, a and b). On this question (and also on the interpretation of the individual canons) see the writings of J. Hefele-Leclercq, *Histoire de l'Eglise*, II, 1085–1110; G. de Plinval, *L'activité doctrinale dans l'Eglise Gallo-Romaine;* P. Lejay, *Césaire d'Arles;* E. Amann, "Semi-pélagiens," in *DTC;* G. Fritz, "Orange," in *DTC;* M. Cappuyns, *L'origine des capitula;* J. Ernst, *Die dogmatische Geltung;* K. Rahner, *Augustinus und die Semipelagianer;* Chene, *Semi-Pélagianisme;* L. R. Piccorelli, *Valor dogmatico.*

According to the most recent investigation by Piccorelli, the following Catholic dogmatic theologians take the whole document as de fide definita: Leclercq, Malnory, Morin, De Groot, Huygens, Natalis, Lercher, Godoy; as de fide: Billuart, Noris, Beraza, Hurter. This list may not be complete but, no matter how the historical question may eventually be decided, Catholic dogmatic theologians agree that the whole document is an integral statement of Catholic teaching—which must not be disputed by anyone. In Denzinger's *Enchiridion* it is said of the Council: "This Council, approved by Boniface II. obtained such authority in the Church that it is worthily held as an infallible norm of faith." Major significance for the history of dogma attaches to the fact that, because the Council was not contained in the majority of medieval collections or compilations, it was unknown to theologians between the 12th Century and the second third of the 16th Century. In general these theologians do not distinguish between Pelagianism and semi-Pelagianism. Even Thomas was aware of semi-Pelagianism only beginning with the *Summa c. Gentes*. It is not before about 1600 that the term "semi-Pelagianism" made its appearance. Cf. H. Bouillard, *Conversion et Grâce,* pp. 92–122, on this whole development.

Now for another look at Canon 22: "No one has anything of his own except lying and sin," and so on (*D* 195). This is considered the crux interpretationis because of its opposition to the condemned proposition 27 of Baius ("Free will without the aid of divine grace avails for nothing except sinning"): *D* 1027; cf. Le Bachelet, "Baius," in *DTC* I, 83–86. For clarification, cf. J. Ernst, *Die Werke und Tugenden der Ungläubigen nach Aug.,* (Appendix), and "Erklärung des XXII Canons von Orange"; Hefele, II, 1100–1103; Fritz, cc. 1098f.; Amann, cc. 1846–1848; Rondet, *Gratia Christi,* p. 161.

We intend to follow the interpretation of Ripalda, Kleutgen, Berlage, Schwand, Hefele, et al. as summed up by Hefele: "When, therefore, only the natural forces in man are involved, the result is only the opposite of morality, namely sin and falsehood" (p. 1100). This interpretation appears to conform better to the Augustinian context from which Canon 22 has been taken (cf. Augustine, *In Joan.,* tract. V, n. 1; *PL,* 35, 1414). Thus the text need not be diminished. The first and negative part of the assertion states that all the good man has in himself and not by grace (in the widest sense) is sin; or vice versa, sin is only what is not by virtue of grace but rather what man has on his own. The second and positive part states that what is of good in us is due to the grace of Jesus Christ. Peccatum then is understood here in the strict sense. Rodet is correct in rejecting the anachronistic interpretation which suggests that the statement had validity only in the "supernatural" sphere. (*Gratia Christi,* p. 161).

And, concerning Baius' proposition 27 (*D* 1027), it seems questionable to insist that this proposition is only partially condemned and does not in any way have to be heretical ("some of them could be maintained in some way," *D* 1080) and that the consultants of Pius V did not have in mind the proceedings of the Council of Orange which had just been rediscovered (Amann, col. 1847f.). Or so we think.

D 1027 is a chapter heading in Baius' work, "De virtutibus impiorum": "That free will without the aid of divine grace avails for nothing except sinning" (lib. II, c. 8, p. 70). Condemned is the statement: "Free will can do no good before justification" (cf. the condemned sentence 35: "Everything the sinner or the slave of sin does is sin," *D* 1035; and *D* 1025, 1065): that is, free will cannot do good without the grace of justification. (Moreover, Baius very clearly did not accept any true gratia habitualis.) The question remains undecided whether the free will could do good without any grace. Baius did not express himself on this point because a "good" work before justification was for him out of the question (*D* 1035). Baius' chief opponent, Ripalda, resolutely defended (with Orange) the proposition that in the present world order, free will could not do good without some kind of grace (*De ente supernaturali,* disp. 20). Marietti's *Commentary on I–II,* q. 109, a. 2, cites, in support of the opinion that in statu naturae corruptae no good work could happen without grace, Capreolus, Contenson, Ariminensis, Gregorius, Vasquez. Rondet holds that the "sine gratia" in this passage of Thomas Aquinas meant gratia habitualis (*Gratia Christi,* p. 217; on the development of doctrine in Scholasticism, cf. Auer, *Entwicklung der Gnadenlehre,* II, 8–26; cf. I, 237).

In this interpretation, the verdict is in accord with both Canon 22 of Orange (*D* 195) and also with the condemnation of Abelard, who had said "that free will is sufficient in itself for any good thing" (*D* 373). With this point of reference one can also understand correctly *D* 1028. On *D* 1388–91, cf. Berbuir, *Natura Humana,* pp. 63–65.

Hence the terminus a quo of justification is the sinner—and not a man who could hold firm in one way or another by his own power, who at least could exist without Christ "as man," having preserved for himself some shred of autonomy. It is the sinner, the man who owes to Jesus Christ all the being left to him despite his sin—the Christ who has sustained it for him for his justification. So the sinner—despite his ability to choose—is not capable on any level of any kind of self-justification. As Trent expressed it at the beginning of the canons on justification: "If anyone says that, without divine grace through Jesus Christ, man can be justified before God by his own works, whether they were done by his natural powers or by the light of the teaching of the Law: let him be anathema" (*D* 811). And by the Council of Orange in Canon 7: "If anyone affirms that without the illumination and the inspiration of the Holy Spirit—who gives to all sweetness in consenting to and believing in the truth—through the strength of nature he can think anything good which pertains to the salvation of eternal life, as he should, or choose, or consent to salvation, that is to the evangelical proclamation, he is deceived by the heretical spirit, not understanding the voice of God speaking in the Gospel: 'Without me you can do nothing'; and that of the Apostle: 'Not that we are fit to think everything by ourselves as of ourselves, but our sufficiency is from God'" (*D* 180).

Here, for the sake of specifying our position, we must for once add a polemical distinction. The fundamental error in the Reformers' stand on sin was not that they took sin too "tragically." Rather, they did not take it "tragically" enough, because they were unaware what an "overwhelming" expenditure of grace is necessitated. The Catholic can agree with the Reformers to this extent, that without grace (in an all-encompassing sense, not in the sense of a "justifying" grace) man is nothing. For then man would indeed be without Christ and, as we saw above, without Christ man would not be. It is true, without grace man would be nothing: ". . . in order to confess the grace of God, from whose work and honor nothing should be entirely taken away" (Index of Celestine, *D* 142).

Yet the Reformers erred when they conceived of the condition of the sinner as one *absolutely without grace*. They overlooked the fact that even the sinful creature exists in Jesus Christ. They overlooked the fact that "although we were displeasing we were loved, so that there might be produced in us (something) by which we might please" (II Orange: *D* 198). They were not radical enough. If sinful man were in an *absolutely graceless* state, then man would not be left like a piece of wood with no will, but rather would be cut off from the earth. But for the Reformers this was obviously in conflict with the evidence and therefore they could not go that far. If they had been radical enough in their thinking they would have affirmed, not only that the sinner deserved to be left to his own resources but that he deserved to be cut off from the earth; that God, however, in Jesus Christ, had allowed grace to be victorious even in sin, preserving the sinner from destruction. With Trent they would then have allowed the sinner the "freedom" to convert himself, not on the basis of a Pelagian autonomy, but rather on the basis of the conserving mercy of Jesus Christ. This was the dominant concern of Trent in its definition: Jesus Christ, in His grace, wills that man should not be left to himself, inert and resigned, but that he should work out his salvation in the spirit of humble penance solely through the power of Christ.

The sinner's inability to achieve any self-justification needs closer definition. We shall answer three questions: (1) Is the sinner free or not? (2) What about the sinner's existence? (3) What about what the sinner does?

25. THE RUIN OF MAN

Is man in sin *free or unfree?* The important role terminology plays at this point is easily overlooked. "Freedom" is known to be an ambiguous concept, and not just since the days of liberalism; it was already so in the time of Jesus. When Jesus Christ proclaimed to His countrymen His word that the truth would make them free, they replied in anger that they were already free: "How is it that you say, 'You will be made free'?" And Jesus answered them: "Truly, truly, I say to you, every one who commits sin is a slave to sin . . . So if the Son makes you free, you will be free indeed" (Jn. 8.31–36).

As Chap. 20 made clear, Sacred Scripture, as the primary norm for theology, is the primary norm for theological terminology as well. The reason is not that the terminology of Jesus Christ (or the sacred writers) has a unique significance as a product of the personal intelligence and depth of religious insight of this particular man. For this terminology is not simply a new invention, but a given fact—since it is the ordinary means of communication for a given community. But though this is a human word, shaped by a limited collectivity, it is at the same time, and in all its historical limitations, the inspired Word of God. As such it has universal bearing, is valid and normative for all men, all times and climes. And since the inspiration of the Spirit does not only affect an abstract content, but a content which has a particular literary guise, it also affects terminology. This, too, has its share in the normative character of the Word of God, especially insofar as it contains in itself contents which are theological. The terminology of Sacred Scripture is of course not "scientific" terminology (in the sense of an exclusive and meticulously observed ordering between specific content and specific concepts) but rather a terminology (though in no way incomprehensible, let alone irrational) of extrascientific human discourse. Like human discourse, Sacred Scripture determines what is meant, not primarily by the place which it assigns a term in the world of concepts; rather it reformulates its meaning at any given moment out of the live totality of the complex of facts at issue within the *range* of meaning which it allows a term to cover. In this of course it aims with divine freedom less at a delimiting and fixing than at a sounding of dimensions and an increasing of range, and in so doing aims at a concentration of verbal meanings. To this extent scriptural terminology shares in the normative character of the Word of God. With this, then, the use of extrabiblical categories is by no means ruled out. To renounce theology in favor of the Word of God would signify a wish to react otherwise than as a thinking man to God's utterance. Thus it becomes even more important to make intelligible and obvious the entire dependence of theology—an inevitable development—on the Word of God even down to details of terminology. All philosophical and theological categories are to be measured against the categories of the Word of God.

The theologian in using the term "freedom" will use for his standard the original range of meaning and the original sense it has in Sacred Scripture. He will not attach another meaning to it without very weighty reasons. Investigation of the New Testament usage of ελευθερια, ελευθερος, ελευθερον shows immediately that in the whole of the New Testament (as before in the Old), these words never mean freedom of choice.

The entries in the lexicons by F. Zorell, W. Bauer, and H. Schlier (*TWNT*) show that in the New Testament it means either social and political freedom (in opposition to being a slave or a political subject) or and more especially (in theologically important statements) religious-moral freedom, the specifically Christian freedom of the children of God. The "freedom" to do evil is revealed as servitude (2 Pet. 2.19).

W. Rudolph (*Menschenbild des Alten Testaments*, p. 241f. summarizes the viewpoint of the Old Testament as follows: "At no moment in the history of Israel was it dismissed from its duty to the Lord, Yahweh. It is not by chance that the term 'freedom', a slogan in the Greek world, occurs only once in the Old Testament (chufscha: Lev. 19.20) and then merely as designating the social aspect of 'free' in distinction from 'slave' (the same is true for the more frequent adjectives chofschi and also naqi which can occasionally be translated as 'free'; it always means only a negative freedom from specific obligations and never expresses anything positive). Though it is consequently not surprising that while the theological lexicon (*TWNT*) normally gives the Old Testament root of Greek terms, in regard to eleutheros there is no reference whatever to the Old Testament."

Cf. S. Lyonnet, *Liberté chrétienne et loi nouvelle;* R. Egenter, *Von der Freiheit der Kinder Gottes;* H. Schlier, *Das vollkommene Gesetz der Freiheit.*

When we want to discuss theologically *that* freedom of which the Holy Spirit Himself speaks, then we talk not of "freedom of choice" but rather of the "freedom of the children of God." "Freedom of choice" is presupposed on every page of Sacred Scripture and for this reason is indispensable to theology; that goes without saying. The great themes of Scripture such as covenant, guilt, punishment, and repentance are meaningless without it. Just as man and even the sinner can think "rightly," so he can act "freely." Yet this is not what Sacred Scripture calls acting "freely."

We do not intend to eliminate the terminology which understands the word "freedom" in the primary meaning of "freedom of choice." The Church has its good reasons for using the word "freedom" also in this sense—especially since Scholasticism, because "freedom of choice" forms the anthropological subsoil of Christian freedom. Without this subsoil it loses (as was just pointed out from scripture) its total meaning as Christian freedom. The Church, precisely in defending "freedom of choice," has taken under her protection "the freedom of the children of God." Thus since the early Middle Ages the Church has set itself against the various varieties of predestinationism, for example, against Spanish heretics in the eighth century (*D* 300); then in the ninth century against Gottschalk and others (*D* 316); and again against Scotus Erigena (*D* 320ff.); in the fourteenth century against Eckhart (*D* 514). In this context the use of the term "freedom" for "freedom of choice" is a legitimate extension of the biblical concept of freedom. (In connection with the Reformation, the concept "freedom of choice" was more precisely defined against Jansenism: *D* 1094, 1291; and also in I Vatican *D* 1805.) But it does not follow that, because of this, scriptural terminology was to be abandoned. After all, the Church never ceased proclaiming "the freedom of the children of God." But perhaps some misunderstandings might be eliminated through a terminological clarification proceeding simultaneously from Sacred Scripture and Catholic tradition.

E. Gilson (*Intr. à l'étude de S. Aug.*) has explained how, for Augustine, the liberum arbitrium is directly identified with the human capacity to choose, and is thus canceled neither by sin nor by grace (pp. 205–208). But for Augustine liberum arbitrium does not yet mean libertas. In the sinner there is liberum arbitrium, but no libertas. Man obtains libertas through grace. While liberum arbitrium also allows for the possibility of sinning, making man responsible for his sin, libertas excludes committing sins. Libertas means actually freedom from sin. Thus Augustine, according to Gilson. It is possible that Gilson has exaggerated the contrast between liberum arbitrium and libertas and that his interpretation does not correspond with all the texts (on the Augustinian concept of freedom see also de Broglie. *De fine ultimo*, pp. 84–87; Merlin, *S. Augustin et les dogmes du péché originel et de la grâce*, pp. 376f.). But it probably has to be conceded that we can find such a fundamental distinction in Augustine. In any case, this terminology has (as Gilson himself observed: pp. 212–214) the obvious shortcoming that the same adjective, liber, must be used both for liberum arbitrium and libertas.

Gilson goes on to note that the Augustinian terminology is clarified and fixed in Anselm. According to Anselm, man always has an arbitrium but this arbitrium is not always liber. (Cf. *De libero arbitrio*, c. 2; 3, *PL*, 158, 492–494.) Libertas (arbitrii) is therefore synonymous with "the ability not to sin" (potestas non peccandi).

In Thomas liberum arbitrium is used in the sense of "freedom of choice," and often libertas is, too. However, the biblical and Christian concept of freedom operates in the terms liberatio, liberare (e.g., *S.th.*, III, q. 46, a. 1–3; q. 49, a. 1–3; q. 52, a. 5–8; q. 69, a. 2; *Summa c. Gent.*, III, cc. 157–158), but also in the word libertas itself, that is, in the commentaries where Thomas distinguishes libertas corporalis from libertas spiritualis (libertas gratiae); (in Jn. 8.31–36, lect. IV, 1–4; cf. also in Rom. 6.18, 22; 8.2, 21). Interesting in this connection are the statements, "not to be able to sin does not diminish freedom" (II–II, q. 84, a. 4, ad 1), and "To desire evil is neither freedom nor a part of freedom, although it is a kind of sign of freedom" (*De ver.*, q. 22, a. 6 co).

More recent Catholic theologians clearly see the terminological problem. For example, Staudenmaier makes the distinction of "a double freedom," freedom "as capacity," (= "freedom of choice"), and freedom "as condition" (*Encyclopedie*, pp. 712ff.; cf. *Dogm.*, III, 207; II, 353–357). Kuhn places "freedom" between "necessity" and "fiat" (*Lehre v. d. Gnade*, p. 113). Baader distinguishes "free choice" from "truly free will" (*Vorlesungen über spekulative Dogm.*, *Werke*, VIII, 108), "formal freedom or freedom of choice" and "freedom of being" (VIII, 120), "freedom of choice" and "effective freedom" (*Erläuterungen*, XII, 94), "ability to choose evil" and "freed from the choice between evil and good" (XII, 334).

On the basis of this biblically grounded Catholic tradition we propose to make a terminological distinction between "the capacity to choose" ("ability to choose"—"arbitrium"; adj. "capable of choice," "capable of decision," etc.) and "freedom" ("libertas"; adj. "free").

Using this terminology, the following theological statements can be made: In God capacity to choose and freedom are identical, insofar as God necessarily would choose good. With men of this world, however, capacity to choose means the ability to choose between good and evil (and here the philosophical and theological problem of determinism comes up). The capacity to choose will be used either well (with grace) or poorly (against grace). If it is used well, the capacity to choose is therefore "free" (1 Cor. 7.22; 2 Cor. 3.17); if it is used poorly, it is therefore "unfree" (Jn. 8.34; Rom. 6.6–17). According to this then, even in sin the capacity to choose still remains preserved in man, who continues to exist by the grace of Jesus Christ. It is truly present even though weakened. Yet man is not "free" but a "slave of sin" (Jn. 8.34). The sinner's arbitrium is therefore a servum arbitrium (which has nothing to do with determinism).

The lost freedom is restored to the sinner in justification through Jesus Christ. The Son makes us free (Jn. 8.36), through His Holy Spirit (Rom. 8.2; 2 Cor. 3.17), in the word produced by the Spirit (Gal. 5.12; Jn. 8.31–32), and in the sign produced by the Spirit (Rom. 6.11). Therefore, we are free from sin (Rom. 6.18–23), from Law (Rom. 7.3–4; 8.2; Gal. 2.4; 4.21–31; 5.1–13), and from death (Rom. 6.21–22; 8.21). This freedom consists in being bound as a servant of Jesus Christ and God, but it is precisely this state of being bound—in opposition to the state of being bound to sin—which frees (1 Cor. 7.22; 1 Pet. 2.16; Rom. 6.16–18). This is the only true freedom, the freedom unto which the Son has made us free (Jn. 8.36); the freedom unto which Christ has set us free (Gal. 5.1); the freedom which we have in Christ (Gal. 2.4).

In this light only is the arbitrium of the justified man a liberum arbitrium. This is not something opposed to grace; it is a fruit of grace. The more man stands under grace, the freer he becomes. Just as the sinner in hell will be finally and completely "unfree" and a servant of sin, so too the justified in heaven will be finally and completely free, with "the glorious liberty of the children of God" (Rom. 8.21).

The careful reader can easily distinguish these explanations from similar sounding statements which have been condemned. The point is radically to exclude any determinism (even in a limited, Jansenist sense). What we can say in favor of the terminology we are using is this: in close conformity with the New Testament, the term "freedom" retains its eminently theological meaning. The servitude of the sinner will not, however, be made light of or blurred by this terminology. Is it not dangerous to call him "free" who is designated as "slave" in Scripture? Besides, this terminology—as was demonstrated—is solidly grounded in Catholic tradition and facilitates a stand for Augustine against the Jansenist position. Finally, it does justice to the various official expressions of dogma which appear to contradict each other. It is defined in Trent (*D* 815; compare the Council of Arles, *D* 160a, where the same thing had already been said; see further *D* 776, 793, 1065, 1094, 1291, 1298, 1388) that in sin a real capacity to choose is preserved though in a weakened state—that is, even the sinner can and must continue choosing. It is also taught that man has in sin lost freedom (see the Index of Celestine, *D* 130: "natural powers . . . deceived by his powers of free choice . . ."). In II Orange, *D* 186 (". . . [have] been lost"), in ratification of which we have Boniface II (*D* 200a) "that [faith] has remained in the free will of man from Adam—which it is a sin to say—and is not even now conferred on individuals by the bounty of God's mercy—and the Council of Quiersy *D* 317 ("The freedom of will which we lost in the first man, we have received back through Christ our Lord; and we have free will for good, preceded and aided by grace, and we have free will for evil, abandoned by grace. Moreover, because freed by grace and by grace healed from corruption, we have free will"; see in this connection *D* 105, 134, 135, 181, 194).

The *whole* man has sinned, not only his sensual nature or reason or will, not only his body or soul, but man as a *person* (". . . and that it was the *whole* Adam, both body and soul, who was changed for the worse . . ." *D* 788; II Orange, *D* 174). For man is entirely "sinful flesh" although he did remain man. He is "evil from his youth" (Gen. 8.21), from the inside out, evil in his "heart"—in the center of his person, in his core (cf. Mk. 7.21–23; Mt. 6.23; 9.4; 12.35; 15.19; 20.15; Rom. 1.21; 2 Cor. 3.5). The whole man is "carnal, sold under sin" (Rom. 7.14); "by nature" he is one of the "children of wrath" (Eph. 2.3), "nothing good dwells" in him (Rom. 7.18).

Cf. W. Schauf, *Sarx. Der Begriff "Fleisch" beim Apostel Paulus;* especially the use of the adjective σαρκινος and σαρκικός pp. 119 and 168f. (and in this connection 1 Cor. 3.3f.).

Also in this perspective, there appears the inability of man to accomplish any self-justifying work of salvation.

K. Rahner says on the question of how freedom can belong to one with whom it is not identical:

"There is no need to spend any time here in showing that the following approach provides no solution. Someone might say: The will is an accident of the substance of the soul (= nature), and freedom is its modality; consequently this cannot be conceived of in such a way that the question should ever arise as to how the freedom could be 'eccentric' to the person. The starting-point of this answer is sound enough in certain respects; yet 'freedom' remains in its intrinsic ontological root supremely central to the person, and thus the question we have tried to put remains. If anyone doubts this, he should consider the fact that this modality of the second act of this accident is, simply speaking, master of the destiny and the decision of the *whole* reality of the free being, and that the free act can thus never be made 'central' enough" (Karl Rahner, *Theological Investigations,* vol. I, pp. 161–162, n. 2).

F. A. Staudenmaier: "Through sin the creaturely spirit renounced what for him is both the beginning and final principle, the first cause and final goal. With this there took place in his primal and fundamental relationship, a total perversion whereby the eternal divine order itself was perverted. The spirit who has fallen from God ceases to acknowledge in God the cause and goal of his being and life. In doing so, however, he ceases to let himself be determined by God and to follow Him in his acts of commission and omission. With one word the divine has ceased to be the ultimate principle of the finite spirit. This perversion penetrates into the total being of the spirit, it permeates the whole order of the life which has deviated from its primal source, so that in this there is nothing more to be found of what is *of* God, *according* to God, and *because* of God. Every reference to God has been lost and what is left is confusion and contradiction. This is in the nature and interest of sin and it happens even where it does not enter into consciousness with full clarity" (*Dogm.,* p. 49).

And the *acts* of the sinner? Are they good or evil? Later on we will go into the question of man's co-operation in justification. Only three points will be referred to here:

(1) From all that has been said, it ought to be clear that no self-disposing autonomous good resides in any act of the sinner. "Sine tuo numine, nihil est in homine/nihil est innoxium": so sings the Church to the Holy Spirit of Jesus Christ. What is true about the being of the sinner is also true about his activity: "No one has any-

thing of his own except lying and sin. . . ." (*D* 195). If there is some good in the sinner's activity, it is certainly only due to the redeeming power of Jesus Christ: ". . . It is from that fountain for which we ought to thirst in this desert, that having drunk some drops of water from it, we may not falter on the way" (*D* 195). Because the Church takes the second and positive part of this statement as seriously as the negative, it condemns the teaching that "all works performed before justification . . . are truly sins" (*D* 817, 1027, 1035, 1038, 1040). From this source—from Christ —the sinner obtains power to do penance and to repent and so to bring about "good" acts.

Isidore, *Sent.* II, 5 (*PL,* 83, 604): "The defenders of free will know that, by its power, nothing can avail for good unless sustained by the assistance of divine grace. Thus also the Lord says through the prophet, 'I will destroy you, O Israel; who can help you?' (Hos. 13.9). It is as if He were saying: 'that you perish is by your merit, that you are saved is by My help.' Divine grace does not discover man's merit in order that it may come, but creates merit after it has come."

(2) But even in this sense the predicate "good" ought to be attached to the works of a sinner only with major reservations and by way of analogy. For no act of a sinner is good in the sense that it is capable of accomplishing something for eternal salvation and thus of being an act of salvation in the strict sense of an act of merit. To this extent one could just as well designate it "sinful" in an analogical sense. The sinner is the bad tree who can bring forth no good fruit (Mt. 7.17–20; 12.33). It is through justification that the man of God is first made capable of good works in the real sense, that is, of acts of salvation in the strictest sense.

J. H. Newman: "They (the good principles) do not exist by themselves in their unmixed nature, as if we could act on them and nothing but them, whatever might be their worth if so exerted; but though good, viewed in themselves, still they are, in fact and as found in us, of a sinful nature. All that we do, whether from better principles or from worse, whether of an indifferent nature or directly moral, whether spontaneously, or habitually, or accidentally, all is pervaded with a quality of evil so odious to Almighty God, as to convert even our best services almost into profanations; or, in the expressive words of St. Paul, 'They that are in the flesh cannot *please* God' " (*Lectures on Justification,* pp. 89f.).

(3) The consciousness of works doubtless exists in varying degrees (there are acts which consciously refer to Jesus Christ and

those which do so unconsciously). Furthermore, there exists the possibility (for example, in philosophy) of a conscious abstraction from Jesus Christ (the possibility or helpfulness of which is not to be debated here). But all of these distinctions must not call in question the fundamental being of man in Jesus Christ. Therefore, after all is said and done, it is not feasible to assume the existence of ultimately *indifferent* acts, let alone acts occurring without grace. To abstract from Jesus Christ ontologically (not only logically or psychologically) is totally impossible, since something would be taken out of τα παντα. An act refers positively or negatively to Jesus Christ (knowingly or unknowingly, explicitly or implicitly, in se or in causa, formally, virtually, or habitually). Even in conscious abstraction from Jesus Christ (as in philosophy) everything depends on whether the abstraction is in good faith (proceeding from Christian faith) or in bad faith (disregarding Jesus Christ in a malicious or neutral and indifferent way and not respecting Him).

Christ says: "He who is not with me is against me, and he who does not gather with me scatters" (Mt. 12.30). Of good works not consciously done in reference to Christ it is said: "He that is not against us is for us" (Mk. 9.40). And this is always true: "*I am* the way, and the truth, and the life" (Jn. 14.6), and: "Apart from me you can do *nothing*" (Jn. 15.5). And in the last judgment Christ will make clear to everybody that all works which were good, were so for His sake ("you did it to *me*") (Mt. 25.40), and that all works which did not have at least an implicitly positive relation to Him were sinful works ("you did it not to *me*"—Mt. 25.45).

For this reason St. Paul said, "So, whether you eat or drink, or whatever you do, do *all* to the glory of God" (1 Cor. 10.31): "And whatever you do, in word or deed, do *everything* in the name of the Lord Jesus" (Col. 3.17).

That is the reason for the very categorical declarations of the Fathers on John 15.5: "Apart from me you can do nothing": for example, Augustine, *In Joan. tract.* 81.3 (*PL*, 35, 1841f.); Pope Leo, *Sermo 38*, 3; *PL*, 54, 261; *Sermo 49*, 4; *PL*, 54, 303) and Gregory, *In Ezech.* I, hom. 11, 45 (*PL*, 76, 905).

On this, see the canons of the Council of Orange, esp. Canons 6–9, 16, 20, 22, 25 (*D* 179ff.); on their interpretation, see Rondet, *Gratia Christi*, esp. p. 161. Special reference is made to *D*, 200 (and *D*, 199): "We also believe and profess for our salvation that in every good work it is not that we make a beginning and afterwards are helped through God's mercy, but rather, that without any previous good merits on our part, God himself first inspires us with faith in him and love of him so that we may faithfully seek the sacrament of baptism, and so that after baptism, with his help, we may be able to accomplish what is pleasing to him" (*D* 200).

For more on this question, see Ripalda, *De ente supernaturali. Disp.* 20. On the indifference of human acts, see Thomas, *S.th.*, I–II, q. 18, a. 8 and 9; Scheeben, *Dogm.*, III, 1004–1005; Marchal, "Moralité" in *DTC, X*, 2470–2472; O. Lottin, *Psychologie et morale aux XIIe et XIIIe siècles*, vol. II, chap. 7, "L'indifférence des actes humains chez S. Thomas d'Aquin et ses prédécesseurs" (pp. 469–489); B. Häring, *Gesetz Christi*, pp. 343–348.

Today the majority of Catholic theologians agree with Schmaus' statement: "So it must be stressed here too that the Church's doctrinal declarations only speak of the possibility of a natural morality, not of its actuality. The Church's teaching thus leaves room for the view that no purely natural good acts exist in fact, but only those which are referred to the community with the heavenly Father . . . The proposition that there is nothing like good action on a purely natural plane is supported by the fact that the whole creation is focused on Christ. Nothing stands apart from the connection with Jesus Christ . . . As a result of this connection with Jesus Christ, mankind was never without grace; no matter how sparingly it might have been given, it never was completely missing. Mankind never had to bear a condition totally without grace, it never had to bear sin in its entire dreadfulness. Baius erred too in taking unbelievers to be men without grace. This error gave birth to the other—that all works of the unbeliever and pagan are sin, and that the virtues of the philosophers are vices" (*Dogm.*, III/2,274f.).

26. A VARIETY OF FOUNDATIONS?

The last five chapters may have convinced the reader that the fundamental questions of the theology of justification are decided in Christology, and therefore connected with the theology of creation and sin. It is regrettable that these fundamental questions had to be treated with such brevity—in spite of the length of the chapters. And why shouldn't it be admitted that we hesitated for a long time before working out these chapters at all? It is so difficult not to get stuck or lost in the extensive net of closely knit questions, while trying to present the infinite riches of Catholic teaching with some degree of definition. And it is also easy to be misunderstood in these very problems. What else was there to do in the dilemma of either tackling the fundamental problems head-on or foregoing real answers to the questions raised? A valid and satisfactory response to the questions traditionally asked of us about the theology of justification cannot possibly be given without anchoring the answer in the foundations of Catholic teaching. The presentation in the first part of this book of Karl Barth's theology of justification should have adequately shown that the reproaches directed against Catholic teaching are aimed not so much at individual doctrinal declarations as at the fundamental Catholic attitude. It is taken to be some kind of veiled unchristian humanism, a secret self-glorification of man, and even as what Karl Barth once used to call the Catholic "analogy of being" (cf. Introduction). And if we examine contemporary Protestant theology we find that, in general, the difficulties about Catholic teaching in modern Protestant theology are rooted in these fundamental questions. Let us cite only a few of today's representative Protestant theologians:

E. Brunner: "The relation between general and special revelation can never be complementary: as, for instance, that of a 'basic revelation' or a 'revelation of truth' (Tillich) as its foundation, and above that, like the second story of a building, the 'revelation of salvation.' This certainly very closely resembles an existing definition of the relation between general and special revelation: that of the Catholic Church. The *Lex naturae,* natural life, natural ordinances, natural knowledge, natural theology, as the foundation; then, overarching the whole, the Kingdom of Grace, the Church, with its 'revealed' truth. This graded scheme of a special revelation erected on the basis of general revelation destroys the significance of the fact of Christ and distorts the image of the 'natural man.' If it is true that the decisive fact lies there, then it can be there and there only, and it cannot be divided into two stages. This division is, however, of the very essence of the Catholic conception, in which the structure of the Church is based upon the natural life of man, whereas theology is built up on the natural (metaphysical) knowledge of God; the good in man is completed by grace, and God and man co-operate in the work of redemption." (*The Mediator,* pp. 32f.).

"Karl Barth's singling out of the analogia entis as the decisive difference between Catholic and Reformation thought was therefore a great insight, proving his theological acumen. The principle of analogy, as understood by Karl Barth, *is* the crossroad." (*Dogm.,* II, 51).

P. Althaus: "The Roman articulation of tensions is 'Catholicity' at the expense of the gospel. To be sure, Rome *also* has the gospel—but only 'also'—that is, in the complexio oppositorum. In this the gospel has to forfeit its unequivocal character and yield its supremacy in order to be capable of being integrated into the great synthesis . . . The modern Catholic concept of fullness, of synthesis, of the articulation of tensions, is not derived from the gospel and cannot be justified according to the gospel. Rather it is condemned by the gospel. For it really implies a compromise between gospel and legalism, gospel and mystery religion, kingdom of God and kingdom of the world; and hence it implies the substitution of an 'as well as' where there is really only an 'either or' " (*Christliche Wahrheit,* p. 236).

H. Asmussen: "The most essential section to be found in Melanchthon's reply is the beginning. Here he shows that his opponents speak of justification on the philosophical level. He writes: 'If we accept the opponents' teaching . . . then we are already Aristotelians and not Christians and there is no distinction between the man of honor and the pagan, between the Pharisaic and the Christian life, between philosophy and gospel.' This is spoken from the heights of evangelical faith. This phrase is expressive of something pertaining to the deepest intent of the Reformation. Though Melanchthon and Luther himself may have erred here and there in presenting their opponents, at this point what was truly at stake becomes. evident. At no time has Rome really been able to absolve itself of the charge that it is dangerously tampering with the clear distinctions between philosophy and gospel, between morality and salvation." (*Warum noch lutherische Kirche,* pp. 70f.)

O. Cullmann: "I often note, in discussions between representatives of the various confessions, that both parties take anxious pains to speak only concerning those questions regarding which there exists a common basis of discussion. The other questions are studiously avoided, even though as a rule the conversation necessarily reaches a point where it should move on to precisely those other questions for which the common basis is lacking. When this point is reached, one should go back to the reason for this lack of a common basis, not—let me repeat—to fight for one's position and not, indeed, with the illusory purpose of converting one's partner, but rather to listen to him. . . ." (*Peter: Disciple—Apostle—Martyr,* Foreword, p. 12.) Cf. also the section on the development of post-Reformation Catholicism in M. Werner, *Protestantische Weg,* I, 861–891.

Under these conditions, it seems better to put up once and for all with the difficulties and deficiencies and at least venture an attempt at answering—rather than lightheartedly sow where the soil remains unworked. We have therefore attempted, as concisely as possible and without the burden of polemic, to make clear the foundations of Catholic teaching on justification. It will not seem too rational now to give a preliminary summary of our inquiries to date, with a brief comparison. It is suggested that chap. 19 be skimmed over once again, especially the moot questions regarding Jesus Christ, creation and sin. Chaps. 21–25 may be assumed to have given a summary answer to these questions. It may be left to the reader to compare the details, since in the previous chapters he is not likely to have lost track of Barth's position. In particular the following comparisons should be made: chap. 18 with chaps. 2–5 (in regard to Jesus Christ), chap. 19 with chap. 5 (in regard to creation), chaps. 23–25 with chaps. 6, 9, and 10 (in regard to sin).

We did not go into the theology of *original sin* because it would fill a book of its own. We can accept Barth's theology of original sin insofar as it is a positive statement (Adam as the exemplar and representative of all men). But this does not as far as we are concerned exhaust the reality of original sin. More must be said, in consonance with Trent. Nevertheless it would seem that we can safely disregard this point for the time being, insofar as Barth would find it relatively easy to improve and deepen it, provided that his Christological basis and his treatment of creation and sin are sound. As a result, Barth's stand on *infant baptism* would also be modified.

Moreover, there is plenty of room within Catholic dogma (cf. the encyclical *Humani Generis*) for theological explanations. We can mention only the differences between the Greek Fathers and Augustine, between De Lugo and Billot. The most recent Catholic discussions (especially in connection with the primitive history of man and the analogical character of "hereditary sin") have shown that even in Catholic teaching on original sin, many points await elucidation. On this: A. Gaudel, "Péché originel," in *DTC;* H. Rondet, *Le mystère du péché originel,* and *Problèmes pour la réflexion chrétienne;* Ch. Hauret, *Origines de l'univers et de l'homme d'après la Bible;* K. Rahner, *Theologisches zum Monogenismus;* G. Feuerer, *Adam und Christus;* A. Verrièle, *Le surnaturel en nous et le péché originel;* M.-M. Labourdette, *Le péché originel et les origines de l'homme.*

The theology of redemption will be studied in the next chapters, insofar as this proves necessary for our purpose.

Our preliminary summary therefore covers the foundations of the theology of justification to the extent that they are in Christology, in the theology of creation, and in that of sin. If we were heard only in this preliminary statement of ours we might easily be open to the suspicion of irenicism. But we justified our procedure in chap. 20, and have come to our conclusion by means of a sober theological presentation. And the preliminary conclusion points to a fundamental agreement between Barth and Catholic teaching.

We exposed ourselves to questions on the Catholic attitude toward Jesus Christ and we saw that living Catholic teaching does not consider Jesus Christ a peripheral figure. We also saw that in Catholic theology Jesus Christ has a primacy which dominates everything else, and that in it He is the beginning and end of all God's ways. We have exposed ourselves to further questions on the Catholic attitude toward creation. And we saw that here, too, there is no room for an unchristian autonomy, since creation is in no way a profane sphere but rather is integrated into the one plan of salvation which God had projected in Jesus Christ—a plan shrouded in the mystery of sin and grace. We exposed ourselves to questions regarding the Catholic understanding of sin. We saw that for us sin is in no way merely a loss of a non-essential accident, affecting man only peripherally. Rather sin impairs man in his heart as well as in all his actions and brings upon him death—from which he is spared and finally prepared for justification only by the prevenient grace of Jesus Christ.

Hence, Barth's fundamental objection to Catholic teaching can be rejected as unjust and untenable—that is, the charge that Catholic theology relativizes the sublimity and sovereignty of God and diminishes Jesus Christ and His grace. But there is no denying that it is not always easy to perceive the living Catholic teaching in its fullness, and that consequently Barth's reproaches against certain presentations of Catholic doctrine might be justified. On this see chap. 20.

At the same time it is clear that on the whole Barth's theology (so far as we have considered it) does justice to Catholic questions. We presented well-founded doubts as to whether Barth's manifestly strong anthropological statements would not in the final analysis prove to be weak and empty verbalizing. The comparison with Catholic teaching demonstrated that these doubts—in spite of the first impression—are unjustified. It cannot be said that Barth has over-valued Jesus Christ in order to devaluate man or that in Barth the autonomy of creation is threatened or that sin, in its very impotence, would be overpowering. For this reason it must be granted that our fundamental doubt about Barth's theology (that is, that it does not take man seriously and ultimately does not take seriously the incarnation of Jesus Christ) is on the whole untenable and not justifiable. But that does not mean to suggest that this is always easy to perceive in Barth's teaching. Whoever gets stuck on an individual declaration will be faced with almost insurmountable obstacles to complete understanding (cf. chap. 1). We might want to have particular formulations and accents changed, but despite this Barth's teaching can be understood with perfect clarity.

Our preliminary conclusion in these initial chapters is therefore this: in regard to the foundations of the theology of justification, Barth, considered as a whole, stands on the same ground as we Catholics do. This is saying a great deal—but by no means everything. One can build all kinds of houses on the same ground. It remains for the concluding chapters to examine the theology of justification in its more limited sense.

B.

The Reality of Justification

The following chapters do not, in the strict sense, present the total outline of Catholic teaching on justification. They are a "response"—sometimes longer and sometimes shorter—to questions raised. So one thing or another will be found missing. But the headings show that the chapters are concerned with the central problems of the theology of justification.

27. GRACE AS GRACIOUSNESS

The reaction to Karl Barth's polemic against Catholic teaching on grace (IV/1, 89–94; cf. our chap. 7) involves mixed feelings. The motivation behind the attack is doubtless a genuine concern for the supremacy of God's grace. This has been fully enough discussed. However, the foreground is still full of a polemic which obscures Barth's concern rather than illuminates it—largely due to the use of the rhetorical question form. The Catholic feels himself either willfully misinterpreted or at least thoroughly misunderstood (cf. E. Riverso, "Caroli Barth in doctrinam catholicam de gratia recentissimae difficultates refutantur"). This is regrettable. For as a result Barth's own concerns and his justifiable questions are in turn misunderstood by those questioned—because they themselves are being misunderstood. This does no one any good. There is one first question which we, in turn, cannot very well suppress. Why is it that all of Barth's other opponents (including people of the most divergent orientations and even philosophers) stand a better chance of being given a fair hearing and fair treatment than representatives of Catholic theology? This is not to say that Barth has not tried again and again, and tried harder than with others, to do honor to Catholic concerns. He does it however in devious ways, without saying to whom in particular he is conceding a point. For the rest, what we find is one-sided polemic. Is the very massiveness of his reproach perhaps a sign of Barth's attempt to disengage himself from something with which he has already become too involved? Is it his intention to reaffirm

Protestant orthodoxy against the "dangers of the brethren"? At this juncture are we to suppose that fear of "Catholicizing" could provide sound theological guidance?

However that may be, unsympathetic polemic will not hinder us from earnestly studying the questions put forward. They deserve this study despite their one-sidedness. We want to begin our work on the problem with an analysis of the term "grace" as used in the Old and New Testaments. We said the *term* "grace," implying that the *reality* of grace cannot be thinned down just to the words חסד or χαρις alone, since Matthew, Mark, and John know the reality very well and yet never use the word (John uses it only in the somewhat stereotyped phrases of the prologue). A whole series of other words must be taken into consideration in order to express the fullness of the grace of God (for example, ζωη, φως, δικαιωσυνη, ειρηνη, and so on, cf. Bonnetain, "Grace," in *DBS*).

Speaking of the term "grace" reminds us of what has been said above regarding theological terminology (chaps. 20–25). That is, the word "grace" is to be used, if possible, in the original sense it had in Sacred Scripture. There it had a well defined meaning, for it expressed a definite aspect not expressible by some other word which might possibly point towards the same reality. For instance, the one and the same reality—the God-man—is called "King" as well as "Son of man" in Sacred Scriptures though the word "King" expresses something not expressed when the word "Son of man" is substituted. As theologians we must not simply impute to "grace" a meaning which, while in agreement with the facts, is not the meaning expressed by *this* word. Therefore we shall attempt to define the unique meaning of the word "grace" in Sacred Scripture.

See the critical remarks of Spicq, *Bulletin de Théol. biblique*, pp. 131f., on the article of Bonnetain: "This is how eventually everything is identified with or assimilated to grace." On the exegetical analysis of the concept of grace we follow especially the article "Gnade," in the Catholic *Bibel-Lexikon* (pub. by H. Haag, 1951ff.). Still the essential points are quite adequately dealt with in the article "Gratia" by I. Knabenbauer in *Lexicon biblicum* (*Cursus S. Script.*, Paris, 1907, II, 427ff.). Additional encyclopedias to be consulted are: for the Old Testament, F. Zorell and Brown-Driver-Briggs; for the New Testament, F. Zorell and W. Bauer.

The Old Testament lacks a word for "grace" as a created supernatural inner endowment. The Hebrew words corresponding to the German "Gnade" mean first of all favor, good will, mercy.

חן, which corresponds roughly to the Greek χαρις (so it is usually translated in the LXX), means charm (lovely or appealing), gracefulness, and hence, goodwill (benevolence, generosity) and favor.

חסד in the LXX almost always is translated by ἔλεος, originally expressing a mutual relationship; when it refers to God it means the helpful act corresponding to the relationship of trust and thus—motivated by God's kindness—favor.

In the New Testament "grace" means first of all the favor and benevolence of God and of Christ, rarely the created inner quality of the soul.

Originally χαρις was something causing joy—like charm, beauty, and therefore favor, benevolent disposition and the expressions of benevolent disposition. "χαρις meant above all the grace of God or Christ, the active and kind disposition, or the token of favor given by God or Christ." (*Bibell.*, p. 590; cf. Zorell: "In the New Testament χαρις means primarily the favor of God or of Christ toward men, the benevolence, liberality and mercy by which he is forbearing toward sinners and gives His gifts to the undeserving.") It occasionally means even the work of salvation (the new order of salvation) and the gospel. Rarely, however, does χαρις designate the supernatural created grace given man (Bibell, citing Rom. 1.5; 2 Cor. 1.12; 12.9). The gifts of grace are generally designated as gifts of the spirit or as gifts (χαρισμα, δωρον, δωρημα). Finally χαρις also means thankfulness, thanksgiving, and reward. We can discover the aspect of favor in the Latin terminology "gratia, gratis" and so on in Forcellini, *Lexicon totius Latinitatis*, II, 621ff.; Du Cange, *Glossarium mediae et infimae Latinitatis*, IV, 104ff.; *Thesaurus linguae latinae*, VI/2,2205.

On the German usage of "Gnade," cf. Trübner, *Deutsches Wörterbuch*, III, 211ff.

What follows from this for the theology of grace? The perspectives of Sacred Scripture must also be the perspectives of theology. When theology uses "grace"—and not some different word expressing another, even though proper aspect—its point of departure must be that grace is the *favor* (benevolent disposition) and the *generous kindness* of God. From this starting point and semantic center of gravity follows everything else contained in the word "grace." "Grace" is thus not primarily a physical entity in the human subject but rather something entirely *personal*—the character and behavior of the living God Himself. God Himself "is gracious" as is always said in Sacred Scripture. "To receive grace" means therefore to receive the favor of God—"His" grace and not simply grace in general. God graciously turns to me, the sinner, and inclines toward me in my wretchedness. The ray of his divine benevolence enlightens my eyes and warms my heart. As it is put in the priestly benediction: "The Lord make his face to shine upon you, and be gracious unto you" (Num. 6.25). "To be in the state of grace" means that I am in favor with God: I stand in the sunshine of His benevolence; He is gracious toward me, well disposed; He smiles on me in friendship, like a good father on his beloved child.

In this is more clearly expressed not only the personal but also the theocentric aspect of grace—in line with its divine, personal nature. Grace always refers primarily to God without intermediates. Grace is not an interfering third party between God and man, but rather is the gracious God Himself. The issue is not *my having* grace, but *His being* gracious. The word "habitus" especially can very easily lead to false conceptions. For in grace it is not in the first instance I who "have" God but God who "has" me.

In Catholic theology "grace" is generally defined correctly in a philological and in an exegetical way, though it is true that this knowledge is neither theologically and systematically nor practically and pastorally made adequate use of.

To our knowledge there has, as yet, been no investigation of the history of the concept χαρις in patristics. Yet usage in the primitive Church must be seen in the light of Wobbe's critical investigation: "Besides the difference between our way of thinking and that of the Greeks must be noted. As far as grace is concerned, the Greeks always think of the source—of the favor and kindness of its Giver. By contrast, we when we pronounce the word grace think more of the receiver of grace, of the gift of grace. In the Greek vernacular χαρις, meaning good graces, benevolent and liberal disposition, is quite normal" (*Der Charis-Gedanke*, p. 32; cf. the appendix "Paulus und der Begriff χαρις," and W. Reinhard, *Das Wirken des Heiligen Geistes*). On patristic literature, see Roslan, *Die Grundbegriffe der Gnade nach der Apostolischen Väter*. The many connotations of "gratia" stand out clearly in Peter Lombard. On this, see J. Schupp, *Die Gnadenlehre des P. Lombardus*, pp. 24–27.

Thomas (in *S.th.*, I–II, q.110, a.1,co) puts it in proper perspective: "According to the common manner of speech, grace is usually taken in three ways: First, for anyone's love, as we are accustomed to say that the soldier is in the good grace of the king, i.e., the king looks on him with favor; secondly, it is taken for any gift freely bestowed, as we would say: I do you this act of grace (favor); thirdly, it is taken for the recompense of a gift given *gratis* inasmuch as we are said to be *grateful* for benefits. Of these three the second depends on the first, since one bestows something on another *gratis* from the love wherewith he receives him into his good *graces*. And from the second proceeds the third, since from benefits bestowed *gratis* arises *gratitude*" (cf. *De Ver.*, q. 27, a. 1, co).

Notton corrects Harnack's interpretation as follows: "Thomas, on the contrary, derives his thesis from the fact that grace is above all the gracious disposition of God. This disposition represents a vital, creative act of love, an apostolic act of will, which consequently produces a corresponding activity in the creature affected . . ." (*Harnack und Thomas*, p. 10).

"Grace" is correctly defined by the following among more recent Catholic theologians: Berlage, *Dogm.*, VI, 414ff.; Dieringer, *Dogm.*, p. 514; Heinrich, *Dogm.*, V, 463ff.; Scheeben, *Herrlichkeiten*, p. 6; Bartmann, *Dogm.*, p. 406; Diekamp, *Dogm.*, II, 355; Pohle, *Dogm.*, II, 337; Van der Meersch, "Grâce," in *DTC*, VI, 1555; Rademacher, *Lebensordnung*, pp. 66ff.; Ott, *Dogm.*, 254; Premm, *Glaubenskunde*, IV, 3f.; Schmaus, *Dogm.*, III/2, 15; Lippert, *Credo*, pp. 303–310; Guardini, *Freiheit*, pp. 160–166; Bonnetain, "Grâce," in *DBS*, IV, 1154ff.

Regarding Catholic exegetes A. Hulsbosch asks: "What Catholic exegete could have any objection to going along with Protestants in interpreting grace as the favor of God?" (*De Genade*, p. 20.)

This data is inadequately utilized from a theological point of view if the particular "gift of grace" is singled out from among various definitions of "grace" without giving any particular reasons and is designated the "theological" definition. The result of this will be that the whole theological enterprise will revolve almost exclusively around the so-called "created grace" (gratia creata). Wobbe's statement is also valid for present day intra-Catholic discussions on the dwelling of the Holy Trinity in the just.

This data is inadequately utilized from a pastoral point of view if an entirely too anthropocentric and materialistic popular notion of grace prevails—grace as a quasi-physical entity and a supernatural-natural fluid or "lump." To cite just one example, the effect of the Sacrament of Penance in people's minds is often not much more than a soul's being made pure again (with God as the condition for this)—a freshly cleaned suit for the soul (as though we had here the problem of getting a nice "white garment"). The question of personal relationship to God, of my again standing in favor with Him, of His being friendly and not looking angrily upon me any more—all this has, in many instances, receded into the background.

If grace is understood as favor and kindness, the *unity of grace* will be convincingly presented—for then it is guaranteed by the one gracious God Himself, who gives us His whole kindness and His whole grace in the one Jesus Christ. Jesus Christ is *the* grace of God, *the* favor, the personified benevolence of God toward us men: "For the *grace* of God has appeared for the salvation of all men" (Tit. 2.11). And everything which is given us in grace is given us in Him: "And from *his* fulness have we all received, grace upon grace" (Jn. 1.16). This is why Paul always speaks of the grace of "our Lord Jesus Christ." All "graces" which are sent to us are nothing but the rays of the "Sun of Justice, Christ Jesus" (Trent, D 792a).

Thomas, *De Ver.* q. 29, a. 5 "And since Christ in a certain manner instills into all rational creatures the workings of his grace, thence it is that he himself in a certain manner is the beginning of all grace for the benefit of mankind, as God is the beginning of all being: hence, as in God the perfection of all being is united, so in Christ the fulness of all grace and virtue is found."

Moeller: "A treatise on grace which does not speak of Christ and of the Trinity on every page of its exposition will be seriously out of focus. Too many Catholic manuals devote the major part of their exposition to the discussions between Molinism, "Banezianism" and other systems which, however interesting they may be, cannot occupy the front of the stage. It is not a matter of silencing schools of theology but of arranging them in a hierarchical order within a total frame of reference" (*Théol. de la Grâce,* p. 44).

And the grace of the Father in Jesus Christ works through the Holy Spirit and is not isolated within the individual. It is not a private grace; it establishes community fellowship through the one Holy Spirit with Jesus Christ, for the sake of unity within the one body of Jesus Christ which is the Church. Grace has an essentially *ecclesiological character*. The grace of God in Jesus Christ has been given us through the Holy Spirit in the Church, sending forth light into the world, drawing it into the Church for the sake of the Church's increase.

When all this is said then something else follows: Grace, as the favor and benevolence of God, is not oriented toward a vacuum. It is not impotent in regard to the sinner, but omnipotent—Verbum Dei efficax. As Paul said: "His grace toward me was not in vain" (1 Cor. 15.10). Grace accomplishes something in man. It transforms him inwardly. It enlightens and revives him in his heart, in the center of his being. It does actually bestow grace upon *man*.

Here, too, the perspectives must not be given a distorted anthropocentric meaning, but what Thomas said must be heeded: "Moreover, when a man is said to be in another's good graces, it is understood that there is something in him pleasing to the other; even as when someone is said to have God's grace—with this difference, that what is pleasing to a man in another precedes his love, but whatever is pleasing to God in a man is caused by divine love, as was said above" (*S.th.*, I-II, q.110, a.1 ad 1).

And what does this bestowal of grace upon man mean? It means that God opens Himself and imparts Himself (His truth, which constitutes His being), and that He thereby allows man to have a share in His divine life. As Sacred Scripture says, the Holy Spirit of Jesus Christ and of the Father takes possession of man and through this Spirit, the Father and Jesus Christ Himself take possession, too: "We will come to him and make our home with him" (Jn. 14.23). The triune God takes up residence in the man who has received grace. This is what the bestowal of grace on man and the favor of God mean: He dwells in us as the Father through the Son dwells in the Holy Spirit, and through the Son in the Holy Spirit we have the power to acknowledge and love the Father.

We refer once again to the quotation from K. Rahner given in chap. 22: The truth of the characteristic relationships between the man given grace and the individual divine persons is to be taken first of all in possessione as in Sacred Scripture, and taken as literally as possible so long as it has not strictly been proved that it is only a question of appropriations.

If God is to be able to do man this favor, if the triune God is to be able to dwell in man in this marvelous way, man must be properly prepared for it. He must have been prepared for it by God Himself. God does this through His own indwelling, but in such a way that in the sphere of created being something actually happens and becomes reality. In Catholic tradition this reality is called created grace (gratia creata). The gratia creata is not the main thing. It is not to be given a principal position which is not due it. This position belongs rather to uncreated grace (gratia increata)—to God Himself in his graciousness. If the gratia creata is correctly understood, there will be no notion of an impersonal interfering third element between God and man.

K. Rahner appeals to the fact that in the entire theology of grace, the theology of Paul as well as that of John and that of the Fathers, the created gifts of grace appear as the consequence of a substantial communication from God to the justified man. Rahner's solution for the relationship between uncreated and created grace is as follows: "In this regard created grace is seen as causa materialis (dispositio ultima) for the formal causality which God exercises by graciously communicating his own Being to the creature. In this way the material and formal causes possess a reciprocal priority: as dispositio ultima created grace is in such a way the presupposition of the formal cause that it can itself only exist by way of the actual realization of this formal causality. From this objective reciprocal priority there follows further the logical justification for inferring the presence of one reality from that of the other" (Karl Rahner, *Theological Investigations*, vol. I, p. 341). Rahner also shows that this solution can be harmonized very well with the teaching of Trent (see also Scheeben, *Dogm.* II, 361f.).

On patristic theology, cf. Hugo Rahner, *Die Gottesgeburt, Die Lehre der Kirchenväter von der Geburt Christi im Herzen der Gläubigen* and J. Gross, *La divinisation du chrétien d'après les Pères grecs.* Rondet notes that the texts cited for created grace in the Greek Fathers and the pre-Augustinian Latin Fathers are not so clear as is often maintained. Most often they refer only to the greatness of the soul rather than to the Holy Spirit Himself (*Gratia Christi*, p. 97).

In regard to the development of dogma during the Middle Ages, the following points must be made (cf. Auer, *Entwicklung der Gnadenlehre*, I, 109–123; Moeller, *Théol. de la Grâce*, pp. 27–35): The theology of created grace was developed especially in opposition to the special teaching of Peter Lombard on charity, which he identified with the direct, unmediated activity of the Holy Spirit. According to Auer, until Albert the Great, created grace and uncreated grace were spoken of with the same emphasis, one group identifying uncreated grace with the Holy Spirit or God within us (so Fishacre, Philipp, Rupella, Peter of Tarantasia and Thomas in his Commentary on the Sentences), the other group identifying it with the God who confronts man in a spirit of acceptance (thus Odo, Bonaventure, Alexander of Alexandria in his first commentary, and especially Hannibaldus and Romanus). It was Albert who first began to emphasize only created grace. Auer credits this development to the deepened philosophical penetration into the entire cosmic reality, a penetration necessitated by the spiritual and biological development of Western culture. Before this, he holds, a naive popular biblical piety which, somewhat refined, was alive in the works of the school of St. Victor, had been lived in a Christian way for a whole Christian millennium without these fine distinctions, and with its help even accomplished the greatest work of the Church of this era, the mission to all the Germanic peoples. According to Moeller the first text on gratia creata is found in the so-called *Summa* of Alexander of Hales about 1245 (p. 81). Why grace is treated as a quality is explained very well in H. Schmidt's *Brückenschlag*, p. 190.

In modern Catholic theology—which proceeds from the Greek Fathers and especially Cyril of Alexandria—the indwelling of the Holy

Spirit (and the most holy Trinity in general) through grace has again moved toward the center of interest, especially through men like Petavius, *De Trinitate,* VIII, chaps. 4–8 (*Dogm. Theol.,* III, 453–495); J. H. Newman, *Lectures on Justification,* pp. 130–154; J. M. Scheeben, *Mysterien,* pp. 125f.; *Dogm.,* pp. 363–385; M. Schmaus, *Dogm.,* III/2, pp. 60–92.

So Barth is vindicated by Catholic teaching in his emphasis on the theocentric aspect of grace. It cannot really seriously differ with him when he defines grace as the free personal favor of God, as His powerful and sovereign act, and when he teaches its unity and indivisibility as the grace of Jesus Christ. On the other hand, Barth has not ignored the anthropological aspect of grace (we refer once more to chaps. 7, 12, 13, 14 and especially chap. 17). Barth realizes that something actually occurs in man through grace; that it is *man* who is graced; that man is altered in his very being. And so we do not hesitate to assert that there is a basic agreement between Barth's and the Catholic position on this fundamental problem of the theology of grace.

In this respect Barth's anti-Catholic polemic makes no real difference. Given a little sympathetic understanding, Barth should not have found it difficult to do justice to Catholic teaching here. Nobody expects him to approve historically conditioned overstatements by Catholic authors. Post-Tridentine theology often overlooked the polemic intent of Trent's condemnation of the proposition that "the grace by which we are justified is only (!) the favor of God" (*D* 821), and did not take seriously enough the fact that grace has the character of favor—a truth clearly asserted in Trent itself. We can readily admit this oversight. And every Catholic theologian will agree, to a greater or lesser extent, that Catholic teaching on grace, in its reaction to the Reformation, is heavily concentrated on man, and that grace is often divided up too much and its unity insufficiently emphasized.

Dumont says in his article, "Le caractère divin de la grâce," p. 62: "It is clear that during the century following the Council of Trent theologians of the various schools occupied themselves too exclusively with sanctifying grace as a created entity. Accustomed by Aristotelian philosophy to subdivide beings in order to define or classify them according to generic or specific, substantial or accidental forms corresponding to each of their properties and operations, they likewise sought to explain the different functions of the supernatural life in terms of infused qualities, graces and virtues, one fitting into another and all of them superimposing themselves like accidents on the normal faculties of the spiritual nature.

"Although it was very careful not to favor one theological system at the expense of another, and even, as far as possible, not to identify itself with any given system, the Council of Trent nevertheless underwent the influence of doctrines prevailing at the time of its convocation, both in the themes it tackled and in the manner in which it expressed itself."

On the decisive influence of Aristotelian categories upon Thomas' theology of justification and upon later Catholic teaching on justification (in regard to the matter-form schema and the specification of grace as *habitus,* quality, and so forth), see Bouillard, *Conversion et grâce chez St. Thomas d'Aquin,* esp. pp. 211–219; and also Auer, *Entwicklung der Gnadenlehre in der Hochscholastik;* Rondet, *Gratia Christi,* pp. 191–195.

In this connection we can refer categorically to what was said in chap. 20 about the development of dogma, about polemic, and about Trent being necessarily anthropocentric. Barth on the other hand may rest assured that what he rightly finds desirable is not prevented from expressing itself in Catholic life and literature, and is now being expressed, as pointed out above.

In particular two misunderstandings of Catholic teaching in Barth's polemic deserve brief comment:

(1) Barth refuses—or so it appears—to call any created gift "grace." This is not a pressing problem since Barth does accept a reality corresponding to gratia creata, as we saw in chap. 17 in connection with the creaturely character of faith. Discrepancies in terminology need not keep us apart. Nevertheless, Barth's refusal does not appear well-founded. Is scriptural usage actually that unequivocal? What if we take a close look at Rom. 1.5; 1 Cor. 16.3; 2 Cor. 8.4, 6, 19; 12.9? And what of the use of terms like χαρισμα, δωρον, δωρημα? (See Rom. 5.14–17.)

Asmussen writes: "We cannot simply take for granted, as I myself used to be in the habit of doing, the identity of grace and favor. One look at Ephesians, for example, shows that grace is a very complicated concept" (*Warum noch lutherische Kirche,* p. 338).

Cf. Schrenk in *TWNT,* II, 208: "In Paul, δικαιοσυνη is simultaneously an imparted and a received δωρεα: Rom. 5.17 (της δωρεας της δικαιοσυνης; gen. appos.). It also means a gift bestowed, in Rom. 8.10, 9.30, 10.6. Thus we can speak of a state of justification because in this giving the whole of the life of faith is founded. Thus what is stressed in Phil 3.9 is the always valid position that faith based on δικαιοσυνη is something given."

We have surely quite another question when we ask whether in present circumstances the expression "gratia creata" is a fortunate expression or is perhaps misleading.

Thus Moeller asks "whether we could not make use of the expression of Father de la Taille—'created actuation by uncreated act'—applying it mutatis mutandis to grace" (p. 40).

Barth's fears that God's grace might become, perniciously, *my* grace are unfounded if we keep in view the fact that grace is mine only as the grace of God; I never "have" it; it is never simply at my disposal. The term habitus is not meant in the sense of "having" grace, but, as Bonaventure explains, "to hold is to be held" (see Moeller, *Théol. de la Grâce*, p. 32). Grace is given to me each day as something completely new. It becomes "my" grace —as a consequence of the incarnation—but always as a grace alien to me, according to the paradoxical formulation of Trent:

"Propria—sed non tamquam ex nobis propria" ("Thus, it is not personal effort that makes justice our own."—*D* 809). The *Index of Celestine* states in Chap. 2: "Unless he who alone is good grants a participation in his being, no one has goodness within himself. This truth is proclaimed by that pontiff (Innocent I) in the following sentence of the same letter: 'For the future, can we expect anything good from those whose mentality is such that they think they are the cause of their goodness and do not take into account him whose grace they obtain each day, and who hope to accomplish so much without him?' " And in Chap. 6: "The same teacher Zosimus instructed us to acknowledge this truth when, speaking to the bishops of the world about the assistance of divine grace, he said: 'Is there ever a time when we do not need his help? Therefore, in every action and situation, in every thought and movement, we must pray to him as to our helper and protector' " (*D* 131 and 135).

S.th., II–II, q. 4, a.4 ad 3: "Grace is cause of faith not merely when faith first begins to be in a man, but also as long as faith perdures. For as was said above, God is always working man's justification, just as the sun is always lighting up the air. Thus grace coming to a believer is not less effective than when it comes to an unbeliever, because it works faith in both—in the one by confirming and perfecting faith, and in the other by creating it anew."

The decree of Trent does not after all use the term habitus any more than it uses the term gratia creata. The expressions gratia inhaerens and gratia infusa permanens emphasize only the true, essential, inner transformation of man.

As far as other expressions are concerned, "state of grace" very often suggests false conceptions, just as does "increase" of grace: "The habitus becomes intensified, that is, the union with God becomes stronger; in this sense, that it acts in a more supernatural way, not that it increases the quantity of the *state* of grace—as though it were a thing, a capital sum yielding interest—but simply *being more acted upon* by the Holy Spirit, being more receptive to Him. Acting in a better way comes down to being better acted upon, just as in the words of St. Bonaventure 'to hold is to be held' " (Moeller, *Théol. de la Grâce,* p. 37).

Bouyer: ". . . the fact that sanctifying grace is a *habitus,* in the Thomist sense, does not mean that it gives us a separate, independent power of acting supernaturally without further need in every instance of a special intervention of God; the exact opposite is the case. Sanctifying grace does not cancel the necessity of a particular actual grace for each meritorious act. The *habitus* of sanctifying grace, far from establishing us in some sort of autonomy in regard to God, involves precisely a permanent hold of God, not only on our actions, but on the source of our being, in so far as this could have been alienated from God by sin, and has to become his again, in the strictest possible sense, in Christ. In consequence, sanctifying grace, so far from conferring any power of our own to perform independently supernatural acts, is simply a disposition maintained in us by God to act no more but under the impulse of actual grace." (*The Spirit and Forms of Protestantism,* pp. 207f.) Cf. Cerfaux, "Justice," in *DBS,* IV, 1487.

(2) Barth misunderstands the meaning of the Catholic divisions of grace. These are not meant to reflect on the question of unity of grace nor the totality of grace given us in Jesus Christ; they are intended only to present the overwhelming and variegated effect on man of God's sovereign action. Grace is one, but it is bestowed upon man who is a complex thing, and it is in regard to him that making distinctions makes sense.

In citing Dumont we have admitted that this tends at times to be overdone on the Catholic side. We subscribe to what Schmaus wrote, in preface to his presentation of the distinctions on grace: "The form of existence made accessible to us in Christ, an existence which resulted from participation in the kingdom of God, presents a unified whole. However one can give an idea of its abundance only by taking the individual layers of the whole and studying them. We must therefore set up distinctions where normally there are none, so that we can gain a better understanding and a living conception of the one stratified and all-encompassing reality of grace" (*Dogm.* III.2, 16f.).

And Staudenmaier: "Grace is distinguished in many different ways.

Not as though there are various kinds of grace; rather the variety is determined by the various human situations and relationships, and it rests on the nature of the human reception of the one and only divine grace" (*Enc.* 710).

Barth might have been able to take more seriously, for example, the statement of the much abused Bartmann who wrote in the passage Barth criticized: "Although grace—insofar as it has its root in the active salvific will of God—is only *one*, it can still be, as Thomas explained . . . distinguished and classified according to the variety of *effects* it has" (*Dogm.*, 410).

Barth should remember that he himself in treating divine activity did the same thing when he distinguished between a praecurrere, concurrere, and succurrere, even though he was dealing with "one single and indivisible activity." But that is the situation: "The fulness of the divine activity must be revealed in the light of its relationship with creaturely activity" (III/3, 131). And an even better example further down: "The divine concursus is not simply as manifold as the *causae secundae.* From the very first and prior to the existence of these *causae,* it is more manifold than they are. . . . It is the operation of One whose power over the creature is so complete because it is differentiated, because it can find and re-determine each one according to its particular nature, because it can use it in its particular place. . . . We must not be led astray at this point by a false conception of the simplicity of the divine essence" (III/3, 137f., cf. 156; on the activity of grace cf. 472). And does not Barth speak of "forms of grace" (IV/2, 89), of a "communication of graces" (IV/2, 84)? And earlier, in a similar case, do we not find a great difference in his concern to understand various distinctions? (Cf. II/1, 590–597 on the various classical distinctions of divine will.)

On what is meant by particular distinctions in the Catholic theology of grace, cf. the article of Riverso, "Caroli Barth . . . difficultates refutantur."

We have said enough here to help clear up misunderstandings on both sides. These misunderstandings are not sufficient to destroy the basic agreement between Barth's and the Catholic teaching on grace. Our path is now clearly mapped out. God is gracious to man. But how does it come about for man the *sinner* that God is gracious to him? And how does it happen that the sinner gets a gracious God? This then is the question: How does the justification of man come about?

28. THE DECLARATION OF THE SINNER'S JUSTICE

We shall once more initiate the presentation of what the Catholic Church teaches with an exegetical analysis—an analysis of the word *"justification."* This is necessarily marked by a certain narrowness inasmuch as the *reality* of justification (as of grace) is much richer than what is directly signified by the *word* "justification." The word expresses only one aspect of what really happens. Nevertheless our procedure is justified and necessary, because in the meaning of the word "justification" we are dealing with the chief and fundamental aspect of the process, the basic meaning on which everything else must build. If we want to speak as theologians of "justification" and not of something else, then we must always begin from the meaning of the term, and of course—since Sacred Scripture is the main font of dogmatic theology—from the basic meaning taught in scripture by the Holy Spirit (cf. chap. 20).

Also, in speaking of "justification" rather than of "justice," we must constantly keep the biblical concept of justice in mind. The word δικαιοσυνη (and in connection with it the adjective δικαιος) represents on the one hand (as δικαιοσύνη Θεου) the antecedent for δικαιουν and δικαιος. On the other hand (as δικαιοσυνη των ανθρωπων and to some extent also as δικαιοσυνη Θεου) it can be conceived of as the consequence of δικαιουν. In any event the complex meaning of δικαιοσύνη must not be arbitrarily restricted in the meaning of the verb δικαιουν. In the exegesis of this we have come a long way from the extreme juridical view and have become aware again that the justice of God is a "saving justice." An exact definition of biblical justice is however very difficult. For this we can refer to the articles of Lyonnet ("De 'justitia Dei' in Ep. ad Rom."), Feuillet ("Isaïe," in *DBS*, IV, 705ff.), Descamps-Cerfaux ("Justice," in *DBS*, IV, 1417–3510), Cazelles ("A propos de quelques textes difficiles relatifs à la justice de Dieu dans l'AT"). Feuillet carefully notes the connection between God's justice and covenant. It is evident from this that justification can be scripturally understood only as an event of salvation in function of the covenant of God with man. This covenant is a "pact," but a pact of pure grace. In what follows we must constantly keep this in mind.

As to the Catholic-Protestant controversy, it is more concerned today with the verb δικαιουν than the adjective δικαιος or the substantive δικαιοσυνη.

What then do the Old and New Testaments say about the meaning of the word "justification"? According to the original biblical usage of the term, "justification" must be defined as a *declaring just by court order.*

In the Old Testament: צדק. Prat states: "We admit without hesitation that the justification of man suggests usually in the Old and even in the New Testament the idea of a divine judgment . . ." (Fernand Prat, S.J., *The Theology of Saint Paul,* II, p. 247).

Thus the word "justification" in the Old Testament meant a divine act of judgment. Lagrange (*Epître aux Romains,* pp. 120ff.) does not deny this but believes that we cannot legitimately generalize from this. However that may be, we can at least say that the main sense of the word צדק would be a "declaring just in a court judgment" (cf. Brown-Driver-Briggs and also Zorell). Descamps (*DBS,* IV, 1458) insists that this is true, at least as far as the pre-exilic prophets are concerned. And Meinertz (II, 115) says: "There is no doubt that Paul started from Old Testament concepts. The just man in the Old Testament is the man who lives according to the will of God, especially as revealed in the law. God's justice manifests itself especially in His active relationship in regard to human activity—a relationship revealed in judgment. Part of this judgment is substantially affected by His mercy. In the strongly juridical thought of the Israelites, the word 'justification' principally suggests a judgment in court and a real declaration of justice occurs—a judgment by God followed by a judgment by the world." Cf. also Cerfaux (*DBS,* IV, 1485); Guillet (*Thèmes bibliques,* pp. 30–38); Tobac (*Justification,* pp. 208–211).

It is significant, as Zorell says, that δικαιουν in the LXX generally means forensic justification. On this cf. the Pauline citation in Rom. 3.20 with Ps. 143.2.

In regard to the *New Testament* meaning of δικαιουν, δικαιωσις and δικαιωμα: the idea of an act like that of a court is indeed not universally present, yet the association with a juridical situation is never absent. Any impartial reading of the text will confirm this without any difficulty, even though it cannot be conclusively proved in every given case. Catholic exegetes also realize this.

Meinertz: A forensic conception is without doubt basic here inasmuch as the image is taken from the context of judicial trial, with man appearing before God as the defendant" (*Theologie des NT,* II, 115f.). Knabenbauer: "The word (to justify, justification) generally implies the idea of declaring and pronouncing someone just, good, guiltless" ("Justificatio" in *Lex. Bibl.*). Newman on the "Primary sense of the term 'Justification' " says: ". . . first, that justification is, in the proper meaning of the word, a *declaration* of righteousness" (*Justification*, p. 66). Tobac: "Thus it follows that the forensic and messianic character of justification will be maintained in Pauline teaching" (*Justification*, p. 211). The same viewpoint can be found in Prat (*Théol. de St. Paul*, II, 297); Mollat (*DBS*, IV, 1365f.); and W. Grossouw ("Rechtfertigung," in *Bibel-Lexikon*, pp. 1405f.).

Cerfaux himself, though he rather leans toward the viewpoint of Lagrange, says: "It must be recognized that a very general forensic meaning ('to declare just') could be attached to the verb δικαιουν from its etymological meaning as much as from Old Testament usage." (*DBS*, IV, 1485; and he refers in this respect to Schrenk, *TWNT*, II, 219ff.; A. Scott, *Christianity according to St. Paul*, 1927, pp. 54ff.; Sanday-Headlam, *The Epistle to the Romans*, 1911, pp. 30ff.).

On λογιζεσθαι, cf. Heidland, *Anrechnung des Glaubens zur Gerechtigkeit;* "λογιζεσθαι," in *TWNT;* and Spicq, *Bulletin de Théol. biblique*, pp. 125f.

There is no place within the compass of this study for the exegesis of individual texts. So we confine ourselves to some hints as to what can be said in favor of the forensic meaning of the word δικαιουν, especially in Pauline usage:

(1) The general dependence of Paul on Old Testament terminology, which is forensic.

(2) The forensic aspect of the teaching on justification of the synagogues—a teaching which is unaffected by the Pauline-Pharisaic controversy. And although the entire Pauline teaching must not be construed a priori to be opposed to Pharisaic teaching, it is nevertheless still true that Paul "was compelled by controversy to take the stand he took and that his terminology was to a large extent taken from the legalistic and juridical usage of the Pharisees" (W. Grossouw, "Rechtfertigung," in *Bibel-Lexikon*, p. 1403). It is interesting in this connection to notice the lexicographical evidence in favor of an almost exclusive limitation of δικαιουν to the major anti-Judaic letters, Romans and Galatians. What is more, δικαιωσις and δικαιωμα are found only in Romans and Galatians; δικαιουν is totally missing in 1 Thess., II Thess. 2 Cor., Eph., Phil., Col., Philem., and is only found twice in 1 Cor. (in connection with Paul's defense of himself against his accusers), and twice in the pastoral letters (in the case of 1 Tim. 3.16, in the special context of a Christological hymn). By contrast δικαιουν occurs eight times in Galatians and fifteen times in Romans plus the fact that δικαιωσις occurs twice and δικαιωμα five times.

(3) The forensic character of the LXX citations in Paul (cf. Zorell).

(4) The equating of "to justify" and "to credit toward justice" (Rom. 4 and Gal. 3.6).

(5) The clearly forensic connotation of δικαιουν in the eschatological passages (Rom. 2.13; Rom. 8.33; 1 Cor. 4.4).

(6) The juxtaposition of δικαιουν and κατακρινειν (Rom. 8.33; 1 Cor. 4.3–6) and the use of the characteristic formulas of judgment, ἐνωπιον αυτου (Rom. 3.20) and παρα τω Θεω (Gal. 3.11; Rom. 2.13).

(7) The usage of δικαιωσις (Rom. 4.25, the connection between justification-judgment-death-resurrection, to which we will return; Rom. 5.18, the polarity between κατακριμα, condemnation) and δικαιωμα (which is a multiple meaning, but is still definitely used in a forensic sense in Rom. 5.16 as the opposite of κατακριμα).

(8) Finally the implicitly juridical tone of all the other δικαιουν passages.

The Latin and German words have strongly juridical connotations too. On this see Forcellini, *Lexicon totius Latinitatis,* II, 971ff.; Du Cange, *Glossarium mediae et infimae Latinitatis,* IV, 472ff.; Trübner's *Deutsches Wörterbuch,* V. 336f.

Individual Catholic exegetes and theologians do not give this biblical evidence sufficient weight. One reason lies in the danger that this forensic concept might compel us to accept the (allegedly) Lutheran notion of a *purely* forensic pronouncement. So in order to evade this purely verbal declaration of justice the verdict of God in justification is often conceived of as a verdict handed down *after* justification—that is, as God going on record in regard to the state of grace of the justified man. But this verdict of God confirming the justification of man must be—in refutation of Luther—secundum veritatem and, so the argument runs, thus presupposes that man has been made just.

This notion of the declaration of man's justice cannot be satisfactory since it would be too anthropomorphic to suppose that God for His own satisfaction must as an afterthought reconfirm the fait accompli. And finally, the divine declaration of justice has this quality in contrast to any human judgment—that it does not justify the just man but the *sinner:* Rom. 4.5 says that we must believe in him "who declares the *unjust* just."

How can justification be defined as a declaring just and at the same time circumvent both an anthropomorphic confirmation of the state of grace and a purely verbal declaration of justice?

Even if the *"justice of God"* is understood (with Lyonnet, et al.) as a saving justice and not as a vindictive or condemning justice, this does not detract from the forensic significance of δικαιουν. It only means that the δικαιουν of God is not an act of juridical reprisal. Thus the door is definitively closed to any exaggerated juridicism.

Yet δικαιουν can be a *juridical* act—not a juridical act of revenge and retaliation but a juridical act *of grace* (a salvific act), for the sake of the ratification and re-establishment of God's universal covenant of grace.

We now turn from exegetical analysis to the theological interpretation of justification as a declaration of justice, as this interpretation develops from the Catholic position.

In this we especially rely on Cardinal Newman's *Lectures on Justification,* published in 1838 when he was an Anglican, and republished in 1874 after his conversion with the addition of corrective notations. Though too little known, this book is one of the best treatments of the Catholic theology of justification. It has recently received praise from H. A. Knight, in *A Neglected Early Work of J. H. Newman;* and from K. Steur, *Notities over de rechtvaardigmaking zooals Katholieken haar zien.*

In Chap. 3, on the "Primary sense of the term 'justification' " (62–84), Newman sets forth the following three principles, founded on Sacred Scripture: "Here I am to consider it, not as it is in fact, but as it is in idea: as an imputation of righteousness, or an accounting righteous; and I shall offer remarks on behalf of three positions, which arise out of what has been said; first, that justification is, in the proper meaning of the word, a *declaration* of righteousness; secondly, that it is *distinct* from renewal; thirdly, that it is the *antecedent* or *efficient cause* of renewal" (p. 66).

The Catholic exegetes cited above can be considered an indication that Newman in no way stands alone. What Catholic tradition says about the term will be discussed shortly.

The term "justification" means a declaring just. It really implies a declaring just, in the sense of a leaving out of account, a not imputing. Justification cannot ignore what man has done nor what he is: Man *has* sinned; he *is* a sinner. Further, God cannot make undone what has been done (*facta infecta fieri nequeunt*). And so there remains no other possibility of justification than this —that God does not "reckon" this event, does not impute the sin and its guilt, "not counting their sins against them," (2 Cor. 5.19). God treats us as though we had not sinned. He hides his face from our sins and thus deletes them (Ps. 51.9). *Despite* the sin, God declares the sinner just: "Blessed is he whose transgression is forgiven, whose sin is covered (*obtectum*). Blessed is the man to whom the LORD imputes no iniquity (*non imputat*)" (Ps. 32.1–2; cf. Ps. 85.2f., and also Rom. 4, where Ps. 32.1 is cited). This is God's declaration of righteousness (cf. also Rom. 5.16–18; 8.23; Lk. 20.35; 21.36; 2 Thess. 1.5; Rev. 3.4).

The term "justification" as such expresses an actual declaration of justness and not an inner renewal. Does it follow from this that God's declaration of justice does not imply an inner renewal? On the contrary. It all comes down to this, that it is a matter of *God's* declaration of justice and not man's word: the utterance of the Lord, mighty in power. Unlike the word of man, the word of God *does* what it signifies. God said, "Let there be light" and there was light. He said, "Be clean" and it was clean. God commands the demons, and they get out. He speaks harshly to the wind and the waves, and there is a deep calm. He says, "This is My body." And it is His body. He says, "Stand up." And the dead man rises. The sinner's justification is exactly like this. God pronounces the verdict, "You are just." And the sinner *is* just, really and truly, outwardly and inwardly, wholly and completely. His sins *are* forgiven, and man is just in his heart. The voice of God never gets lost in the void.

"The voice of the LORD is powerful, the voice of the LORD is full of majesty. The voice of the LORD breaks the cedars, the LORD breaks the cedars of Lebanon. He makes Lebanon to skip like a calf, and Sirion like a young wild ox. The voice of the LORD flashes forth flames of fire. The voice of the LORD shakes the wilderness, the LORD shakes the wilderness of Kadesh. The voice of the LORD makes the oaks to whirl, and strips the forests bare; and in his temple all cry, 'Glory!' " (Ps. 29.4–9; cf. Ps. 147.18).

Hence God's declaration is not a mere recording of past fact, nor a testimonial to an established one, nor the announcement of something wholly in the future. Much less is it a declaration of something which never was and never will be. The declaration of justice is the cause of something which before now was *not,* but now *is.* What man accomplishes by action, God accomplishes by speech, through His Word, filled with spirit and power: "Is not my word like fire, says the LORD, and like a hammer which breaks the rock in pieces?" (Jer. 23.29; cf. Ezek. 12.25). It is the efficacious Word of God; His verdict is the creative fiat of the Almighty. In brief, God's *declaration* of justice is, as God's declaration of justice, at the same time and in the same act, a *making* just.

It is no longer customary in exegesis to break down the whole of Pauline theology into a "juridical" and a "mystical" schema. Neither must be lost sight of: δικαιωσις ζωης expresses both facets. It is outside the scope of our "response" here to go into all the questions concerning the "mystical" aspect. We refer again to the leading lines laid down in the last chapter, in other words, to grace as living communion with Christ within one body, the Church; to the idea of being seized by the Holy Spirit of Jesus Christ; to the indwelling of the Trinity.

At the same time care must be taken to leave to the process of justification its peculiar character. Undoubtedly the event which took place in Jesus Christ in the fullness of time is an extraordinarily rich and many-faceted reality, which can and must be considered from many sides. For this event means life (God has made us alive), cleansing (our sins have been washed away), peace (Christ has established this), love (which has been poured out through the Holy Spirit), the body of Christ (into which we have been incorporated), return to the Father, salvation from the world of evil, and so forth. It is impossible to separate these from justification, since this *one* central event in Jesus Christ means all these things simultaneously. This is especially true in view of the "objective" character of the event of justification (see the next chapter). In spite of this, it would be harmful to the many-splendored abundance of the one experience if the various aspects were simply identified. Each facet must be allowed its individuality. This is especially true for the one facet to which scripture has given the name "justification," and which was assigned a special place precisely in the Pauline corpus. It is true that Jesus Christ as the God-man is at once both King and Prophet. But we do justice to the full abundance of His person only when we endeavor to take seriously both kingship and prophetic office in their distinct uniqueness. It is to the credit of modern exegesis that it has painstakingly investigated the aspects of the one Person in their various colors and has sought to present them in a living fashion. Only thus has the figure of Jesus Christ been freed from that all-embracing and therefore often colorless and abstract universality which so often accompanied the name of Christ in theology: His image was rediscovered in the concrete and variegated diversity of His historical life. Much the same thing is true of the justification which came about through Jesus Christ. It is true that the same central experience in Christ is at once both "justification" and "sanctification." (The exact relationship between these concepts will be discussed in a later chapter.)

But the full richness of this one central concept will be given its due only when the tones peculiar to each of these two sides are not merged in a general and homogenizing gray; but only when justification is permitted to be justification (Newman is a particularly good example here for us Catholics). And justification, following Sacred Scripture's teaching, means a declaring just, a judicial event—though it is a truly special kind of judgment, not simply a judgment of just wrath, but primarily and above all a judgment of saving grace. It is not human justice, but rather, and with all the justice involved, divine love; it is not a judgment that declares the just to be just, but one which fashions the justice of the *un*just. In this judgment the dead is made alive, is cleansed, made holy, and reconciled. It establishes peace and pours out love through the Spirit, incorporating the lost sinner into the Body of Christ and bringing him back to the Father. Justification is all this and much more. It is indeed no formalistic juridical deed done by a vindictive divine justice; but it is nevertheless a declaration of justness, a wonderfully gracious saving justice—coming from a loving and faithful covenant God who brings life through His justice.

A declaring of justice which makes just: this expression needs further explanation. For the moment, it is easily established that here there is no essential difference between the Barthian and the Catholic position. No serious difficulty, despite Trent? Barth has leveled vehement criticisms at the Council: (IV/1, 624–626; IV/2, 497f.; cf. chaps. 10, 15). And the Fathers of Trent have no complaint about any excess of understanding and empathy on Barth's part, as far as their "theologically wise and in many respects not unsympathetic document" is concerned. Yet this decree can be correctly understood only within the context of the total history of dogma.

To avoid dealing unfairly with whole theological epochs, we must remember that not all the truths of faith need be grasped with equal force in every age. Differences will prevail, especially in regard to justification, and such differences are very noticeable even in scripture itself—differences for example between the Synoptics and John and Paul. And note the differences even within the lifetime of Paul. In the captivity and pastoral letters the idea of a declaration of justice is certainly not forgotten, but who would insist that this is among the vitally significant central themes in those later letters? And who would reproach Paul on this account? How unfair it is, on the other hand, to disparage patristic and medieval theology for not expressly stressing the idea of a forensic declaration of justice.

Protestant historians of dogma, and especially the earlier theologians of controversy (e.g., Hamelmann, Chemnitz, and Gerhard) diligently searched for forerunners. But it has since been discovered that these existed, if at all, only in very limited numbers (cf. A Ritschl, *Rechtfertigung und Versöhnung*, I, esp. pp. 105–109; 129–135).

It must be remembered that the belief in justification without works was for Paul involved in his polemic against the Judaizing spirit. This problem no longer preoccupied him once the heresy itself had receded into the background. (Note the difference between Romans and Galatians on the one hand and 1 and 2 Corinthians on the other.) But after the Judaistic heresy, there was nothing like it in the primitive Church until Pelagianism (if we except the case of Manicheism, against which the Fathers had to defend human freedom of choice). Only at the beginning of the fifth century did Pelagianism and then semi-Pelagianism lead Augustine to an express development of the priority of divine grace over human works (chiefly in connection with the initium fidei). In place of grace as participation in the divine nature (cf. J. Gross, *La divinisation des chrétiens d'après les Pères grecs*), grace as liberating grace comes into prominence. With this one exception, justification was, on the whole, no problem for the Fathers. And thus we do not find in them any systematization or special treatment of the theology of justification. In exegesis and in sermons, of course, one or another aspect was repeatedly touched on (cf. J. Rivière, "Justification," in *DTC*, VIII, 2078).

The situation in the *Middle Ages* remained essentially the same, despite the rational penetration of the deposit of faith and the new syntheses of truths contained in it. It was then that the categories of habitus and qualitas were taken over from Aristotle and the notion of infused virtues took shape. Thus the accent, in the matter of actual grace, was shifted from what is now called "actual" grace (the liberating delectatio) to "habitual" grace (grace as form), from preparation for justification to co-operation with it, from justification as a gradual process of conversion to justification as instantaneous happening and as metaphysical reality seen from the viewpoint of the matter-form schema. Cf. Auer, *Entwicklung der Gnadenlehre in der Hochscholastik*, I and II; Flick, *L'attimo della giustificazione secondo S. Tommaso;* Rivière, "Justification," in *DTC*, VIII; Rondet, *Gratia Christi*, esp. pp. 191–199; Bouillard, *Conversion et grâce*, pp. 212–219; Dhont, *Le problème de la préparation à la grâce*. On the late scholastic period: Vignaux, *Justification et prédestination au XIVᵉ siècle*.

This whole development, complicated and not without problems, led to countless scholastic controversies. But the Church (except for the apparently neo-Pelagian Abelard interlude, which had a number of repercussions in early scholasticism) remained safe from any serious heresies such as might have forced it to formalize its teaching on justification, perhaps even in dogmatic form.

Nominalism brought a decisive turn. It is easy to discredit this theology; its weak philosophy and especially its pelagianizing voluntarism make it unappealing. But it did have its constructive side. (And it was considered, after all, to be Catholic theology.) It heralds modern times in its accent on individuality and historical contingency. And it is correct to say that Nominalism emphasized anew—and unfortunately in a one-sided and extrinsic way—that justification consists in a non-imputation. In sharp rejection of neo-Pelagianism, Luther adopted this style of thought, and evoked the reaction of the Church. The problem of justification as a declaration of justice was thus formally reinstated as a problem.

On *nominalism,* cf. Feckes, *Die Rechtfertigungslchre des G. Biel und ihre Stellung innerhalb der nominalistischen Schule* (on Biel, pp. 23–58; on the followers of Occam in general, pp. 91–144); Vignaux, "Nominalisme," in *DTC,* XI; *Justification et prédestination au XIVe siècle;* Rivière, "Justification," in *DTC,* VIII, 2126–2129; Rondet, *Gratia Christi,* pp. 244–247.

As to Luther, it is not easy to deal with him adequately: cf. Lortz, *Reformation in Deutschland,* I, 381–437. In any case, there were many factors driving him to rethink the theology of justification—the sanctimonious fuss being made about good works, nominalistic theology, reflection on Sacred Scripture and Augustine, his own unique personality, and the religious experience of 1513. There has been much discussion about whether Luther really taught a purely extrinsic justification. The Lutheran Ruckert (*Rechtfertigungs Lehre auf dem Tridentinischen Konzil,* p. 105) has asserted, in connection with the wellknown studies of K. Holl, that the Tridentine condemnation affected only Melanchthon, who had taught that a declaration of justice did not imply a making just.

Trent reacted sharply and with good reason against the extrinsicist exaggeration. The massive attack of the Reformers called for an equally massive counterattack. We have already pointed out in chap. 20 how the Reformers actually provoked a certain anthropocentricity in the Council.

How can the Council be reproached for failing to emphasize as forcefully the theocentric and forensic aspects? In Luther's polemic, it was not always easy to detect his primary concern. And if the Council did not wish to be misunderstood, it had to place its accents clearly on the opposite side. The Council simply continued the great Western tradition in that it created, for all practical purposes, a synthesis between the Augustinian and Thomistic views of justification. For the rest, however, what Cardinal Newman wrote about a certain one-sidedness in the Catholic theology of justification cannot be denied: "This charge only comes to this, that when Roman schools are treating of one point of theology, they are not treating of other points. When the Council of Trent is treating of man, it is not treating of God. Its enunciations are isolated and defective, taken one by one, of course" (*Lectures on Justification*, p. 31).

But the Council in no way excluded the forensic and theocentric aspect. It is included. Only the exclusively extrinsic character is con-demned—that is, the idea "that men are justified either through the imputation of Christ's justice *alone,* or through the remission of sins *alone*" (*D* 821); the truth rather is that "not *only* are we reputed just, but we are truly *denominated* just, and we are just . . ." (*D* 799). The imputation or the act of forgiving sin and with it the juridical act of justification are consequently included. And in the description of justification in chap. 4 of the decrees (*D* 796: "a transfer from the state in which man is born a son of the first Adam, to the state of grace and adoption as sons of God"), "trans-fer" must be understood in a double sense, following the consensus of interpretation. Not only does it have a passive sense, implying a becoming just; but it has (and this is primary) an active sense, implying the sovereign justifying act of God. This distinction is already clearly presupposed in Thomas, in his treatment of the quaestio on justification (I-II, q. 113, a.1). And the same thing is meant, in the final analysis, in Augustine's conception of justifica-tion as the gracious freeing of the sinner, as well as in the Greek Fathers' conception of it as a being seized by the Holy Spirit with a reception of the Spirit. Even the strictly juridical aspect is notice-able on the periphery, time and again. The development of the Catholic theology of justification is missed completely if its true continuity is ignored.

Thomas, too, was well aware of the basically juridical character of the word "justification." On Rom. 2.13 (Lect. III) he wrote: "But we must say that being justified can be taken in a threefold sense. In the one sense it can be taken as a matter of imputing justice, as someone is then said to be justified when he is reputed just. And according to this it can be so understood: 'They that do the law are justified," that is, they are reputed just before God and men." And one can find many passages in him like the following: "God does not receive us as just, but this being received makes us acceptable" (*De Ver.*, q. 27, a. 1). Bouillard has correctly noted that such typical Aristotelian and

Scholastic notions as *qualitas*, as *motio divina*, as *auxilium Dei speciale*, etc., were adopted in the treatment of justification precisely in order to emphasize the fact that justification is the work of a totally free grace (*Conversion*, p. 219).

In studying the *Acta* of Trent it is interesting to note that the questions of the legates of the theological commission concerning the essence of justification elicited answers like: "Passive justification is the covering up or nonimputation of sins"; "justification is the remission of sins and the nonimputation of divine punishment through the righteousness given to us by Christ" (*CT*, V, 279; cf. 262–280). And in the second draft of the decree (*CT*, V, 423) the formula can be found: "For His justice is then communicated and imputed to us when we are justified."

The stand in favor of *double justification*, as represented by the Catholic school of Cologne (Gropper, Pflug, and Pigge), by the papal legate from the Diet of Ratisbon, Contarini, by Cardinal Morone and the president of the Council, Cardinal Pole—and in the Council itself by the Augustinian superior general, later cardinal and Council president, Jerome Seripando—was discretely eliminated by the Council after long discussion (cf. *CT*, V, 335; 371–375; 486–488; 496; 523–675). "Finally, the *only* formal cause is the justice of God, not the justice by which He is Himself just, but the justice by which He makes us just" (*D* 799). The Council wished to exclude any theory which would in any way question the full reality of intrinsic justification. The formal statement of the problem, formulated by Seripando himself for the Council's discussions, is instructive: "Whether the justified man who has done good works by grace . . . so that he retains his inherent justice . . . must be judged to have satisfied divine justice enough to merit and acquire eternal life, or whether besides this inherent justice he has need of the mercy and justice of Christ . . . by which what is lacking in his own justice is supplied . . ." (*CT*, V, 523). The Council did not overlook Seripando's real concern in the second member of the disjunction (more on this below), but it could not accept the expression as such. It would have amounted to a questioning of the reality of justification, if besides inherent justice (through justification) there were needed yet a second, imputed justice (in the final judgment). Instead, man is justified in the one justice of God, to which we gain access through Jesus Christ (*D* 799; *CT*, V, 710). On the doctrinal development here, see Hefner, *Entstehungsgeschichte des Dekretes*, pp. 165–276). The idea of double justification was actually a compromise, splitting the unity of the act of justification (which is simultaneously imputation and communication) into two disparate acts (and, besides, putting the forensic act after rather than before the act of renewal). Thus Bellarmine (*De iustificatione*, II, c.2, c.7) correctly maintains that man is not justified partly by internal renovation and partly by the imputation of the justice of Christ. And similarly, much later, in the nineteenth century, C. von Schäzler said correctly—in opposition to Kuhn and Linsenman during the well-known debate over grace, that the *one* act brings about simultaneously forgiveness of sin and inner renewal (cf. *Neue Untersuchungen über das Dogma von der Gnade,* pp. 317–332; esp. 321; and before this, *Natur und Übernatur,* pp. 333–336).

So it is very vitally important that the relationship between the declaration of justice and making just be precisely defined, as we did above—that is, as the single act which simultaneously declares just and makes just. This is how several Catholic writers have expressed it:

Bellarmine: "When God justifies the sinner by declaring him just He also makes him just, for God's judgment is according to truth" (*De iustificatione,* II, 3).

Vasquez: "The word of the Lord and His will are efficacious, and by this very fact that He declares someone to be just, He either considers him to be just, or He makes him just in fact, that His Word may not be false. And in this God's judgment differs from man's judgment that when man by his judgment declares someone to be just, he cannot make him just but considers him to be so; God, however, can." (Quaest. 112, disp. 202, c. 5).

And in more recent Catholic theology:

Prat: "For a man to be just before God and for God to pronounce him just, one of two things is necessary: either that God has made him just previously, or that he makes him just by this pronouncement itself. In the latter hypothesis, the justification of the wicked would be declaratory in form but effective in reality. The divine sentence of justification would then produce its effect after the manner of sacramental formulas, like the words of consecration or like the words of Christ when working miracles. In this way, there would be kept for the word "justification" that judicial meaning which many modern exegetes regard as essential, while excluding that fictitious justification due to a divine judgment contrary to truth" (*Theol. of St. Paul, II,* pp. 248–249).

J. Knabenbauer: "If God is said to justify someone, i.e., to declare and to pronounce him to be just, this, in consideration of the truthfulness and holiness of God, ought to be so understood that he is truly absolved from guilt, free from the charge of sin, and just before God; therefore on these grounds the meaning of this word, by necessary inference, can be established as *to make just,* i.e., to make him what God wants him to be" ("Justificatio," in *Lex. Bibl.*).

The same is the case in Meinertz (*Theol. aes NT,* II, 116); Schmaus (*Dogm.,* III/2, 113f.); Rademacher (*Übernat. Lebensordnung,* pp. 70ff.); and Grossouw ("Rechtfertigung," p. 1405). Newman and Tobac have already been cited.

It is important to note how Catholic theology stresses the forensic character of justification in the third sense (cf. *CT,* V, 281). The forgiveness of sins *in the Sacrament of Penance* is considered an act of judgment, a declaration of justice which as such signifies also a making just.

Trent's teaching on justification can be correctly understood only in the context of history of dogma. In this context, however, it can and must be understood correctly. This, for the time being, is our preliminary answer to Karl Barth's polemic against Trent. Protestants speak of a declaration of justice and Catholics of a making just. But Protestants speak of a declaring just which includes a making just; and Catholics of a making just which supposes a declaring just. Is it not time to stop arguing about imaginary differences?

29. JUSTIFICATION IN CHRIST'S DEATH AND RESURRECTION

Justification is the life-giving act by which the sinner is declared just. But when is the sinner declared just? When does God's gracious saving judgment of the sinner occur? According to Sacred Scripture, God's judging must not be conceived of in too human a fashion, in terms of so much busy-work—as though God's solemn judgment need be pronounced in every individual case (e.g. in the moment of individual conversion or baptism). This matter does of course deserve some consideration, and we shall have to return to it later. But for Sacred Scripture the real judgment of God is inexorably bound up with the crucifixion and resurrection of Jesus Christ. In *the death and resurrection of Jesus Christ* the sinner is declared just: "But now the righteousness of God has been manifested . . . the righteousness of God through faith in Jesus Christ for all who believe. For there is no distinction; since all have sinned and fall short of the glory of God, they are *justified* by his grace as a gift, through the *redemption* which is in Christ Jesus, whom God put forward as an expiation by his blood, to be received by faith. This was to show God's righteousness, because in his divine forbearance he had passed over former sins; it was to prove at the present time that he himself is righteous and that he justifies him who has faith in Jesus" (Rom. 3.21–26). We are "*justified* by his *blood*" (Rom. 5.9); Christ "was put to death for our trespasses and *raised* for our *justification*" (Rom. 4.25).

Rom. 3.24ff. is known to be one of the most difficult passages in the New Testament. Reference may be made to the detailed exegesis (with many witnesses from tradition) by S. Lyonnet in *Verbum Domini* 25 (1947) 129–144; 193–203; 259–263; Lyonnet also puts special stress here on the saving character of "God's justice."

In the previous chapter it was pointed out that the juridical character of justice did not exclude consideration of "God's justice" as a saving justice, but rather presupposed this.

D. Mollat, in his "Jugement dans le NT" (*DBS*, IV, 1344–1394) gave an excellent idea of the judgmental character of Christ's coming. We should note especially the preaching of the Baptist, the teaching of Jesus, and the teaching of Paul and John. On Romans Mollat writes: "From all this it follows that, while the idea of justification, because of its mystical fulness, goes beyond the juridical framework, nevertheless it must not be separated from it. The forensic meaning of justification by faith has been exaggerated; yet it must not be disregarded. Some texts are expressly opposed to it: Rom. 2.13; 3.20; 8.33. It is significant that the most mystical development to be found in the Letter to the Romans (chap. 8.) takes place, as we have just seen, within the framework and vocabulary of judgment. Mystical and juridical elements fuse intimately and finally merge into one another (*DBS*, IV, 1365f.). Cf. the discussion s.v. "κρινω" by Büchsel and Herntrich in *TWNT* III, 920–955, esp. 936–942.

In reading texts which speak of justification in connection with the death and resurrection of Jesus Christ, it is striking to note that all of them referred emphatically to *faith* as well (for example, Rom. 4.5, 20–25). Only he who believes is justified. The task consequently is to relate the "objective" act of justification which happened on the cross with its "subjective" realization. On the one hand, the justification accomplished on the cross must not be separated from the process which reaches down to the individual man: this would in one way or another lead to apokatastasis. On the other hand, personal justification must not be separated from the general act of justification on the cross; this would in one way or another lead to predestinationism. Rather both must be seen as the two sides of a single truth: *All* men are justified in Jesus Christ and only the *faithful* are justified in Jesus Christ. The generic act of justification on the cross is the "permanently actual presence of salvation, accessible for personal appropriation" (Schrenk, S. V. "δικη" in *TWNT*, II, 220f.). The divine character of the declaration of divine justice and grace which took place on the cross once and for all and for all men, makes possible a relation between "objective" and "subjective" justification.

It is the task of this chapter to stress the "objective" aspect of justification. In the chapter on faith we will return to the "subjective" aspect. The coming of Jesus Christ is a coming unto judgment as proclaimed in threatening terms by the prophets, as loudly heralded by the Baptist, and as seen by the Synoptic writers (Mt.

10.34, "not . . . to bring peace, but a sword"!), and especially by John: "And this is the judgment, that the light has come into the world, and men loved darkness rather than light" (Jn. 3.19; cf. 5.19–30; 12.47–48; 16.11). It is a judgment whose climax ("my hour") is the crucifixion: "Now is the judgment of this world" (Jn. 12.31; cf. the essential agreement with 2 Cor. 5.18–21).

This, therefore, is the event: In the death and resurrection of Jesus Christ, God's gracious saving judgment on sinful mankind is promulgated. Here God pronounces the gracious and life-giving judgment which causes the one just man to be sin and in exchange makes all sinners free in Him: "He [God] made him to be sin who knew no sin, so that in him we might become the righteousness of God" (2 Cor. 5.21; cf. Gal. 3.13; Rom. 8.3). And in this ("objective") sense we can say that through Jesus Christ all men are justified, because "one has died for all" (2 Cor. 5.14; cf. 1 Tim. 2.6). "Then as one man's trespass led to condemnation for all men, so one man's act of righteousness leads to acquittal and life for all men. For as by one man's disobedience many were made sinners, so by one man's obedience many will be made righteous" (Rom. 5.18–19; cf. 5.12–17; 8.32; 11.32).

One for all: The vital biblical term in this passage—υπερ—according to Zorell (*Lexicon Graecum NT,* p. 1361; in agreement with Protestant exegetes such as W. Bauer in his *Wörterbuch*) together with the meaning "in favor of" and in connection with the substitutionary death of Christ, can have the additional meaning of "for someone" or "in *place* of someone." And so "to this many passages which deal with Christ's vicarious death can be referred." Zorell gives καταλλασσω, καταλλαγη two meanings: (1) to change, a change; (2) to reconcile, reconciliation (*loc. cit.,* p. 674f.). As to just how redemption can be simultaneously reciprocity and solidarity, cf. the citations from Schmaus and Medebielle given below.

And so justification (like grace in general, cf. chap. 27) is never a purely private affair, but one which concerns the community. In the Pauline perspective especially, justification never stands in isolation as a purely personal event; it has its place in the total framework of salvation history, of the redemption of all mankind. Those justified on the cross and in the resurrection are "the many," the "all." The object of justification, as the prophets proclaimed, is Israel, the people of God, and in the new Israel, all people on earth. In Jesus Christ all men were justified and thereby called to the

Church and even germinally integrated into it. The Fathers were right in linking the founding of the Church with the incarnation and with the crucifixion and resurrection. In the death and resurrection of Jesus Christ the eternal design for salvation—which God conceived in Jesus Christ, which He already secretly established in creation, and which He mercifully maintained even in sin—is made public, is confirmed and is made fully operative: "to unite all things in him, things in heaven and things on earth" (Eph. 1.9–10: cf. chaps. 21–25). This, God's mystery of grace hidden in creation, the salvation of all men in Jesus Christ—Jews as well as Gentiles—is now "made known . . . through the Church" (Eph. 3.9f.). Through faith, the individual shares the general justification, and so justification, as it occurs in the death and resurrection of Jesus Christ, is essentially *ecclesiological* in character.

Tobac: "It seems to us that there is no doubt that justification envisaged as an effect procured immediately by the death of Christ has in the eyes of Saint Paul a collective meaning . . . The divine decree of justification affects the community directly and individuals only indirectly. The latter are not incorporated into the messianic community because they are justified, but they participate in the collective justification because they have received membership in the community." (*Justification*, pp. 224f.).

H. Schlier: "The mystery of Christ is indeed disclosed more fully. What His crucified body contains and guarantees is disclosed in His body the Church. In it is that all-encompassing and overflowing breadth of life of the God who is present to her, a breadth of life which His body on the cross has opened to all mankind is marked out and made available in history and in its everchanging presence." ("Die Kirche als Geheimnis Christi," p. 392).

Soiron: "This means, however, that Christ as the eternal Word, combining the words of the Father concerning the whole of creation and all mankind, and Christ as the eternal Word who has assumed the nature of all minkind *as it appears since the fall of Adam, germinally constitutes the 'we' of mankind.* In the Word, Christ and mankind, head and body, are embryonically integrated into the one divine-human person. This leads to the important conclusion that all He did as God-man—what He said, suffered, sacrificed, and prayed for—all this is done for mankind. And more than this, embryonically humanity has done all this in Him, in His spirit. And so mankind is in principle redeemed in Him and is freed from the weight of sin and called and summoned into that community with God in which Christ Himself stands with God as the Son of God. Mankind is called into the community of the children of God . . . In His incarnation Christ is already established as head and body. Over the manger the bell sounding the first hour of the founding of the Church has tolled. The founding reached its consummation as Christ on the cross surrendered to death the old man and received the new man for His own in His resurrection." (*Kirche*, p. 219f.).

"The objective fact of justification is accomplished in the redemptive death of Christ, in connection, of course, with the resurrection. And so Rom. 5.9 can insist that we are justified in His blood, and by way of complement, in Rom. 4.25, that Christ was raised up for our justification" (Meinertz, *Theologie des NT*, II, 116). Catholic theologians do not normally speak of justification in connection with the death and resurrection of Christ. They prefer to the term "justification" (which is ordinarily understood as "subjective") the terms "redemption," "atonement," and so forth. But we saw that the term "justification" is used here in perfect agreement with scripture, revealing a deep and ultimately indispensable meaning. The example taken from Meinertz shows that this terminology and conception of justification is by no means unknown on the Catholic side.

Further examples: Tobac: "If justice comes to us by the law, says Paul, then Christ died in vain" (Gal. 2.21). The death of Christ has therefore, in the Apostle's view, the objective of obtaining justice for us. The Law administers condemnation. By contrast the Gospel administers justice (2 Cor. 3.9). The Gospel is therefore the proclamation of the justice procured by Christ's death. It is by God that we are in Christ Jesus who has become, through God, our wisdom, our justice, our sanctification, our redemption (1 Cor. 1.30). Christ has become our justice. It is in our union with Christ that we find justice. God has made Christ sin for us so that we might become the justice of God in Him (2 Cor. 5.21), that is, so that we might be made subject in Him to the justifying justice of God. And as we find justice in Christ, we also by the very fact and mediation of this justice, find in Him our justification." (*Problème de la justification*, pp. 219f.) Tobac refers in conclusion to Gal. 2.17; Rom. 3.24; 5.9.

Bover: "We can express in one word what St. Paul understood by the formal act of redemption—justification. To verify this, it is enough to analyze the concept of justification and to compare with it what the Apostle teaches us concerning redemption" (Teol. de S. Pablo, p. 107; cf. 108–114).

Cerfaux too touches upon the justifying character of the crucifixion of Christ, "We can speak of a justification and of a reconciliation" (p. 101); "justification and reconciliation are synonyms" (*Le Christ*, p. 111; cf. p. 238). Cf. also Guillet, *Thèmes bibl.*, pp. 91f; Rivière, "Justification," in *DTC*, VIII, 2080: "The objective and subjective aspects of justification."

Recently J. Dupont has brought out with special emphasis the "objective" aspect of the justification event and connected it with the redemption event, *La réconciliation dans la Théologie de S. Paul:* "At first glance the two affirmations would seem equivalent; the blood of Christ has justified us (Rom. 5.9), His death has reconciled us (Rom. 10). These are only two aspects of the same reality, two ways of expressing the same teaching. But as we look more closely it seems that we can recognize a certain gradation between the two affirmations. Verse 1 expresses the idea which anticipates the theme of verse 10: 'Now that, thanks to faith, we have been justified, we are at peace with God, through our Lord Jesus Christ.' To be at peace with God is precisely the result of reconciliation, the condition of the reconciled. This seems to say more than 'to be justified' for justification gives us new relationships with God. Slight as the difference may seem, it assures a certain logical priority to justification. The reconciliation which God accorded us presupposed that we had been justified of our shortcomings. Sin had made us enemies; it had to be destroyed so that we might be reconciled," (pp. 30f.). "The death of Christ has changed everything, 'the old has passed away, behold everything is new' (2 Cor. 5.17). That which was old was sin. From now on God no longer keeps account of it (v. 19) . . . Reconciliation coincides concretely with the fact that God no longer keeps an account of men's sins. The purely negative expression 'does not impute' which Paul uses under the influence of Ps. 32 is the exact equivalent in meaning of what vs. 21 expresses positively; "we have become the justice of God." Rom. 5.1,9 says 'we have been justified.' In justifying us from sin, God has reconciled us to Himself. Considering this context, we should be less surprised at the rather juridical character of reconciliation" (p. 31f.).

And cf. Prat: "Note the insistence with which Paul extends justice to *all* who believe (Rom. 1.16; 3.22; 4.11; 10.4–11, etc.), and makes of all men potential believers (*Theol. of St. Paul,* I, p. 208, n.2.)

Finally the Scholastics meant nothing else when they said that the death and resurrection of Christ is the "cause" (causa) of our justification, or that in His death Christ has "merited" justification.

It will be clear now why even before presenting Barth's teaching on justification we warned against applying too narrow a concept of justification as a yardstick, since this could block any access to the teaching of Barth. It would not even be noticed that what Barth and with him many Protestants call "justification" largely coincides with what we Catholics call "redemption" and that many expressions that sound heretical ought to be understood as completely orthodox (e.g., *"all* men are justified in Christ," although it agrees with Scripture may seem to Catholic ears to imply apokatastasis which Barth, however, categorically rejects. In ordinary Catholic usage—and in agreement with scripture—this would mean nothing other than the totally orthodox statement that "*All men are 'redeemed' in or by Jesus Christ.*") On the basis of our presentation up to this point there is no doubt that the Barthian concept of justification coincides with the Catholic. If Barth had been fully aware of this fact, his critique of Trent would have turned out differently. Everything does indeed depend on the proper definition of the relationship between "objective" and "subjective" justification (cf. Bover's distinction between virtual and actual or formal justification, *Teologia de San Pablo,* p. 114). This problem still requires more thorough investigation.

An exposition and critique of the theology of redemption, of soteriology in general, is not within the compass of this study of the theology of justification. Yet it can be said—and the exposition up to this point is an indication of this—that here, too, the teaching of Barth, seen in its totality, agrees with Catholic teaching. This can be illustrated by a long citation from Schmaus' *Dogmatics* on the matter of judgment in Christ's death and resurrection. It should be compared with the corresponding section of Barth's presentation (see chap. 11):

"In regard to the death of Christ as seen *from God's point of view,* the Father, wishing to free the world from sin, lets sin take its course with His incarnate Son. When He became man the Son of God chose to bear the curse of sin and to take it upon Himself even to the point of sacrificial death on the cross. Thus the Father *sat in judgment* on sin in the crucifixion of His Son. It was a terribly severe judgment. In it the abysmal depths of sin were demonstrated. The death of Christ shows most clearly what sin is.

"What occurred in the divine judgments before Christ was, as was every other divine revelation in the pre-Christian era, directed to the judgment of God which took place at the crucifixion. Consequently these pre-Christian judgments had the character of promise. On the cross the holiness of God came with His indwelling power over Christ, who was the representative of sinful mankind even though He Himself was without sin. When we say that God pronounced *judgment,* the term 'judgment' is not meant in a proper sense but has a broader meaning. It signifies the equivalent of an *act of sovereignty.* In one sovereign act, proper to Him who is Lord of creation, God demonstrated His holiness in one man. This meant death for the man met by the impact of divine holiness. Under the impact of divine holiness man can no longer live but only die. Thus God proved Himself to be Lord, the Lord who can dispose of man in sovereign superiority. In this disposition He established the presence of His holiness in the world. Thus at one place and in one period of history God's rule of the cosmos was re-established. God Himself made His rule real. He established His kingdom. The death of Christ meant the *establishment of the Lordship of God, of the kingly rule of the Father, and of the kingdom of God.*

"Terrible though the judgment was in which the holy God sent Christ to His death, it is nevertheless a *judgment of love.* This comes out in two ways. First, God imposed upon no other than His own beloved Son the terror and pain of death. Second, on the basis of this death, He has accorded the incarnate Logos the transfiguration and elevation of His own human nature, and has accorded all other men freedom from sin and eternal life. Death was the demise of the past form of existence, the form for which sin was responsible. At the same time, for Christ, it was also the transition to another and incorruptible form of existence in the glory of the Father. The goal of death was the resurrection and ascension. Everyone is to have a part in the fullness of life and power of existence which Christ won by death. Therefore, the judgment of the Father on the Son was a *judgment of grace.* It merited salvation. Salvation demands the triumph over sin and the realization of divine holiness in the world. Making present divine holiness and divine glory, to which man in sin sets himself in opposition, meant death for sinful man. In demanding the death of His beloved Son God was not giving utterance to His wrath, which could only be satisfied by blood and tears. Rather it was a sign of His love and justice" (*Dogm.,* II, 765–767).

"Hence, His obedience and love is our obedience and love, His death and resurrection our death and resurrection. He accomplished it in our place. *He offered Himself up as representative of all.* In Him mankind stood on Golgotha before God's face, bowing to the judgment of the Father. In Him mankind gave satisfaction to the justice of God" (*Dogm.,* II, 800). Cf. also *Dogm.,* II, 777–779, 785; III/2, 106. Cf. also A. Médebielle, "Expiation," in *DBS,* III, 2–262; esp. 175–185.

On the *various aspects of the Catholic doctrine of redemption,* see *S. th.,* III, q. 22–26; 46–49; Rivière, "Redemption," in *DTC,* XIII, 1912–2003 (with an extensive bibliography); Kirchgaessner, *Erlösung und Sünde im NT.* A systematic treatment similar to the Barthian theology of redemption, though not contained in the same kind of close-knit and comprehensive synthesis, can be found in Staudenmaier, *Encyclopedie,* pp. 620–766; Dieringer, *Dogm.* pp. 398–714; Scheeben, *Dogm.* V/1 and V/2, etc. We can find here—as earlier in Thomas, Suarez, Petavius, et al.—what later treatises on the offices and states of Christ often neglected—references to doctrinal passages from the Old Testament.

A question much debated today among Catholic theologians is just *where to put the emphasis on soteriology.* So there is no need here for a conclusive judgment on the matter of emphasis in Barth. Catholic theologians are making an effort to eliminate an extreme juridical emphasis by going back to scripture (and to scriptural terminology). This will require some caution. We must not understress certain emphases, which after all may really be present in scripture, in favor of others. As to Barth, he does accent juridical categories but we cannot charge him with extremism in this regard. Barth not only affirms the legitimacy of other approaches but also takes account of grace in justice and justice in grace. He in no sense defines biblical justice as exacting and vindictive justice. He defines it rather as God's loyalty to Himself and also sees the connection between justice and life, and so on. This is of course not to deny that this and that might be stated in a more scriptural and thus more satisfactory way (Cf. the interpretation of Rom. 3.24–26 in Barth, in II/1, 328f., and in Lyonnet in "Justitia Dei").

The center of present discussions on the theology of redemption is very properly the often neglected *meaning of the resurrection of Jesus Christ* in regard to salvation. Compare the pertinent statement of Lyonnet in *Bulletin d'exégèse paulinienne*. Among recent publications dealing with this theme (along with older works like Staudenmaier, *Encyclopedie,* pp. 703f.; Berlage, *Dogm.,* VI, 39f.; Scheeben, *Dogm.,* V/2, 176–178) the following are noteworthy: D. M. Stanley, *Ad notationes quaedam pro historia exegeseos Rom. 4.25;* J. Schmitt, *Jésus ressuscité dans la prédiction apostolique;* I. Bonsirven, *Théol. du NT,* pp. 110–127, 301f.; F. Prat, *Théol. de S. Paul,* II, 250–254; J. Bover, *Teología de S. Pablo,* pp. 419–431; T. Zapelena, *De Eccl.,* II, 398–432; Cerfaux, *Le Christ,* pp. 57–72; 85–94; F. X. Durrwell, *La résurrection de Jésus, mystère de salut;* B. Vawter, *Resurrection and Redemption;* Goossens, *De valore soteriologico resurrectionis et ascensionis Christi;* F. Holtz, *La valeur sotériologique de la résurrection du Christ d'après S. Thomas d'Aquin.*

Put without polemics then, the justification of the sinner means the declaration of justice by God who at the cross and in the resurrection of Jesus Christ declares all sinners free and just, and thereby makes them just, though this act can, for the Church, have its consequences in the individual only if the individual submits in faith to God's verdict. Some things relegated to the background in many presentations seem to stand out more clearly in this view. Let us single out three important points (the ecclesiastical dimension has already been alluded to) in some brief statements.

Only thus does the *personal* character of justification find adequate expression. For it is not a matter of an organic process of nature (by means of "graces") but a matter of taking a personal stand with Christ before the Father.

Only thus does the *seriousness* of justification find adequate expression. Faith is not simply diluted in love, as though it were a harmless matter of two lovers making up after a quarrel. The issue is the just (and gracious) judgment of the Lord of heaven and earth.

Only thus is adequate weight given to the *theocentricity* of justi-fication. It is not primarily a matter of a process of salvation taking place within man, of a not-having followed by an infusion of habitus and grace—that is of justification considered as passive. Rather the primary issue is the wrath and grace of *God, His* divine act of gracious and judicial decision, of justification considered as active; it is not primarily "peace to men on earth," but "glory to God in the highest." It is not primarily the justification of man, whereby man receives justice, but the *self-justification of God,* whereby God, willing from eternity salvation and creation, is proven just.

"Therefore say to the house of Israel, Thus says the Lord God: It is *not* for your sake, O house of Israel, that I am about to act, but for the sake of my holy name, which you have profaned among the nations to which you came. And I will vindicate the holiness of my great name, which has been profaned . . . among them; and the na-tions will know that *I* am the LORD, says the Lord GOD, when through you I vindicate my holiness before their eyes" (Ezek. 36.22–23; cf. 36.31–32; Rom. 3.26).

Thus the accent is not on the "subjective" but on the "objective" aspect of justification. It is true that everything depends on this having its effect within individual men, on its realization in the individual, on human participation in it. It is true, too, that only he who believes is actually (subjectively) justified. Yet the de-cisive element in the sinner's justification is found not in the indi-vidual but in the death and resurrection of Christ. It was there that our situation was actually changed; there the essential thing hap-pened. What afterwards happened in the individual man would be impossible to conceive of in isolation. It is not man in his faith who originally changes the situation, who does the essential thing. It is not a matter of completion of the central salvation event in Jesus Christ, but rather an active acknowledgment, and this solely by the power stemming from the central event (cf. chap. 31, on faith). In the death and resurrection of Christ, justification is established with final validity. It has happened once and for all and irrevocably (ἐφάπαξ).

Dupont: ". . . Man is 'reconciled' in that he sees his situation before God changed. The change is accomplished at the time of the death of Christ. It precedes every change in the personal attitudes of man. Christ has made peace once for all. Henceforth the world finds itself at peace with God.

"But reconciliation does not stop there. Second Corinthians notes a second stage. God has reconciled the world to Himself; the world is reconciled with God; this is what is accomplished. But it yet behooves each man to reconcile himself positively and personally with God. Each one must appropriate reconciliation by changing his own attitudes. Each one must make effective for his own account the reconciliation which God has already granted to the world" (*Réconciliation*, pp. 18ff.).

Just as in the chapter on grace as favor so, too, after these two chapters on justification as declaration of justice, we can record a basis agreement between Barthian and Catholic teaching (on ontological inner justification, see the following chapter). And once again Barth's critique of Catholic teaching must be rejected as an unjustified critique. In regard to his critique of the decree of Trent, he has treated the matter superficially.

Above all Barth has failed to see that the Tridentine concept of justification should be understood not as closed but as open, that is, as complementary. Barth understands by "justification" primarily the judgment of God in Christ's death and resurrection. The Council of Trent understands by "justification" primarily the process of justification in man (and as we pointed out this was for good historical reasons). It turns out that these two do not exclude but rather include one another. Barth, speaking as he did of the inner justification of man, in no way overlooked this. Yet in his critique of Trent, Barth played off his concept of justification against the Tridentine concept, instead of assessing active and passive justification as two complementary sides of one reality. Thus he failed to take into account differences in usage. As it turned out, the "objective" event of salvation on the cross, to which Barth applies the scriptural term "justification" is generally designated by Catholics "redemption" (an equally Scriptural term) to distinguish it from "justification" as a "subjective" saving event. But instead of sensibly comparing his "justification" with Catholic "redemption" on the "objective" level (where the result could have been positive), he unconsciously compared his ("objective") justification with the Catholic ("subjective") justification. So we need not be astonished at the results, especially the charge of a lack of light from above, of "another gospel" and of misjudging the divine sovereign act. But how could Barth ignore the fact that in the decree of Trent the chapter on justification in the "subjective" sense (Chaps. 3ff.: *D* 795ff.) is prefaced (pre!) by a short (after all, there was no quarrel about this aspect) yet very informative chapter on "redemption"—that is, on justification in the "objective" sense? Does this not say essentially and concisely (which was all that was needed) everything Barth wants to see said about justification in an "objective" sense, that is, that the redemption or justification of all men is in the crucifixion of Jesus Christ?

Chapter 2: "And so it came about that, when the glorious fullness of time had come (*see Eph. 1:4; Gal. 4:4*), the heavenly Father, 'the Father of mercies and the God of all comfort' (*II Cor. 1:3*), sent Jesus Christ his Son to men. Christ had been announced and promised to many holy Fathers before the Law and during the time of the Law (*see Gen. 49:10, 18*). He was sent that the Jews, who were under the Law, might be redeemed, and that the Gentiles, who were not pursuing justice, might secure justice (*see Rom. 9:30*), and that all might receive the adoption of sons (*see Gal. 4:5*). God has set him forth as a propitiation by his blood through faith for our sins (*see Rom. 3:25*), not for our sins only, but also for those of the whole world (*see I John 2:2*)" (D 794).

This relieves much of the puzzlement. For example, that whereas in his positive teaching Barth does defend man's being made inwardly just, in his negative polemic he protests against a kind of process within man. What Catholic has ever tried to reduce the "objective" justifying event which took place on the cross to the dimensions of an intra-human process? Or, for another example, that whereas Barth defends a "subjective and active" appropriation of the "objective" justifying event, yet he protests the language of "to assent to and to co-operate with" used by Trent. How could Trent possibly have spoken of a co-operation in the objective event which took place on the cross?

The Council meant nothing but what Barth himself has written in another section of his *Dogmatics:* "But when we see man, we do not see any kind of being. Whatever it may or may not signify in detail or in a more general context, we see the being which is constantly realizing its existence in acts of free determination and decision. And we the observers are ourselves the primary evidence. To use the older terminology we see a *creatura rationalis,* a thinking, willing, feeling creature, a spiritual being. . . . The well-known passage in the Formula of Concord (*Sol. dec.* II, 19) does not say that man is a 'stone and a log' but that Holy Scripture compares his heart with a 'hard stone which resists rather than yields in any way to human touch, or to an unhewn timber, or to a wild, unbroken animal'. . . . If it does not belong to our freedom to put ourselves in this position, it is none the less our freedom which we exercise in this position. If there is no 'cooperation on the part of our will in man's conversion' (44), there can and must be once we assume the work of the Holy Spirit on man: 'as much and as long as God rules him through his Holy Spirit, guides and leads him.' If God were to withdraw His gracious hand from us, in that case 'man could not remain in obedience to God for one moment' (66)" (I/2, 364).

Similar remarks could be made about the rest of his charges—about the certainty of salvation; about the "perfection" of justification by good works; about the growth of the grace which justifies; about the "repetition" of justification. We still have much to review.

There remains the final question of terminology: Can the term "justification" also be used in a passive sense? At one time Barth appears to oppose any "biological and psychological" interpretation of the "great concepts of justification and sanctification" in the sense of an individual and personal process of salvation (IV/1, 149f.). At other times he speaks of a "subjective" side to the theology of *justification* covering the range of topics we have dealt with here (IV/1, 551f.). In general Barth uses the term "justification" only for God's act of judgment.

We have consciously tried to focus the term "justification" on the "objective" events. Yet it still seems valid to apply it to what it accomplished in individual man by means of divine judgment (though *not* independently of faith). The term "providence" in itself expresses God's act of solicitude, but it also can be used legitimately for what happens in the world as a result of this act. And so, too, the term "justification" (which taken in itself means God's judgment) can be legitimately applied—and also in conformity with Scripture—to what is effected in man by this judgment. And just as the term "providence" was enriched by this extension, so, too, by an analogous broadening, the wealth of meaning in the term "justification" begins to become manifest. It can only be to the detriment of the divine declaration of justice if in nominalistic fashion the two aspects of the one event of justification are torn apart. Everything turns on the *one* act, looked at from two points of view: active and passive, in its source and in its fulfillment, in what God does and in what man receives, in the declaring of justice and the becoming just, in the doing and its result. Why divide what God has joined together? A complementary self-justification of man can also in this way be avoided altogether. Either aspect ought to be dealt with in a balanced fashion, and this was not always done on the Catholic side. But still, who has a right to blame Trent if, in response to the massive doubts raised by the Reformation in regard to the second aspect, the Council put special (and seemingly one-sided) emphasis on the second—precisely to safeguard the first?

30. SIMUL IUSTUS ET PECCATOR

God in His gracious judgment justifies man. The declaration of justice by the divine judge is identical with making man just. What does God's justification mean for *man?* What does it mean to say that man is just?

According to Barth justification by God means three things: forgiveness of sins; the granting of the right of the children of God; and the granting of the inheritance of eternal life (see chap. 13). This is also the teaching of Trent (see, for example, *D* 796 and 799).

The only question is whether Barth overemphasized the eschatological character of justification (justice as promise). In order to solve the problem let us tackle the old controversial question—that is, to what extent does the just man remain sinner? (see chap. 13.)

It is to be presupposed that the justified man is *truly* just—inwardly in his heart. At this point Barth does side with Trent against the Reformation (see chap. 14). Justification is not merely an externally pasted-on "as-if." Man is not only *called* just but he *is* just. He is a new man—not just outwardly but *inwardly,* not just partly but *totally,* not just negatively but *positively.* That is an indisputable presupposition.

Therefore, our question regarding the "simul iustus et peccator" cannot under any circumstances be the Reformation question. It cannot challenge the authenticity of divine justification. Rather, our question is whether or not there is sense in calling a man who is fully justified inwardly a sinner. Can he be a sinner? Is there such a thing as a Catholic "simul iustus et peccator"? If the expression is correctly understood no Catholic can deny its truth. Proceeding this once from the evident facts of the matter we can leave their theological interpretation for later.

Perhaps the most impressive example of the Catholic "simul

iustus et peccator" is the *Roman Mass*. We have to allow these texts to speak for themselves and to remember that the Church is severely strict in demanding of the celebrating priest the "state" of grace. Hence it is presupposed that the one who prays these texts, at least the priest, stands before God as just. In spite of this we find throughout—especially at decisive points in the Mass—a declaration of a state of sin and a prayer for forgiveness of sin put in the most outspoken terms. It should be noted, too, that the reform of the Mass was instigated by the very Council which issued the decree on justification, and that consequently the Catholicity of these texts is precisely the Catholicity of this Council.

We shall quote extensively from the Mass texts to show that this is no mere matter of a few random utterances.

The Roman Mass [in the form in which it has been offered for long centuries up to 1964] begins with the solemn confession of sin by priest and people: "I confess to almighty God . . . that I have sinned exceedingly in thought, word, and deed by my fault, my fault, my very grievous fault." The people say to the priest exactly what the priest says to the sinner in the confessional: "Almighty God have mercy on you, forgive your sins, and lead you into life everlasting." The priest requests for himself and the people what he requested for the sinner in the confessional: "May the almighty and the merciful Lord grant us pardon, absolution, and the forgiveness of our sins." The same formulas are prayed by the faithful for those who have been readied by this sacred preparation to receive the Lord.

In awareness of the state of sin the priest steps up to the altar, even after this confession: "O Lord, we pray Thee, take away from us our sins, that with pure hearts we may be worthy to enter the holy of holies. . . . We pray Thee that Thou wouldst deign to pardon all my sins." Before he dares to sing the praise of God in the Gloria, he prays again with the people: "Lord have mercy. . . . Christ have mercy." In the Gloria itself: "Thou that takest away the sins of the world, have mercy upon us; Thou that takest away the sins of the world, receive our prayer." Before the proclamation of the Gospel: "Cleanse my heart and my lips, almighty God, who didst cleanse the lips of the prophet Isaiah with a burning coal; thus do Thou vouchsafe to cleanse me by Thy grace and mercy that I may be able worthily to preach Thy holy Gospel." After the Gospel: ". . . May our sins be wiped out by the words of the Gospel."

With the offering of gifts the priest prays: "Accept, O holy Father, almighty, eternal God, this immaculate host which I, an unworthy servant of Thine, offer unto Thee, my living and true God, for my innumerable sins and offences and failings." Somewhat later: "With humble spirit and contrite heart may we be received by Thee, O Lord. . . ." In the most sacred part of the canon, just before the consecration, he prays, ". . . command that we be saved from eternal damnation and numbered with Thine elect." After the transubstantiation: "And also to us, Thy sinful servants, who hope in the multitude of Thy mercies, do Thou condescend to grant some portion and fellowship with Thy holy apostles and martyrs . . . and with all Thy saints, into whose company we pray Thee to admit us, not considering our merit but freely granting us pardon."

The holy meal is prepared through the prayer of the Lord: "and forgive us our debts . . ." continuing, "and deliver us, O Lord, we pray, from all evils that are past, present, and to come. . . ." Then three times: "Lamb of God, who takest away the sins of the world, have mercy upon us." Finally, most urgently, right before the *sumptio corporis et sanguinis Domini:* ". . . receiving the body and blood of the Lord: Lord Jesus Christ . . . do not look upon my sins but upon the faith of Thy Church! . . . Deliver me by this Thy most holy body and blood from all mine iniquities and from all evils; and make me ever to adhere to Thy commandments and let me never be separated from Thee. . . . May the reception of Thy body, Lord Jesus Christ, which I unworthily presume to receive, not redound to my judgment and condemnation. . . . Lord, I am not worthy that Thou shouldst come under my roof; but speak the word only and my soul shall be healed." The Mass is concluded with ". . . grant that the sacrifice which I who am unworthy have offered before the eyes of Thy majesty may be acceptable to Thee and, by Thy mercy, salutary to me and to all. . . . Through Christ, our Lord. Amen."

Cf. also the prayers of the Mass, i.e. the collects of the Fourth Sunday after Epiphany, the Monday after the Second Sunday in Lent, Passion Sunday; the Secreta of the Sixth Sunday after Epiphany, Quinquagesima, the Tuesday after the Second Sunday in Lent, Thursday after Passion Sunday, the Second Sunday after Pentecost; the postcommunion of the Fourth Sunday in Advent, the Wednesday after the Fourth Sunday in Lent, the Eleventh Sunday after Pentecost. It is true as Schmaus said, "that we encounter an image of man in the liturgy in which he is simultaneously justified and sinful" (*Dogm.,* III/ 2, 231).

Another fact of significance is the *recurrent confessional formula* which involves the confession and request for remission of sins that have already been confessed and forgiven. This kind of formulary is admitted by the Church and even recommended. Thus, although he is justified, a man may, as a sinner, lament anew the sins forgiven him and pray for their remission.

There can be no doubt that these facts clearly proclaim a Catholic "simul iustus et peccator." But how is this to be explained theologically?

It should be taken for granted that this is not a more or less pious bit of hypocrisy. It should be obvious that statements so often and forcefully repeated in acts as vital for the Church as the Mass and the Sacrament of Penance are to be taken at face value. The Church here and in its total life of prayer carries out the mandate of the Lord who said, "When you pray, say . . . forgive us our sins" (Lk. 11.2, 4). And it also thinks on the words of the apostles, "For we all make many mistakes" (Jas. 3.2); and "If we say we have no sin, we deceive ourselves, and the truth is not in us" (1 Jn. 1.8).

It is for this reason that the Church has defined the "simul iustus et peccator."

The *XVI Council of Carthage* says in Can. 6: "They have likewise decreed: Whoever thinks St. John the Apostle's statement—'If we say that we have no sin, we deceive ourselves, and the truth is not in us' (I John 1:8)—is to be taken in the sense that he is saying we have sin because humility demands us to say so, not because we actually do have sin: let him be anathema" (*D* 106).

Can. 7, "Whoever says that the reason why the saints say, 'forgive us our debts' (Matt. 6:12) in the Our Father is not that they are requesting this for themselves—for such a request is not necessary for them—but that they are requesting it for others of their people who are debtors . . . : let him be anathema" (*D* 107).

Can. 8, "They have likewise decreed: Whoever says that, when the saints pray the Our Father, they say 'forgive us our debts' (Matt. 6:12) humbly rather than truthfully: let him be anathema. For who would tolerate the thought of a man praying and lying, not to men but to the Lord himself, since he says with his lips that he wishes to have his debts forgiven, but denies in his heart that he has anything to be forgiven?" (*D* 108). For an interpretation, cf. Rondet, *Gratia Christi,* pp. 128–130.

But how is this to be explained without, in effect, denying the inner justification of man, or at least casting doubt on it?

In the *Council of Trent* we can isolate a double series of assertions which will clarify the Catholic "simul iustus et peccator."

The *first* series stresses the following truths: In justification man is reborn not to glory (and thus not to a total justness) but rather to the *hope* of glory. Man is in via; he is not yet there where "the just shine like the sun." The Council emphasizes this aspect when it treats of such topics as: (a) the fomes peccati, which remains in the just man, too, as a kind of kindling wood—although not as sin —and has a very close connection with sin since it is from sin and continually inclines toward it (*De pecc. orig.:* Can. 5, *D* 792);

(b) the necessity of perfection and growth in justification (*De justificatione:* Chap. 10, *D* 803); (c) the uncertainty of salvation (Chaps. 9 and 12, *D* 802 and 805); (d) the special privilege without which man could not avoid even venial sin (Chap. 9 and Can. 23, *D* 804 and 833); (e) in the statement that the just "Knowing that they are reborn unto the hope of glory (see I Pet. 1:3) and not yet unto glory itself, they should be in dread about the battle they must wage with the flesh, the world, and the devil. For in this battle they cannot be victors unless with God's grace . . ." (*D* 806).

Schmaus: "Luther's formula" *simul iustus et peccator* "is not affected by the condemnation of Trent if it is meant not metaphysically but concretely and historically . . . The justified man, who is free from sin and yet always tempted toward it, approaches a condition in which he is freed also from temptation to sin—that state of perfection in which, in the contemplation of God, he is totally immersed in God's love and holiness. His earthly life is lived in a tension between his present, in which he is free from sin and still continually threatened by it, and his future which is free from every threat of sin. It is for this reason that justification has an *eschatological* character" (*Dogm.,* III/2, 117f.).

Lyonnet: "Therefore, although the charge of guilt is forgiven, man remains a *debtor to retribution*, which the theologians, especially Saint Thomas, consider remedial, by which man, so to speak, *must be purified* whether it be on earth or whether it be after death in 'Purgatory.' Before that, man, however righteous he may be, is plainly not fit for that intimate union with God which will be enjoyed when we shall see Him with our eyes; in other words, *an obstacle resulting from sin* has not yet been fully removed. Therefore Catholic doctrine declares that in a true sense man is 'at the same time a just man and a sinner' " (*Quaest. de soteriologia,* p. 149).

The *second* series of statements stresses that all that man possesses of justice is given him by grace and thus in origin is alien to man. This series of statements only develops the consequences of Canon 22 of Orange: "No one has (anything) of his own . . ." (*D* 195).

The Council stresses this aspect in the following instances: (a) when it designates the justice of God as the sole causa formalis of justification (Chap. 7; *D* 799); (b) when it condemns the idea that man could be justified without the justice of Christ (Can. 10; *D* 820); (c) when it says that justice is indeed ours but is not ours due to ourselves (Chap. 16; *D* 809).

Schmaus: "The justice of Christ becomes our justice. We have seen again and again that the life of Christ becomes our life in a real but purely analogical way. In regard to its source, our justice can be called an 'extrinsic' justice but this justice, though received from 'without,' so penetrates man that it inheres in him, not as a possession which he can dispose of at will, and not as in the case of the owner of some capital funds. It inheres rather as a gift of grace granted to him in a continuous divine declaration of grace—a gift for which he is answerable" (*Dogm.*, III/2, 133).

Cerfaux: "The relation between faith and justice persists therefore in Paul's thinking, even when justice is conceived of as the permanent condition of the Christian. We have received justice thanks to our insertion by faith into the work of salvation. And if we would lose sight of the permanent subordination of the gift, we would make of justice our own possession. It would be the justice of man and no longer the justice of God. At any moment, therefore, justice remains what it has been continuously, that is something obtained by faith, determined by the character which essentially pervades it, which character we must constantly remain conscious of, 'the justice which comes from God, which depends on faith; that I may know him (Christ) and the power of his resurrection, and may share his sufferings' (Phil. 3.9–10); cf. "Justice," in DBS, IV, c. 1487.

And so we see how the Catholic teaching of Trent on the "simul iustus et peccator" is grounded: (1) The justified man is capable of sin afterward as well as before. He remains in the danger zone of sin (wherein the full and complete annulling of the culpability of sin is not yet visible, while the concrete sinfulness of man is decidedly visible) and he is nevertheless bound continually to pursue perfection, moving from the past into the future (Phil. 3.12–14). (2) The justice characteristic of the justified man remains something which in the final analysis is "alien" and "extrinsic" to him. Although it does really dwell in him, he must constantly receive it afresh from Christ as a grace which never originates with himself.

These statements made in Catholic teaching are nothing but a faithful echo of the words of Sacred Scripture itself. The following are some examples: "Blessed are those who *hunger* and *thirst for* righteousness" (Mt. 5.6). "For through the Spirit, by faith, we *wait* for the *hope* of righteousness" (Gal. 5.5). "And your life is *hid* with Christ in God. When Christ who is our life appears, then you also will *appear* with him in glory" (Col. 3.3–4). "But we ourselves, who have the first fruits of the Spirit, groan inwardly as we wait for adoption as sons, the redemption of our bodies. For *in this hope* we were saved. Now hope that is seen is not hope. For who hopes for what he sees? But if we hope for what we do not see, we *wait* for it with patience" (Rom. 8.23–25). "Not that I have already obtained this or am already perfect; but I press on to make it my own, because Christ Jesus has made me his own. Brethren, I do not consider that I have made it my own, but one thing I do, forgetting what lies behind and straining forward to what lies ahead, I press on toward the goal for the prize of the upward call of God in Christ Jesus. Let those of us who are mature be thus minded; and if in anything you are otherwise minded, God will reveal that also to you" (Phil. 3.12–15). Not to be overlooked is the fact that δικαιον very often has not a present but a *future* sense (Rom. 2.13; 3.20, 30; Gal. 2.16; etc.).

Tobac has been reproached for exaggerating the eschatological aspect of justification and it is true that here and there a future tense must be taken as a logical future. But no one will deny that the justification of the individual becomes fully and conclusively valid only in the final judgment.

In his exegesis Barth took *Romans 7* as the classical passage for the "simul iustus et peccator" (IV/I, 580–591). Whether that chapter applies to the justified man or to the unjustified (if this is the problem at all) is disputed. In any case there is no need to take this up with Barth since there is in the Catholic tradition a sufficient number of important witnesses who interpret the passage as applying to the Christian.

Before Augustine there were: Hilary, Gregory of Nazianzus, Ambrose, Cyprian, Jerome (cf. Platz, *Der Römerbrief in der Gnadenlehre Augustins,* p. 163, along with Cornely and Prat); after Augustine (in the anti-Pelagian controversy), Gregory the Great, Peter Lombard, Thomas, Cajetan, Salmeron, Estius . . . (cf. Lemonnyer, "Justification," in *DTC,* VIII, 2052–2054).

No matter how these passages are interpreted no one will be able to argue away the spiritual experience of a continual conflict within the individual Christian, between the old sinful and the new justified man (cf. Rom. 6.11–14; Gal. 5.16–18; Eph. 4.17–24; etc.). From this viewpoint no one in the Catholic tradition has paraphrased Romans 7 more beautifully than Racine:

> "Mon Dieu, quelle guerre cruelle!
> Je trouve deux hommes en moi:

L'un veut que plein d'amour pour toi
Mon coeur te soit toujours fidèle.
L'autre, à tes volontés rebelle
Me révolte contre ta loi.

L'un, tout esprit, et tout céleste,
Veut qu'au ciel sans cesse attaché,
Et des biens éternels touché,
Je compte pour rien tout le reste;
Et l'autre, par son poids funeste,
Me tient vers la terre penché.

Hélas! en guerre avec moi-même,
Où pourrai-je trouver la paix?
Je veux, et n'accomplis jamais.
Je veux, mais, ô misère extrême!
Je ne fais pas le bien que j'aime,
Et je fais le mal que je hais.

O grâce, ô rayon salutaire,
Viens me mettre avec moi d'accord;
Et domptant par un doux effort
Cet homme qui t'est si contraire,
Fais ton esclave volontaire
De cet esclave de la morte."
(*Cantiques Spirituels,* Cantique III)

Catholic theology plainly and openly speaks—despite the *totus iustus*—of a *simul iustus et peccator*. What was said up to now could be easily elaborated by a closer consideration of the truths in question. It will be enough to take a short look at three concepts —the past, concupiscence, and sin.

(1) In this problem it is too often the obvious that is overlooked. For time is not an infinite series of single "objective" moments arranged one after another. Past, present, and future are not three epochs standing beside one another with the past increasing at the point of the present by exactly the amount by which the future decreases. Rather time is one continually flowing movement, which I possess as my own time, and in which I can distinguish various moments, without however being able to isolate

them. My time is a personal, single and indivisible entity. What is behind me is not simply past, but rather *my* past; what lies before me is not simply future, but rather *my* future. What has happened or will happen I cannot separate from myself. It is absurd to deny one's past or not to take one's future seriously. For the past is also present—though as something past, and the future is present—though as something future. So it is understandable how a man can be weighted down with his past (although it has gone by) or by his future (although it is still far away). Man is, after all, simultaneously the man he will be as well as the man he was.

This seems to be behind an apparently absurd petition made by the Church: "Deliver us from the evils that are past." And it seems to be behind what she does when she permits the reconfession of sins already remitted, and when she continues to speak of justified sinners as "poor sinners." Man indeed *was* a sinner because *his* sin is truly forgiven and not just "hidden" or "overlooked" but man *is* the one he *was*. In other words, the sinful past is his past; he can never say, "No, I am not such a one, with him I have nothing to do." Rather he must honestly acknowledge his past. Being at once humble and happy, he must carry his past—as past —out of the present into the future, until, all at once, through God's new grace he definitively sheds his past and his future becomes eternally present.

Schmaus seems to be making this point when he says: "Through the forgiveness of sin the *reatus culpae* is taken away—that is, the sinful nature of sin; but the sin as *historical fact* is by no means annulled, for there is no reversal of history. Rather, whatever has become historical fact remains forever an element of history." (*Dogm.*, III/2, 107).

And Thomas says very clearly: "Interior penance is that whereby one is sorry for a sin he has committed and this penance ought to last until the end of life" (*S.th.*, III, q. 84, a. 8 co).

(2) As Karl Rahner has demonstrated (in his essay on the theological concept of concupiscence), the idea of concupiscence is ambivalent and can be understood positively or negatively. In Trent it is understood negatively—as a kind of kindling wood for sin. Concupiscence taken in this sense is a radical threat to man's condition of justice "because it is from sin and inclines toward sin." (*D* 792). The past which has been disposed of time and again as temptation, turns into an anxious present. Justified man, too, has a continual inclination to sin, a heavy burden which

always pulls him down. If man does not fall prey to this inclination, it is due to the grace of Jesus Christ rather than to himself. But who could readily diagnose for himself whether he is still marching forward or whether he is slipping imperceptibly? Who could so readily draw the line for himself between what is and what is not sin? How the moral theologians struggled for clear lines of division, only to realize that real life can time and again spill over what appear to be solidly established borders. What justified man would have the self-assurance to assert that for him everything was really pure, that worship of self played no part in his worship of God? Was it not the great saints who suffered—as it seems, excessively —under the sinfulness of even their best deeds? Was it not just *because* they were just and united with God that they knew that much better about the smoldering kindling, the "remnant of sin" among the saints (Augustine), the residue of an ultimate disorder even in the hearts of the saints, the simple fact that they were poor sinners? Finally, must not every one of us be extremely grieved when he says what is dearest to his God: "Lord, you know that I love you"? That is what so greatly troubles the just man in this world: whoever looks upon himself as just is a sinner, and whoever looks upon himself as a real sinner is just. The latter goes home justified, the former does not.

When John of the Cross lay on his deathbed and a friend attempted to comfort him, pointing out the things he had accomplished, John answered, "Don't tell me, Father, don't tell me that, tell me my sins!"

(3) Sin is never merely private guilt. It is always sin against Jesus Christ and His body. Every sin has an "(a-)social" character. This is true even when we look at its author. Man is of course not simply the product of his environment, and there is no collective guilt which cancels out personal responsibility. Yet man is in his being linked with his fellowman in his acts of commission and omission. He participates in good and also bears his share of evil. In sin and guilt how could the line between mine and yours be so easily drawn? The curse of an evil action is that it goes on forever producing evil consequences. All men live in one world; they are bound together in one world; and the world is the sphere of reality where sin holds sway.

The trouble with the Church is that it is not something on the inside shuttered away from the world outside. No, it is inside the world and the world is in it; the battlefront where world and Church face one another always runs straight through the heart of man. "Indeed, we desire one thing because we are in Christ, and we desire another thing because we are still in this world" (Aug., *In Joh.,* tr. 81, 4; *PL,* 35, 1842). The Church is a communion of saints, but it is simultaneously a communion of sinners. It is precisely the Catholic Church that has maintained, in opposition to all heresies of all times, that sinners, too, belong to the Church—and thereby the Church has definitely rejected the appeal to an allegedly "pure" Church. The Church is holy, certainly. But it is holy—and this also applies to the individual—only from *Christ.* It is holy, not through the spirit of its sinful members, but through *His* Holy Spirit. It is holy not through its words and actions, but rather through *His* teaching and Sacraments. *This* kind of holiness manifests itself in individuals and also in a special way among those who are especially beloved by God. The following words are also true for the community: "No one has anything of his own except lying and sin. But if man has any truth and justice, it is from that fountain for which we ought to thirst in this desert, that having drunk some drops of water from it, we may not falter on the way" (*D* 195).

This, then, is the Church as she is—the holy Church of Jesus Christ, the holy bride of Jesus Christ, but simultaneously, as the Church of sinners, the sinful Church. Sin does not belong to her being but to what in her is the opposite of being—as the guilt-laden contradiction of the innocence decreed for her by her Lord. This is the great and unfortunate ecclesiological implication of the "simul"—that the ecclesia is simul iusta et peccatrix.

K. Rahner: "If all we said was, 'Of course there are sinners in the Church but this fact does not have anything to do with the Church proper,' we would be assuming an idealistic concept of the Church, which theologically is very questionable. The 'Church' would then be an ideal of something which ought to be something asymptotic, always to be merely approximated and never to be reached. Something like that one can always love and be pledged to as something intangible, never touched by everyday misery, something to which, from the standpoint of real life, a legal appeal might be addressed. However, this is not what is really meant in the theological concept of the Church. In this conception the Church is a real entity—that is, the only Church which exists and is believed in; it is the always and ever visibly and legally organized sum total of those who are baptized, and are united in public confession of faith and in obedience to the Roman Pope. And of this Church it is quite impossible to say that it has nothing to do with the sins of its members. Naturally it does not sanction sin. Naturally there are men within it (and maybe even a lot) who must be called saints in some true sense of the word (a sense not to be dwelt on here). But if it is something real, then if its members are sinners and as sinners continue to remain members, it is itself sinful. Then the sins of its children are a blemish and a spot on the most holy and mysterious body of Christ Himself. The Church is a sinful Church— that is a truth of faith, not a primitive fact of experience. And it is a shocking truth" (*Kirche der Sünder*, pp. 14f.).

Of interest in this connection are the results of the historical investigation by P. Nautin on the third article of faith. Significantly enough, in the earliest times the attribute "holy" was seldom applied to the Church and even then the primary meaning was not the moral holiness of its members, but the Church's connection with God (holy as celestial), and especially with the Holy Spirit (holy as spiritual) (*Je crois à l'Esprit*, pp. 54–63). In the apostolic tradition the baptismal question was originally: "Do you also believe, in the Holy Spirit within the Holy Church, in the resurrection of the body?" (p. 27).

On the theological significance and on all the necessary distinctions, cf. Pilgram, *Physiologie der Kirche*, pp. 128–136; Y. Congar, *Vraie et fausse réforme*, pp. 63–132 (particularly the doctrine of Scripture, the Fathers, and the magisterium, pp. 72–91, and the theological synthesis, pp. 127–130); Ch. Journet, *L'Eglise du Verbe incarné*, vol. I, xiii–xiv, vol. II, 395f., and esp. vol. II, 893–934. Cf. also the other theologians cited by Congar: E. Mersch, Dom Vonier, K. Adam, Pinard de la Boullaye, J. Bernhart, P. Couturier, H. Rahner. On the double aspect of the Fathers' use of the bridal image for the Church, see H. de Lubac, *Katholizismus*, pp. 61f.

To finish this chapter it seems fitting once again to point out the limits of the Catholic simul iustus et peccator.

"Luther's 'simul iustus et peccator' is a formula with many meanings. It could express an extreme opposition to what is Catholic, and again as Robert Grosche has pointed out, if interpreted in meliorem partem, it could represent a Catholic position. In a general way it might be said that the formula is correct for what Luther wished to express. On the other hand, it expresses the status viatoris, in which the justice of man before God is not consummated but is rather involved in general historical process, in daily turning away from the old man and turning toward the new, in a dying and a being born. On the other hand, it expresses the fact that man's justice is a gift from start to finish, coming to him from above and from without and thus, though given him for his own, is not really his own. Only in two cases does Luther's formula become untenable for Catholic dogmatic theology: first, when the idea is mixed up through an exaggerated eschatological attitude so that justice is consigned to man only as hope and not also as present reality; or second, when due to a legalistic nominalism the idea is twisted to mean that justice can never become man's possession as an intrinsic reality. For in these cases the formula expresses either genuine contradiction—the sinner is just as sinner and inasmuch as he is sinner—or it expresses an assessment actually not at all applicable to him as sinner; for the sinner, though in himself nothing but a sinner, is nevertheless judged by God to be just on the basis of Christ's merits (H. U. von Balthasar, *Karl Barth,* pp. 379f.; cf. R. Grosche, *Simul peccator et iustus*).

31. SOLA FIDE

The justification of the sinner is the work of God, but it is accomplished in man. How does man behave in this work? What is man's attitude in God's justification? That is the last question we are able to deal with out of the welter of problems raised by the event of justification.

Barth's answer to the question of man's behavior in divine justification is the answer of Luther—sola fides. Man has to respond to the justifying activity of God with faith and indeed *with faith alone*. What is the Catholic to say about this formula?

The controversy began when in 1521 Luther translated Romans 3.28 as, "That a man be justified . . . by faith *alone*." This has earned him much abuse from the Catholic side, even the reproach of falsifying Scripture. We do not have to investigate how Luther himself understood the formula; he did not always express himself with the same precision. In his commentary on Romans he still accepted good works, after justification as well as before, as long as they did not occur "in pursuit of justification" (pro quaerenda iustificatione).

The formula sola fide can be taken for orthodox since the "alone" may be understood as a plausible way of making clear the statement in Romans 3.28. This much is certain—the "alone" in the translation is not Luther's invention. Even *before* the Reformation there were already such translations. According to Lyonnet (ad Rom., p. 117) the German Bible's (Nürnberg, 1483) reading of Gal. 2.16 is "gerechtfertigt . . . *nur* durch den Glauben." The same reading occurs in three Italian translations, according to Oltramare: "ma solo per la fede" or "per la sola fede" (Genoa 1476, Venice 1538 and 1546). Nor did the Council of Trent intend to say anything against the formula in itself.

Villette (*Foi et sacrement,* IV, 111f.) noted in his section on Trent that the earlier redaction of the famous ninth canon read as follows

(*D* 819): "Faith alone . . . *in the sense in which this is understood by the heretics of our time."* This was later dropped out because it was self-evident. In the condemnations the term "faith," it was argued, even if used absolutely, was always to be understood in the sense intended by the heretics. And for Trent, too, the procedure of condemnation of Baius and Jansen ought to apply—that is "although some of them could be maintained in some way, yet in the strict and proper sense intended by those asserting them, we condemn them." (*D* 1080; cf. 1098, 1099).

Even more significant than the translations is the fact that the formula definitely belongs to Catholic tradition. Bellarmine (*De iustificatione* II, 25) realized this and cited the following for the Reformation formula: Origen, Hilary, Basil, Chrysostom, Augustine, Cyril of Alexandria and especially Ambrosiaster and Bernard. It is enough for us here to cite an even later witness of the tradition. Thomas Aquinas commented on 1 Tim. 1.8: "We know that the law is good, if one uses it lawfully . . ." Here the gloss distinguishes between moral precepts and ceremonial precepts. Thomas, however, continues: "But the Apostle seems to be talking about morality, for he adds that the law was laid down because of sins (vs. 9) and these are moral precepts. The use of these is lawful when man does not assign to them more than they contain. The law was given that sin might be known, for if the law did not say, 'You shall not covet,' I should not have known what it is to covet (Rom. 7.7), as the *commandments* teach. *There is therefore no hope of justification in them, but in faith alone.* We hold that a man is justified by faith without the works of the law (Rom. 3.28)." So the question is not the formula itself but the meaning of the formula.

Along with the Fathers and theologians cited, see among modern writers: Lemonnyer, "Justification" in *DTC,* VIII, 2066; Rivière, "Justification" *DTC,* VIII, 1080; Bouyer, *Protestantism,* p. 14; Lyonnet, *loc. cit.;* Meinertz, *Theol. des NT,* II, 129.

For the position of the theologians of Trent in regard to this patristic tradition, see Stakemeier, *Glaube und Rechtfertigung,* p. 201 (notice especially the explanation of Lippomano).

Now what is the correct meaning of "sola fide"? (Along with Rom. 3.28 the parallel passages, especially Gal. 2.16, Phil. 5.9, Eph. 2.8–9, have to be considered).

"Sola fide" makes good sense when it is used to express what was stressed in the foregoing chapters—that is, the total incapacity of man for any kind of self-justification. In justification the sinner can give nothing which he does not receive by God's grace. He stands there with his hands entirely empty. Just as Abraham in Gen. 15.6 and Rom. 4.3 and as the Israelites before Moses in Ex. 4.31: "And the people believed; and when they heard that the LORD had visited the people of Israel and that he had seen their affliction, they bowed their heads and worshiped." This man is a man who knows that he has nothing to build for God, but he accepts God's word, like David. "Would you build me a house to dwell in? . . . Moreover the LORD declares to you that the LORD *will make you* a house" (2 Sam. 7.5, 11). This man is a man who will not dash off on a charger, but whose power lies in quietness and trust (cf. Isa. 30.15–16), who receives the kingdom of God like a little child (Mk. 10.15) and who says nothing else than a Marian "let it be to me" (Lk. 1.38); a man who expects nothing from himself, but expects all from God, who is completely open to that which is his only refuge—this man is the man who does not work but *believes* and therefore radically excludes any "self-boasting." "Then what becomes of our boasting? It is excluded. On what principle? On the principle of works? No, but on the principle of faith. For we hold that a man is justified by faith [alone] apart from works of law" (Rom. 3.27–28; cf. Rom. 4.2, 5–6; 5.11; 9.30–32; 10.4–6; 1 Cor. 4.7; 2 Cor. 12.9). "Yet [we] know that a man is not justified by works of the law but through faith in Jesus Christ, [so] even we have believed in Christ Jesus, in order to be justified by faith in Christ, and not by works of the law, because by works of the law shall no one be justified" (Gal. 2.16; 3.6; Phil. 3.9; etc).

Which works are excluded? The works of the Mosaic ceremonial law perhaps? No, *all* works are excluded, even the works of the moral law (the Ten Commandments and so forth). This is the opinion of many others, including St. Thomas in his comment on Rom. 3.28; cf. the above citation of 1 Tim. 1.8. What is true is precisely what Lyonnet remarked on this citation: "In fact *all moral works* on the one hand and *faith alone* on the other are opposed" (p. 117).

Thus it is already apparent from scripture that the antithesis between faith and works is to be equated with the antithesis between grace and works. (Rom. 4.16; 6.14; 11.5–6; Gal. 2.21).

Lyonnet also makes reference to *S.th.* I–II, q. 106, a. 2 co, where it is taught that the new law justifies only insofar as it is not written, namely, insofar as it is grace: "But in so far as it contains teachings concerning faith and precepts regulating man's conduct and man's acts . . . the new law does not justify. . . . The letter kills, the spirit makes alive. And Augustine explains that by the 'letter' any Scriptures existing outside of men, *also moral precepts such as are contained in the Gospel.* Whence even the letter of the New Testament kills, unless the healing *grace of faith* be present in them (i.e. in men)."

The Council of Trent defined: "We may be said to be justified freely, in the sense that nothing that precedes justification, neither faith nor works, merits the grace of justification" (*D* 801).

Bouyer: "Furthermore, that faith *alone* saves us means, if it means anything, that we on our part must add nothing to it, nothing outside it or independent of it. Any such addition would result necessarily in a negation of the essential, for if, though believing in principle in the saving action of God, we felt constrained to add anything at all in which we would rely on our own initiative, what would be the result? We would fall back at once into the impossible situation from which grace had rescued us; we would have to accomplish one part of our salvation, trusting God to do the rest. But our actual state of wretchedness comes from our incapacity for any effective initiative, even incomplete, in regard to salvation; in short, we have not only to be assisted in order to save ourselves, but in order to be saved" (Bouyer, *Protestantism*, p. 12).

Thus man is justified through God's grace alone; man achieves nothing; there is no human activity. Rather man simply submits to the justification of God; he does not do works; he believes: "In this that he believes in God who justifies, he submits to his justification and thus receives its effect" (Thomas Aquinas In Rom. 4.5).

That is why Paul (as also the Synoptics and John) always links justification with faith and not with love. Justification occurs through faith *alone,* inasmuch as no kind of work, not even a work of love, justifies man, but simply faith, trust, abandoning oneself to God, giving oneself over to God's grace in response to God's act, the "sese subiicere iustificatione et ita recipere eius effectum."

Bouyer: "What it (the formula) rejects or wants to reject is the idea, and nothing but the idea, of our adding our personal contribution, *extrinsic to these two things, grace which gives, and faith which receives.* Understood in this way, such an addition amounts to saying that we are saved neither by grace nor faith. Faith in divine grace would assure us that only one part of our salvation need no longer concern us. Now precisely that insight of Luther which is preserved in the type of Protestantism most faithful to its origins and most truly Christian, is that *all* is grace, and that, consequently, *all* in our salvation comes to us by faith. If this all is compromised, the very heart of

Protestant spirituality is wounded mortally" (Bouyer, *Protestantism,* p. 13; cf. Rondet, *Gratia Christi,* p. 60; Schillebeeckx, *Sacramentele Heilseconomie,* p. 563).

Faith is therefore actually *trust.* It is the faith of Abraham (Rom. 4). "Take heart, my son: your sins are forgiven" (Mt. 9.2; Mk. 2.5; cf. *D* 798). Our faith as it appears in Sacred Scripture is a trusting faith. This is the faith demanded of man in justification. Interestingly enough, however, the most recent and most thorough presentation of the biblical concept of faith in the article πιστις in *TWNT,* VI (Weiser, Kittel, Bultmann) shows that the biblical usage of "faith" does not permit of the smallest degree of simplification. Even if faith is taken in the active and specifically Christian sense, it would be pointless to look everywhere for the connotation of "trust" because the primary meaning of faith in the New Testament is not this but the acceptance of the Christian kerygma.

Bultmann says of the specifically Christian usage: "πιστις is here understood as the acceptance of the Christian kerygma and therefore as *saving faith* which in acknowledging the work of God, accomplished in Christ, makes it his own. Naturally, πιστις contains here also the sense of faith as a giving of credentials and in addition the elements of obedience, trust, hope and steadfastness might be connoted—just as, vice versa, where one of these meanings is primary the reference to Christ may be connoted. But the primary meaning of πιστευειν in the specific Christian usage is 'the acceptance of the kerygma of Christ'" (*TWNT,* VI, 209; cf. for the Pauline concept, esp. 218–220).

After Trent (*D* 789) the Vatican Council took pains to elaborate the intellectual and cognitive aspect of faith (*D* 1795).

But at the same time the fact remains that there is the closest connection between faith and trust; the element of trust is included in biblical faith. This is especially true when faith is discussed in reference to justification (for example Rom. 4.17–20; 9.33; 10.11).

The Old Testament האמין means both faith and trust; cf. Heinisch, *Theol. des AT,* p. 149; Prat, *Théol. de S. Paul,* II, 283; *Bibel-Lexikon,* "Glaube," p. 578. Cf. the lexicon article of Zorell and of Brown-Driver-Briggs. Cf. Weiser's definition of "faith" as "to say 'Amen' to God" (*TWNT,* VI, 186ff.).

And faith and trust also belong together in the New Testament in the expressions πιστις and πιστευειν, when it is a question of the religious act of man; cf. the lexicon article of Zorell, Bauer, Knabenbauer (*Lex. Bibl. II*); in addition *Bibel-Lexikon,* pp. 580f.; Tobac, "Justification," pp. 226f.; Prat, *Théol. de S. Paul,* I, 202, 204f.; II,

282f., 290; Antoine, "Foi," in *DBS*, III, 278; Meinertz, *Theol. des NT,* II, 126; Bonsirven, *Théol. du NT,* p. 132; Bartmann, *Paulus und Jacobus,* pp. 42f.; Schmaus, *Dogm.,* III/2, 306; H. Schmidt, *Brücken-schlag,* pp. 195f. (cf. also Bultmann in *TWNT,* VI, 203f.; 206f., 209, 219).

In justification man bows before God, with nothing at hand but his faithful trust. Cerfaux: "The Jew sought justice which to him consisted in observing the entire law . . . with God acknowledging this justice of men who expected it to be publicly rewarded at the future judgment. It is precisely the opposite in the case of the Christian, who puts his trust in God by giving himself to the work of salvation accomplished in Christ, and God justifies him ("Justice," in *DBS,* IV, 1474).

Huby: "Man can give only his faith, which is, in the essential relationship between faith and justice, not at all a 'work' but an attitude of total agreement with the divine work of salvation through Christ, an act of knowledge and an offering of obedience intertwined, the two reciprocally conditioning one another" (*Epître aux Rom.,* p. 71).

Indeed it is not a question of a blind dogmatic trust (*D* 802, no "boasting," iactare! cf. *D* 822), nor of an indolent tranquil trust (*D* 802, quiescere! cf. *D* 822), and most certainly not a trust that trusts itself, that relies on its own justification (*D* 824; cf. *D* 802). On the contrary, it is a trust in which man—looking at himself and his own sinful weakness—fears and trembles (*D* 823; cf. *D* 802, 818), is humbly and hopefully expecting everything from God (*D* 798, 802), and believing in the divine promise (*D* 798), especially the forgiveness of sin which occurs in Christ (*D* 798). Thus it is clear what interpretations of *fides sola* (*D* 819) and *fiducia sola* (*D* 822) are condemned by Trent and how, at the same time, the trusting faith alone is "the beginning, the foundation and source of man's salvation and of all justification" (*D* 801).

Villette says that Chapter 6 of the decree on justification "obviously aims at only one aspect of the reformation teaching on faith, at the affirmation which is essential to it, the subjective certitude and assurance of being justified. It is this assurance which the Council declares vain and unholy, not directly the faith which it accompanies" (*Foi et sacrement,* IV, 114).

"Canon 12, on the other hand, by virtue of the clear reservations twice occurring in the text (Nihil aliud esse quam . . . et eam fiduciam solam esse) surely indicates the insufficiency of this faith and confidence to elicit justification, but it does not go so far as to say that this faith and confidence is evil in itself or harmful" (IV, 114).

Yet, faith in the sense of confidence is inserted in Chapter 6 (*D* 798) under the name of hope. "This description of hope corresponds almost literally to that of the confident faith of the Reformers; however, it requires two precise and important distinctions. First, the basis of the confidence is not the subjective feeling of believing and of being justified, but the objective promise of God; second, this confidence does not concern itself with a present and realized object (justification already granted) but with a future object (Deum sibi propitium fore). These shades of meaning make it possible to distinguish between simple confident faith, whose legitimacy the Council recognizes and which corresponds to the necessary movement of theological hope, and that which is called "fiducial faith" or "special faith," a purely subjective conviction condemned by the Council. In the measure, therefore, that the Reformers affirm the necessity of simple "confident faith" for justification or for the Sacraments, their thought conforms to that of Catholics. In the measure, on the other hand, that Protestants adhere only to "fiducial faith" they are condemned by the Council which has declared such faith vain, useless, and dangerous. It is without valid foundation and runs the risk of causing man to forget how weak he really is and how undependable his intentions." (IV, 115).

On the Tridentine discussion of the certainty of grace, cf. Hefner, *Entstehungsgesch. des Rechtfertigungsdekretes*, pp. 297–328 (esp. on the expression, "which cannot be subject to error," see p. 323); A. Stakemeier, *Gnadengewissheit*, pp. 167–170, 171–181, esp. pp. 174f.

What O. Karrer writes on the certainty of faith agrees with its historical results: "A characteristic peculiarity of the faith of justification is the solid and faithful *certainty* of God's mercy combined with confident hope regarding final salvation because of this divine love. The apostolic proclamation is full of such encouragement and so are the religious writings and the message proclaimed by the Church throughout the centuries. This trust is based on divine omnipotence and mercy in Christ and has a part in the certainty of faith as Thomas and Bonaventure point out in reference to Rom. 8.24; Heb. 6.19; etc. (See Jos. Pieder, *Hoffnung*, pp. 37ff.). The only thing *uncertain* is whether the believer will persist in his faithful hope; and so, well aware of the human weakness which always remains as a dangerous element, he will not lull himself into absolute certainty . . ." (*Galaterbrief*, p. 34). Thus also Schmaus, *Dogm.*, III/2, 222. Was Luther really referred to in the definitions? A. Stakemeier expresses doubts: pp. 173–175.

This faithful trust is not primarily an assent to abstract truths but an affirmation of a person. It is trusting faith in God and the One whom He sent. Faith in God depends upon belief in *Jesus Christ*. He is *"the* truth." "This is the work of God, that you believe in him whom he has sent" (Jn. 6.29). Jesus Christ always demands belief in Himself, and the center of the apostolic kerygma is faith in Christ as Lord, faith in the death and resurrection of Jesus Christ. So it is that the faithful have been called "Christians" since

Antioch, because they believe in God through Jesus Christ and through none but Him.

The *personal* character of faith has recently been emphasized by J. Mouroux in his *Je crois en toi*. Of special importance are the citations from Thomas. We restrict ourselves to quoting the motto of his book. "Now, whoever believes, assents to someone's words; so that, in every form of belief, the person to whose words assent is given seems to hold the chief place and to be the end as it were; while the truths which are held in assenting to that person hold a secondary place. Consequently he that holds the Christian faith aright, assents, by his will, to Christ, in those things which truly belong to His teaching" (*S.th.*, II–II, q. 11, a. 1, co.) Cf. also Mouroux, *Expérience chrétienne*.

On its *christological* character, cf. Mouroux, *Je crois*, pp. 36–41; Huby, *De la connaissance de foi*, pp. 389–392; and the biblical theological works cited above.

The sinner is justified through faith alone, but not through a faith which stands opposed to works done in living community of will with Christ or out of love grounded in faith and all other virtues. Love is not missing in justification and it cannot be so. The faith through which man is justified is indeed faith in the full sense of the word. It is a living faith, fides viva. It does not insist upon acts of love since it wants to receive everything from God. But faith, even "dead" faith, (*D* 798) has the seed of love in it. How else could it grasp God's mercy without a seed of love? How could it have trust in the Redeemer without a secret longing for Him? But neither the sinner pulling himself together nor man stimulated by God's grace effecting a change of heart in him can achieve justification (*D* 801). For this purpose what is needed is God's taking a hand, God's justifying grace which overcomes and gives life to these human acts (*D* 800).

In Scholastic language this event is expressed in the theology of faith, hope, and love as habitus infusi. According to Cornely (Ep. ad Rom., p. 261), the Fathers of Trent did not wish to give an authentic interpretation when they related Rom. 5.5 in chap. 7 of the decree on justification (*D* 800) to the virtue of love. Instead, they used the words of Paul only in such a way that they might apply them somehow to their argument. They are of themselves most appropriate for its expression.

Living faith, which alone justifies, does not exclude but rather includes sorrow for sin. It does not bring about any works (not even works of faith) in order to justify itself. Justification through living faith in no sense means justification by faith *and* works. But it wants to be active in works, "faith working through love" (Gal. 5.6). How should it be otherwise? For "if I have all faith, so as to remove mountains, but have not love, I am nothing" (1 Cor. 13.2).

Moehler: "Thus also the medieval schools knew a faith of which they said that it alone justifies. It is designated as fides formata. To them this was the soul of faith and had love as its enlivening and forming principle (forma), and therefore it is also designated fides caritate formata, animata, fides viva, vivida" (*Symbolik,* p. 150).

On this basis we can understand why San Felice, Bishop of La Cava (*CT,* V, 295) and J. Contarini, Bishop of Bethune (*CT,* V, 325) could defend sola fides at the Council, and how it was sufficient to rebut the strong attacks which followed to say that this ought to be understood of fides formata caritate.

We have already explained how faith also includes the other dispositions (*D,* 798). It is noteworthy that in Chapter 6 the Council wished to define neither the sequence nor the indispensability of any one act nor the exclusiveness of these acts (Pohle, *Dogm.,* II, 502; Schmaus, *Dogm.,* III/2, 300). The concern of the Council was not psychology but theology. Everything is pinned to faith, which is and remains the fundamental disposition. Everything else is a sign for the genuineness of faith. Faith, seen in its fullness, is the surrender of the whole man.

Prat has described faith perfectly in the full Pauline sense: "For Paul, the Gospel is not a system, a theory, a collection of dogmas, but a divine economy containing the truths to be believed, an ethic to practice, and redemptive institutions to be put to work. And faith is not a simple intellectual adherence to revealed truth, but the spontaneous entry of man into the economy of the Gospel, the total gift of one's self to the divine Saviour, at the same time that one takes possession of all the promised divine benefit" (*S. Paul,* p. 130).

Yet "he who believes and is *baptized* will be saved" (Mk. 16.16; cf. Jn. 3.5). Baptism belongs to justification (*D* 796, 798, 799, 861). The same Paul who speaks so impressively of faith, speaks just as impressively about Baptism (Rom. 6.3–5; Gal. 3.26–29; Col. 2.12), and he says exactly the same thing about Baptism in Rom. 6.3–9 that he says about faith in Gal. 2.16–20. At this point we cannot dwell on the details of the connection between faith and Baptism. This we must leave to sacramental theology. What is all important is that faith and Baptism belong together, and neither should empty out the other. There is no Baptism without faith (the Catholic Church requires faith even for infant Baptism, though naturally in another form than with adults). Also, there is no faith without a reference to Baptism (even "Baptism of desire" has its power in relation to the Sacrament). Faith calls for Baptism, and Baptism rests on faith. Faith wants to become visible in the Church through the visible sign. Therefore Baptism is nothing but embodied visible faith. It is the sacramentum fidei (D 799), a sign of faith, which however is not empty, but rather charged with reality.

Cf. Schmaus, Dogm., III/2, 321–324; Coppens, "Baptême," in DBS, I, 900–902; Schlier, Die Zeit der Kirche, pp. 47–56, 107–129; Fortmann, Geloof en Sacrament, pp. 4–17.

Baptism makes visible, according to the will of the Lord, the fact that faith is not a purely individual concern. Certainly justification is not only corporate; the individual is caught up in it. But as this individual, the believer becomes a member of the Body of Christ which is the Church. Baptism is the visible sign of visible incorporation into the visible Church. Thus Paul can say that man is justified in Baptism (1 Cor. 6.11).

Villette, in his systematic section (V), gives special stress to the role of the Church. The causality of the Sacrament is not simply a question of the relation between ritual and grace.

Here special reference must be made to the comprehensive work on the Catholic theology of the Sacraments by H. Schillebeeckx, De sacramentele Heilseconomie (it has a valuable bibliography; the second volume will among other items develop a Christology of the Sacraments). Also see E. Walter, Quellen lebendigen Wassers; R. Graber, Le Christ dans ses sacrements; Aus der Kraft des Glaubens; E. Biser, Das Christusgeheimnis der Sakramente.

Schillebeeckx notes that in the Tridentine decrees on justification the emphasis is entirely on faith, which is viewed as more necessary than Baptism: D 799 "The Sacrament of Baptism, which is the sacrament of faith; without faith no one has ever been justified" (Sacramentele Heilseconomie, I, 563f.). It is significant, moreover, that according to Thomas "ex opere operato" means simply "ex opere Christi" or "deriving its efficaciousness from the passion of Christ" (I, 641–646); cf. in addition the section on "S. Thomas' synthesis of the 'efficacia ex opere' and the 'efficacia ex fide' in the sacraments" (I, 647–657).

Let us review this chapter. What is its relation to Barth's teaching? Comparing it with chaps. 15 and 17, we have to acknowledge a fundamental agreement in regard to the sola fides formula. The formula means the same thing in Catholic teaching as it does in that of Barth: no human works, not even the best works, are responsible for justification. Man is justified by God on the basis of faith alone. In faith the sinner submits himself to divine justification which has occurred for all men in the crucifixion and resurrection of Jesus Christ. This is where justification gets its "subjective" character. Thus justifying faith, proceeding from a trust which includes repentance and penance, involves both acknowledgment and realization of God's declaration of justification which has happened once and for all in Jesus Christ. God Himself achieves the justification of the sinner—not man through some work of his own (the work of faith, for instance). Man simply acknowledges the work of God.

Is faith, then, in no sense a condition of justification? It follows from this chapter, in basic accord with Barth, that faith is obviously not a condition for "objective" justification, which occurs for all in the death and resurrection of Christ. But what of faith in relation to "subjective" justification? We have seen that it is not faith that effects justification but rather God, both "subjectively" and "objectively": "Nothing that precedes justification, *neither faith nor works,* merits the grace of justification" (*D* 801). Yet, faith is indeed a condition (on this see chap. 15 and Barth's second positive assertion on the function of faith), inasmuch as it is man *alone* who has subjectively realized in himself the "objective" justification, who actively submits to divine justification. And in submitting (sese subiicere) he is not doing works but is relying in trust on the Lord. To this extent we can say that there is no justification without faith and we can speak with Scripture of a justification "through" faith.

We must forgo a discussion of the nature of the conditionality (or causality) which faith exercises (especially in connection with Baptism). On this, cf. e.g., B. P. Antoine, "Foi," in *DBS,* III, 299–302; Lyonnet, "De Rom. 3.30 et 4.3–5 in Conc. Trid. et apud S. Rob. Bellarm."; Huby, *Epître aux Rom.,* pp. 169ff.; Prat, *Théol. de S. Paul,* II, 296f.; and the various manuals. After long discussions the Council found it unnecessary to formulate its stand. The point is to emphasize that it is truly God Himself who justifies man. "Just as it would be false indeed to conceive of faith as a precondition of salvation, necessary at one stage but later dispensable, so too it would be false to regard faith as such as a cause which effectively contains within itself justification and develops it through a simple unfolding of its own capability." (E. Stakemeier, *Glaube des Sünders,* p. 431).

But doesn't this turn faith into a purely cognitive process? From the viewpoint of Catholic teaching, isn't there something more going on in "subjective" justification than an acknowledging acceptance? This question affords us the opportunity to return again to the ontological aspect of Barth's theology of justification. Barth doubtless put a strong emphasis on the iustitia Christi, the alien justice, the element of hope. There are passages where, despite all his statements to the contrary, we cannot help asking whether it is not after all something exclusively extrinsic that happens—whether this history develops perhaps only in Christ and not in any way in us, and whether the justice of man remains in the end merely a promise. Such sharp emphasis does suggest a certain anxiety on Barth's part about the consequences of a "systematization" of the theology of sin, which might lead to Catholic conceptions of the Church and of the Sacraments (the Sacrament of Penance!). Yet we can correctly understand Barth where the ontological aspect of faith is concerned. We have to, unless we insist on harping on individual statements to the point of neglecting others. We must not overlook the fact that statements which often sound one-sided are to be found in just those sections where "objective" justification is under consideration, where it is correctly said that redemption took place in Christ and not in us. Yet there remains the decisive question whether something ontological happens within the *"subjective"* sphere. However, Barth had already pointed out when he discussed "objective" justification that forgiveness of sin (and to some extent also sonship of God and the inheriting of heaven) does not remain in the area of *pure* promise whose present consists only in the certainty of its future fulfillment. Barth says that when men completely rely on this promise, the forgiveness of sin does actually *occur;* it goes beyond mere promise (cf. chap. 13). Moving from this to the "subjective" realization of justification, we would search in vain for Aristotelian and Scholastic phraseology in Barth (for example the largely psychological explanations of the process whereby man is made just—in conformity with various faculties of the soul or of the substance of the soul, in line with the matter-form schema, by means of various actual and habitual graces, etc.). Yet there remains the question whether Barth's explanation has neglected essential scriptural affirmations on the ontological and intrinsic character of justification. We must say that Barth has not neglected these affirmations if we consider the fact that Barth conceived of justification in a *concise way* with the result that various aspects of the process of redemption which would generally be treated by Catholics within the category of "justification" are discussed instead under "sanctification" or "vocation"; cf. chaps. 28 and 32 and also the short statements at the end of chap. 8; the process of redemption as light, liberation, acknowledgment, peace, and life (IV/2, 280–319).

And so, does something concrete and ontological actually happen in the "subjective" appropriation of "objective" justification? Is there a beginning of a new concrete condition of existence? According to Barth this question would have to be answered with an unconditional affirmative—despite and precisely because of the fact that faith is a purely cognitive process. He has expressed himself very clearly on this point and in two regards. First, believers and only they are moved and possessed by the Holy Spirit; nonbelievers are devoid of the Holy Spirit (cf. the beginning of chap. 17). This is what Catholic theologians call gratia increata or inhabitatio Spiritus Sancti (the indwelling of the Holy Spirit). Second, it is precisely in faith that a new and special existence becomes something real (cf. chap. 17 on the constitution of the Christian) —a new, special, objective, real, living kind of being. In faith man is in fact reborn and newly created in the root of his being. The sinner and the just man are radically distinct. And in this special new being of the believer we doubtless have what would be called by most Catholic theologians gratia creata (with all that this implies for the individual faculties). Indeed, the agreement goes so far that Barth, in a fashion parallel to that of the decree of Trent (chap. 7, *D* 799f.), distinguishes between what in faith comes from below, directly from man, and what is a gift from above, directly from God. Trent distinguished between the act of faith (we saw how, despite the different acts, the sola fides is not impaired) and the "infused virtues," those which are not earned by man but are a direct gift of God, the new reality of grace coming from above. Correspondingly Barth distinguishes between faith as a human act and the special new kind of being brought about directly by the grace of Jesus Christ. Trent said that all human acts (even faith as an act) cannot earn justification, nor in themselves call forth a change of being; rather they must cling to and be informed by the ("infused") reality of grace given by God in Christ. Barth, in similar fashion, maintains that faith as a human act cannot produce justification by itself any more than any other act, that it can call forth no radical change and in itself has only a "cognitive" and not a "creator-like" character. The believer is wholly dependent on God's action which allows a new state of existence to become real in him and only thus makes him capable of the true faith necessary for justification. To this extent and clearly in an indirect way, through the grace of Jesus Christ, faith now has a *"creator-like"* character. Thus it is proper to assume that Barth's stand on intrinsic justification fulfills the requirements of Catholic dogma. The differences do not fall outside the scope of the recognized schools of theological thought, which on this point, depending on period and party allegiance, were always marked by extraordinary discrepancies.

The theology of Baptism was only briefly touched upon because it has been necessary for us to omit from our consideration here the problems of sacramental theology. There is another reason: Barth wrote in the foreword of his most recent volume, IV/2: "Baptism and the Lord's Supper are given only incidental mention in the present volume. But they are not forgotten, and will be given what seems to be their appropriate and worthy place as the basis and crown of the fourth and ethical section of the doctrine of reconciliation. I know that this will expose me in advance to many suspicions. The *Evangelisch-Lutherische Kirchenzeitung* (as well as the angels) has long since known that this is how things would turn out. But I must bear this cheerfully, and with a good courage" (IV/2, Preface, xi–xii).

On the intra-Protestant controversy concerning infant Baptism, cf. especially K. Barth, *Die kirchliche Lehre von der Taufe;* O. Cullmann, *Die Tauflehre des Neuen Testamentes, Erwachsenen-und Kindertaufe;* F. J. Leenhardt, *Le baptême chrétien, son origine, sa signification.*

We have seen once again how unfounded was Barth's polemic against the Council of Trent. It may have become clear now that, according to Catholic and Tridentine teaching on justification too, there is no other recourse for the sinner than to place his whole trust in the Lord.

In the problem of the certainty of faith, Barth's misunderstanding of the strictly "subjective" character of the Tridentine concept of justification shows up once again. Obviously, Trent did not intend to question the certainty of, and absolute confidence in, that ("objective") justification which took place for everyone in the death and resurrection of Christ. But in the question of certainty as to the ("subjective") realization of justification, and in the matter of trust in this having happened, the Council intended to make sure that its approach was tempered by an awareness of human frailty and sinful unreliability.

But this discovery is not enough for an answer to our questions. We need further clarification. What about human co-operation, sanctification, and merit?

32. SOLI DEO GLORIA

The conclusion of Chapter 29 was this: If justification (in the "objective" sense) is understood as the verdict of God in the death and resurrection of Jesus Christ, then there is no co-operation on man's part. Justification is the work of God alone in Jesus Christ. Through Him all men are redeemed. No one except the one God-man, Jesus Christ, is the Redeemer. It becomes clear just how Barth misunderstood the "cooperari" of the Council of Trent. Trent did not defend any cooperari in the "objective" event of salvation ("redemption" in Trent's own terminology: see *D* 794), but rather only in the "subjective" process of salvation ("justification" in Trent's terminology: see *D* 795, 797). The justification of all through redemption in Christ by God's verdict is exclusively God's work. This is Catholic teaching.

But how about the "subjective" salvific event? Here, too, the Council took its departure from the sinner's absolute incapacity for any kind of self-justification (cf. the first canons of the decree, *D* 811–813). God's verdict comes down upon the sinner for whom nothing remains to do except to subject himself to this judgment in faith. The sinner himself is incapable of doing anything for his justification. But through God's grace man is highly active, precisely in his passive receptivity. God's verdict, powerful in Jesus Christ, makes him alive and ready for the cooperari and the assentire (*D* 797, 814–816). It is a co-operation (Mitwirken) not in the sense of collaboration (Mitwerken) but of involvement (Mitmachen). "Works" are asked from the man already justified. The man yet to be justified is called upon to co-operate in faith, meaning a full and living faith as described in the foregoing chapter. Assentire then means, despite his passivity, the highly active "Yes and Amen" of the repentant sinner awakened by God's gracious verdict. Cooperari means getting oneself involved in what God alone has put into execution. The God who justifies in Christ remains, even in justification, the God of the covenant who—by reason of His new gracious election—wants a true partner, not a robot or a puppet, but a man responding to him with a personal, responsible, active, and heartfelt Yes. For this purpose He has, through His prevenient grace, preserved in the perishing sinner the power, the understanding, and the ability to choose. He now renews the offer of His grace with urgency but without compulsion. He does not manipulate man by force but calls him to come and go along. God's justification requires man's repentance, in the way in which it is asked on every page of Scripture: "We beseech you . . . be reconciled to God" (2 Cor. 5.20).

Kirchgaessner: " 'Be reconciled with God!' This means man must respond to the redemptive will of God so as to have his mind changed in regard to God. Faith and conversion is thus the second step, made necessary as soon as God has taken the first. At first man is passive. God acts on him as an object, but it is precisely through this activity of God that he is made active" (*Erlösung*, p. 105).

Therefore, Trent's cooperari implies no synergism in which God and man pull on the same rope. It is never as though justification came *partly* from God and *partly* from man. It has been sufficiently emphasized that the sinner can do nothing without the grace of Jesus Christ. "What have you that you did not receive?" (1 Cor. 4.7). "For God is at work in you, both to will and to work for his good pleasure" (Phil. 2.13). "Not that we are sufficient of ourselves to claim anything as coming from us; our sufficiency is from God" (2 Cor. 3.5).

Everything comes from God, even what man does. A "supplementation" of divine justification is out of the question, God's glory is not belittled. God wants man's highest activity, but this can grow only from a complete passivity, from a receptivity brought about by God. The vital point is that God accomplishes *everything*. But it does not follow from this that He accomplishes it *alone*. On the contrary the greatest marvel of God's accomplishing everything is that man accomplishes *along with Him* as a result of God's accomplishment. Sacred Scripture makes both points, as does Trent (*D* 797): "Restore us to thyself, O LORD, that we may be restored!" (Lam. 5.21), and "Return to me, says the LORD of hosts, and I will return to you" (Zech. 1.3).

Among the doctors of the church no one has put it so well as Bernard of Clairvaux: "What, then, you say, is free will for? I will answer briefly: *It is saved.* Take away free will and there will be nothing to save; take away grace, and there will not be anything by which salvation is wrought. This work cannot be accomplished without these two: the one by which it is done, the other to whom or in whom it is done. God is the author of salvation, free will has only the capacity for salvation: only God can bestow it (salvation); only free will is able to receive it. What therefore is given only by God and only to free will can no more be without the consent of the recipient than without the grace of the giver. And thus free will is said to cooperate with grace as it works salvation, when it consents, that is, when it is saved.

"What then? is this the entire work of free will, is this alone its merit, that it agrees? It is indeed. Not indeed that itself, in which all its merit consists, were of itself; for we are not sufficient to think (which is less than consenting) anything by ourselves as being of ourselves (2 Cor. 3.5). The words are not mine but the apostle's, who attributes all the good things that can be—that is, thinking and willing and accomplishing (anything)—to God (Phil. 2.13), and not to free will. . . . It is by God therefore without doubt that the beginning of our salvation is made, not through us at all nor with our co-operation. Yet consent and the work, though they are not of us, are now not without us. We must therefore beware lest, when we feel these things going on invisibly within us and with our concurrence, we attribute them either to our will, which is weak, or to God's need, of which there is none, but to grace alone, which is abundant. Grace arouses free will when it plants reflection; grace heals it when it changes the desire; grace strengthens free will that it may lead it to action; it preserves it from thinking of defection. But grace so works with free will that only grace at the beginning is prevenient, thereafter it accompanies; for this purpose grace takes the initiative that free will may soon co-operate with it. Yet in such a way that what is begun by grace alone is accomplished equally by both, that jointly and not singly, at the same time and not by turns, in unified undertakings they work together. *Not grace separately, nor free will separately,* but rather both, each by its own activity, accomplish the entire work. Free will accomplishes the entire work and grace performs the entire work; in such a way, however, that *the entire work is in the will, precisely because the entire work is from grace."* (*De gratia et libero arbitrio, PL,* 182, 1002, 1026f. Scheeben, *Dogm.,* IV, 65; Schmaus, *Dogm.,* III, 12, 286f.; Kirchgaessner, *Erlösung,* pp. 147, 152).

Thus faith, as far as cooperari is concerned, means simultaneously nothing and everything for justification. Nothing, insofar as even it does not produce justification and is neither an achievement nor a good work. Rather, faith wants God to work on itself. God Himself produces justification.

"We may be said to be justified freely, in the sense that nothing that precedes justification, neither faith nor works, merits the grace of justification" (*D* 801).

But faith is everything, insofar as justification has no meaning for the individual without faith. Faith involves a humble, obedient participation of man. Faith is, in its passivity, the active readiness to receive from God. And this not only in the special experience of justification but throughout the entire life of the justified man. It enlightens anew the instant of the alienness of justice and the continually new state of appropriation of the gift of justice.

"We may then be said to be justified through faith, in the sense that 'faith is the beginning of man's salvation,' the foundation and source of all justification, 'without which it is impossible to please God' (see Heb. 11:6) and to be counted as his sons" (D 801). For an extended discussion on chap. 8, cf. Hefner, *Entstehungsgeschichte,* pp. 277–279.
The Cardinal legate Cervini interpreted the chapter this way: ". . . therefore the words seem to have been presented according to the consensus of the Church; for in the preparation as in the instant of justification, in its exercise and in its increase, faith is the foundation and root of justification" (*CT,* V, 734).
And Moehler: "Faith is therefore the *beginning* of salvation, but it is not a beginning which could ever be abandoned during this life-time . . . for it is also the continuing *foundation* on which the whole structure of salvation is being erected. But it is not to be taken only as a layer of material set underneath without any organic connection with the rest of the structure. In other words, faith is the root of justification. In other words, its power and efficacy are those of justifying grace . . . endowed with divine love though even faith does not merit this grace" (*Symbolik,* pp. 148f.). Cf. *S.th.,* II–II, q. 4, a. 4, to 1: *"Deus semper efficit iustificationem."*

What could Barth have to say against such a "participation"? It is, after all, nothing other than what he himself presents in his statement on faith and on the "subjective" appropriation of the grace "objectively" consigned to us (see the end of the preceding chapter).

The proper interpretation of "prevenient grace" in the sense intended by Trent is given in the study of P. Huenermann on the nature and necessity of actual grace as taught by the Council.

These basic considerations make it possible, finally, to describe the relationship between justification and sanctification. Many misunderstandings stem from an insufficient awareness of the ambiguity of the term "sanctification." The Catholic understands by "sanctification" primarily the objective and ontological holiness (*heiligkeit*) achieved in man by God. The Protestant emphasizes the subjective and ethical sanctification (*heiligung*) brought about by man. Both are valid provided the differences are seen in their unity.

Inasmuch as justification occurs through faith alone, and not through works of man, it is *not* identical with sanctification (in the strictly objective and ethical sense). Otherwise, divine justification would become the self-justification of man (as is clearly stated in Trent *D* 801). In this sense sanctification *follows* justification.

Everything said in Chapter 28 should be considered in this context too.

"It is patently obvious that for Paul justification includes the cancellation of sins and positive sanctification. But it is equally certain that the Pauline vocabulary of justification in itself does not *formally* express this correspondence since it has a forensic ring reminiscent of court language. As soon as the subject of justifying and justification comes up, it is immediately defined in terms of an act of God by virtue of which man is recognized by God as just. (Grossouw, *"Rechtfertigung,"* in Bibel-Lexikon, p. 1405).

In general the expression "sanctification" (1 Thess. 5.23; Rom. 6.19, 22; Heb. 12.14) is not used by Scripture in the objective and ontological sense (parallel to justification as "making just") but rather in the subjective and ethical sense. From this point of view the term "renovatio" used by Trent is preferable to "sanctificatio" whenever the term "sanctification" designates the ontological holiness or "making holy."

Furthermore, insofar as justification, considered as the efficacious divine just judgment, makes man really just or holy, it is *identical* with sanctification (in the sense of an objective and ontological making holy brought about by God). Otherwise, divine justification would be an empty, purely verbal assertion (this aspect is discussed by Trent in *D* 709 and 821).

Schrenk (art. "δικαιοσυνη" in *TWNT*, II, 213) refers to Rom. 6.13, 16, 18, 19, 20 and states: "The concept of an absolving forensic justice merges with the concept of justice as a life-force, which overcomes sin without any difficulty or contradiction being felt. The gift of justice links the believer to the life-force of δικαιοσυνη. Once more it is δικαιοσυνη which initiates man into the status of ἁγιασμος. This justice, as the power which is binding on all of life, emerges as the overpowering of ἀδικια and ἁμαρτια (6.13, 17, 18, 20). Hence, in Paul, δικαιοσυνη can designate absolving justice as well as the life-force which overcomes sinful limitation. Thus the thought of a justice within life is not to be excluded in reference to Paul's teaching.

If these distinctions are not attended to, communication breaks down. But now, how does the objective and ontological making-holy relate to subjective and ethical sanctification? It can be put this way: Justice or holiness given to man through the justification of God is the necessary foundation for any moral sanctification of man and vice versa. Sanctification is holiness as established through justification becoming operative and real. Human sanctification without the holiness given by God is worthless—for the former is based on the latter. God-given holiness without grace-inspired human sanctification is sterile. As faith must be operative in love, so justification must be operative in sanctification. Whatever there is of human sanctification, it goes without saying that human sanctification can never be considered a human complement but only an after-effect of divine activity. "You shall . . . therefore be holy, *for I* am holy" (Lev. 11.44; cf. 19.2; 20.7f).

Bonnetain: "It (justice) appears occasionally together with sanctification (1 Cor. 1.30, the two nouns; 1 Cor. 6.11, the two corresponding verbs) or holiness (Luke 1.75; Eph. 4.24). Justification and sanctification designate practically the same reality, but under different aspects. Justification is logically anterior, and in series appears first in order (1 Cor. 1.30); 1 Cor. 6.11 however reads 'You have been sanctified, you have been justified.' The same is true of the respective order of 'justice and holiness' (Eph. 4.24) or 'holiness and justice' (Lk. 1.75)" ("Grâce," in *DBS,* 1275).

Huby: "The description of the Christian life in St. Paul presents two successive aspects which one can designate by two different words, justification and sanctification. Justification and sanctification are not two different things any more than the light at dawn differs from the light of the sun at noon or the life of the rosebud differs from the full flower. They are the merciful gift of God's justice. The term justification corresponds to the pouring out of this justice, this holiness, *at its first moment.* It designates the act by which God causes a soul to pass from the state of sin to the state of grace, of the divine friendship. *Sanctification* will be the development in the course of the Christian life of this justice, this holiness, received in the act of justification" (*Epître aux Rom.,* p. 205). Cf. Prat, *Theol. of St. Paul,* II, 251f.

What could Barth have against such a conception of sanctification? He has never quarreled with sanctification as such, but only with a reducing of divine justification to human sanctification. We have seen that there is also in the Catholic conception a definite distinction to be drawn between the act of God and the act of man. With this, we have refuted Barth's attacks on Trent. Although Barth since then (see vol. IV/2, 497) has started to speak of the "Roman terminology" which includes "sanctification" in "justification," he has, nevertheless, (IV/1, 625), not sufficiently noted that the Council has various statements about "justification" which in a different vocabulary would pertain to "sanctification." We need not stumble over this. The Catholic, too, can understand justification as the gracious judgment carried out in the death and resurrection of Jesus Christ, which, since it has happened once and for all, bears upon all men without exception. And no Catholic would speak of an uncertainty, a growth, a repetition, or a consummation of this "justification" (though he might prefer instead to call it "redemption"). And after all Barth has said (especially in Vol. IV/2) that even he could not deny that in the sphere which he calls "sanctification," there can be something like uncertainty, growth, repetition, and consummation.

Moeller: "Of central importance is the distinction introduced by Calvin between justification and sanctification. This distinction was not taken into consideration in the definitions of Trent. The Council was satisfied to affirm in regard to *justification* a series of things which the Reformation refused to admit, preferring to attribute them instead to *sanctification*. This point must be carefully considered" (*Théol. de la Grâce*, p. 41).

Prat: "If, in order to distinguish them, justification and sanctification are compared, the latter appears like a positive perfection, susceptible of indefinite progress, while the former presents itself under its negative aspect—the remission of sins—which does not seem to permit such progress at all" (*Theol. of St. Paul*, II, p. 251).

Can we speak of "merits" in the sanctification of man? So much is certain, that the thought of reward cannot be eliminated by any arguments from the Old and New Testaments (cf. Preisker, "μισθος," in *TWNT*, IV). It is found in the Synoptics as well as in Paul, just as clearly as the threat of punishment is. Still the question remains: Will this reward be given on the basis of "merit"? The term is hardly at all used in this connection in the New Testament. And why? In Scripture the morality of merit is Pharisaic morality. The Pharisee boasted of his merit and spoke of it before God and man, but he did not return home justified (Lk. 18.14). Christ spoke out sharply against the Pharisaic morality of merit: "Does he [the Lord] thank the servant because he did what was commanded? So you also, when you have done all that is commanded you, say, 'We are unworthy servants; we have only done what was our duty'" (Lk. 17,9–10).

The Catholic exegete J. Schmid (*Der Lohngedanke im Judentum und in der Lehre Jesu*, in substantial agreement with Preisker in *TWNT*) establishes the following distinctions between the teaching of Jesus Christ and Jewish thinking on merit: (*a*) in Jesus merit is thought of in an eschatological way; (*b*) what counts is not the works but the intention with which they are done; (*c*) man confronts God not as a partner with equal contractual rights, but always as an unworthy servant who receives from God a reward of grace (reward not as a legal claim but as promise); (*d*) there is no equality between reward and achievement (man is always behindhand in his responsibility, but God's reward is overflowing); (*e*) the thought of reward is not the major ethical motive, but is subordinated to motives of obedience and especially love, gratitude and imitation of God.

Schmid: "The moral worth of an activity is not defined in terms of reward, as though the morally good would be identical with what is somehow profitable to man, but the will of God. One acts immorally if he fulfills the moral demands of God purely with a view to reward. His morality is pure egoism, and 'he moves in a sphere of thinking which lies outside the higher justice demanded by Jesus' (Tillmann). Jesus specified that in giving alms the left hand should not know what the right one does (Mt. 6.3), which is meant to exclude any calculation of heavenly reward. And in the picture of judgment in Mt. 25.31–46, the astonishment of both the 'blessed of the Father' and the unjust proves that in doing as they did they had not thought of the Judge who rewards" (*Lohngedanke*, p. 227).

Schmid's studies of Jesus' teaching agree with G. Didier's on Paul (*Désintéressement du Chrétien. La rétribution dans la morale de S. Paul*); cf. the thorough analysis of individual texts (pp. 22–218) and especially the final conclusions (pp. 219–233). "Because they have neglected to note the context of the verses of a chapter or a letter which they cite, certain apologists for Catholic dogma, and occasionally also Protestants, have considerably exaggerated the number and importance of the passages where Paul appeals to fear of punishment or desire for reward. In doing so they expose themselves to the simplifications of lay moralists who try to turn the entirety of Christian ethics into eudaemonic calculation. . . . In the great majority of cases

Paul speaks of sanctions without any underlying intention of moral exhortation, just as he most often justifies his moral exhortation without appeal to the idea of sanction" (Didier, p. 221).

A reading of Chapter 16, on the idea of merit (*D* 809f.) in Trent's decree on justification will reveal five distinctions: "(*a*) To the end . . . eternal life; (*b*) for those who hope in God; (*c*) as being the grace that God, through Jesus Christ, has mercifully promised his sons, and 'as the reward' which, according to the promise of God himself, must assuredly be given; (*d*) beyond all measure—in many things we all offend—neither should anyone pass judgment on himself, even if he is conscious of no wrong, because the entire life of man should be examined and judged not by human judgment, but by the judgment of God . . . ; (*e*) your work and the love . . . who love His coming" (*D* 809f.). The Tridentine theology of merit is summed up in one sentence: "Nevertheless, a Christian should have no inclination either to rely on himself or to glory in himself instead of in the Lord [see 2 Cor. 10:17], whose goodness towards all men is such that he wants his gifts to be their merits" (*D* 810).

So the teaching of the Council had nothing in common with pharisaic teaching on merit. As in Scripture, the Council's only concern is that man should not remain in a state of indolent passivity, burying his talents, but put them to use. It is a summons not to an idle basking in the sun but to earnest fear of God and active obedience. "Merit" thus must not be understood in a pharisaic way. In this sense, then, and only in this sense, did Barth deny the idea of merit (cf. chap. 16), though he fully accepted the idea of reward (cf. e.g. IV/2, 586f.; III/2, 137).

Karrer: "If Catholic teaching paraphrases the objective soteriological meaning of moral and religious struggle in the state of sonship by using the term 'merit,' then it can be granted that in such a context the expression does not appear in the New Testament. And naturally, as a transposition of human relationships into our relationship with God, it has only analogical meaning (see Stakemeier, p. 171). That is, with regard to the situation pointed to by Scripture, e.g., a 'heavenly reward,' the expression is inadequate— dissimilar as well as similar. (See B. Bartmann, *Dogm.*, II/117). The word of Jesus and the experience of all religious educators tell us that the notion of 'merit' that is, something practically equivalent to reward, ought to be viewed as only an expedient—which on the other hand should not be disregarded. Naturally, what is emphasized about this from the Protestant side is completely correct—that is, what obviously is the *essential intention* of the 'battle against the doctrine of merit'—that one cannot 'boast' of his works before God since ultimately they are God's gifts, and that likewise he cannot 'place his trust in them'—the whole stability of trust is oriented instead toward God. Nor does it make sense to 'keep an account' of the quality of one's life of grace and virtue. Though a Christian does well to be aware with Paul of his 'good fight,' this could not, of course, be in the sense of self-glorification or as though he could 'estimate his own merits.' If he were to entertain such a notion, then it should be rather in the spirit of Psalm 130.3: 'If thou, O Lord, shouldst mark iniquities, . . .' Actually, in the evaluation of all such items there is no division of opinion between Catholic and Protestant theologians and educators, though there is much mutual recrimination! At the most there is a division of opinion on whether the term 'merit,' which Scholasticism took over from Augustine, was a felicitous expression to convey the intended meaning. The fight about words can be quite a spectacle if all we want is to have the last word. But at the heart of the matter—as to how the believer is to estimate his openness to grace, and his works due to grace—there is no division of opinion in theological and in reasonably good devotional Christian literature. There would be absolutely no sense in examining all the varieties of questionable commodities produced by the religious 'industry.' In interconfessional discussions the only issues are the fundamental themes of Christian teaching and education which in practice may very often have been shelved, and even now continue to be shelved, unfortunately, in favor of the 'needs of the people.' (But this is also a Protestant complaint in regard to conditions in their own camp, see W. A. Hauck, p. 61; Köberle, p. 174). Yet it is undeniable that such pedagogical deficiencies do not continue uncorrected—partly thanks to the Protestant 'thorn' " (*Galaterbrief*, p. 32).

Bernard of Clairvaux: "For he is disgusting and foolish who puts his trust in other merits of life, in any other religion or philosophy but that of humility alone. Before the Lord we cannot have rights" (*De diversia sermo,* 26, 1; *PL,* 183, 610).

Cyprian: "We have nothing to boast of since nothing is ours" (*Testim.,* III/4; *CSEL,* III/1, 116).

K. Rahner, *Trost der Zeit,* pp. 242–244; Schmaus, *Dogm.,* III/2, 403–405; on the development of dogma in the period of high Scholasticism, Auer, *Entwicklung der Gnadenlehre,* II, 58–111.

The great theological battle cries—soli Deo gloria, sola gratia, sola fides, sola scriptura—were in the final analysis identical for the Reformers and are so for Karl Barth, in that they expressed one great concern, zeal for God. In this sense they are grounded not only in theory but in religious existence, so that no one should "glory" in himself but in the Lord (cf. Rom. 3.27; 1 Cor. 4.7; 1.29, 31; 2 Cor. 10.17; Gal. 6.14). This is the root of all polemic against "good works," "co-operation," and "merit." Here a merely theological and theoretical answer will never do.

Prayers can often give a better theological answer than doctrinal statements:

Teresa of the Child Jesus—four months before her death: "I am very happy that I am going to heaven; but when I think of this word of the Lord, 'I shall come soon, and bring with me my recompense to give each one according to his works,' I tell myself that this will be very embarrassing for me, *because I have no works.* . . . Very well! He will render to me *according to His works* for Himself" (*Histoire d'une âme*, p. 302).

And in her "Offrande a l'Amour misericordieux": "In the evening of this life I shall appear before Thee *with empty hands,* because I do not ask Thee, Lord, to *count my works.* All our just acts have blemishes in Thine eyes. Therefore I want to *wrap myself up again in Thy justice,* and to receive from Thy love the eternal possession of Thee Thyself."

Claude de la Colombière: "O Lord, in hope alone hast Thou established me. Men can take away both wealth and honor. Sickness may take away the strength and the means to serve Thee. *I can even lose Thy grace through sin;* but I shall never lose my hope: I shall keep it to the last moment of my life. Others may support themselves on the innocence of their lives, on the strictness of their penitence, on the number of their charities, or on the fervor of their prayers. Thou O Lord in hope alone hast established me. For me, Lord, this is all my confidence, it is my confidence itself" (cited in Lyonnet, *Ad Rom.,* p. 149).

In the Liturgy: the collect of the Fifth Sunday after Epiphany, "Guard thy family in persevering piety so that they will rest only in the hope of thy heavenly grace . . ."; the collect of Sexagesima Sunday, "O Lord God, who seest that we put not our trust in anything that we do . . ."; the collect of the Second Sunday in Lent, "O God, who seest that of ourselves we have no strength . . ."; the Common of Confessors, ". . . that we who put no trust in our own justice . . ."; and in Prime, "To the King of the ages, immortal and invisible, *to God alone be honor and glory* forever and ever."

33. DIVIDED IN FAITH?

We have come to the end of our Catholic response, and yet it can be no more than a beginning. To think of the many themes only briefly touched upon: Jesus Christ, creation, sin, death, grace, judgment, faith . . . ! These are endless themes and no more than an attempt could be made to harmonize them, yet this much we may have learned from the attempt: We have here a melody from which certain harmonies cannot be excluded with impunity. The theology of justification coming from grace through faith is interwoven with the theology of creation and sin, and all of it receives its profound resonance from Christology. This unity justifies the diversity of themes and their rapid review.

This was by and large a self-appraisal in the light of Christian revelation, and, as self-appraisal, our response to Karl Barth. We could have satisfied ourselves with what is often done in similar works—with more or less brief and critical footnotes on our author. This would have been a less precarious and especially a more comfortable way out, and many troublesome details (not the least of which were the many citations) could have been dispensed with. But this would have been a less fruitful method. Many truths in Barth's teaching would hardly have appeared to us to be truths. Chap. 20 demonstrated the difficulties confronting not only Protestant but also Catholic theologians who try to see the measureless abundance of Catholic teaching in its truly Catholic openness. Only an untiring return to the sources can offer any hope of a successful outcome—whose success would at best be highly relative anyway. If then the total upshot of our investigation is so very positive, we cannot attribute this to a soothing irenicism—which we reject—but to a deliberate and unpolemic reflection on Catholic teaching on the basis of its sources. Nevertheless, much of what we have discussed might have sounded more convincing and less one-sided had we given a more expanded treatment to Scripture within tradition. And yet it was not our intention to rewrite Catholic dogmatic theology but simply to respond to the questions of Karl Barth.

It is all really one question—the question about God and man in the process of salvation, which is the question about God's becoming *man* and about the becoming-man of *God*. It is a question about Jesus Christ and thus about all of us. It is a question about creation and sin, about grace and justification. It is certainly not a question of two great powers dealing on even terms, but rather a question put to the God who has been so gracious to us, asking Him to tell us what He wants to say about Himself and thus about ourselves. The question concerns the *sovereignty* of the *gracious* God and the *justification* of *sinful* man. God's answer is given to man in Jesus Christ. It is for this answer we have been looking all along; and our response was to be nothing but the most faithful possible—and yet so pitiably unfaithful—copy of this one divine response.

The results can be summarized in brief statements; yet we could emphasize that such a summary can be correctly understood only in the light of the corresponding chapters.

Barth's question to Catholic theology was: Does Catholic theology take justification seriously as the gracious act of God's sovereignty in Jesus Christ? It turned out that living Catholic theology does take justification seriously as God's act of sovereignty in Jesus Christ. The God who is gracious to us in Jesus Christ is beginning, middle, and end of everything. In Him the justification of the sinner was powerfully predetermined from all eternity (chap. 21); in Him creation was achieved in its totality and its details, and it has in Him, and in Him only, its permanence (chap. 22). In Him a good creation is preserved beforehand from the fatal corruption of sin. In Him the sinner who has forfeited his life can go on existing (chap. 23). But in Him, too, the frightfulness of sin is made manifest as sin against the incarnate God and His body (chap. 24). And thus sin affects man himself in the very center of his being, in his freedom and consequently in all his acts (chap. 25). But in Him that grace is also manifest which, as the favor of God, powerfully graces man (chap. 27). In Him the sinner is declared just (chap. 28). In Him, in His death and resurrection, justification is accomplished once and for all (chap. 29). In Him, however, it must be appropriated by man in faith (chap. 31), and in serious stewardship must be carried to heaven (chap. 32) by man as the justified sinner (chap. 30).

It is obvious that within Catholic theology these points are not always and everywhere elaborated with equal precision and clarity, but we have shown (chap. 20) that this cannot be expected. However, from all that has been demonstrated we can say without qualification that, regardless of limitations, it *is* definitely *Catholic* teaching. Who could make the assertion that in Catholic teaching the gracious act of God's sovereignty in Jesus Christ is not taken with unreserved seriousness?

Now as far as the teaching of Barth is concerned, the question of Catholics was: Does Karl Barth take justification seriously as the justification of *man?* After having investigated the corresponding Catholic teaching we must acknowledge that Barth does in fact take the justification of man seriously. In Jesus Christ God has from eternity been gracious to man as a subsistent creature (cf. chaps. 4 and 21). In Him man and the whole creation was created good (chaps. 5 and 22). In Him the covenant remains in effect even in opposition to the sin of man, and man thus remains man even in sin (chaps. 6, 10, 23–25). In Christ, however, the existence of man confronts anew the free grace of God (chaps. 11–14, 27) because in Him God makes the sinner interiorly just (chaps. 8, 11–14, 28–30), though it is up to man—as a new creature in faith who through love wants to be active in works—to actualize it (chaps. 14–17, 31–32).

We must not then reject the positive statements of Barth nor accuse him of vital omissions: yet we do have to reject resolutely his anti-Catholic polemic, especially against the Catholic theology of grace and the Tridentine decree on justification. Our positive presentation may be assumed to have clarified the misunderstandings. In addition to the chapters on these topics, we recommend to special consideration the introductory chapter on methodology (chap. 20) illuminating the development of dogma and the sources of Catholic teaching. These misunderstandings, however, do not jeopardize the positive results of our study since it is undeniable that there is a fundamental agreement between Karl Barth's position and that of the Catholic Church in regard to the theology of justification seen in its totality. Within the scope of the questions treated, Barth has no genuine argument for separation from the ancient Church.

We must now specify what is implicit in the problem area we treated. The intransigence of Barth's opposition to Catholic teaching, especially in the area of Church and Sacrament (ecclesiastical tradition, the primacy of the Pope, Mariology and, beyond that, in regard to the "natural" knowledge of God) has been sufficiently publicized. This casts a dark shadow on Karl Barth's theology of justification. And so a man will be met with skepticism and incredulity if he ventures to suggest that there is a substantial agreement in the matter of justification. How could that be possible? Furthermore, Barth explicitly formulated the connection between the fundamental Christological problems and the theology of redemption on one hand, and the further problems of Church and Sacrament on the other hand. His rejection of the Catholic position in regard to the latter is based upon his opposition to the former (see the Introduction).

Our analysis has at least shown that Barth's statements about the theology of justification lend themselves to a positive interpretation. On the basis of our inquiries we believe that this is done with good reason. What then makes Barth draw false consequences for the second problem area, despite his beginning from a fundamentally correct position? Three partly overlapping factors appear to be responsible.

(a) Every school of theology has its own particular direction of flow or inclination, different for Greek patristic theology and for the theology of Augustine, different for Thomists and for Scotists. This flow does not in itself imply an overflow into error but it does imply limitation. No particular gradient ought to claim absolute authority; the water can pour into the valley by many different routes. Perhaps one riverbed channels the waters more swiftly and impressively than another—without meanderings or stagnation. Yet its flow will be finite and circumscribed, not comparable to the all-inclusive infinity of the ocean. The direction of flow determines the strengths and weaknesses of any theology. Strength, because in the direction of the incline all flows easily and is swiftly carried along. Seemingly immovable log jams of problems are sped downstream with the utmost ease. But also weaknesses, because as a result of its fall the current may readily leave its channel, undercut banks and overrun dams. Any theology, even the best, can in its own way become a victim of its own inclination. Any theology, even the best, has its most dangerous currents precisely at the point of maximum flow. God's Word alone is the all-encompassing ocean, alive yet at rest.

Barth's theology has its direction of flow, too, and we have become acquainted with it in its unmitigated force. However, even this gradient implies weaknesses in its very strengths. Barth's theology, too, has its dangerous inclinations.

These inclinations lead Barth not only to misunderstandings but into anti-Catholic polemic which misses the point. They also allow certain tendencies to gain prominence, tendencies which—while they are not erroneous in Barth's closely knit synthesis—do, when misapprehended, lead very easily into dangerous errors. The fundamental motive of Barth, to underline the gracious sovereignty of God in everything, tends in the theology of election toward apokatastasis; in the theology of creation, toward devaluing creaturely self-continuity; in the theology of sin, toward minifying and justifying sin; in the theology of redemption, toward neglecting the ontological and creaturely aspect. In the theology of justification proper, we would mention the tendency to overemphasize the "sinner," "alien justice," the man who is "in hope" at the expense of the "just," "my justice," and the man who is "in fact"; the tendency to cancel the essential distinction between the just man and the sinner, between the tares and the wheat, between good and bad fish, between believers and unbelievers; the tendency to resolve justification into a continuous flux without a sharp break, without the sharp caesura which the Word of God effects in the here and now of the justifying of this particular man; and finally, a tendency to deny a true advance and increase in grace and the possibility of a fall from grace.

These trends, while present in Barth's fundamental position, do not become errors nor irresponsible exaggerations. They form the organic inclination of Barthian theology, which in different form is found in Catholic theologians, and even in a Thomas Aquinas. In all this we must not overlook the fact that Barth, like any theologian who has undergone a true development, is burdened with his past (negatively and positively). Just as Augustine, during his whole lifetime, bore the marks of his neo-Platonism and Manicheism, so too, Barth will continue to bear the marks of his idealistic faith and of his antihumanistic, dialectical existentialism (negatively and positively) throughout his life.

These trends in the flow of Barthian theology do not, at least in the fundamental problems, go beyond the rather considerable differences of opinion found within Catholicism (for example, the Greek and Scholastic theologies of the Trinity and grace). In this sense they cause no special concern. They do arouse concern, however, within the scope of the theology of the Church and the Sacraments, where Barth would permit these currents of thought to carry him beyond the dams which God, as Catholics see the matter, appears to have set up in His revelation.

The gracious sovereignty of God is also the major concern of Catholics. It emerges in Catholic theology—in Catholic teaching on election, creation and redemption—just as much as in Barth's presentation; it is the absolute norm for the other problem areas too. However, it does not seem to us Catholics to entail a negative and subversive calling into question of the primacy of Peter and his successors, of the soteriological status of Mary, of the normative character of tradition, of the effective character of the Sacraments and the "natural" knowledge of God.

(b) Polemically one-sided Catholic accounts of the theology of the Church and the Sacraments appear to us to be a further reason why Barth should proceed, from a correct basic position, to negative conclusions in this sector of problems. We spoke in chap. 20 about the assessment of such one-sided Catholic presentations. Unfortunately a one-sided presentation is bound to evoke a one-sided echo. How often, precisely in the theology of justification, do the viewpoints clash head-on without really coming to grips with each other. How many presentations were not really *conceived of* as openly polemic. On the other hand, how many target areas are permitted to disappear in calm and unpolemical presentations. We would venture to make the claim, though it cannot be substantiated here, that in the theology of the Church and the Sacraments, too, a large portion of the divergences could be removed through a well-balanced (though not a compromising) and simultaneously theologically sound presentation. For example, the discussion of the primacy might profit if the stress on the theological thesis of primacy were matched by an equal stress on the fact that while the Pope is the vicar of *Christ,* he is only the *vicar* of Christ. The debate on the Church might profit if the emphasis on its unity with its Head were to be matched by putting in focus, with equal conviction, its distance from the Head, the unlimited rule of Jesus Christ *over* His Church. The discussion on the "natural" knowledge of God might profit if it were based not on all sorts of philosophoumena or theologumena but rather on creation in Jesus Christ. And similarly, for various questions in Mariology and the theology of Sacraments. Whatever is to be said about these individual instances, one thing appears to be true in any case: If in regard to these problems we had a greater number of well-balanced Catholic presentations (which does not preclude our taking a clear stand) and, what is more, theologically well-founded (a quality which many well-intended ecumenical writings appear to lack), then at least Barth (and other Protestants) would find it rather difficult to develop anti-Catholic consequences out of a correct basic position.

(c) Theology is life, and life is theology. Whoever would want to separate life and theology would fall victim to untheological and dead abstraction. While the interdependence of ecclesiastical life and theology can be very fruitful for theology, it can also be very oppressive. Precisely because theology is always evaluated as an expression of the Church's life, the finest theology is useless unless it is vindicated by the practical life of the Church. The best theology can appear superstitiously hollow to those of other faiths if the actual life of the Church contradicts these theories. The best treatise on the Catholic theology of justification will not convince those of other faiths if the life of the Church does not proclaim justification by faith but rather by works.

There are three reasons why the Lutheran theology of justification had such enormous consequences in contemporary history (according to H. Schmidt, *Brückenschlag zwischen den Konfessionen*, p. 162):

"(1) Against a widely externalized Christianity it demanded with passionate intensity *an internalization of religious life.*

(2) It *restored pre-eminence to the work of God* in justification, something which had seemingly been diminished through overemphasis on the work of man.

(3) It was *a declaration of war against the Roman curia,* which many Christians then viewed as the real cause of evil, seeing how many worthless people had ascended the throne of Peter. The curia aroused particular antagonism in Germany among princes and people because of excessive tithing and eventually because of the propaganda for indulgences which was probably quite often ill-considered."

Of course we have made headway in the Catholic reform during the past 400 years, although much remains to be done in the struggle to bring actual religious practices into fuller harmony with orthodox Catholic belief (cf. Pascher, *Das inwendige Leben in Werkgefahr*). However, is not Catholic theology especially embarrassed before Protestants in the problem area of Church and Sacraments because of ecclesiastical life? Protestants are very often discreetly silent about this, but in every interconfessional discussion we can easily see just how difficult certain phenomena of Catholic life are to put up with—for instance, the theology of the Church, the primacy of the pope, the teaching on Mary, the Sacraments, and tradition. While they do not charge the Catholic Church with "abuses" which might occur anywhere, there is a question just where the boundary is between use and abuse, between non-use and abuse.

In the ecumenical discussion of these problems, everything depends on not losing sight of the unity between theology and life. The fact that proper Catholic living does not always back up good theology, is another reason why Barth does not think these problems through all the way to their conclusions.

Despite these details we hold to our finding—that is, that on the whole there is fundamental agreement between the theology of Barth and that of the Catholic Church. Within this area of discussion Barth has no valid reason for a separation from the ancient Church.

This finding is significant, not so much in view of Barth (we had stated in the beginning that this was not a matter of being "for or against Barth"), but rather in view of the renewed awareness of the gospel of Jesus Christ in the service of the unity of the Church. The results are significant on account of the unity of the Church. For Barth does not stand alone; he represents many others in the Protestant camp. What is especially significant, however, is that the greater number of leading contemporary Protestant theologians have given up the purely extrinsic declaration of justice.

As representative of the position that forgiveness of sin and renewal comprise *one* reality (under two aspects), O. Karrer cites among modern Protestant theologians: Luthardt, Beth, Schaeder, Wobbermin, Lietzmann, Wetter, Koeberle, Riggenbach, Wernle, Troeltsch, Soederblom, Heiler, Otto, Tillich, Hauck, Luettge, Engelland, Rueckert, Ellwein, Schlatter, v. d. Leew (*Galaterbrief,* p. 142).

We would like to add just a few witnesses from recent years:

Althaus: "If, consequently, renewal cannot be thought of without justification, the reverse is likewise true. Justification occurs in view of renewal. God accepts the sinner as he is into His fellowship in order to make him new. He could not accept him if He did not, in so doing, renew him to faith and new obedience" (*Christliche Wahrheit,* p. 635; cf. *Lutherische Rechtfertigungslehre,* pp. 9f.).

Schlink: with references to the Apology for the Augsburg Confession and to the Schmalcald Articles: "If the sinner is considered as just, then he is not only reputed just but he is just. If he is *'called'* totally just and holy for the sake of Christ, then he also *'is'* totally just and holy . . . For God's justifying judgment never is 'only' a verdict: Rather, it establishes reality . . . It would be a denial of the truth and reality of the thoughts and words of God (by which He imputes and adjudges) if declaring just were not to be taken as simultaneously making just, if nonimputation of sin were not to be taken as simultaneously a new birth." (*Theologie der Lutherischen Bekenntnisschriften,* p. 140; in the same sense Koeberle also appeals to the Apology, cf. *Rechtfertigung und Heiligung,* p. 119).

Lackmann: " 'God's justice is the basis of salvation.' But God *requites* even if in the presence of His judgment we *are* what He wills to make us. This same divine 'justice' *gives* as well as *judges.* We cannot bring God anything that He has not already given us before. But as those who have received, we are also *supposed to bring* to Him what we have from Him.

"Insofar as God's creating word (Jas. 1.18) is through Christ a Yes to Godless man, this man, through faith, does *become* a just man in God" (*Zur reformatorischen Rechtfertigungslehre,* pp. 82ff.; cf. also Lackmann's earlier publication, *Sola fide*).

Asmussen: "Lutherans and Catholics miss one another's point inasmuch as Catholics using the term 'justification' are primarily thinking of the process of salvation, of making holy. By contrast the Lutheran Church has in mind that experience by which a man becomes a Christian before God. No one denies that a man who becomes a Christian must go through a process in which man changes. It is a legitimate matter to raise questions about this process. But no one ought to deny that the decisive moment in this process is that in which God pronounces the judgment, 'Now you stand on My side.' The Reformers viewed this moment as the decisive one" (*Warum noch lutherische Kirche?* p. 74; cf. the section on grace, p. 78).

Heidland: "Because it is the believer who alone is ready to live by God's grace, this grace is imparted to him as God's justice . . . What was said about the tendency of the judgment toward actuality turns out to be important at this point. The declaration of justice does not exist as a fiction alongside reality. If God reckons faith as just, then man is wholly just in God's eyes. The reality of God's judgment is decisive for man. Through God's λογιζεσθαι he turns into a new creature. Therefore in Gal. 3.2–6 justification can become equivalent to receiving the Spirit, and Gen. 15.6 can be adduced as a prooftext for justification" (art. "λογιζωμαι," in *TWNT,* IV, 294; cf. by the same writer, *Die Anrechnung des Glaubens zur Gerechtigkeit.* Heidland points out that both Th. Zahn and H. Cremer [in his biblical-theological dictionary] come close to this sense of λογιζεσθαι).

Cf. also Schrenk, "δικαιοσυνη," in *TWNT*, II, 194–229; esp. pp. 207f., 213f.

The Lutheran, Hofer, gives a survey of the contemporary situation regarding the Protestant theology of justification (*Die Rechtfertigungsverkündigung des Paulus nach neuerer Forschung*). After indicating the vast amount of Protestant literature on the theology of justification between 1895 and 1939 (pp. 4–11), he asks what direction recent Pauline research has taken, and answers that it is toward a "justification of Paul's theology of justification" (p. 12), inasmuch as it "does not have a purely juridical or imputative meaning, but in a mystical dimension, so to speak, encompasses the entire Christian life of salvation, including the state of the unconscious (Eph. 4.23). Therefore, justification in Paul is not only the forgiveness of sin but also vocation, transformation, mobilization, a 'new' life and activity" (p. 12f.).

It might be a good idea if there should be an exacting historical investigation by Catholics as well, into what extent the Reformers did after all take a stand for purely forensic justification. What is going on in this area is frequently based on notions about the opponent which are entirely too stereotyped. On the basis of the research of K. Holl, Hofer asserts that the young Luther proposed an intrinsic connection between the declaration of justice and making just (p. 1). It was only in the wake of Melanchthon that the *pure* declaration of justice was advocated, but it was immediately fought by Osiander and, also, for example, by Pietism (p. 2). He holds that it is only in our own time that the anti-Catholic style of disputation characteristic of the past has been discarded in favor of a return to the data of the New Testament (p. 3).

Interesting in this connection is the fact that just as the Lutheran theologian E. Schlink refers to the Lutheran confessional writings, so too the Reformed theologian Karl Barth refers in the ontological statements of his theology of justification to Calvin.

This is how things stand today in the discussion of justification. It is without any doubt, then significant that today there is a fundamental agreement between Catholic and Protestant theology, precisely in the theology of justification—the point at which Reformation theology took its departure. Despite all the difficulties, have we not, after these 400 years, come closer to a meeting of minds, and this in a way which is theologically decisive?

Excursus:
The Redeemer in God's Eternity

The chapter on Jesus Christ showed that the pre-existent Christ is identical with the Redeemer, and therefore Christ—as the Word to become incarnate—has something to do with redemption. The incarnation is powerfully prepared from eternity in God's unalterable decree. This appears to be the general Catholic teaching and, more than that, the integral expression of Christian revelation.

How this pre-existence of the Redeemer is to be theologically explained is another question. Because it is theology and not revelation, this question is of secondary importance and does not stand in a necessary relationship to the above statement about revelation. Nevertheless, it is of significance and can cast new light on various problems. It is true, though, that it has not been treated too often and all we want to try here is a tentative interpretation.

Our starting point is this: Even creation is a mystery, a mystery in Jesus Christ. But this statement must not be allowed to nullify the next: the mystery of creation must never be placed on a par with the mystery of the incarnation of God. The mystery of creation is integrated within the encompassing mystery of the incarnation of God (since the incarnation calls for creation). And it must, in the last analysis, be understood in this light. But the mystery of God's incarnation cannot be resolved into the mystery of creation. The incarnation is not just a type of creation; rather it is in essence more than creation. The whole Christian tradition, purified by the Arian heresy especially, says that the mystery of the incarnation of God (and in it clearly the mystery of the Holy Trinity) is a mystery in the strictest sense—indeed, the fundamental mystery of Christian revelation, which surpasses all other mysteries. Therefore, there is a qualitative difference between the mystery of the incarnation and that of creation. Why?

A clear indication of the qualitative distinction is already contained in Scholastic terminology. The concept of the productio rei, which describes creation generally (= productio rei secundum totam suam substantiam), is insufficient to describe the incarnation. Although necessary for the description of the source of the human nature of Christ, it is pushed into the background in favor of the concepts of unio and assumptio. Here the element of qualitative difference comes clearly to light. While the relationship of God to creature in creation can of course be described as unio (that is, as unio participativa), it remains true that only in the incarnation is there any unio personalis (See *S.th.,* III, q. 3, 4 co). The element of qualitative difference then is the hypostatic unity, which consists "in a substantial union of the human nature with the divine hypostasis or person, whereby the human nature forms *one* totality with the divine, or is rounded out by the divine into one hypostatic union and, being appropriated by the divine hypostasis, in turn constitutes this a human hypostasis" (Scheeben, *Dogm.,* VI/I, 186).

The mystery of creation bears directly upon the creature (and therefore points indirectly to God); therefore, it can be deduced from the creature under certain circumstances. The mystery of the incarnation, however, cannot be positively deduced from the creature, for which it is a strict mystery. It bears directly on God Himself. It bears upon the Creator who becomes creature, the Eternal who becomes temporal. It is not just somebody who became man; it is the Eternal One. That is why the incarnation is not a historical fact like other historical facts.

Of course it is a historical fact, too, not a myth, but history: it occurs at a definite time, in a definite place. This the Church has always insisted upon with great energy. And one of the major concerns of Scholastic Christology was just this—to present the historical uniqueness of the incarnation with conceptual precision. In this process, Scholastic Christology was able to learn from the centuries-old struggle against the various forms of gnosticism, and from the gnostic evaporation of the temporal incarnation into some kind of incomprehensible "eternal" transcendental sphere. As the Gospel of John proves, this struggle had already begun in primitive Christendom, right after the foundation of the Church. In recent years a significant discussion has developed about the attitude of the primitive Church to the temporal incarnation and to time in general.

Motivated by Harnack's *History of Dogma,* detailed investigations of the relationship between the Israelitic-Judaistic and the Greek-Hellenistic forms of thought have been carried forward, with the relationship generally regarded as one of dynamic-static polarity. For our problem it is significant that different conceptions of time were also compared in these investigations. After E. von Dobschütz (*Zeit und Raum in Denken des Urchristentums*) and J. Guitton (*Le Temps et l'Eternité chez Plotin et S. Augustin*), O. Cullmann has given special attention to this in his *Christ and Time*. Cullmann's special merit is that he forcefully demonstrated the distinctly temporal character of all statements concerning faith, and showed Jesus Christ to be the unique temporal center of the total history of salvation—and this directly from New Testament revelation and through precise analysis of its temporal terminology.

Cullmann's chapter, "Time and Eternity" (pp. 52–59), bears upon our question directly. It is his intention to see the Greek-Platonic concept of eternity radically minimized in favor of the truly "biblical" concept according to which "Eternity is time without end" (p. 53). If it were true that, according to Sacred Scripture, eternity is actually nothing but a time without beginning and end, then our theological explanation of the pre-existence of Jesus Christ would encounter major difficulties. It would even be "dangerous" because this eternal pre-existence would be "set in opposition to the historical sphere," "as though it existed, so to speak, 'behind' all history in a timeless sphere" (cf. p. 87).

It is not our task to check this idea against biblical and historical evidence. (Th. Boman, for example, has pointed out that in the New Testament the temporal element is supplemented by a spatial element, that in its thinking a beyond conceived in terms of space does play a role, and that, after all, there is a very strong intermingling of Greek and Hebrew thought in the New Testament and in the history of dogma. (See *Das hebräische Denken im Vergleich mit dem griechischen,* pp. 140–142.) It is certain that it was precisely this concept of biblical eternity which was attacked most frequently by Cullmann's Catholic and Protestant critics. This prompted Cullmann to refine his arguments in the foreword to the section edition (1948). First of all he refers to the chapter, "God's Dominion over Time," which, though often overlooked, did indeed stress "the fundamental distinction between the endlessness of God's time and the finite character of time as comprehensible to and limited by man" (p. 8). Actually, in this chapter also, the pre-existence of the Redeemer is clearly affirmed (p. 60; cf. 79).

Secondly, in regard to the problem of eternity, Cullmann specifically says: "Moreover I would grant that my book does not solve many questions which dogmatic theologians must ask" (p. 8). We believe that the theological interpretation of the pre-existence of Jesus Christ is among those questions. Besides we would grant readily that the Scholastic concept of eternity must also be tested against the biblical concept of which it must form a transposition. Even the scholastic concept of eternity demands no absolute "non-temporality" (which would have to be in contradiction to eternity as *eminent* time, the transcendental "now" which includes all the fullness of temporality, as well as to the nature of the living God who is powerful in history). Still, Scholasticism justifiably denied any absolute temporalizing of eternity; the truly divine supratemporal character of eternity must remain preserved. As Cullmann's book itself proves, the biblical basis for a true supra-temporality does not seem to be lacking: he mentions that "the New Testament faith traces back the historical incarnation beyond the period of preparation proper into the beginnings of time" (p. 92), and that the *whole* line of the history of salvation "is from the beginning a christological line" (93). One can prescind from Christ, neither "before creation" (93) nor "in the course of creation itself" (94) nor in the "election of the people of Israel" (94).

As Cullmann correctly saw, the dogmatic theologian cannot confine himself to a simple listing of the biblical findings lest he renounce theology. He must therefore put questions to the biblical facts. The problem at this point is how to interpret theologically this supra-temporal simultaneity of Christ with the whole history of salvation, and especially His existence before creation. In this theological interpretation the theologian cannot manage without philosophical categories. When he least intends to philosophize, he does philosophize, as Cullmann's historical and exegetical book has demonstrated. The theologian in this task has the choice between several philosophical systems, and indeed the interpretation of God's eternity has already been attempted according to various systems of categories. If we hold to the Greek and Scholastic categories (especially those shaped by Plato) at this point, we do so particularly because even Cullmann's book has in no way proved the intrinsic incompatibility of these categories with biblical revelation, and above all, because in this work—consistent with the framework of the "Catholic response"—we attach special importance to the continuity of Catholic thinking.

The incarnation of God is a temporal fact. But it is not a temporal fact like any other. It is at the same time more than a temporal fact. Jesus Christ is in an eminent way in time, because He is rooted in God's eternity. He can be in time in this incomparable way only because He transcends all times. This is what Sacred Scripture (cf. e.g. Jn. 1) says. The theologian cannot therefore consider the incarnation only sub specie temporis, he also must attempt to see it sub specie aeternitatis—no matter how fragmentary his results are bound to remain when he does so.

What is the ontological reason for the supra-temporality of Jesus Christ? It is His Godhead. In Jesus Christ the temporal human nature is integrated with the second divine Person in a substantial unity. He is not only a communion of God with man, but the unity of God with man. It is imperative to be fully aware of this so as to distinguish the eternity of Jesus Christ from the presence of all created things in God's eternity.

For *all* created things can be spoken of as present in God's eternity, that is, in God's eternal act of creation. To quote de Finance, echoing Thomas Aquinas and the example of Aureolus on the Antichrist: "Although the Antichrist does not yet exist, has not yet been created, in a certain sense we can say that God creates him provided we strip this verb of all temporal connotation. In relation to us the Antichrist is future. In relation to God he is present, but the now of his presence is not the temporal now from which we are speaking" (*La présence* . . . , p. 50). Again, to quote Garrigou-Lagrange as cited by de Finance: "Things to come do not indeed exist in themselves now, in time, nor in eternity as consequences of passive creation, but they exist from eternity as *appointed times of actual eternal action.* And in this respect the thing created is nevertheless not only possible, nor only to come, but *really present in eternity,* for thus it is within the scope of divine nature which is not only able and willing to create but which *actually does create*" (p. 59). Quite properly the emphasis here is on the fact that the created beings are present to God's eternity, not only "ideally" but "really," precisely in virtue of the *actually* operative will of God as Creator.

Yet what must be said of the human nature of Christ cannot be said of any other created being. What happens is in fact the physical and ontological "assumption and acceptance to and into the person" (*"An-und Aufnahme an und in die Person,"* Scheeben,

Dogm., VI/1, 91)—into the person of the Son of God. The union effected is not just verbal or moral or accidental but (despite the complete discreteness of the natures) a genuine and real substantial union which is not a mere indwelling (inhabitatio) or a merely external joining (coniunctio), but (despite the two completely distinct natures) a union in which the divine Person Himself is the goal, that is, "assumptio humanitatis in Deum" (*Symb. Quicumque, D* 40; cf. *S.th.,* III, q. 3, a. 1 co). Scheeben, guided by the precedent of patristic formulations, gave proper emphasis to this aspect (cf. *Dogm.,* VI/1, 91–99): In addition to "assumption and acceptance to and into the person" (προσληψις, ἀναληψις), he used also the expressions "fastening to" (περιπηξις), "articulation with" or "integration" (καταρτισμος), "organic conjunction" (συμφυια), "interpenetration" (περιχωρειν εἰς ἀλληλα), the "raising and infusing of the form of mankind into the divine person" (ἀναπλασις εἰς μιαν ὑποστασιν, cf. *Symb. Epiph., D.* 13).

What happens is that the divine Person receives human nature "as something intrinsically bound to it, receiving it *into the whole to be constituted together with it,* and thus receiving it *into itself as the ruling principle of this whole* and to that extent bearing it and possessing it and having it *within itself"* (pp. 156f.).

And Thomas, who certainly did not go too far in this direction, did say: "For the grace of union is the *personal being* that is given gratis from above to the human nature in the Person of the Word, and is the *term* of the assumption" (*S.th.,* III, q. 6, a. 6); "Personal grace and capital grace are ordered to an act; but the grace of union is not ordered to an act, but to the *personal being"* (*S.th.,* III, q. 8, a. 5 ad 3); "But by the incarnation human nature . . . is said to be united to the divine nature itself in the Person of the Son" (*S.th.,* III, q. 2, a. 10 ad 1).

This, in Scholastic phraseology, is the same decisive point we tried to make all along. This indeed is the frightening mystery of the incarnation: the created object, unlike creation in general, is not outside God but within God Himself in the second divine Person. Simply by correlating the above formulations with the fact that human nature is a temporal nature and that the divine Person is an eternal Person, it will be seen how utterly perplexed and difficult our problem is. The issue is the "assumptio humanitatis temporalis in Deum aeternum" (following *D* 40), and the mysterious acceptance and assumption of a *temporal* nature into an *eternal* subject. Let us try to grope our way somewhat closer to the subject.

No excuses are made for radically excluding the rationalistic and neo-gnostic explanations of the pre-existence of Christ (especially in connection with Phil. 2.5ff), none of which do justice to the divine-human person of Jesus Christ—for example, the theories about Christ in the cosmic-economy-of-salvation form of epiphany (J. Müller) or in the form of an epiphany of God (Klöpper, B. Weiss, H. J. Holtzmann, Cone, and so on) or in ideal pre-existence (Bunsen), pre-existent divine man (Strauss, Beyschlag, Holsten, Pfleiderer, Krüger). See on this Schumacher, *Christus in seiner Präexistenz und Kenose*, II, 245–266; P. Henry, "Kénose," in *DBS*, V.

Let us put it once more sub specie temporis: On the basis of our *temporal* images we can speak of a *time* in which the Son of God had "not yet" become man. And from our standpoint in time, we can ask how the Logos was *before* the incarnation. Then we would speak of an "un-incarnate" Logos. This is the manner of speaking employed by John in his prologue, in order to remind us that this Jesus Christ, who dwelt among us and whose glory we have seen, is not a creature like any other creature, but rather was with God in the beginning since He was identical with the eternal Son of God (for the exegesis see chap. 21 above).

And now sub specie aeternitatis: When we reason from the viewpoint of God's eternal manner of existence, we must abandon transitory and temporal conceptions. God has time in its fullness without end; His time is not fragmented into a sequence of present, past, and future. Rather it is the unity of the before, the now, and the hereafter—of beginning, middle and end. This is His eternity. It is erroneous to conceive of the divine Logos as if He had "already" become man in some "pre-temporal" eternity, just as it would be wrong to imagine that the divine Logos had "not yet" become man in some "pre-temporal" eternity. From this viewpoint there is no such thing in God Himself as an eternity *before* the incarnation. This would amount to dissolving *eternity* into an inferior *time* of unlimited duration. "The *simultaneously whole and perfect* possession of interminable life" (*S.th.*, I, q. 10, a. 1) would be resolved into a "perpetual succession" (cf. I, q. 10, a. 4). On the basis of our temporal images we can ask: What is the Son of God *before* the incarnation? From the standpoint of eternity, however, the most we can ask is: What would the Logos be *without* the incarnation?—a question possibly helpful in formulating the absolutely free graciousness of the incarnation. In the realm of eternity, it is impossible to speak simply in the strict sense of a non-incarnate Logos, of a prehistorical, pre-Christian, or post-Christian epoch. In this connection, all terms expressing a "pre" (like predetermination, prevision, predestination, pre-existent Christ) easily mislead, since they result, often unconsciously, in the application of inferior temporal images to God's eternity.

We must not overlook the primacy in knowing which existent act has over all forms of potency. To think of God's knowing as first focused on the yet-undefined, on the potential and possible and only thereafter on the actual and real, on the final existential definiteness of things, is an anthropomorphism. It is deceiving to imagine that for God knowledge of possibilities (possibilia) could be an anterior prerequisite for knowing existing things or for deciding to create them. Equally deceiving is the notion that God's knowledge of what is *necessary* in His person (for instance, His omnipotence or the Trinity of Persons) could be an anterior prerequisite for knowing what is *free* in Himself (for example, the human nature of the Son). Of course God knows that He in no way *has to* become man. And yet, God has of Himself only a single and indivisible knowledge through which He knows Himself as the one who freely became man in the Son. Hence the eternal Logos knows Himself as Logos only by knowing Himself simultaneously as incarnate; and only as Logos incarnate is the eternal Logos known also by the Father and the Holy Spirit.

We can easily see how difficult it is not only negatively to eliminate misconceptions, but positively to articulate the truth of faith. The reason is that in a mystery properly so called, all images and directly explanatory conclusions will and must fail. What is possible is to give a few hints. The eternal generative act of the Father has for its formal object the divine person of the Word as such, while the divine act of incarnation has for its formal object the hypostatic union, or better, the unified being itself, the Word become flesh, the divine person of the Word hypostatically joined with human nature (cf. Scheeben, *Dogm.,* VI/1, 236f.).

The mystery, then, consists in this: The Father's eternal begetting is in His unchangeable supratemporality, is in the now of His eternity which simultaneously embraces everything. This eternal begetting of the Father happens and perdures also in the generation and perduration of the hypostatic union, so that this eternal begetting, in its eternity, has for its object as a matter of fact the divine person of the Word which subsists in human nature. Scheeben points out how generatio aeterna and actio unitiva "work together in the begetting of Christ as the proper product of the actio unitiva. For Christ as such comes to be or to be generated in that the hypostasis of the Logos, proceeding from the Father through the eternal and hence continuing act of begetting, is formed into one whole with human nature by virtue of the actio unitiva. Consequently both actions work together in the generation of Christ in such a way that in regard to this product they constitute a total action which *as such* cannot be called a simple *generation* but is a *begetting of Christ by God the Father and from him.*" (*Dogm.,* VI/1, 241f.).

Sub specie aeternitatis, this might be briefly formulated as follows: In His eternity and thus unchangingly and yet in a totally free way, God, the Father, sees and loves (begets) His Son who is man. The incarnation becomes reality in a specific space-time point of our history. Yet, in the eternity of God the incarnation of the Son is, and really is, fixed in God's decree where no shadow of alteration exists. Thus in His eternity, God decrees Himself in His Son to be man. So the pre-existent Jesus Christ is indeed identical with the Redeemer.

So much for the attempt at a theological interpretation of the "pre-existence" of Jesus Christ, of the verbum incarnandum. In the light of this interpretation the facts of revelation, as they are presented in the chapter on Christ, along with some other questions, may appear less obscure. Let us mention a few things.

Our explanation is entirely in line with the New Testament witness and serves to accent some statements which may often have been taken not literally enough—for example the "lamb without blemish or spot" who "was destined before the foundation of the world but was made manifest at the end of the times" (1 Pet. 1.-19–20), the "Lamb slain from the foundation of the world" (Rev. 13.8 KJV), especially the many passages about the eternal "mystery" which though hidden, has always been reality. It is clear that here a philosophical and theological interpretation has the support of a solid base in Scripture. In the chapter on Jesus Christ and on creation many statements of exegetes were cited which stress the soteriological aspect of the scriptural texts on the pre-existent Jesus Christ. Only two citations especially important for our explanation will be added here:

Cerfaux: "The Old Testament provided St. Paul with the idea of pre-existence, in the sense that the Christ foreseen for Israel had been prepared from all eternity and had existed from all eternity in the purposes of God. This person who would come to accomplish God's work is called, in the thought of God, His Christ. We know how Jewish apocalyptic had concretized this idea of pre-existence, so as to make of Christ, become the 'Son of Man' of Daniel, a pre-existent being. Having renounced the expression 'Son of Man' and because, moreover, the title 'Kyrios' points to Christ's exaltation and 'Son of God' is an epithet and does not really play the role of a substantive, it remained for St. Paul to follow the line of the Old Testament and the apocalypses and to call ὁ Χριστος the pre-existing Christ, who exercises His salvific causality from the side of His pre-existence. The Christ is to be the one who comes to accomplish the work of God in the world" (*Le Christ*, pp. 373f.).

Bonsirven: "In all the passages in which he deals with the incarnation of Jesus and its consequences, St. Paul affirms His identity in His three states: His pre-existence, His earthly life, and His exaltation in glory. It is always the same subject and is considered in the glory of the exalted Christ (cf. Col. 2.3 and 1 Tim. 3.16). From this we can understand better how the Apostle, without arriving at our theological precision, speaks of the pre-existence of Christ. It is neither a kind of predestination, nor an ideal existence in the plans of the Creator, nor a projection into the time prior to the Incarnation of Christ first earthly and then glorified, but a Christ considered always as a creature" (*Théol. du N.T.*, p. 256). "The first stanza and first stage of the divine blessings, 'before the foundation of the world,' the only means (Jn. 17.24, 1 Pet. 1.20) to make it clear that the order of predestination is supra-temporal, is anterior both logically and ontologically to the whole creation" (p. 272). On the connection with the Old Testament, see A. Feuillet, *Le Fils de l'homme de Daniel et la tradition biblique;* on the connection with late Judaism, G. Kretschmar, *Frühchristliche Trinitätslehre* (esp. p. 219, n. 2).

Sub specie aeternitatis, Paul's idiosyncrasy in always speaking of the God-man, Jesus Christ (whether he refers to Jesus Christ in the bosom of the Father or to Jesus Christ in the flesh), is not to be construed as a primitive and undifferentiated style of speech, but must be appreciated as a profoundly theological manner of speaking. This is not to say that Paul had a philosophical and theological meaning of this type consciously in mind. What he certainly was conscious of was the inestimable meaning and power of the eternal divine decree and the unity of the divine plan of salvation.

From this viewpoint it is not overly important to determine which specific passages of Paul refer to Christ as man or Christ as God. We will have to agree with Brinkmann (*Die Kosmische Stellung des Gottmenschen in Paulinischer Sicht,* p. 8), who asserts along with other authors that the Apostle always referred to the concrete historical God-man and "not by any means only to Christ as God or Christ as man." And we can go along with Durand ("Le Christ 'Premier-né,'" p. 58) in his analysis of the confusion which prevails in the interpretation of Col. 1.15–17. "Probably this would not have happened if exegetes had not started with the unwarranted assumption that the Apostle was supposed to speak here distinctly of the divine nature *or* the human nature. In reality, his thought moves directly to the universal and sovereign mediation of Christ as it is manifest in the unity of one and the same person. It is true that this mediation presents two aspects and that it has known two moments: as cosmic Mediator, the Christ is Creator (Col. 1.15–17); as mystic Mediator, the Christ is Redeemer (Col. 1.18–20). It is likewise correct that the prerogative of Christ as Creator is based definitely on His pre-existence in the divine life, and that His function as Redeemer presupposes the incarnation. But it does not seem that the Apostle here intended all these precise definitions. It was enough for him, at the moment, to maintain the transcendence and plenitude of the mediation of Christ Jesus."

Our explanation also appears to be *in line with patristic theology.* What Spindeler says (*Cur Verbum caro factum*) is doubtless true: Almost all the Fathers . . . simply equate the Logos, the Son of God, with 'Christ'" (p. 87). Now we do not think that this manner of speaking is in need of correction, since behind it there is the same thing we tried to bring out—the meaning of the eternal decree of God as well as the unity of the person and the work of Jesus Christ, and the unity of the history of salvation (we will shortly return to the Fathers' Christological interpretation of the Old Testament).

It is significant that even Irenaeus, called the Father of Catholic theology, came out very plainly for the unity of Jesus Christ. E. Scharl says of him: "Regardless of how present-day exegetes and dogmatic theologians wish to interpret this word (Col. 1.15ff.), whether as referring to Christ as man or Christ as God, Irenaeus, in Chap. 16 of Book 3 where he uses it, does not admit this division. He consistently explains against various groups of Gnostics, who would wish to split up the personal unity of Jesus Christ, that there is one single Word of God, one single Jesus Christ. 'We must not assume that Jesus and Christ are different persons, but must be aware that He is one and the same' " (*Recapitulatio mundi,* p. 100). And P. Galtier says approvingly about Irenaeus: "He holds that Adam was created to be saved, because of the fact that the Son of God pre-existed from eternity as the Savior" (*De incarn.,* pp. 475f.).

And with respect to Augustine, J. Guitton said: "In sum, the incarnation finds only a support in chronology. In the world of spirits it is at the center, and it is history which vibrates in it. It is the only efficacious working of the divine. Through it the Eternal comes to the aid of the temporal, and the temporal takes its place in the Eternal" (*Le Temps et l'Eternité,* pp. 323f.).

In this connection it is of interest that Thomas, on the question "whether it is true that the man (Christ) always existed," instead of denying it as one might expect, rather affirms it: "And we must say that this is true because of the fact that the use of the term man implies an eternal presupposition. Thus in the last chapter of Hebrews (13.8) it is said: "Jesus Christ, the same yesterday, today, and forever." Yet a proposition of this kind is not reduplicatively true. For it was not according to His manhood that He was always man but *according to His being as Son of God.*" (On Rom. 1.4, Lect. 3; cf. III, Sent., Dist. 12, q. 1; *S.th.,* III, q. 16, a. 9). The "non reduplicative" is important: If Jesus Christ is in God's eternity it is not by virtue of His human nature but by virtue of His divine Person. Together with the negative aspect of the answer the positive aspect (hanc .esse veram) must be weighed in its total meaning and theological profundity. (See Bonaventure, Dist. II, 2, q. 2).

It should be noted how according to *S.th.,* II-II, q. 2, a. 7, the mystery of the incarnation and with it the mystery of the Trinity, (a.8) permeates the whole of human history.

Perhaps on this basis the gracious activity of Jesus Christ in the Old Testament also becomes a little clearer. This "prelude to the incarnation" (*Prat, Theol, of St. Paul,* II, 148f.), is described to us in the text on the rock which, from the historical point of view, followed the Israelites but despite that, since it was reality in the bosom of the Father, was already there when they drank from it (1 Cor. 10.4). It is a universal Catholic teaching that the grace of Jesus Christ was already operative in the Old Testament (even as justifying grace): "However, it was possible at the time of the law for the minds of the faithful to be united by faith to Christ incarnate and crucified; so that they were justified by faith in Christ," (*S.th.*, I-II, q. 103, a. 2 co; I, q. 43, a. 6 ad 1; I-II, q. 98, a. 3, ad 4; q. 103, a. I ad 3; a. 3 ad 2); on Augustine, cf. Rondet, *Gratia Christi*, p. 139. Yet it would require explanation how the incarnation is able to radiate its power into *all* ages, why "the effects of the redemption could be shared by all mankind and thus from the very beginning" (Scheeben, *Dogm.*, VI/1, 19), and how the "anticipated reception of the fruits" of redemption (p. 21) was made possible. And to what could such an explanation be traced if not to the eternity of the divine decree of salvation in Jesus Christ?

It is in patristic theology that many treasures still lie hidden regarding the soteriological activity of Jesus Christ in the Old Testament. The Fathers regard this activity of Jesus Christ in the Old Testament as a very plain and concrete fact. All of the ante-Nicene and most of the post-Nicene Fathers up to Leo the Great and Isidore of Seville take it for granted that the Son has appeared in the Old Testament, with the majority thinking exclusively of the Son and some individuals even asserting the impossibility of the appearance of the Father.

Among the ante-Nicene Fathers only Clement of Alexandria and Origen express doubts about this being impossible (cf. de Régnon, *Etudes sur la Trinité*, III/1, 63–66; 88–101). This teaching was even defined against Photinus at Sirmium in 351. Hilary, who defended the orthodoxy of this Council, has preserved its canons for us (*op. cit.*, pp. 88f.).

It can be claimed that where the Old Testament shows God acting and speaking, the Fathers generally take this as the second person of the Godhead whom they designate as Christ, Word, Son, the Lord Jesus, without any set order. For example, Jesus Christ created the world, made Adam out of dust and was with him in paradise, appeared to Abraham and the patriarchs, to Moses in the burning bush on Sinai, wandered with the people through the wilderness, etc. Especially important in this connection, next to the figure of the "Angel of the Lord," is the activity of "Wisdom" (for which there does exist an unbroken theological tradition from the

Fathers via Thomas, Bonaventure and Suarez to Kuhn, Staudenmaier, Franzelin and Scheeben; on this see Heinrich, *Dogm.*, IV, 98; cf. 50ff.). Moreover, the Fathers (in close connection with Scripture) see "figures" of Jesus Christ throughout the Old Testament, not only in persons (Adam, Abel, Noah, Abraham, Melchizedek, Isaac, Joseph, Moses, Job, David, Jeremiah, Jonah, etc.) but also in objects (paschal lamb, ark, burning bush, the pillar of cloud, Jacob's ladder, manna, the rock, sacrificial animals, the serpent in the wilderness, tabernacle, the fleece of Gideon, and so on).

These conceptions appear in the Fathers from the very beginning; they are already in the "nontheological" Apostolic Fathers (especially Ignatius, and later in Justin and Irenaeus), where there is less reason to suspect philosophical influences (Platonic and Philonic) than is true somewhat later in the school of Alexandria (for example, with regard to the invisibility of the Father). It is Augustine who first departed from this exegesis of the appearances of Jesus, because of the danger of a distinction in substance between the Father and the Son, coming from Arianism (see on this development of dogma, Kuhn, *Dogm.*, II, 14f., 20). But it must be remembered that the rest of the Fathers engaged in this exegesis saw no distinction in essence but only in person.

It is worth the effort to reconsider whether this patristic teaching cannot be reconciled with the principles of the theology of the Trinity which have been elaborated since then. Even authors like Billot and Ch. Pesch keep open the possibility of "visible missions" in the Old Testament "in the manner of a kind of beginning or prelude to the future economy of the incarnation" (Billot, *De Deo uno,* p. 610; cf. Ch. Pesch, *Praelectiones,* II, 333); others like J. von Kuhn and H. Schell (*Das Wirken des dreieinigen Gottes*) go further.

In such considerations caution is certainly in order. Still why should we not continue—with new caution—to meditate on Scripture? Did not K. Rahner's article, "Theos im Neuen Testament," show that "Theos" in the New Testament always means the Father; and does this not have great significance for his special "invisibility" (Jn. 1.18)? Has the meaning of the Scholastic proposition, "the Father is not sent," really been exhausted within the scope of our problems? Has everything been done to fathom the concept and scope of "appropriation" (cf. de Régnon, *Etudes sur la Trinité,* I,

315–319)? Does not the principle, "the operations of the Trinity ad extra are one," remain inviolate even in the incarnation of the one divine Person? Isn't there still some treasure hidden in the Old Testament, even with due regard to the big bracket according to which the Old Testament is not the New Testament?

K. Rahner, too, is aware of possibilities for deepening present-day Christology: "The question suggests itself whether there might not be a formula for salvation history as God's progressive taking possession of the world in history, as the manifestation, ever clearer and more hidden at once, of God in the world as his quasi-sacramental mysterium. The Christ would appear as the summit of this history and Christology as its *sharpest* formulation, just as inversely, salvation history would appear as the prelude to and extension of Christ's own history. Perhaps the ancients had a better idea of all this than we usually have today, with our still very pale and vague idea of the time before Christ as the preparation for the fullness of times. The old speculation about the Logos, which ascribed to him an activity and history in creation 'before Christ but Christ-like,' distinct from the invisible Father, would be well worth rethinking, after being purified of its subordinationist elements. It is still by no means established that the extraction of this waste matter would inevitably lead to the ruin of these early speculations" (Karl Rahner, *Theological Investigations,* vol. I, pp. 166–167).

Finally, on this basis, the predominant *place of Mary in God's plan of salvation* might be more firmly founded and be made more convincing in the eyes of the non-Catholic. Catholic Mariology is often rejected because it does not show the courage of its Mariological convictions, because it does not dare radically to link Mary with Jesus Christ (that is, in knowledge and love in the bosom of the Father), insofar as Jesus Christ is seen and loved by the Father in eternity as the Son of Mary. Here the Church shows the way between undogmatic Mariological sentimentalism and an equally undogmatic Mariological minimalism by interpreting, with unaccustomed courage, the Wisdom literature not only on the Christological and ecclesiological but then also on the Mariological level. If seen in the proper light all this is anything but pious allegory.

It should be noted how Pius IX put it at the beginning of the Bull "Ineffabilis Deus" (8 Dec. 1854): "From the beginning and before creation, God chose and ordained for His only begotten Son a Mother from whom, made flesh, in the blessed fullness of time,

He should be born." And he adds: "The very words with which the divine Scriptures speak of uncreated Wisdom, and of His eternal origin—those are the words the Church was accustomed to present both in the breviary and in the sacred liturgy, referring them to the origin of that Virgin who was determined beforehand in one and the same decree with the incarnation of divine Wisdom."

In conclusion it should once more be stressed that the whole of the mystery of Christ is a *mysterium in the strict sense*. Whoever wants to form any concrete images out of all this, or even only an idea clara et distincta (especially of the God-man in the bosom of the Father) is on the wrong track to start with. Both things are true: Jesus Christ is in eternity and Jesus Christ is temporal. Time and eternity must not be mixed up nor should they be severed.

We have attempted an interpretation of this mystery—an interpretation which is open to discussion, though it would be an illusion to overlook the significant difficulties connected with it. So we want to formulate some of the difficulties ourselves in the form of questions. For difficulties are not a call to resignation but to go on questioning and thinking.

What does it mean to say that God's relation to the creature, and thus the relation of the Logos to human nature, is only a rational relation? (cf. *Contra Gent.*, II, c. 12–14; *S.th.*, I, q. 13, a. 7; cf. on this, Krempel, *Doctrine de la relation chez S. Thomas, pp.* 563–570.). If this means that God does not lose His independence in the incarnation and that He does not enrich Himself by this and if the "asynchytos" of the Chalcedonian formula is to be stressed in this manner, is this sufficient to explain the "adiairetos"? Does this make it clear that now, after all, the Word of God *itself* has become man—that the incarnation is actually the history of God Himself?

In Christ what does the *"communication of characteristics"* (communicatio idiomatum) mean? (Cf. *S.Th.*, III, q.16, a. 4–5.) The stress on the noncommingling of the two natures—which only says that the same Christ is truly God and truly man and not of a third intermediary kind—does this warrant the neglect of the unity between the two natures? In spite of the noncommingling, is not the *unio* still the greatest of unions (*S.th.*, III. q. 2, a. 9.) if one looks at what unifies them? Does the substantial hypostatic, perduring and indispensable unity of the two natures really imply more than a formal, abstract, and ultimately somehow empty unity? Is the desire to take the unity in a somewhat more plastic and concrete way satisfied if the human reality is only *predicated* of the divine Word, without this divine Word being in some way effected? Is not the "communication of characteristics" a rule of linguistic expression because it is a rule of thought? And in addition, is it not a rule of thought because it is a rule of the *"object"* of this thought, namely, the God-man? Does the communicatio idiomatum mean only that this or that predication (e.g., Thomas' "Iste homo semper fuit") is logically correct, or does it mean much more—that is, that here a *truth* is expressed about the *being* (of that man)? And is the kenosis of the Son of God, which is described in Sacred Scripture, really a kenosis (even if not in the sense of the kenoticists), or is it in the final analysis only a ready image lacking in depth? Does it actually affect Jesus Himself when He emptied Himself and became humble (Phil. 2.7f.), gave Himself (Gal. 1.4; 1 Tim. 2.6), surrendered Himself (Gal. 2.20; Eph. 5.2), offered up Himself (Heb. 7.27; 9.14)? Does His obedience really affect Himself inwardly (Phil. 2.8; Heb. 5.8)?

We refer once more to K. Rahner who mentions in this connection: "The only way in which Christ's *concrete* humanity may be conceived of in itself as diverse from the Logos is by thinking of it *in so far as* it is united to the Logos. The unity with the Logos must constitute it in its diversity from him, that is, precisely as a human nature; the unity must itself be the ground of the diversity. In this way, the diverse term as such is the united reality of him who as prior unity (which can thus only be God) is the ground of the diverse term, and therefore, while remaining 'immutable' 'in himself', truly comes to be *in* what he constitutes *as* something *united* (geeinte) with him *and diverse* from him. In other words, the ground by which the diverse term is constituted and the ground by which the unity with the diverse term is constituted must as such be strictly the same. But if what makes the human nature ek-sistent as something diverse from God, and what unites this nature with the Logos, are *strictly* the same, then we have a unity which (a) cannot, as uniting unity (einende Einheit), be confused with the united unity (geeinte Einheit) (this is not permissible); (b) which unites *precisely by* making existent, and *in this way* is grasped in a fullness of content without any relapse into the empty assertion of the united unity; and finally (c) which does not make the ἀσυνχύτως look like a sort of external counterbalance to the unity, always threatening to dissolve it again, but shows precisely how it enters into the *constitution* of the united unity as an intrinsic factor, in such a way that unity and distinction become mutually conditioning and intensifying characteristics, not competing ones."

And as a footnote he adds: "It follows from this statement that the assertion of God's 'immutability', of the lack of any real relation between God and the world, is in a true sense a dialectical statement. One may and indeed must say this, without for that reason being a Hegelian. For it is true, come what may, and a dogma, that the Logos himself has become man: thus that he himself has become something that he had not always been (*formaliter*); and therefore that what has so become is, as just itself and of itself, God's reality. Now if this is a truth of faith, ontology must allow itself to be guided by it (as in analogous instances in the doctrine of the Trinity), must seek enlightenment from it, and grant that while God remains immutable 'in himself', he can come to be 'in the other', and that *both* assertions must really and truly be made of the same God as God" (Karl Rahner, *Theological Investigations,* vol. I, pp. 181–182, and n. 3, p. 181).

Bibliography

A. CHAPTERS 1–19 (The Doctrine of Karl Barth)

1. The Works of Karl Barth

A complete list of Barth's publications that includes 406 titles up to December, 1955, has been compiled by Miss Charlotte von Kirschbaum in: *Antwort, Karl Barth zum 70. Geburtstag,* Zürich, 1956, pp. 945–960. Only a few works which are of special importance in connection with our study are listed here.

Der Römerbrief. 1st ed. Bern 1919.
Der Römerbrief. 2nd ed. München 1922.
"Das Wort Gottes und die Theologie," *Ges. Vorträge.* München 1924.
"Das Halten der Gebote," *Zwischen den Zeiten,* V, 1927, 206–227.
"Rechtfertigung und Heiligung," *Zwischen d. Z.,* V, 1927, 281–309.
"Die Theologie und die Kirche," *Ges. Vorträge.* München 1928.
"Schicksal und Idee in der Theologie," *Zwischen den Zeiten,* VII, 1929, 309–348.
"Evangelium und Gesetz," *Theol. Existenz heute,* No. 32, 1935.
Rechtfertigung und Recht. (Theol. Studien, No. 1). Zollikon-Zürich 1938.
Die kirchliche Lehre von der Taufe. (Theol. Studien, No. 14). Zollikon-Zürich 1943
Die protestantische Theologie im 19. Jahrhundert. Ihre Vorgeschichte und Geschichte. Zollikon-Zürich 1947.
Rudolf Bultmann. Ein Versuch, ihn zu verstehen. (Theol. Studien, No. 34). Zollikon-Zürich 1952.
Die Kirchliche Dogmatik, Zürich 1932ff:
I/1   *Die Lehre vom Worte Gottes* (1932).
I/2   *Die Lehre vom Worte Gottes* (1939).
II/1   *Die Lehre von Gott* (Die Erkenntnis Gottes, die Wirklichkeit Gottes) (1940).
II/2   *Die Lehre von Gott* (Gottes Gnadenwahl, Gottes Gebot) (1942).
III/1   *Die Lehre von der Schöpfung* (Das Werk der Schöpfung) (1945).
III/2   *Die Lehre von der Schöpfung* (Das Geschöpf) (1948).
III/3   *Die Lehre von der Schöpfung* (Der Schöpfer und sein Geschöpf) (1950).
III/4   *Die Lehre von der Schöpfung* (Das Gebot des Schöpfers) (1951).
IV/1   *Die Lehre von der Versöhnung* (Jesus Christus, der Herr als Knecht) (1953).
IV/2   *Die Lehre von der Versöhnung* (Jesus Christus, der Knecht als Herr) (1955).

1a. Works of Karl Barth in English

A list of the above publications which have been translated into English, with two more recent volumes of the *Dogmatics*.

The Epistle to the Romans: Tr. from the 6th ed. by Edwyn C. Hoskyns, London, New York, 1953.

The Word of God and the Word of Man. Tr. by Douglas Horton. Boston, Chicago, 1928.

Theology and Church: Shorter Writings, 1920–1928. Tr. by Louise Pettibone Smith. New York, 1962.

The Teaching of the Church regarding Baptism. Tr. by Ernest A. Payne. London, 1954.

Protestant Thought: From Rousseau to Ritschl. Translation of 11 chs. of *Die protestantische Theologie im 19. Jahrhundert,* by Brian Cozens. New York, 1959.

Church Dogmatics. Editors: G. W. Bromiley and T. F. Torrance. Edinburgh, 1936–62.

I/1   *The Doctrine of the Word of God.*
I/2   *The Doctrine of the Word of God.*
II/1   *The Doctrine of God* (The Knowledge of God, The Reality of God).
II/2   *The Doctrine of God* (The Election of God, The Command of God).
III/1 *The Doctrine of Creation* (The Work of Creation).
III/2 *The Doctrine of Creation* (The Creature).
III/3 *The Doctrine of Creation* (The Creator and His Creature).
III/4 *The Doctrine of Creation* (The Command of God the Creator).
IV/1   *The Doctrine of Reconciliation* (Jesus Christ, The Lord as Servant).
IV/2   *The Doctrine of Reconciliation* (Jesus Christ, the Servant as Lord).
IV/3   *The Doctrine of Reconciliation,* First Half (Jesus Christ, the True Witness).
IV/4   *The Doctrine of Reconciliation,* Second Half (Jesus Christ, the True Witness).

2. Books on Barth by Catholic Authors

The important works which have appeared in book form since 1945. For more extensive bibliographies, cf. Riverso, pp. 407–415, especially the articles by L. Malevez, G. Rabeau, and E. Przywara.

BALTHASAR, H. U. VON, *Karl Barth, Darstellung und Deutung seiner Theologie,* Köln 1951.

EBNETER, A., *Der Mensch in der Theologie Karl Barths,* Zürich 1952.

FRIES, H., *Bultmann–Barth und die katholische Theologie.* Stuttgart 1955.

GHERARDINI, B., *La parola di Dio nella teologia di Karl Barth.* Roma 1955.

GROOT, J. C., *Karl Barth en het theologische kenprobleem.* Heiloo 1946.

HAMER, J., *Karl Barth, L'Occasionalisme théologique de K. Barth, Etude sur sa méthode dogmatique*. Paris 1949.

RIVERSO, E., *Intorno al pensiero di Karl Barth, colpa e giustificazione nella reazione antiimmanentistica del "Römerbrief" barthiano*. Padova 1951.

———, *La Teologia esistenzialistica di Karl Barth. Analisi, interpretazione e discussione del sistema*. Napoli 1955.

VOLK, H., "Die Christologie bei Karl Barth und Emil Brunner," *Konzil von Chalkedon*, III, 531–611. Würzburg 1954.

3. Additional Authors Cited in the First Part

BOUYER, L., *The Spirit and Forms of Protestantism*, tr. A. V. Littledale. London and Westminster, Md., 1956.

LORTZ, J., *Geschichte der Kirche in ideengeschichtlicher Betrachtung*. 16th ed. Münster 1950.

———, *Die Reformation in Deutschland*. 2 vols. 3rd ed. Freiburg i. Br. 1949.

———, *Die Reformation als religiöses Anliegen heute*. Trier 1948.

B. CHAPTER 20 (Development of Dogma, Trent, Scripture, and Tradition)

ACTA ET DECRETA SACRORUM CONCILIORUM RECENTIORUM. *Collectio Lacensis*. Book VII (Vaticanum) Friburgi Br. 1890.

ADAM, K., *Das Wesen des Katholizismus*. 11th ed. Düsseldorf 1946.

———, *Jesus Christus*. 5th ed. Augsburg 1938.

ASMUSSEN, H., *Warum noch lutherische Kirche? Ein Gespräch mit dem Augsburgischen Bekenntnis*. Stuttgart 1949.

BALIC, C., "Il senso cristiano e il progresso del dogma," *Gregorianum*, 33 (1952) 106–134.

BALTHASAR, H. U. VON. See under A.

BAUMGARTNER, CH., "Tradition et magistère," *RechScRel*, 41 (1953) 161–187.

BEA, A., "Il progresso nell'interpretazione della S. Scrittura," *Gregorianum*, 33 (1952) 85–105.

BELTRAN DE HEREDIA, V., "Controversia de certitudine gratiae entre Domingo de Soto y Ambrosio Caterino," *Ciencia Tomista*, 62 (1941) 133–162.

BOSSUET, J.-B., *Exposition de la doctrine de l'Eglise catholique sur les matières de controverse*. Paris 1671.

BOUILLARD, H., *Conversion et grâce chez St. Thomas d'Aquin*. Paris 1944.

BOUYER, L. See under A.

BOYER, C., "Relazione tra il progresso filosofico, teologico, dogmatico," *Gregorianum*, 33 (1952) 168–182.

BROGLIE, G. DE, "Letter to the author from G. de Broglie, S.J., in Bouyer, L., *The Spirit and Forms of Protestantism*, 1956, p. ix; also Note by de Broglie, pp. 230ff.

BUUCK, F., "Zum Rechtfertigungsdekret," in Schreiber, *Weltkonzil,* pp. 117–143.

CAVALLERA, F., "La session VI du Concile de Trente," *Bull. de Littérature ecclésiastique 1942–1953.*

CHENU, M.-D., "Vocabulaire biblique et vocabulaire théologique," *NRTh,* 84 (1952) 1029–1041.

CONCILIUM TRIDENTINUM, Diariorum, actorum, epistularum, tractatuum Nova Collectio. (Ed. Goerresiana). Friburgi Br. 1901ff.

CONGAR, Y. M.-J., *Chrétiens désunis. Principes d'un "Oecuménisme" catholique.* Paris 1937.

————, *Vraie et fausse réforme dans l'Eglise.* Paris 1950.

CRISTIANI, L., *L'Eglise à l'époque du concile de Trente.* Paris 1948.

CULLMANN, O., *Die Tradition als exegetisches, historisches und theologisches Problem.* Zürich 1954.

DEJAIFVE, G., "Bible, Tradition, Magistère dans la théologie catholique," *NRTh,* 78 (1956) 135–151.

DENEFFE, A., *Der Traditionsbegriff. Studie zur Theologie.* Münster 1931.

DENZINGER, H., *Enchiridion symbolorum.* 25th ed. Barcelona 1948.

DHANIS, E., "Révélation explicite et implicite," *Gregorianum,* 34 (1953) 187–237.

FILOGRASSI, G., "Tradizione Divino-Apostolica e Magistero della Chiesa," *Gregorianum,* 33 (1952) 135–167.

FLICK, M., "Il problema dello sviluppo del dogma nella teologia contemporanea," *Gregorianum* 33 (1952) 5–23.

FRANZELIN, J. B., *Tractatus de divina Traditione et Scriptura.* 2nd ed. Roma 1875.

FRIES, H. See under A.

GEISELMANN, J. R., *Lebendiger Glaube aus geheiligter Überlieferung.* Mainz 1942.

————, J. A. MÖHLER, *Die Einheit der Kirche und die Wiedervereinigung der Konfessionen.* Wien 1940.

————, *Das Missverständnis über das Verhältnis von Schrift und Tradition, und seine Überwindung in der kath. Theologie (Unam Sanctam 11).* Paris 1956.

GRABMANN, M., "Das Konzil von Trient als Fortschrittsprinzip der katholischen Dogmatik," Schreiber, *Weltkonzil,* pp. 33–53.

HARNACK, A. VON, *Dogmengeschichte.* Vol. III. 4th ed. Tübingen 1910.

HEFNER, J., *Die Entstehungsgeschichte des Trienter Rechtfertigungsdekretes.* Paderborn 1909.

HENNINGER, J., *S. Augustinus et doctrina de duplici iustitia (Seripando).* Mödling 1935.

HEYNCK, V., *Untersuchungen über die Reuelehre der Tridentinischen Zeit* (Franz. Studien 29 [1942] 25–44 [Vega]; 120–150 [Medina]; 30 [1943] 53–73 [Soto]).

————, *A Controversy at the Council of Trent concerning the Doctrine of Duns Scotus.* (Franciscan Studies 9 [1949] 88–103; 129–148).

————, "Zum Problem der unvollkommenen Reue auf dem Konzil von Trient," in Schreiber, *Weltkonzil,* pp. 231–280.

————, *Zur Kontroverse über die Gnadengewissheit auf dem Konzil von Trient* (Franz Studien 37 [1955] 1–17; 161–188).

HOLDEN, H., *Divinae fidei analysis, seu de Fidei christianae resolutione libri duo.* Parisiis 1652.

HÜNERMANN, F., *Wesen und Notwendigkeit der aktuellen Gnade nach dem Konzil von Trient.* Paderborn 1926.

JEDIN, H., *Geschichte des Konzils von Trient.* Freiburg 1949ff.

LENNERZ, H., "Das Konzil von Trient und die theologischen Schulmeinungen," *Scholastik,* 4 (1929) 38–53.

————, "Voten auf dem Konzil von Trient," *Gregorianum,* 15 (1934) 577–588.

LORTZ, J. See under A.

LOTZ, J. B., "Zur Geschichtlichkeit der Wahrheit," *Scholastik,* 27 (1952) 481–503.

MERSCH, E., "L'objet de la Théologie et le Christus totus," *RScRel,* 26 (1936) 129–157.

MOELLER, CH., "Bible et Oecuménisme," *Irénikon,* 23 (1950) 164–188.

————, "Tradition et Oecuménisme," *Irénikon,* 25 (1952) 337–370.

MÖHLER, J. A., *Die Einheit in der Kirche oder das Prinzip des Katholizismus dargestellt im Geiste der Kirchenväter der drei ersten Jahrhunderte.* Tübingen 1825.

————, *Symbolik oder Darstellung der dogmatischen Gegensätze der Katholiken und Protestanten nach ihren öffentlichen Bekenntnisschriften.* Regensburg 1832. 12th ed. 1924.

————, *Neue Untersuchungen der Lehrgegensätze zwischen den Katholiken und Protestanten.* Mainz 1834.

MÜLLER, O., "Zum Begriff der Tradition in der Theologie der letzten hundert Jahre," *MünThZ,* 4 (1953) 164–186.

OLZARAN, J., "La controversia Soto-Caterino-Vega sobre la certeza de la gracia," *Estudios Eclesiasticos,* 19 (1942) 145–183.

PAS, P., "La doctrine de la double justice au Concile de Trente," *EphTheol-Lov,* 30 (1954) 5–53.

PREMM, M., *Das Tridentinische "Diligere incipiunt."* Graz 1926.

PRUMBS, A., *Die Stellung des Trienter Konzils zu der Frage nach dem Wesen der heiligmachenden Gnade.* Paderborn 1909.

RAHNER, K., "Über den Versuch eines Aufrisses einer Dogmatik," *Schriften z. Theol.,* 1, 9–47. Einsiedeln-Zürich 1954.

————, "Zur Frage der Dogmenentwicklung," *op. cit.,* I, 49–90.

————, "Probleme der Christologie von heute," *op. cit.,* I, 169–222.

————, "Über die Schriftinspiration," *ZkTh,* 78 (1956) 137–168.

RAMBALDI, G., "Immutabilità del dogma e delle formule dogmatiche," *Gregorianum,* 33 (1952) 58–84.

RIVIÈRE, J., "Justification," *DTC,* VIII, 2077–2227. Paris 1925.

RONDET, H., *Gratia Christi. Essai d'histoire du dogme et de théologie dogmatique.* Paris 1948.

RÜCKERT, H., *Die Rechtfertigungslehre auf dem Tridentinischen Konzil.* Bonn 1925.

SARTORY, TH., *Die ökumenische Bewegung und die Einheit der Kirche.* Augsburg 1955.

SCHEEBEN, M.-J., *Handbuch der Katholischen Dogmatik* (ed. by J. Höfer, *Ges. Schriften* Vol. IIIff). Freiburg 1948ff.

SCHIERSE, F. J., "Das Trienterkonzil und die Frage nach der christlichen Gewissheit," in Schreiber, *Weltkonzil,* pp. 145–167.

SCHMAUS, M., *Katholische Dogmatik.* 5 vols., 4th ed. München 1949ff.

SCHREIBER, G., *Das Weltkonzil von Trient.* Freiburg 1951.

SOTO, D., *Ad sanctum concilium Tridentinum de natura et gratia.* Venetiis 1547.

SPIAZZI, R., "Rivelazione compiuta con la morte degli Apostoli," *Gregorianum,* 34 (1953) 24–57.

STÄHLIN, W., *"Allein." Recht und Gefahr einer polemischen Formel,* Stuttgart 1950.

STAKEMEIER, A., *Das Konzil von Trient über die Heilsgewissheit.* Heidelberg 1947.

STAKEMEIER, E., "Das Trienter Konzil über den Glauben im Stande der Ungnade," *Röm. Quartalschr.,* 42 (1934) 147–172.

————, "Glaube und Busse in den Trienter Rechtfertigungsverhandlungen," *op. cit.,* 43 (1935) 157–177.

————, "Die theol. Schulen auf dem Trienter Konzil," *Theol. Quartalschrift,* 117 (1936) 188–207; 332–350; 466–504.

————, *Glaube und Rechtfertigung.* Freiburg Br. 1937.

————, *Der Kampf um Augustin. Augustinus und die Augustiner auf dem Tridentinum.* Paderborn 1937.

————, "Trienter Lehrentscheidungen und reformatorische Anliegen," in Schreiber, *Weltkonzil,* pp. 77–116.

STAUDENMAIER, F. A., *Der Protestantismus in seinem Wesen und in seiner Entwicklung.* 2 vols. Freiburg Br. 1846.

STEFFES, J. P., "Die Lehrbestimmungen des Tridentinums und die moderne Weltanschauung," in Schreiber, *Weltkonzil,* pp. 55–75.

STEGMÜLLER, F., "Zur Gnadenlehre des spanischen Konzilstheologen Domingo de Soto," *op. cit.,* pp. 169–230.

THILS, G., *Histoire doctrinale du mouvement oecuménique.* Louvain 1955.

TROMP, S., *De sacrae scripturae inspiratione.* 4th ed. Roma 1945.

UTZ, A. F., *Anmerkungen und Kommentar zu Thomas v. Aquins: Glaube als Tugend* (Deutsche Thomasausg. 15). Heidelberg 1950.

VAN LEEUWEN, B., "Regula credendi," *Genade en Kerk,* pp. 331–337, Utrecht-Antwerpen 1953.

VERONIUS, F., *Règle générale de la foi catholique séparée de toutes autres doctrines.* 1646.

VILLALMONTE, A. DE, "Andreas de Vega y el proceso de la justificación según el Concilio Tridentino," *Rev. espanola de Teologia,* 5 (1945) 311–374.

ZAPELENA, TH., *De Ecclesia Christi.* 5th ed. Vol. I. Roma 1950; Vol. II Roma 1954.

C. CHAPTERS 21–26 (Christ, Creation, Sin, Excursus)

ADAM, K. See under B.

ALTHAUS, P., *Die christliche Wahrheit. Lehrbuch der Dogmatik.* Gütersloh 1947. 3rd ed. 1952.

AMANN, E., "Semi-pélagiens," *DTC*, XIV, 1796–1850. Paris 1939.

ARNOLD, F. X., "Das gott-menschliche Prinzip der Seelsorge und die Gestaltung der christlichen Frömmigkeit," *Konzil von Chalkedon,* III, 287–340. Würzburg 1954.

ASMUSSEN, H. See under B.

AUER, J., *Die Entwicklung der Gnadenlehre in der Hochscholastik.* 2 vols. Freiburg Br. 1942. 1951.

BAADER, F. VON, *Sämtliche Werke.* 16 vols. Leipzig 1851–1860.

BAIUS, M., *Opera.* (Ed. Gerberon). Köln 1696.

BALTHASAR, H. U. VON, "Der Begriff der Natur in der Theologie," *ZkTh,* 75 (1953) 452–461.

———, "Christlicher Universalismus," *Antwort. K. Barth zum 70. Geburtstag.* pp. 237–248. Zürich 1956.

BAUCHER, J., "Liberté," *DTC,* IX, 660–703. Paris 1926.

BAUER, W., *Griechisch-Deutsches Wörterbuch zu den Schriften des NT und der übrigen urchristlichen Literatur.* 4th ed. Berlin 1952.

BERBUIR, E., *Zeugnis für Christus. Eine Auslegung des Johannesprologs.* Freiburg 1949.

———, *Natura humana.* München 1950.

BEUMER, J., "Die altchristliche Lehre einer präexistenten Kirche und ihre theol. Auswertung," *Wissenschaft und Weish.,* 9 (1942) 19–32.

———, "Die persönliche Sünde in sozialtheologischer Sicht," *Theologie und Glaube,* 43 (1953) 81–102.

Bibel-Lexikon (ed. by H. Haag). Einsiedeln-Köln 1951 ff.

BICHLMAIR, G., *Der Mann Jesus.* 2nd ed. Wien 1946.

BILLOT, L., *De Deo uno et trino.* 6th ed. Roma 1920.

BOISMARD, M.-E., *Le Prologue de S. Jean.* Paris 1953.

BOMAN, TH., *Das hebräische Denken im Vergleich mit dem griechischen.* 2nd ed. Göttingen 1954.

BONSIRVEN, J., *Les enseignements de Jésus Christ.* Paris 1943.

———, *Théologie du Nouveau Testament.* Paris 1951.

———, *L'Apocalypse de S. Jean.* Paris 1951.

BOUILLARD, H. See under B.

BOUSSET, W., *Kyrios Christos.* 4th ed. Göttingen 1935.

BOUYER, L. See under A.

BRINKMANN, B., "Die kosmische Stellung des Gottmenschen in Paulinischer Sicht," *Wissenschaft und Weisheit,* 13 (1950) 6–33.

BROGLIE, G. DE, *De fine ultimo humanae vitae. Tractatus theologicus, pars prior positiva.* Paris 1948.

BRUNNER, H. E., *The Mediator: A study of the central doctrine of the Christian faith,* tr. Olive Wyon, London, 1934; Philadelphia, 1947.

———, *Dogmatik.* 2 vols. Zürich 1946. 1950.

———, *Der Mensch im Widerspruch. Die Lehre vom wahren und wirklichen Menschen.* 2nd ed. Zürich 1941.

BULTMANN, R., "θανατος," *TWNT*, III, 7–25. Stuttgart 1938.

CAPÉRAN, L., *Le problème du salut des infidèles.* 2 vols. 2nd ed. Toulouse 1934.

CAPPUYNS, DOM M., "L'origine des 'Capitula' pseudo-célestiniens," *Rev. Bénéd.*, 41 (1929) 156–170.

———, "L'origine des 'Capitula' d'Orange," *Rech. de Théol. Anc. et Méd.*, 6 (1934) 121–142.

CAZELLES, H., "Loi israélite," *DBS*, V, 497–530. Paris 1953.

CERFAUX, L., *Le Christ dans la théologie de S. Paul.* 2nd ed. Paris 1954.

———, *La Théologie de l'Eglise suivant S. Paul.* 2nd ed. Paris 1948.

CHARLES, R. H., *A Critical and Exegetical Commentary on the Revelation of St. John.* 2 vols. Edinburgh 1920.

CHÉNÉ, J., "Que signifiaient 'initium fidei' et 'affectus credulitatis' pour les semi-pélagiens," *RechScRel*, 35 (1948) 566–588.

———, "Le Semi-pélagianisme du midi de la Gaule d'après les lettres de Prosper d'Aquitaine et d'Hilaire à Saint Augustin," *RechScRel*, 43 (1955) 321–341.

CONGAR, Y. M.-J., "Sur l'inclusion de l'humanité dans le Christ," *RevScPhil-Théol*, 25 (1936) 489–495.

CORNELY-ZORELL, *Commentarium in Sapientiam* (Cursus Scr. Sacrae). Parisiis 1910.

CULLMANN, O., *Peter: Disciple—Apostle—Martyr: A historical and theological essay,* tr. F. V. Filson, Philadelphia, 1953.

———, *Christ and Time: The primitive Christian conception of time and history,* tr. F. V. Filson, Philadelphia, 1950.

DANIÉLOU, J., "Christologie et eschatologie," *Konzil von Chalkedon,* III, 531–611. Würzburg 1954.

———, "La doctrine de la mort chez les Pères de l'Eglise," *Le Mystère de la mort et sa célébration,* pp. 134–156. Paris 1953.

DANIEL-ROPS, H., *Jésus en son temps.* Paris 1945.

DEMAN, TH., "Péché" *DTC,* XII, 140–275. Paris 1933.

DIERINGER, F. X., *Lehrbuch der kath. Dogmatik.* Mainz 1847, 4th ed. 1865.

DILLERSBERGER, J., *Der neue Gott. Ein biblisch-theologischer Versuch über den Epheserbrief.* Salzburg-Leipzig 1935.

———, *Das Wort vom Logos. Vorlesungen über den Johannesprolog.* Salzburg-Leipzig 1935.

DOBSCHÜTZ, E. VON, "Zeit und Raum im Denken des Urchristentums," *Journal of Biblical Literature,* 46 (1922) 212 ff.

DUPONT, J., *Essai sur la christologie de S. Jean.* Bruges 1951.

DURAN, A., "Le Christ 'Premier-né,'" *RechScRel*, 1 (1910) 56–66.

EGENTER, R., *Von der Freiheit der Kinder Gottes.* Freiburg 1941.

ERMECKE, G., "Die Stufen der sakramentalen Christusebenbildlichkeit als Einteilungsprinzip der speziellen Moral," *Festschr. f. Tillmann.* Düsseldorf 1950.

ERNST, J., *Die Werke und Tugenden der Ungläubigen nach St. Augustinus* (*nebst einem Anhang über den 22. Canon des Arausicanum II*). Freiburg 1871.

——, "Zur Erklärung des XXII Kanons von Orange," *ZkTh*, 19 (1895) 177–185.

——, "Die dogmatische Geltung des 2. Konzils von Orange," *ZkTh*, 30 (1906) 650–670.

FELDER, J., *Jesus von Nazareth*. Paderborn 1937.

FELDMANN, F., *Buch der Weisheit*. Bonn 1926.

FELDMANN, J., *Paradies und Sündenfall*. Münster W. 1913.

FÉRET, H.-M., "A propos de la primauté du Christ," *RevScPhilThéol*, 27 (1938) 69–72.

——, "Creati in Christo Jesu," *op. cit.*, 30 (1941) 96–132.

——, "La mort dans la tradition biblique," *Le mystère de la mort et sa célébration*, pp. 15–133. Paris 1951.

FERNÁNDEZ, A., *Vida de Nuestro Señor Jesu Cristo*. Madrid 1948.

FEUERER, G., *Adam und Christus als Gestaltkräfte und ihr Vermächtnis an die Menschheit. Zur christl. Erbsündenlehre*. Freiburg Br. 1939.

FEUILLET, A., "Le Fils de l'homme de Daniel et la tradition biblique," *Rev. Bibl.*, 60 (1953) 170–202; 321–346.

FINANCE, J. DE, "La présence des choses à l'éternité d'après les scolastiques," *Archives de Philosophie*, 19 (1956) 24–62.

FISCHER, J., *Das Buch der Weisheit (Echter-Bibel)*. Würzburg 1952.

FREUNDORFER, J., *Erbsünde und Erbtod beim Apostel Paulus*. Münster W. 1927.

FRITZ, G., "Orange," *DTC*, XI, 1087–1103. Paris 1931.

FUCHS, J., *Lex naturae. Zur Theologie des Naturrechts*. Düsseldorf 1955.

——, "De valore legis naturalis in ordine redemptionis," *Periodica* (1955) 45–64.

GALTIER, P., *Aux origines du sacrement de Pénitence*. Roma 1951.

——, *De incarnatione et redemptione*. 2nd ed. Paris 1947.

GAUDEL, A., "Péché originel," *DTC*, XII, 275–606. Paris 1933.

GEISELMANN, J. R., *Jesus der Christus*. Stuttgart 1951.

——, "J. A. Möhler und das idealistische Verständnis des Sündenfalles," *Scholastik*, 19 (1944) 19–37.

GILLEMAN, G., *Le primat de la charité en théologie morale*. Paris 1952.

GILLON, L.-B., *La théorie des oppositions et la théologie du péché au XIIIe siècle*. Paris 1937.

GILSON, E., *Introduction à l'étude de S. Augustin*. 3rd ed. Paris 1949.

GIORDANI, I., *Gesù di Nazareth*. 2 vols. Torino 1945 f.

GOOSSENS, W., *L'Eglise corps du Christ d'après S. Paul*. Paris 1949.

GRANDMAISON, L. DE, *Jésus-Christ*. 2 vols. Paris 1928.

GROSS, J., *La divinisation du chrétien d'après les Pères grecs*. Paris 1938.

GUARDINI, R., *Wesen des Christentums*. Würzburg 1938.

——, *Der Herr. Betrachtungen über die Person und das Leben Jesu Christi*. 5th ed. Basel 1943.

GUILLET, J., *Thèmes bibliques. Etudes sur l'expression et le développement de la Révélation*. Paris 1951.

GUITTON, J., *Le Temps et l'Eternité chez Plotin et S. Augustin.* Paris 1933.

GUNKEL, H., *Genesis.* 3rd ed. Göttingen 1910.

GUTWENGER, E., "Natur und Übernatur. Gedanken zu Balthasars Werk über die Barthsche Theologie," *ZkTh,* 75 (1953) 82–97.

———, "Der Begriff der Natur in der Theologie," *op cit.,* 461–464.

———, "Zur Ontologie der hypostatischen Union," *ZkTh,* 76 (1954) 385–410.

HAAS, J., *Die Stellung Jesu zu Sünde und Sünder nach den vier Evangelien.* Fribourg 1954.

HÄRING, B., *Das Gesetz Christi. Moraltheologie.* 2nd ed. Freiburg Br. 1955.

HARNACK, A. VON, *Dogmengeschichte.* 3 vols. 4th ed. Tübingen 1910.

HAURET, CH., *Origines de l'univers et de l'homme d'après la Bible (Gen. I-III).* Luçon 1950.

HEFELE-LECLERCQ, *Histoire des conciles d'après les documents originaux.* Vol. II. Paris 1908.

HEINRICH, J. B., *Dogmatische Theologie.* 10 vols. Mainz 1873 ff.

HENGSTENBERG, H. E., *Das Band zwischen Gott und Schöpfung.* Regensburg 1948.

HENRY, P., "Kénose," *DBS,* V, 7–161. Paris 1950.

HILD, J., "La mort, mystère chrétien," *Le mystère de la mort et sa célébration.* pp. 210–249. Paris 1951.

HOLTZ, F., "La valeur sotériologique de la résurrection du Christ d'après S. Thomas d'Aquin," *EphTheolLov,* 29 (1953) 609–645.

HUBY, J., *L'Epître aux Romains.* Paris 1946.

———, *Les Epîtres de la captivité.* Paris 1947.

HUMMELAUER, *Commentarium in Genesim* (Curs. Scr. Sacrae). Paris 1895.

IGNACIO DE LOYOLA, *Obras Completas.* Madrid 1952.

JOURNET, CH., *L'Eglise du Verbe incarné.* 2 vols. Bruges 1941. 1951.

JUNGMANN, J. A., *Die Stellung Christi im liturgischen Gebet.* München 1925.

———, *Die Frohbotschaft und unsere Glaubensverkündigung.* Regensburg 1936.

KÄPPELI, TH., *Zur Lehre des hl. Thomas v. Aquin vom Corpus Christi mysticum.* Fribourg 1931.

KÄSEMANN, E., *Leib und Leib Christi.* Tübingen 1933.

———, "Eine urchristliche Taufliturgie," *Festschr. R. Bultmann,* pp. 133–148. Stuttgart-Köln 1949.

KENNY, I. P., "Reflections on Human Nature and the Supernatural," *Theol. Studies,* 14 (1953) 280–287.

KIRCHGÄSSNER, A., *Erlösung und Sünde im Neuen Testament.* Freiburg 1950.

KITTEL, G., "λογος," *TWNT,* IV, 100–140. Stuttgart 1938.

KNABENBAUER, I., *Commentarium in Ezechiel.* Paris 1890.

KONZIL VON CHALKEDON. *Geschichte und Gegenwart* (ed. by Grillmeier-Bach. 3 vols. Würzburg 1951 ff.

KRAUS, J., "Zum Problem des christozentrischen Aufbaus der Moraltheol.," *Div. Thom.* (Freiburg) 30 (1952) 257–272.

Krempel, A., *La doctrine de la relation chez S. Thomas. Exposé historique et systématique.* Paris 1952.

Kretschmar, G., *Studien zur frühchristl. Trinitätstheologie.* Tübingen 1956.

Kuhn, J. von, *Katholische Dogmatik.* 3 vols. Tübingen 1846 ff.

Laberthonnière, L., *Le réalisme chrétien et l'idéalisme grec.* Paris 1904.

Labourdette, M.-M., *Le péché originel et les origines de l'homme.* Paris 1953.

Lagrange, M.-J., *L'évangile de Jésus-Christ.* Paris 1928.

Lakner, Fr., "Das Zentralobjekt der Theologie," *ZkTh,* 62 (1938) 1–36.

Landgraf, A. M., "Sünde und Trennung von der Kirche in der Frühscholastik," *Scholastik,* 5 (1930) 219–247.

La Taille, M. de, "Actuation créée par acte incréé," *RechScRel,* 18 (1928) 253–268.

Le Bachelet, X., "Baïus," *DTC,* I, 38–111. Paris 1905.

Lebreton, J., *La vie et l'enseignement de Jésus-Christ.* 2 vols. Paris 1931.

——, *Histoire du dogme de la Trinité des origines au concile de Nicée.* 2 vols. Paris 1927f.

Leclercq, J., *L'enseignement de la morale chrétienne.* Paris 1950.

Lejay, P., "Le rôle théologique de S. Césaire d'Arles," *Rev. d'hist. et de litt. rel.,* 10 (1903) 217 ff.

Lohmeyer, E., *Die Offenbarung des Johannes.* 2nd ed. Tübingen 1953.

Lottin, O., *Psychologie et morale aux XIIᵉ et XIIIᵉ siècles.* 3 vols. Gembloux 1942 ff.

Lubac, H. de, *Katholizismus als Gemeinschaft.* Einsiedeln-Köln 1943.

——, *Surnaturel. Etude historique.* Paris 1946.

Lyonnet, St., *Liberté chrétienne et loi nouvelle. Institut Biblique* (Manuscript) Rome 1953.

Malevez, L., "La gratuité du surnaturel," *NRTh* 75 (1935) 561–586; 673–689.

——, "L'Eglise dans le Christ," *RechScRel,* 25 (1935) 257–291; 418–440.

Marchal, L., "Moralité de l'acte humain," *DTC,* X, 2459–2472. Paris 1929.

Mauriac, F., *Vie de Jésus-Christ.* Paris 1936.

Menoud, Ph., *L'évangile de Jean d'après les recherches récentes.* Neuchâtel-Paris 1947.

Merlin, N., *S. Augustin et les dogmes du péché originel et de la grâce.* Paris 1931.

Mersch, E., *La théologie du Corps Mystique.* 2 vols. 3rd ed. Paris 1949.

——, *Morale et corps mystique.* 3rd ed. Bruxelles 1949.

——, "Le Christ centre de la Théologie comme science," *NRTh,* 61 (1934) 449–475.

——, "La morale et le Christ total," *NRTh,* 68 (1946) 633–647.

——, "Filii in Filio," *NRTh,* 65 (1938) 551–582; 681–702; 809–830.

——, See also under B.

Michel, A., "Mort," *DTC,* X, 2489–2500. Paris 1929.

Montcheuil, Y. de, *Leçons sur le Christ.* Paris 1949.

Mussner, F., *Christus, das All und die Kirche.* Trier 1955.

O'BRIEN, J., *The life of Christ*. Paterson 1944.

ORBE, A., "Cristo y la Iglesia en su Matrimonio anterior a los siglos," *Estudios eclesiasticos*, 29 (1955) 299–344.

PAPINI, G., *Storia di Cristo*, 14th ed. Firenze 1950.

PASCHER, J., "Christus gegen die geistige Zersetzung der Welt," *Theol. und Glaube*, 30 (1938) 245–255.

PERCY, E., *Die Probleme der Kolosser- und Epheserbriefe*. Lund 1946.

PESCH, CH., *Praelectiones dogmaticae*. 9 vols. Friburgi Br. 1894 ff.

PETAVIUS, D., *Dogmata theologica*. 8 vols. Parisiis (Vivès) 1865–67.

PHILIPS, G., "La grâce des justes de l'Ancien Testament," *EphTheolLov*, 23 (1947) 521–556.

PICCORELLI, L., *Valor dogmatico de la doctrina catolica sobre el "Initium Fidei" según la controversia semipelagiana*. (Diss. Gregoriana) Roma 1953.

PILGRAM, F., *Physiologie der Kirche*. Mainz 1860. 2nd ed. 1931.

PIROT-CLAMER, La Sainte Bible. Vols. I. II. VI. Paris 1940 ff.

PLINVAL, G. DE, "L'activité doctrinale dans l'Eglise Gallo-Romaine," in Fliche-Martin, *Histoire de l'Eglise*, IV, 397–419. Paris 1948.

POSCHMANN, B., *Paenitentia secunda. Die kirchliche Busse im ältesten Christentum*. Bonn 1940.

———, *Busse und Letzte Ölung. Handbuch der Dogmengesch*. IV/3. Freiburg 1951.

PRAT, F., *La théologie de Saint Paul*. 2 vols. 38th ed. Paris 1949.

———, *Jésus-Christ, sa vie, sa doctrine, son œuvre*. 2 vols. 21st ed. Paris 1953.

PRIBILLA, M., "Die Kirche von Anbeginn," *Stimmen der Zeit*, 117 (1929) 241–254.

PRÜMM, K., "Sammelbericht zu Urchristentum, Biblischer Theologie und Religionsgesch. II," *Biblica*, 33 (1952) 258–273.

QUELL-BERTRAM-STÄHLIN-GRUNDMANN, "ἁμαρτια," *TWNT*, I, 267–320. Stuttgart 1933.

QUOIDBACH, TH., *Le Christ cet Inconnu*. Paris 1947.

v. RAD-BERTRAM-BULTMANN, "ζωη," *TWNT*, II, 833–877. Stuttgart 1938.

RAHNER, H., "Die Gottesgeburt. Die Lehre der Kirchenväter von der Geburt Christi im Herzen der Gläubigen," *ZkTh*, 59 (1935) 333–418.

RAHNER, K., "Augustin und der Semipelagianismus," *ZkTh*, 62 (1938) 171–196.

———, "Zur Theologie des Todes," *Synopsis*, No. 3, pp. 87–112. Hamburg 1949.

———, "Theos im Neuen Testament," *Schriften z. Theol.*, I, 91–167.

———, "Theologisches zum Monogenismus," *op. cit.*, I, 253–322.

———, "Über das Verhältnis von Natur und Gnade," *op. cit.*, I, 323–345.

———, "Zur scholastischen Begrifflichkeit der ungeschaffenen Gnade," *op. cit.*, I, 347–375.

———, "Die Gliedschaft in der Kirche nach der Lehre der Enzyklika Pius' XII. 'Mystici Corporis,'" *op. cit.*, II, 7–94.

———, "Vergessene Wahrheiten über das Busssakrament," *op. cit.*, II, 143–183.

————, "Bemerkungen über das Naturgesetz und seine Erkennbarkeit," *Orientierung,* 19 (1955) 239–243.

————, "Über das Verhältnis des Naturgesetzes zur übernatürlichen Gnadenordnung," *op. cit.,* 20 (1956) 8–11.

————, See also under B.

RÉGNON, TH. DE, *Etudes de théologie positive sur la Sainte Trinité.* 5 vols. Paris 1892 ff.

RICCIOTTI, G., *Vita di Gesù Cristo.* Milano 1941.

RIPALDA, J. M. DE, *De ente supernaturali disputationes theologicae.* Paris (Palené) 1870.

RONDET, H., *Le mystère du péché originel.* Le Puy 1943.

————, *Problèmes pour la réflexion chrétienne.* Paris 1946.

————. See also under B.

RUDOLPH, W., "Das Menschenbild des Alten Testamentes," *Dienst unter dem Wort. Festschrift H. Schreiner.* pp. 238 ff. Gütersloh 1953.

SASSE, H., "αἰων," *TWNT,* I, 197–209. Stuttgart 1933.

SCHARL, E., *Recapitulatio mundi. Der Rekapitulationsbegriff des hl. Irenäus und seine Anwendung auf die Körperwelt.* Freiburg Br. 1941.

SCHAUF, W., *Sarx. Der Begriff "Fleisch" beim Apostel Paulus unter besonderer Berücksichtigung seiner Erlösungslehre.* Münster W. 1924.

SCHEEBEN, M.-J., *Die Mysterien des Christentums.* Freiburg 1951.

————, See also under B.

SCHELL, H., *Das Wirken des dreieinigen Gottes.* Mainz 1885.

SCHLIER, H., *Christus und die Kirche im Epheserbrief.* Tübingen 1930.

————, "κεφαλη," *TWNT,* III, 672–682. Stuttgart 1938.

————, "ἐλευθερος," *TWNT,* II, 484–500. Stuttgart 1935.

————, "Die Kirche als Geheimnis Christi (nach dem Epheserbrief)," *Theol. Quartalschr.,* 134 (1954) 385–396.

————, "Über das vollkommene Gesetz der Freiheit," *Festschrift R. Bultmann,* pp. 190–202. Stuttgart 1949.

————, *Die Zeit der Kirche. Exegetische Aufsätze und Vorträge,* Freiburg 1956.

SCHLIER-WARNACH, *Die Kirche im Epheserbrief.* Münster W. 1949.

SCHMAUS, M., "Reich Gottes und Busssakrament," *MünThZ,* 1 (1950) 20–36.

————, See also under B.

SCHNEIDER, O., "Gedanken zu Vinzenz Palottis Selbstbezeichnung 'nihil et peccatum,'" *Zeit. f. Asz. und Mystik,* 13 (1938) 229–232.

SCHRENK, G., "ἀθικια," *TWNT,* I, 150–163. Stuttgart 1933.

SCHUMACHER, H., *Christus in seiner Präexistenz und Kenose. Nach Phil. 2, 5–8.* 2 vols. Roma 1914. 1921.

SÉJOURNÉ, P., "Les trois aspects du péché dans le 'Cur Deus homo,'" *Rev. d. Sciences Rel.,* 24 (1950) 5–27.

SICKENBERGER, J., *Leben Jesu nach den 4 Evangelien.* Münster 1933.

SIWEK, P., *Psychologia metaphysica.* Roma 1948.

SKINNER, J., *A Critical and Exegetical Commentary on Genesis.* Edinburgh 1930.

SOIRON, TH., *Die Kirche als der Leib Christi. Nach der Lehre des hl. Paulus.* Düsseldorf 1951.

SPICQ, C., "Le Siracide et la structure littéraire du prologue de Saint Jean," *Mémorial Lagrange*, pp. 183–195. Paris 1940.

SPINDELER, A., *Cur Verbum caro factum? Das Motiv der Menschwerdung und das Verhältnis der Erlösung zur Menschwerdung Gottes in den christologischen Glaubenskämpfen des 4. und 5. christlichen Jahrhunderts.* Paderborn 1938.

STARCKY, J., "Logos," *DBS*, V, 479–496. Paris 1952.

STAUDENMAIER, F. A., *Die christliche Dogmatik.* 4 vols. Freiburg 1844 ff.

STEGMÜLLER, F., *Repertorium biblicum medii aevi.* 2 vols. Matriti 1950.

———, *Repertorium commentariorum in Sententias Petri Lombardi.* 2 vols. Herbipoli 1947.

STROHM, M., "Der Begriff der 'natura vitiata' bei Augustin," *Theol. Quartalschr.*, 135 (1955) 184–203.

SWETE, H. B., *The Apocalypse of St. John.* London 1906.

TERNUS, J., "Chalkedon und die Entwicklung der protestantischen Theologie," *Konzil von Chalkedon*, III, 531–611. Würzburg 1954.

TILLMANN, F., *Handbuch der kath. Sittenlehre.* 4 vols. 4th ed. Düsseldorf 1950.

VERRIÈLE, A., *Le Surnaturel en nous et le Péché originel.* Paris 1932.

WALTER, EUGEN, *Christus und der Kosmos. Eine Auslegung von Eph. 1.10* Stuttgart 1948.

WELTE, B., "Homoousios hemin. Gedanken zum Verständnis und zur theologischen Problematik der Kategorien von Chalkedon," *Konzil von Chalkedon*, III, 51–80. Würzburg 1954.

WERNER, M., *Der protestantische Weg des Glaubens.* Vol. I. Bern 1955.

WIKENHAUSER, A., *Die Christusmystik des hl. Paulus.* Münster 1928.

———, *Die Kirche als der mystische Leib Christi nach dem Apostel Paulus.* Münster 1937.

ZERWICK, M., *Analysis philologica Novi Testamenti Graeci.* Roma 1953.

ZORELL, F., *Lexicon Graecum Novi Testamenti.* 2nd ed. Paris 1931.

———, *Lexicon hebraicum et aramaicum Veteris Testamenti.* Roma 1939 ff.

D. CHAPTERS 27–33 (Grace, Justification, Faith)

ALTHAUS, P., *Die lutherische Rechtfertigung und ihre heutigen Kritiker.* Berlin 1951.

———. See also under C.

ANTOINE, P., "Foi," *DBS*, III, 276–310. Paris 1934.

ASMUSSEN, H. See under B.

AUER, J. See under C.

BALTHASAR, H. U. VON. See under A.

BARTMANN, B., *Lehrbuch der Dogmatik.* 2nd ed. Freiburg 1911.

———, *St. Paulus und St. Jacobus über die Rechtfertigung.* Freiburg 1897.

BAUER, W. See under C.

BELLARMINE, R., *De iustificatione*, disp. vol. IV. Venetiis 1721.

BERLAGE, A., *Christkatholische Dogmatik.* 7 vols. Münster W. 1839 ff.

BIBEL-LEXIKON. See under C.

BISER, E., *Das Christusgeheimnis der Sakramente.* Heidelberg 1950.

BONNETAIN, P., "Grâce," *DBS,* III, 701–1319. Paris 1938.

BONSIRVEN, J. See under C.

BOUILLARD, H. See under B.

BOUYER, L. See under A.

BOVER, J., *Teología de San Pablo.* 2nd ed. Madrid 1952.

BRAUN, H., *Gerichtsgedanke und Rechtfertigungslehre bei Paulus.* Leipzig 1930.

BROWN-DRIVER-BRIGGS, *A Hebrew and English Lexikon of the Old Testament.* Oxford 1952.

BÜCHSEL-HERNTRICH, "κρινω," *TWNT,* III, 920–955. Stuttgart 1938.

BULTMANN-WEISER, "πιστις," *TWNT,* VI, 174–230. Stuttgart 1955.

CAZELLES, H., "A propos de quelques textes difficiles relatifs à la justice de Dieu dans l'AT," *Revue Bibl.,* 58 (1951) 169–188.

CERFAUX, L., "Justice," "Justification chez S. Paul," *DBS,* IV, 1471–1496. Paris 1949.

———. See also under C.

CONCILIUM TRIDENTINUM. See under B.

COPPENS, J., "Baptême," *DBS,* I, 852–924. Paris 1928.

CULLMANN, O., *Die Tauflehre des NT. Erwachsenen- und Kindertaufe.* Zürich 1948.

DENIFLE, H., *Die abendländischen Schriftausleger bis Luther über Justitia Dei (R 1, 17) und Justificatio.* Mainz 1905.

DESCAMPS, A., *Le· christianisme comme justice dans le premier évangile.* Louvain 1946.

———, "Justice," "Justification," *DBS,* IV, 1417–1471; 1496–1510. Paris 1949.

———, *Les Justes et la Justice dans les évangiles et le christianisme primitif hormis la doctrine proprement Paulinienne.* Louvain 1950.

DETTLOFF, W., *Die Lehre von der Acceptatio divina bei Johannes D. Scotus mit besonderer Berücksichtigung der Rechtfertigungslehre.* Werl/Westf. 1954.

DHONT, R.-CH., *Le problème de la préparation à la grâce. Débuts de l'Ecole Franciscaine.* Paris 1946.

DIDIER, G., *Désintéressement du Chrétien. La rétribution dans la morale de S. Paul.* Paris 1955.

DIEKAMP, F., *Kath. Dogmatik nach den Grundsätzen des Hl. Thomas.* 3 vols. 2nd ed. Münster W. 1917.

DIERINGER, F. X. See under C.

DOMS, H., *Die Gnadenlehre des sel. Albertus Magnus.* Breslau 1929.

DU CANGE, *Glossarium mediae et infimae Latinitatis,* Vol. IV. Niort 1885.

DUMONT, P., "Le caractère divin de la grâce," *RevScRel,* 14 (1934) 62–95; 13 (1933) 517–552.

DUPONT, J., *La réconciliation dans la Théologie de S. Paul.* Paris 1953.

DURRWELL, F. X., *La résurrection de Jésus, mystère de salut. Etude biblique.* Mulhouse 1950.

FECKES, C., *Die Rechtfertigungslehre des Gabriel Biel und ihre Stellung innerhalb der nominalistischen Schule.* Münster W. 1925.

FEUILLET, A., "Isaïe," *DBS,* IV, 647–729. Paris 1947.

FLICK, M., *L'attimo della giustificazione secondo S. Tommaso.* Roma 1947.

FORCELLINI, A., *Lexicon totius Latinitatis.* Vol. II. Patavii 1940.

FORTMANN, H. J. H., *Geloof en Sacrament.* Utrecht 1949.

GOOSSENS, W., "De valore soteriologico resurrectionis et ascensionis Christi," *Coll. Gandavenses,* 24 (1937) 9–17.

GRABER, R., *Le Christ dans ses sacrements.* Paris 1947.

———, *Aus der Kraft des Glaubens.* Würzburg 1950.

GROSCHE, R., "Simul peccator et iustus," *Catholica,* 4, 3 (1935) 132–139.

GROSS, J. See under C.

GROSSOUW, W., "Rechtfertigung," *Bibel-Lexikon* (ed. by Haag), pp. 1403–09. Zürich 1955.

GUARDINI, R., *Freiheit, Gnade, Schicksal.* München 1949.

GUÉRARD DES LAURIERS, M.-L., *Dimensions de la foi.* 2 vols. Paris 1952.

GUILLET, J. See under C.

HARENT, S., "Foi," *DTC,* VI, 55–514. Paris 1924.

HEFNER, J. See under B.

HEIDLAND, H. W., "λογιζομαι," *TWNT,* IV, 287–295. Stuttgart 1942.

———, *Die Anrechnung des Glaubens zur Gerechtigkeit.* Stuttgart 1936.

HEINISCH, P., *Theologie des Alten Testamentes.* Bonn 1940.

HEINRICH, J. B. See under C.

HOFER, H., *Die Rechtfertigungsverkündigung des Paulus nach neuerer Forschung.* Gütersloh 1940.

HOLTZ, F. See under C.

HUBY, J., "De la connaissance de foi dans saint Jean," *RechScRel,* 21 (1931) 385–421.

———. See also under C.

HULSBOSCH, A., "De Genade in het Nieuwe Testament," *Genade en Kerk,* pp. 20–100. Utrecht-Antwerpen 1953.

HÜNERMANN, F. See under B.

JOURNET, CH. See under C.

JUAN DE LA CRUZ, *Obras.* Madrid 1950.

KARRER, O., "Der Galaterbrief," *Liturgisch-bibl. Monatsschrift,* 9 (1949) 31–35; 92–95; 115–118; 142–144; 164–167; 174–178.

KIRCHGÄSSNER, A. See under C.

KNABENBAUER, I., "Gratia und Justificare," "Justificatio," *Lex. Biblicum.* Paris 1907.

KNIGHT, H. A., *A neglected early work of J. H. Newman: The "Lectures on Justification." A study of their doctrine of grace.* Diss. Lyon 1951.

KÖBERLE, A., *Rechtfertigung und Heiligung.* 3rd ed. Leipzig 1930.

KUHN J. VON. See under C.

LACKMANN, M., *Sola fide. Eine exegetische Studie über Jakobus 2 zur reformator. Rechtfertigungslehre.* Gütersloh 1949.

———, *Zur reformatorischen Rechtfertigungslehre.* Stuttgart 1953.

LAGRANGE, M.-J., *Epître aux Romains.* 2nd ed. Paris 1931. "Note sur la justice de Dieu et la justification," pp. 119–141.

LANDGRAF, A. M., *Dogmengeschichte der Frühscholastik.* 4 vols. Regensburg 1952 ff.

LEENHARDT, F. J., *Le baptême chrétien, son origine, sa signification.* Neuchâtel-Paris 1946.

LEMONNYER, R. P., "Justification (Ecriture)," *DTC,* VIII, 2043-2077. Paris 1925.

LIPPERT, P., *Credo.* Freiburg Br. 1949.

LORTZ, J. See under A.

LUBAC, H. DE. See under C.

LYONNET, ST., "Bulletin d'exégèse paulinienne III," *Biblica,* 32 (1951) 432–439.

―――, "De 'justitia Dei' in Ep. ad Romanos," *Verbum Domini,* 25 (1947), 23–34; 118–121; 129–144; 193–203; 257–263.

―――, *Quaestiones de soteriologia: de peccato et de redemptione* (Manuscript) Roma 1953–1954.

MÉDEBIELLE, A., "Expiation," *DBS,* III, 1–262. Paris 1934.

MEINERTZ, M., *Theologie des Neuen Testamentes.* 2 vols. Bonn 1950.

MOELLER, CH., "Théologie de la Grâce et Oecuménisme," *Irénikon,* 28 (1955) 19–56.

MÖHLER, J. A. See under B.

MOLLAT, D., "Jugement dan le Nouveau Testament," *DBS,* IV, 1344–1394. Paris 1949.

MONSE, F. S., *Johannes und Paulus. Ein Beitrag zur neutestamentlichen Theologie.* Münster i. W. 1915.

MOUROUX, J., *Je crois en toi. Structure personnelle de la foi.* 2nd ed. Paris 1954.

―――, *L'Expérience chrétienne. Introd. à une théologie.* Paris 1954.

NAUTIN, P., *Je crois à l'Esprit Saint dans la Sainte Eglise pour la Résurrection de la chair.* Paris 1947.

NEWMAN, J. H., *Lectures on the Doctrine of Justification.* London 1838; 3rd ed. 1874.

NOTTON, M., *Harnack und Thomas von Aquin. Eine dogmengeschichtl. Studie über die Gnadenlehre.* Paderborn 1906.

OTT, L., *Grundriss der Katholischen Dogmatik.* Freiburg 1952.

PAS, P. See under B.

PASCHER, J., *Das inwendige Leben in Werkgefahr.* München 1940.

PETAVIUS, D. See under C.

PHILIPS, G., "La grâce des justes de l'Ancien Testament," *EphTheolLov,* 23 (1947) 521–566.

PILGRAM, F. See under C.

PLATZ, PH., *Der Römerbrief in der Gnadenlehre Augustins.* Würzburg 1938.

POHLE-GIERENS, *Lehrbuch der Dogmatik.* 3 vols. 9th ed. Paderborn 1936.

PRAT, F. See under C.

PREISKER-WÜRTHWEIN, "μισθός," *TWNT,* IV, 699–736. Stuttgart 1942.

PREMM, M., *Katholische Glaubenskunde. Ein Lehrbuch der Dogmatik.* 4 vols. Wien 1951 ff.

QUELL-SCHRENK, "δικη," *TWNT,* II 176–229. Stuttgart 1935.

RADEMACHER, A., *Die übernatürliche Lebensordnung nach der Paulinischen und Johanneischen Theologie. Eine dogmatische-biblische Studie.* Freiburg 1903.

RAHNER, H. See under C.

RAHNER, K., *Die Kirche der Sünder.* Freiburg 1948.

————, "Trost der Zeit," *Stimmen der Zeit,* 81 (1956) 241–255.

————. See also under B and C.

REINHARD, W., *Das Wirken des Heiligen Geistes im Menschen nach den Briefen des Apostels Paulus.* Freiburg Br. 1918.

RITSCHL, A., *Die christliche Lehre von der Rechtfertigung und Versöhnung.* 4th ed. Bonn 1900 ff.

RIVERSO, E., "Caroli Barth in doctrinam catholicam de gratia recentissimae difficultates refuntantur," *Angelicum,* 31 (1954) 31–45.

RIVIÈRE, J., "Rédemption," *DTC,* XIII, 1912–2003. Paris 1937.

————. See also under B.

RONDET, H. See under B and C.

ROSMAN, A., " 'Justificare' est verbum causativum," *Verbum Domini,* 21 (1941) 144–147.

ROSLAN, W., "Die Grundbegriffe der Gnade nach der Lehre der Apostolischen Väter," *Theol. Quartalschrift,* 119 (1938) 200–225; 275–317; 470–503.

ROUSSELOT, P., "La grâce d'après S. Jean et d'après S. Paul," *RechScRel,* 18 (1928) 87–104.

RÜCKERT, H. See under B.

SCHÄTZLER, C. VON, *Natur und Übernatur. Das Dogma von der Gnade und die theologische Frage der Gegenwart.* Mainz 1865.

————, *Neue Untersuchungen über das Dogma von der Gnade und das Wesen des christlichen Glaubens.* Mainz 1867.

SCHEEBEN, M.-J. See under B.

————, *Natur und Gnade.* 4th ed. Freiburg 1949.

————, *Die Herrlichkeiten der göttlichen Gnade.* 17th ed. Freiburg 1949.

SCHILLEBEECKX, H., *De sacramentele Heilseconomie. Theologische bezinning op S. Thomas' sacramentenleer in het licht von de traditie en van de hedendaagse sacramentenproblematiek.* Antwerpen 1952.

SCHLIER, H. See under C.

SCHLINK, E., *Theologie der lutherischen Bekenntnisschriften.* München 1940.

SCHMAUS, M. See under B.

SCHMID, J., "Exkurs über den Lohngedanken," *Das Evangelium nach Matthäus.* Regensburg 1952, pp. 222–228.

SCHMIDT, H., *Brückenschlag zwischen den Konfessionen.* Paderborn 1951.

SCHMITT, J., *Jésus ressuscité dans la prédication apostolique. Etude de théologie biblique.* Paris 1949.

SCHUPP, J., *Die Gnadenlehre des Petrus Lombardus.* Freiburg 1932.

SPICQ, C., "Bulletin de Théol. biblique (NT)," *RevScPhilThéol,* 27 (1938) 123–125.

STANLEY, D. M., "Ad historiam exegeseos Rom 4, 25," *Verbum Domini,* 29 (1951) 257–274.

STAUDENMAIER, F. A. See under C.

STEUR, K., *Notities over de rechtvaardigmaking zooals Katholieken haar zien*. Bussum 1945.

Thesaurus linguae latinae. Vol. VI/2. Leipzig 1925–34.

TOBAC, E., *Le problème de la justification dans S. Paul*. Louvain 1908.

——, "Le problème de la justification dans S. Paul et dans S. Jacques," *Rev. d'histoire ecclésiastique*, 22 (1926) 797–805.

TRÜBNER, *Deutsches Wörterbuch*. 3 vols. Berlin 1939.

VAN DER MEERSCH, J., "Grâce," *DTC*, VI, 1554–1687. Paris 1924.

VASQUEZ, G., *Commentarium ac Disp. in Primam Secundae S. Thomae*. Vol. II. Lugduni 1631.

VAWTER, BRUCE, "Resurrection and Redemption," *Catholic Bibl. Quarterly*, 15 (1933) 17–23.

VIGNAUX, P., "Nominalisme," *DTC*, XI, 717–784. Paris 1931.

——, *Justification et prédestination au XIVe siècle*. Paris 1934.

——, *Nominalisme au XIVe siècle*. Montréal 1948.

VILLETTE, L., *Foi et sacrement*. Diss. Paris 1954.

VÖLKER, W., *Das Vollkommenheitsideal des Origenes*. Tübingen 1931.

WALTER, E., *Quellen lebendigen Wassers*. Freiburg 1953.

——, *Glaube, Hoffnung und Liebe im NT*. Freiburg 1940.

WETTER, G. P., *Charis. Ein Beitrag zur Geschichte des ältesten Christentums*. Leipzig 1913.

WOBBE, J., *Der Charis-Gedanke bei Paulus*. Münster 1932.

ZAPELENA, TH. See under B.

ZORELL, F. See under C.

INDEX

D

E